KYOTO AREA STUDIES ON ASIA

CENTER FOR SOUTHEAST ASIAN STUDIES, KYOTO UNIVERSITY

VOLUME 15

Myths and Realities

KYOTO AREA STUDIES ON ASIA

CENTER FOR SOUTHEAST ASIAN STUDIES, KYOTO UNIVERSITY

The Nation and Economic Growth: Korea and Thailand
YOSHIHARA Kunio

One Malay Village: A Thirty-Year Community Study
TSUBOUCHI Yoshihiro

Commodifying Marxism:
The Formation of Modern Thai Radical Culture, 1927–1958
Kasian TEJAPIRA

Gender and Modernity: Perspectives from Asia and the Pacific
HAYAMI Yoko, TANABE Akio, TOKITA-TANABE Yumiko

Practical Buddhism among the Thai-Lao:
Religion in the Making of a Region
HAYASHI Yukio

The Political Ecology of Tropical Forests in Southeast Asia:
Historical Perspectives
LYE Tuck-Po, WIL DE JONG, ABE Ken-ichi

Between Hills and Plains:
Power and Practice in Socio-Religious Dynamics among Karen
HAYAMI Yoko

Ecological Destruction, Health and Development:
Advancing Asian Paradigms
FURUKAWA Hisao, NISHIBUCHI Mitsuaki, KONO Yasuyuki, KAIDA Yoshihiro

Searching for Vietnam:
Selected Writings on Vietnamese Culture and Society
A. Terry RAMBO

Laying the Tracks: The Thai Economy and its Railways 1885–1935
KAKIZAKI Ichiro

After the Crisis:
Hegemony, Technocracy and Governance in Southeast Asia
SHIRAISHI Takashi, Patricio N. ABINALES

Dislocating Nation-States: Globalization in Asia and Africa
Patricio N. ABINALES, ISHIKAWA Noboru and TANABE Akio

People on the Move: Rural–Urban Interactions in Sarawak
SODA Ryoji

Living on the Periphery: Development and Islamization among the Orang Asli
NOBUTA Toshihiro

Myths and Realities: The Democratization of Thai Politics
TAMADA Yoshifumi

East Asian Economies and New Regionalism
ABE Shigeyuki and Bhanupong NIDHIPRABA

The Rise of Middle Classes in Southeast Asia
SHIRAISHI Takashi and Pasuk PHONGPAICHIT

KYOTO AREA STUDIES ON ASIA
CENTER FOR SOUTHEAST ASIAN STUDIES, KYOTO UNIVERSITY
VOLUME 15

Myths and Realities

The Democratization of Thai Politics

TAMADA Yoshifumi

Kyoto University Press

The publication of this volume was partially funded by the JSPS Global COE Program (E-04): In Search of Sustainable Humanosphere in Asia and Africa.

First published in 2008 jointly by:

Kyoto University Press
Kyodai Kaikan
15-9 Yoshida Kawara-cho
Sakyo-ku, Kyoto 606-8305, Japan
Telephone: +81-75-761-6182
Fax: +81-75-761-6190
Email: sales@kyoto-up.gr.jp
Web: http://www.kyoto-up.or.jp

Trans Pacific Press
PO Box 164, Balwyn North, Melbourne
Victoria 3104, Australia
Telephone: +61 3 9859 1112
Fax: +61 3 9859 4110
Email: tpp.mail@gmail.com
Web: http://www.transpacificpress.com

This paperback edition published in 2009

Copyright © Kyoto University Press and Trans Pacific Press 2008

Text set by digital environs, Melbourne. Figures and tables set by Kyoto University Press.

Printed in Melbourne by BPA Print Group

Distributors

Australia and New Zealand
UNIREPS
University of New South Wales
Sydney, NSW 2052
Australia
Telephone: +61(0)2-9664-0999
Fax: +61(0)2-9664-5420
Email: info.press@unsw.edu.au
Web: http://www.unireps.com.au

USA and Canada
International Specialized Book Services (ISBS)
920 NE 58th Avenue, Suite 300
Portland, Oregon 97213-3786
USA
Telephone: (800) 944-6190
Fax: (503) 280-8832
Email: orders@isbs.com
Web: http://www.isbs.com

Asia and the Pacific
Kinokuniya Company Ltd.

Head office:
Shin-Mizonokuchi Bldg. 2F
5-7 Hisamoto 3-chome
Takatsu-ku, Kawasaki 213-8506
Japan
Telephone: +81(0)44-874-9642
Fax: +81(0)44-829-1025
Email: bkimp@kinokuniya.co.jp
Web: www.kinokuniya.co.jp

Asia-Pacific office:
Kinokuniya Book Stores of Singapore Pte., Ltd.
391B Orchard Road #13-06/07/08
Ngee Ann City Tower B
Singapore 238874
Telephone: +65 6276 5558
Fax: +65 6276 5570
Email: SSO@kinokuniya.co.jp

All rights reserved. No production of any part of this book may take place without the written permission of Kyoto University Press or Trans Pacific Press.

ISSN 1445–9663 (Kyoto Area Studies on Asia)
ISBN 978-1-920901-84-4 (Hardcover)
ISBN 978-1-920901-41-7 (Softcover)

Contents

List of Figures — vi
List of Tables — vii
Preface — ix

Introduction: Background to the Democratization of Thai Politics — 1

Part I: The May 1992 Incident

1 The Large-Scale Rally: Cause and Effect — 31
2 Political Decline of the Military: Reasons and Processes — 69

Part II: Calls for Political Reform and a New Constitution

3 The 1997 Constitution and its Political Significance — 115
4 The 2000 Senate Election: Return of the House of Public Officials — 175
5 The 2001 General Election: Did it Change Politics? — 201

Epilogue: Democratization of Thai Politics — 250

Notes — 267
Bibliography — 330
Name Index — 348
Subject Index — 353

List of Figures

0.1	MPs among the cabinet ministers, 1946–2001	15
1.1	Map of Bangkok	40
2.1	An example of matrimonial relations of Army leaders (The Sasiprapha family)	78
2.2	Royal Thai Army unit organization chart (major units only)	80
2.3	The succession plot of the post of Commander-in-Chief of the Army	87
2.4	The number of graduates and the number of divisional commanders by Academy class, 1980–2002	103
3.1	The 1997 Constitution drafting process	133
4.1	A breakdown of appointed legislators by occupation, 1932–1996	176
4.2	Example of the introduction of an election candidate (Pramot Maiklat)	183
4.3	Example of the introduction of an election winner (Pramot Maiklat)	185

List of Tables

2.1	Prime ministers, defense ministers, supreme commanders and commanders-in-chief (since 1980)	76
2.2	Personnel changes in the Army leadership (1), 1980–1991	82
2.3	Punitive personnel reshuffle, 1 August 1992	91
2.4	Personnel changes in the Army leadership (2), 1992–2002	94
2.5	The number of officers in key posts by Academy class, 1980–2001	104
3.1	The path to establishing the Constitution Drafting Assembly	118
3.2	The CDA work schedule	135
3.3	Proportion of university graduates in the total population (%)	143
3.4	Educational qualification of lower house candidates and winners in recent years	153
4.1	Senate elections, 2000–2002	180
4.2	Higher ranked candidates in five rounds of voting in Ubon Ratchathani	181
4.3	A breakdown of the 2000 Senatorial election candidates by occupation	184
4.4	A breakdown of the 2000 Senate election candidates and winners by occupation	187
4.5	A breakdown of the 2000 Senate election winners by occupation	189
4.6	Distribution of people with a higher education (university or higher) in 2000	193
4.7	Numbers, education and places of work of national public officials in 1999	194
4.8	A breakdown of the 2000 Senate election winners by education	198
4.9	Number of former public officials in the April 2001 Senate by-election	200
5.1	Red- and yellow-carded candidates and by-election winners by party	203
5.2	Single-seat district winners by party and region	204
5.3	District-based seats won in the 2001 election and in the previous four elections	205
5.4	Seats won by party in the 2001 election	206
5.5	Number of branches and members of major parties	208
5.6	State subsidy for major parties, 1999 and 2000 (in Baht)	209

5.7	Breakdown of income of major parties, 1998 and 1999	210
5.8	Donations to major parties, 1998–2000 (in Baht)	211
5.9	Example of the impact of electoral changes	216
5.10	Number of incumbent MPs and former candidates among candidates of major parties, 2001	226
5.11	Members of the House of Representatives in the Thaksin Cabinet, February 2001	232
5.12	Comparison of votes polled by major parties in party-list and single-seat districts	233
5.13	Votes polled by major parties in Chanthaburi province	236
5.14	Votes polled by major parties in Nakhon Sawan province	236
5.15	Votes polled by major parties in Khon Kaen province	237
6.1	Most respected prime minister, by region 1994 (%)	255
6.2	Votes polled by Thai Rak Thai and other major parties in party-list district in 2001, 2005 and 2006	261

Preface

It all began during my exciting days in Bangkok, capital city of Thailand, between April and September 1992. The political turmoil in May of the same year was irrefutably one of the most crucial turning points in the process of democratization in Thailand. Successive political events I witnessed were real eye-openers and provided me with a rich perspective. Quite naturally and irresistibly, I was guided towards the theme of this book – democratization in Thailand since the 1990s.

After years of research work on this topic, I am still, and increasingly, overwhelmed by the extent to which these events influenced the course of democratization of Thai politics in the following decade. The May 1992 turmoil eventually fostered the momentum for political reform and a new constitution. This was promulgated in 1997, almost coincidentally at a time of economic crisis. The 1997 Constitution radically – or in hindsight, terribly to some – changed Thai electoral and parliamentary politics; a shift which became apparent only in 2001 after the first general election under the new constitution. Without doubt, this very change paved the way for Thaksin's premiership from 2001, allowing Thaksin to further restructure Thai politics and society. Under Thaksin's leadership, Thailand was able to rise from the ashes of the 1997 economic crisis and once again made her presence felt in ASEAN and the world. In September 2006 however, Thaksin was toppled by a military coup.

The majority of this book is based upon research conducted in 1999 and 2000 under a grant from the Ministry of Education, Science and Culture of Japan. The research report, submitted immediately after the 2001 general election, was updated and published in Japan in 2003 by Kyoto University Press with university financial support. The book received the Ōhira Masayoshi Memorial Prize in the same year.

For this English edition, I opted not to make major alterations from the 2003 Japanese edition except for correction of factual errors and the insertion of a brief explanation of the 2006 coup in the form of a postscript in the Epilogue. Part of my analyses and judgments in 2003 turned out to be off the mark today. However, my main arguments, framework and analyses remain relevant and convincing. This book is therefore useful for those who want to understand politics in Thailand in the last three decades. Unfortunately, my prediction in the 2003 edition that democracy would face a crisis under the overly-stable Thaksin administration proved right in 2006. The coup was staged and supported by forces opposing the full realization of electoral politics.

In studying Thai politics I am indebted to just too many people. Allow me to mention only a few Thai names for this edition. During my student days from 1983 to 1985 at the faculty of political science, *Sing Dam*, Chulalongkorn University, under the scholarship of the Ministry of Education, Science and Culture of Japan, the late Professor Phornsak Phongpaew was my adviser and generously extended his kindness and hospitality to me. My classmates of 'B6' and 'B7' at the faculty, many of whom are now government officials, taught me the Thai way of thinking. The Thai language skills I acquired during that time opened the door for me to continue to form a wider circle of acquaintances. These friends have always been good teachers for me on Thai politics, society or history. Especially noteworthy are Nakharin Mektrairat of Thammasat University and Atthachak Sattayanurak of Chiang Mai University, both from my generation. These friends are the best drinking companions, and stimulating discussions with them over glasses of beer helped me a great deal in gaining new insights on a range of subjects. Several Thai students who came to study in Japan fell victim to, but endured, a barrage of questions about their society from this curious Japanese professor. Khwanthida, Viengrat, Lakkhana, Achakorn and Kriangchai are among these ill-fated students. To all my unnamed friends who helped me in the understanding of Thailand, I extend my deepest gratitude.

This publication would not have been possible without a generous grant from the Japan Society for the Promotion of Science (JSPS). My gratitude also goes to Kyoto University Press and Trans Pacific Press which carried out all the necessary arrangements. Pasuk Phongpaichit and Jojo Abinales read the early version of the English manuscript and gave most valuable comments and advice, which I hope I was able to incorporate. Uchida Haruko diligently perused every page of the Japanese edition and English manuscript, and her assistance was indispensable in translation and editing. I appreciate all the support from other unnamed friends and colleagues.

I alone, of course, am responsible for any factual or interpretive errors.

1
Introduction: Background to the Democratization of Thai Politics

The aim of this book is to empirically examine the democratization of Thai politics, focusing primarily on the 1990s.[1] Since the early 1990s, the democratization has been generally understood in terms of a theory that locates the urban middle class at center stage. It came to be generally accepted among researchers in the field of Thai politics that the Thai middle class played a central role in the May 1992 incident, thus proving to be the main pillar of democratization. Then, beginning with the premise that the middle class is the central or primary force for democratization, it is assumed as axiomatic that the political reform movement that began in the mid-1990s with the middle class's support has significantly contributed to the further development of democracy. In other words, the proponents of this view claim that the emergence of the middle class has put slow-moving democratization on a fast track.

However, this interpretation seems to be full of holes. First, the middle class-led democratization theory may be able to shed some light on the democratization of the 1990s, but it has little relevance whatsoever to the pre-1990s era. Further, the processes of democratization clearly did not suddenly emerge in the 1990s; although progress was very slow, advancing in fits and starts, it had in fact begun decades earlier at a time when the Thai middle class was virtually nonexistent. There is no doubt that the size of the middle class was increasing but the middle class, as a social class rather than individual members, never played a significant role in the world of politics in either action or discourse.[2] It is therefore misguided to attempt to explain democratization only in terms of the middle class. We must, instead, develop a theory that can account for the continuity between the 1980s and 1990s, rather than cutting the former off from the latter.

Second, the dominant interpretation of the May 1992 incident appears to be the only 'evidence' that the middle class is the primary force behind democratization. There can be no doubt that this incident was an extremely important event in the democratization of Thai politics, but there are very solid grounds for doubting that the middle class was the leading actor. Third, objectives and effects of the 1997 Constitution must be considered in detail before we can determine if the political reform movement of the 1990s will contribute to deepening the roots of democracy. To cite one example, the 1997

Constitution stipulated that members of parliament and the cabinet must have a bachelor's degree in spite of the fact that only 5% of the total population were qualified in 1990. Why did the 1997 Constitution, praised as very democratic, restrict eligibility for election to a small number of university graduates? The 'middle class-led democratization thesis' is unable to provide answers to these simple questions.

Pro-democracy researchers tend to pay more attention to proponents for democratization and search for such proponents. The middle class is often regarded as a part of the proponents. However, my perspective is that opponents are more crucial than proponents for democratization. Opponents usually have vested interests in the previous non-democratic regime and are often politically powerful enough to resist democratization. As far as such powerful opponents do not comply with democratization, chances of successful democratization must be low. Therefore, the appeasement of the opponents is no less crucial than emergence or empowerment of the proponents.

As I will explain in detail, the democratization of Thai politics can be divided into two phases: the transition phase and the consolidation phase. While the former began in the 1970s and ended in the 1980s, the latter began in the 1990s. A significant characteristic of the transition phase is a conservative pact that deprived radical or progressive aspects of party politics. Leftist parties were purged and politics came to be dominated by conservative parties. Due to this moderatism, democratic transition became possible. Conversely, the consolidation phase started in 1992 after the military retreated from politics. This book runs counter to the popular perception of the middle class-driven democratization and argues that the key role played by the middle class was moderation rather than promotion of democracy. The middle class achieved discursive power after the May 1992 incident and prevented the numerical majority of the population, rural residents and urban lower class people, from gaining the hegemony.

Middle class-centered argument and its problems

Emergence of the argument
The most commonly accepted view in the study of Thai politics up to the 1980s was the bureaucratic polity theory. According to this model, first proposed by Riggs (1996), the bureaucracy controlled politics because other forces were weak. According to Riggs, one manifestation of this bureaucratic control was the overrepresentation of military and civil bureaucrats in the cabinet. This bureaucratic polity theory is based on three principal assumptions:

1. A bureaucratic polity is non-democratic.
2. A bureaucratic polity was possible because opposing 'extra-bureaucratic forces' (parliament, political parties, business community, student organizations, labor unions, peasants' groups etc.) were weak.
3. Conversely, the bureaucratic polity would collapse if extra-bureaucratic forces gained power.

Both the substance and the application of this model are problematic. Broadly speaking, the model was used for two purposes. One was to identify various political and administrative problems and to attribute them to the bureaucratic polity. The other was to identify the emergence of extra-bureaucratic forces that would defeat the bureaucratic forces. Both approaches interpret Thailand's political history and current situation in a negative light and criticize the 'bureaucracy.' The model appears to have been used primarily as a tool for critique rather than analysis.[3] There are at least four serious problems with this 'model.' First is the fact that many of the researchers using this model do not differentiate the political role of the military from that of the administrative bureaucrats, lumping them together as the 'bureaucracy.' For example, Chaianan Samutthawanit (Chai-anan Samudavanija), regarded by many as the leading researcher of Thai politics, discusses the history and characteristics of the administrative bureaucracy, then suddenly switches his topic to the 'bureaucratic polity' and criticizes political intervention by the military in his paper on the 'bureaucracy' (Chaianan 1987). Perhaps it is easier and more convenient to treat the military and the administrative bureaucracy together as the 'bureaucracy' than to handle them separately. Furthermore, their critiques of bureaucratic power tend to follow simple stereotypes with little corroborative evidence. Second, they typically appear to begin from the assumption that excessive bureaucratic power hampers democratization, overlooking problems on the side of the non-bureaucratic forces. Because they expected the extra-bureaucratic forces to challenge and compete against the bureaucratic force, any evidence of cooperation between the extra-bureaucratic and bureaucratic forces was assumed to be subordination and dependency of the extra-bureaucratic forces, and therefore dismissed. Third, they overemphasized changes in the proportion of bureaucrats in the cabinet, assuming that higher proportions of extra-bureaucrats could be read as a sign of democratization. In particular, the increasing number of businesspeople in the cabinet in the 1980s was hailed as evidence of democratization. Emphasis was placed on the fact that these businesspeople were not bureaucrats, but few researchers paid proper attention to whether they had any merits or virtues beyond their business skills. This bureaucratic polity theory was so popular that analysts ignored the fact that whether or not the cabinet members were bureaucrats was not a very meaningful measure of democracy. The proportion of elected MPs among cabinet ministers is actually the more important measure of democracy; whether elected MPs have military or bureaucratic backgrounds is of secondary concern. Fourth, Thailand's bureaucracy is neither very autonomous nor very efficient; it is certainly not as strong as the bureaucratic polity theorists seem to expect (Tamada 1988). Chai Uengphakon (Ji Ungpakorn) makes the following observation on this point:

> From the viewpoint of the poor who have always been ill-treated by soldiers, policemen and government officials, Thailand's bureaucracy may appear strong. In reality, however, the Thai bureaucracy is a weak entity that oppresses and abuses those who are weaker than it. It is like a savage dog that bites children on the roadside, yet is scared of its master. Those researchers who consider the excessive power of the bureaucracy as the real impediment to democratization do not understand the essence of a capitalist country or the nature of a modern state. (Chai et al. 2000: 57)

Up to the 1980s when the bureaucratic polity model was the commonly accepted theory, the military and the bureaucracy were considered to be the biggest villains in the struggle for democracy. The good guys were 'extra-bureaucratic' party politicians and the businesspeople who supported them. However, the military withdrew from politics in the 1990s. About the same time, bureaucrats also moved down in the ranking of villains. Party politicians soon emerged as the new impediment to democratization, and quickly came to be regarded as the villains of the story.

From the bureaucratic polity to the middle class

Interestingly, even as the party politicians 'fell from grace,' so to speak, the businesspeople—who had been supporting the party politicians since the 1970s—remained the 'good guys.' How do we explain this? First, we might begin with Anek's analysis (1992) that has had a significant influence on Thai studies. Anek emphasized the importance of corporatist-type political participation via business associations rather than parliamentary politics. This was perhaps one of the reasons that researchers on Thai politics tended to pay more attention to corporatist politics rather than party politics when they analyzed the relationships between businesspeople and politics in the 1990s. For example, Surin and McCargo (1997: 145) argue that '[e]lections have become the domain of a broad coalition of three strategic political groups: veteran politicians (across all parties), bureaucrats (particularly from the Interior Ministry) and provincial business people. This political-bureaucratic-business "iron triangle," or rather "vicious triangle"—which is essentially conservative in its political orientation—is making the electoral process increasingly exclusionary.' Further, 'electoral politics...can easily become a vehicle for consolidating the power of the conservative triumvirate.' As the Interior Ministry has played a powerful role in the provinces, this 'iron triangle' is portrayed as a triangle of provincial forces. It suggests that provincial businesspeople have formed an alliance with party politicians and bureaucrats through which they can control the national government. Yet such analyses overlook the fact that there are only small to medium sized businesses in Thai provinces; all large corporations are located in the national capital, and these large corporations have long maintained close connections with political power.[4] Hence, the claim that provincial forces control national politics is totally false—but it has effectively protected the capital's business community from the criticisms of party politics.

Second, businesspeople themselves are now commonly stereotyped in two groups: the 'good businesspeople' in the capital are portrayed as 'international and civilized' while the 'bad provincial businesspeople' are seen as parochial and backwards, trying to take advantage of party politics to protect their illegal ventures. Many party politicians are provincial businesspeople and have recently become targets of criticism. This framework ignores the important fact that provincial businesspeople are not the only supporters of party politics. Indeed, it is primarily provincial businesspeople who run for national elections and support election campaigns, but the political parties that muster these provincially-elected MPs are based in the capital, and their financiers are large corporate businesspeople in the capital. In a sense, party politics have been supported by provincial businesspeople from below and by the metropolitan businesspeople from above (Tamada 1988). It is safe to say, then, that 'Political parties are representatives of the capitalists' (*Matichon Sutsapda*, 14 July 2002).

In 1997, Narong likened Thai politics to theatre, explaining that politicians are merely actors who perform according to their director's instructions. If they perform poorly, they are simply replaced by another. The director is the financier who is never replaced, and never changes the plot. Thus, for example, when the Asian currency crisis broke out in July 1997, Thanin Chiarawanon (Dhanin Chearavanont), an owner and CEO of the CP Group met former Prime Minister Prem, Prime Minister Chawalit (Chavalit) and other prominent politicians in a series of meetings, and the government accommodated his wishes. The government pays close attention to the opinions of the business community, and while Thai people question whether their government is good or bad, they seem to shut their eyes to the misdeeds of the business community, assuming it to be good (Narong 1997). Yet if the party politics is corrupted by fiscal politics, the financier is none other than the business community. The businesspeople in the capital have managed to sustain a 'good guy' image despite having consistently supported party politics.[5]

In the 1990s, the middle class, particularly the urban middle class, assumed the central position in the good guy camp. The May 1992 bloodshed became a turning point for the middle class. The uprising was interpreted as a democratization movement of the urban middle class, which led, in turn, to this group being regarded as the core democratizing force. Thailand's economy grew steadily from the 1960s until the late 1980s, after which it experienced growth in spurts. There can be no doubt that the size of the middle class grew with the economy. The proportion of the middle class based on occupational classification (professionals, managers and administrator, and clerks) gradually increased from 2.6% in 1960 to 4.7% in 1970, 10.2% in 1980 and 13.0% in 1990 (Hattori et al. 2002: 289). It is also clear that the middle class concentrates in cities, particularly in the capital. These facts lend credence to the modernization approach's view that economic growth expands the urban middle class and thereby promotes the democratization of politics. Thus the interpretation of the urban middle class as the primary democratizing force has become widely accepted.

Once the middle class was recognized as the driving force of democratization and the symbol of the good guy camp, more people wanted to join in, and researchers began to revise the concept of the middle class. As a result, the good guys are now described as the 'citizenry' (*phonlamueang*), 'civil society' (*pracha sangkhom*), the 'public' (*satharana*)[6] and so on, each of which is a slightly broader concept than the 'middle class.' Or, following Surin and McCargo, 'internationalist capitalists, the middle class, the media and intellectuals... can broadly be called the reformists' (1997: 146). The media, NGOs, intellectuals and businesspeople were lumped together under this broad term. It is not always clear who the term refers to. Only two things are clear; that this category is assumed to be the driving force behind democratization and that it excludes rural residents and the urban poor. Its highly abstract nature and lack of specificity seem to have made it a rather convenient concept in political discourse. Any political movements in the 1990s that were allegedly supported by such forces were regarded as democratization movements.

Problems with the middle class-centered theory

Attempting to explain democratization as driven by the urban middle class causes inconsistencies. Although many researchers try to attribute the pre-1990s developments to the role of the middle class as well, this is unfounded. The urban middle class played no significant role in politics before 1992, despite its steady expansion. Proponents of this view, therefore, either have to mount a farfetched argument that the middle class played an important role in the 1970s and 1980s as well, or admit that the middle class was sleeping until 1992. The latter position will inevitably lead to either a self-contradictory view that democratization is a phenomenon peculiar to the period after 1992 or an acknowledgement that democratization was driven by forces other than the middle class until the 1990s. While it is undeniable that the middle class was an important political protagonist in the 1990s, overestimating its influence by stretching it back into the past is problematic. The tendency to restrict one's vision to a narrow window of the 1990s seems to be one reason for overrating the role of the middle class. In order to better understand the democratization in the 1990s, we should locate the changes in the decade in a broader historical context.

Overview of theories of democratization

As Tilly observes, 'old Thailand provides a textbook case of military rule' (1992: 212). There were ten successful military coups during the six decades after 1932. However, in the wake of the May 1992 incident political parties took the place of the military as the main players, and elections seemed to become established as the normal mode of regime change.

How was politics democratized in Thailand? In seeking an answer to this question, I begin with a brief overview of theories of democratization in the fields of political science and Asian studies.

Approaches to democratization

Democratization means a transition from a non-democratic regime to a democratic one. Josepf Schumpeter defined democracy as a system for 'arriving at political decisions in which individuals acquire the power to decide by means of a competitive struggle for the people's vote' (cited in Diamond 1999: 8). Countless slightly modified versions of this definition have been published, but this is the more or less accepted theory. For example, Huntington defines a political system as democratic when 'its most powerful collective decision makers are selected through fair, honest, and periodic elections in which candidates freely compete for votes, and in which virtually all the adult population is eligible to vote' (1995: 7).

Democratization has occurred in many parts of the world since the mid-1970s. From the mid-1980s, as the cases of democratization increased, 'the study of democracy and democratization has come to occupy center stage in the field of comparative politics' (Bunce 2000: 703). Huntington (1991) called this succession of democratic changes from the mid-1970s 'the third wave of democratization' and attributed it to four factors: external actors, changes in the Catholic Church, snowballing effect (transmission), and economic growth. Huntington's study has provided a strong stimulus and shaping influence on studies of democratization since the 1990s. The absence of any definitive recipe for democratization is heating up the discussion.

Potter (1997) categorized explanations of democratization according to three frameworks: the modernization approach, the transition approach and the structural approach. The modernization approach, led by Lipset, argues that socioeconomic development changes variables such as income levels, telephone ownership rates, literacy rates, education standards and urbanization, and as a consequence, politics becomes democratized. This method is characterized by its generalizing tendency—attempting to explain many countries by focusing on a single variable. Although it emphasizes the correlation between variables and democratization, the modernization approach cannot adequately explain any causal relationship. Secondly, the transition approach, pioneered by Rustow, regards democracy as the product of decisions made by elites in the course of history. Many studies tend to focus on the choices and behavior of the elites in power and in opposition during the last two phases—the transition phase and the consolidation phase—of the four-phase democratization model proposed by Rustow. Finally, the structural approach argues that social or economic transformation over a prolonged period can change the power structure between classes and thus can lead to democratization. The key is the power relations between the classes for and against democracy. Since a real-life democratization process is complex and multifaceted and cannot be explained by any single approach, many analysts began to adopt some sort of synthesis of all three approaches during the 1990s (Potter 1997: 10–24).[7]

Whether one focuses on modernization, elites or social structure, the following six factors are frequently identified as promoters of democratization. First is economic development, a very important factor, particularly in the modernization and structural approaches. Modernization theorists have paid particular attention to the correlation between economic growth and democratization, focusing their efforts on trying to discover the parameters of this relationship. Structural theorists assume that the impact of economic growth on politics is not homogeneous and contend that causal links between economic growth, class structure and democratization need to be analyzed on a case-by-case basis. Second is social segmentation, which can be broadly classified into economic and cultural types. Class, for example, is an economic form of segmentation. Lipset (in Potter 1997) contends that modernization helps the bourgeoisie (middle class)[8] expand, leading to democratization. In contrast, structural theorists such as Rueschemeyer et al. (1992) argue that the attitude of a particular class toward democratization is dependent on its relationship with other classes, and that the bourgeoisie does not necessarily aspire to democracy. Third is state and political institutions. Both modernization and structural theorists argue that democratization is difficult when the state is too strong. Fourth is civil society. All of the approaches consider that a strong and pluralistic civil society becomes a counterforce to state power and contributes to democratization. The structural approach, however, cautions that civil society consists of several classes and not all of them are invariably democracy-oriented. Fifth is political culture. Modernization theorists think that culture becomes more democracy-friendly (participatory, moderate, and tolerant toward dissent, for example) as modernization progresses. In contrast, the structural theorists regard democratic political culture as merely a result of democratization, not a cause. Transitional theorists, however, argue that how different groups of elites view their gains and losses from democratic compromise is the key and leave cultural values out of consideration. The sixth factor is the influence from the international community, including the effects of war, the attitudes of world powers and international organizations, and borderless economic and information flows (Potter 1997: 24–31).

Bunce (2000: 715) conducted a review of analyses of democratization and concluded with five generalizations:

> These generalizations are that high levels of economic development function as a virtual guarantee of democratic continuity, political leaders are central to the founding and design of democracy and to its survival or collapse under conditions of crisis, parliamentary system are a far better investment in the continuation of democratic governance than the presidential system, settlement of the national and state questions are crucial investments in the quality and survival of democracy, and old and well-established and new and fragile democracies have, as their common ground, uncertain results but, as their defining contrast, certain versus uncertain procedures.[9]

Bunce reveals that we can detect regional characteristics in democratization,[10] comparing Latin American and Southern European countries with former Soviet bloc countries. In the former, pacts made between authoritarian elites and leaders of the opposition forces were more beneficial for democratization than a popular uprising. By 'using pacts as a way to bridge the old and new orders, authoritarian leaders and leaders of the opposition forces have both the incentives and the capacity to cooperate with each other' (Bunce 2000: 716). Meanwhile, making pacts was 'no more desirable than those transitions that involve substantial mass protest and/or a sudden collapse of the authoritarian rule' in the post-Socialist European countries (Bunce 2000: 716). In other words, we can pose a contrast 'between regime transitions that bridge authoritarian and democratic rule and those that involve a sharp break with the authoritarian past....the first approach has tended to be the most successful in producing full-scale and sustainable democracies in the south...and the second approach the most successful strategy in the east' (Bunce 2000: 717). Bunce did not, however, mention the Asian regions.

Democratization in East and Southeast Asia
Democratization began in some of the countries of East and Southeast Asia during the 1980s. The number of studies that compare several countries in the region has been increasing since the 1990s. A notable example is the study by Pei (1998). His comparative study of democratization in South Korea, Taiwan, the Philippines and Thailand points to five factors underpinning democratization. First is the internal decay of authoritarian institutions. This applies to the collapse of the Marcos regime in the Philippines. A transition to democracy triggered by such a collapse is prone to instability. Second is a 'managed transition,' that is, a top-down process of democratization, which applies to Taiwan, South Korea and Thailand. This process entails gradual liberalization, including moderate improvement in the fairness and competitiveness of local and national elections, greater freedom granted to opposition forces, and considerable reductions in the government's control of mass media, in the lead up to the end of an authoritarian regime. Third is the rise of civil society, indicating the increased activism of various interest groups and social movements led by the dissident intelligentsia (university professors, students and journalists). Fourth is socioeconomic change, which, since the 1960s, has expanded the middle class which constitutes the core of various civic groups. As society becomes more affluent, the people begin to demand from their government not only economic growth but also political freedom and participation. Fifth is external pressure. For the Philippines, the US gave up on Marcos and moved to support the Aquino government. In South Korea, the military refrained from suppressing the democratization movement in 1987 because of pressure from the US and concerns that their hosting of the Olympics might be at stake. For Taiwan, which became internationally isolated in the 1970s, democratization was necessary to secure support from the US, which was vital for its survival (Pei 1998: 66–71).

Note that Pei does not mention two of the factors that Huntington highlights: the importance of the Catholic Church and the transmission effect. This is perhaps because the Philippines is the only country in the region to which the former is relevant.[11] As for the transmission effect, some have argued that the Philippines' political upheaval in 1986 influenced South Korea's declaration of democratization in 1987, Myanmar's (Burma) anti-military government movement in 1988 and China's Tiananmen Square incident in 1989. This effect should not be exaggerated, however, since only South Korea succeeded with democratization. Focus should therefore be on external actors and economic growth, which are common factors cited by Potter (1997), Huntington (1995) and Pei (1998).[12]

'External actors' refers to pressure from the international community to promote democratization. Taiwan, South Korea, and the Philippines fell under this category as mentioned above. Malaysia and Singapore, in contrast, barely acknowledge similar democratization pressures, and Myanmar's military rule continues despite harsh external criticism. Furthermore, although dramatic changes following the end of the Cold War have left only five single party (socialist) dictatorships around the world at the end of the twentieth century, four of them are in Asia: China, North Korea, Vietnam and Laos. These countries have begun to introduce market economies, but have made almost no changes to their political systems.

Arguably, external pressures from world powers only work effectively when a particular regime is largely dependent on them (Iwasaki 2001).[13] Pressure from the US appears to have had some effect on Taiwan, South Korea and the Philippines, but it has been less effective for countries that are less dependent on the US, especially militarily. One example of this is Thailand, from which US troops were withdrawn in the mid-1970s. In addition, the world powers tend to apply less pressure on those countries that are politically and economically important for them. Examples include China, and Indonesia under Soeharto. Conversely, they can apply stronger pressure to smaller countries in which they have little direct interest, Myanmar being a typical example. Thus, external actors cannot be regarded as a definitive cause of democratization. Therefore, the circumstantial evidence of external involvement in democratization processes must be analyzed carefully in conjunction with diverse domestic factors (Tsunekawa 2000: 4).

As mentioned above, economic growth is typically cited as the most important domestic factor contributing to democratization. Modernization theorists argue that economic growth fosters the growth of the middle class or civil society, which invariably demands democracy and initiates democratization. Huntington (1991), who primarily adopts a modernization approach, argues that what is important in the relationship between economic growth and democratization is not income levels but industrialization. Where economic growth involves industrialization, the economy develops into a more complex structure than what an authoritarian regime can handle. More directly, economic growth changes the values and fabric of society and gives rise to aspirations for democracy.

Huntington points out five specific changes. First, improved living standards lead to higher levels of mutual trust and life satisfaction which are compatible with democracy. Second, economic development results in improved education standards, which in turn instill in the people necessary characteristics of democracy such as mutual trust, satisfaction and an ability-oriented view. Third, economic development increases the gross amount of resources available for distribution and thus makes it easier to reach acceptable compromises. Fourth, economic growth increases the international interdependence of economies, and foreign pressure becomes unavoidable. Fifth, economic development promotes the expansion of the middle class, including businesspeople, professionals, shop owners, teachers, public servants, managers, engineers, office workers and retail workers (Huntington 1991: 65–6).

Huntington's main focus is the middle class: 'In virtually every country the most active supporters of democratization came from the urban middle class' (1991: 66). However, certain conditions had to be satisfied for the middle class to join in the democratization forces.

> In its early phases, the middle class is not necessarily a force for democracy. At times in Latin America and elsewhere, middle class groups acquiesced in or actively supported military coups designed to overthrow radical governments and to reduce the political influence of labor and peasant organizations. As the process of modernization continued, however, rural radical movements had decreasing leverage on the process, and the urban middle class increased in size compared to the industrial working class. The potential threats democracy posed to middle class groups thus declined, and those groups became increasingly confident of their ability to advance their interests through electoral politics. (Huntington 1991: 66–7)

Huntington argues that '[i]n the Philippines, middle class professionals and businesspeople filled the ranks of the demonstrations against Marcos in 1986,' that the core actors for political change in Taiwan were the newly emergent middle class intellectuals, and that the most important players in South Korea's 1987 democratization movement were 'the managerial and professional classes of Seoul.' Further, in the Philippines, 'the business community, which had previously supported the creation of authoritarian regime[s], played crucial roles in promoting the transition to democracy' (Huntington 1991: 67–8).

However, as Fujiwara (1987: 15) points out, 'the association between the middle class... status and its political behavior cannot be unambiguously determined,' and as Huntington also acknowledges, it is 'not necessarily a force for democracy.' We therefore should not exaggerate the role of the middle class. It is often suggested that the middle class in Malaysia and Singapore are supportive of their authoritarian political systems despite these countries' relatively steady economic growth rates and high middle class demographics. It is also argued that the middle class in the East and Southeast Asian region are generally the beneficiaries of economic growth and gravitate toward order and stability to protect their vested interests (Jones 1997: chapter 3).[14] Kitahara, for example, observes that 'the middle class in East Asia does not necessarily prefer a democratic political system and more often than not would not recognize the urban lower class and small farmers as citizens (2002a: 17). In South Korea, for example, although the middle class participated in the democracy movement of June 1987, it did not oppose the military takeover in 1979 and became gradually more conservative after June 1987 (Moriyama 1998: 114, 118–21).[15] Iwasaki also states that

> Strangely contrasting views are held by academics in the US and Asia in regard to the analysis of political attitudes of the middle class (in Indonesia, Singapore and Malaysia); Political scientists in the US tend to assume that the middle class are supporters of democratization while researchers in the field of Asian area studies contend that they are either conservative or politically apathetic. One of the reasons for this appears to be that the former views Asian civil society ideologically and the latter is looking at the circumstances of each country individually. (1998a: 27; also 1998b: 99–104)

We must therefore be cautious about associating the formation and expansion of the middle class with democratization.[16]

Then what about civil society? Anek, a modernization theorist, also argues that strengthening civil society is the key to democratization, while economic development is 'neither a necessary nor a sufficient condition for democratic transition' (1997: 17).[17] Yet Endō, a researcher on Africa, maintains that civil society can be regarded as an extension of the middle class,[18] and argues that

> Not enough work has been done in the past…to establish a clear theory about the logic or causal relationship of how the increased activity of a force generally categorized as 'civil society' comes to support democratization. Other parameters need to be considered in regard to this question. (2000: 19)

This applies to Asia as well as Africa. It should be reminded that civil society is rife with inequalities and its expansion contributes to democratization only when it helps to strengthen the weak, such as peasants and laborers (Rueschmeyer et al. 1992: 50). Itō cautions against expecting too much of civil society, arguing that it 'should be seen as an arena for "struggles between various groups" for "hegemony"' (2002: 21). *A priori* assumptions of a glorified and abstract conception of civil society as a promoter of democratization may be an effective campaign slogan, but it is not very useful for accurate analysis. Tilly goes so far as to suggest that 'scholars and political leaders who seek keys to democratization should stop looking for the elusive realm called "civil society" and abandon attempts to strengthen it' (2000: 14).

Thus it is difficult to identify forces or factors that promote democratization decisively. Nevertheless, it is certain that Thai politics has been democratized in the last three decades. Why and how? Let's take a look back on the democratizing process.

Democratization of Thai politics: phases and characteristics

Phases of democratization in Thailand

In order to examine a process of democratization, it is necessary to identify when it progressed. Applying the transition approach allows us to separate the transition and consolidation phases of democratization.

To begin with, it is necessary to define what democratization means in Thailand. Thailand maintains a parliamentary government system under a constitutional monarchy. Its highest policy makers include the prime minister and the cabinet ministers. Therefore, Thai politics can be regarded as democratic when competitive and fair elections are held, government changes according to the election results, and the prime minister and other cabinet members are appointed from the elected members of parliament or MPs.[19] Up to 2001, a total of twenty general elections were held, namely in 1933, 1937, 1938, 1946, 1948, 1952, February and December 1957, 1969, 1975, 1976, 1979, 1983, 1986, 1988, March and September 1992, 1995, 1996 and 2001.[20] Until the 1990s, a new government was created according to election results only four times (1946, 1975, 1976 and 1988). In contrast, all five general elections since 1990 have seen the defeat of the then ruling party and a change of government. Finally, the proportion of popularly elected members of the parliament in the cabinet was, of course, zero before the establishment of the parliament in 1932, also zero from 1932 to 1944, then an average of 35% or so from 1944 to 1957 although it fluctuated greatly,[21] and zero again for more than sixteen years from October 1958. The proportion jumped to over 96% in the mid-1970s following the collapse of the military regime, and reverted to zero again at the time of the 1976 coup d'état but has been rising steadily ever since. Although it was only 19% after the general election in 1979, it steadily increased from around 40% to over 80%

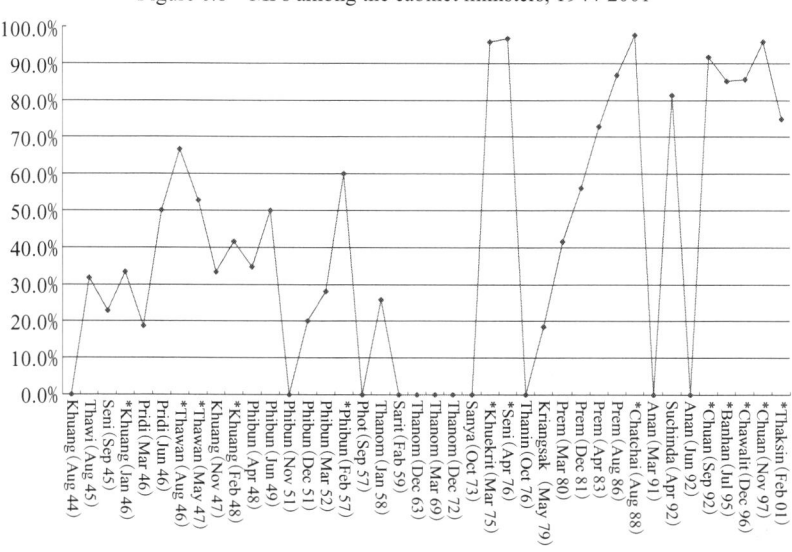

Figure 0.1 MPs among the cabinet ministers, 1944-2001

Source: Prepared by the author based on the lists of cabinet members and MPs.
Note: The names of prime ministers are listed underneath the horizontal axis. * denotes those who were elected MPs at the time of appointment.

under the Prem administration between 1980 and 1988, finally reaching 98% in 1988 under the Chatchai government. Since then, it has remained constantly above 80% except for two periods under the premiership of Anan Panyarachun. In contrast, it has declined to as low as 75% under the Thaksin administration which came to power in 2001 following the 1997 political reform.

Despite the fact that a general election had been held every few years except for a long hiatus before 1969, the election results were barely reflected in the composition of the cabinet—only a small number of elected MPs were included because the cabinet was dominated by military officers and administrative officials. Inclusion of a growing number of elected MPs in the cabinet based on election results was a necessary precondition for democratization. Accordingly, the best way to identify the period of democratization is to investigate the changes in the proportion of popularly elected MPs in the cabinet. There are two identifiable peaks in the course of change (see Figure 0.1). The first is a sudden jump from 0% to 96% in the mid-1970s, and the second is a stunningly steady climb from 0% in October 1976 to 98% in August 1988. After that, it remained at around 80% except for a couple of brief interruptions from 1991 to 1992. During this period, as mentioned, a new premier was chosen after each election. It is thus clear that the most important period of transition to democracy is the period of Prem's administration from 1980 to 1988. The proportion of popularly elected MPs in the cabinet increased to 42%, 56%, 73% and 87% after each cabinet reshuffle under Prem, from a mere 19% under the preceding Kriangsak government. The 1990s, then, can be regarded as the consolidation phase of democracy. The progress made during the Prem administration supported by the elected MPs, the monarchy and the military is what Pei (1998) characterizes as 'managed transition.' Taking a lesson from the failure in the mid-1970s, the democratization attempt from the end of the 1970s was implemented from top down. Although this managed democratization clearly went off the tracks twice after the 1980s—the February 1991 coup and the May 1992 incident—it recovered quickly each time, heading towards the consolidation phase from 1992. The 1990s must be understood as part of this gradual democratization process.

Granting that the 1997 Constitution marks the consolidation of democracy, it took a quarter of a century to realize democratization. This history of twists and turns must be taken into account in examining the democratization process from 1992 onward, when the role of the middle class became more prominent. The most significant of these turns were the dramatic rise and fall of party politics in the mid-1970s and another shift towards it at the end of the 1970s. Why did such dramatic changes come about?

Bunce offers some clues: 'There is widespread agreement that political elites play a central role in democratization' (2000: 707).

> If political leaders, for various reasons, are understood to be the founders of democracy, then they also often function, after that initial breakthrough, as its sustainers or its underminers. Thus, for example, they design political institutions (which affect the quality and, perhaps, the very survival of democracy); they decide to be more or less constrained by the rules of the democratic game (which affects quality and sustainability…); and in periods of political and/or economic difficulties, they can use their power to either protect democracy or destroy it. (Bunce 2000: 709)

However, 'once founded, the course of democracy depends on a complex array of factors, only one of which involves elites, their attitudes, and their behavior' (Bunce 2000: 709). As Bunce points out, the role of political elites was significant during the transition period from the 1970s to the 1980s. Answers to the questions as to why democracy was denied in 1976 and how its resumption was possible can be found in concerns about the rise of left-wing forces and the elimination of these concerns. Here we should recall Rueschmeyer et al.'s observation that forces that oppose democracy are decisive for democratization

(1992). Not everyone welcomes democracy. There are many who worry that their interests may be eroded by parliamentary politics. Hence, successful democratization requires not only the emergence of democratizing forces, but also the successful appeasement of opposing forces (Rueschmeyer et al. 1992: 287, 296–7). In what follows, then, I examine the democratization of Thailand in the 1990s, focusing on the appeasement of forces opposing democratization rather than the achievements of the forces that are supposedly driving it.

Before analyzing democratization in the 1990s, though, I briefly review the democratization process that began in the 1970s,[22] in order to better understand the main political currents to the end of the 1980s, by shedding light on the appeasement of the passive forces of resistance during the transition phase. This will provide important background for a fuller discussion of what happened during the 1990s.

The transition phase in Thai democratization

The transition phase can be seen to begin with a popular revolt against military rule in 1973. However, the crucial part of this phase was a 'conservative' pact negotiated and institutionalized in the 1980s.

Political turbulence in the 1970s

The military government led by Thanom Kittikhachon (Prime Minister, Defense Minister and Supreme Commander) and Praphat Charusathian (Prapass Charusthira) toppled on 14 October 1973 following a political upheaval that mobilized hundreds of thousand of protesters and left more than seventy dead. The university students who triggered this incident were hailed as heroes and the incident was dubbed the 'Student Uprising.' This incident became a landmark for democratization and the university students were long revered as the 'October 14th generation.' However, rallies and demonstrations were actually attended by people from a wide range of social strata and the students of secondary and vocational schools played as important a role as the university students.[23] Moreover, although the massive crowd and the deaths were perhaps necessary conditions for the ensuing democratization, they were not, of themselves, sufficient. For sufficient conditions we must look to the military and the King.

The military's personnel changes had been stagnant since the 1960s and frustration was growing among the officers. Krit Siwara, who was finally promoted to the position of Commander-in-Chief of the Army on 1 October 1973 after seven years of waiting, abandoned the government leaders when the anti-government uprising broke out and defied orders to subdue the demonstrators.

The King delivered the final blow to Thanom and Praphat by ordering them to resign and leave the country. He then appointed Sanya Thammasak as Prime Minister. Sanya had retired as the Chief Justice in 1967 and had been appointed as a Privy Councilor the following year. His appointment as Prime Minister meant the formation of the 'King's government' for the first time in his reign, hence the event is also called the 'royal coup' (Withaya 1983: 513). Sanya held a general election on 26 January 1975 to complete the important transition to party politics. He was appointed as President of the Privy Council on 5 December 1975.[24]

In the lead up to the general election in January 1975, businesspeople had formed a number of political parties. Businesspeople did not play any notable role in the overthrow of the military junta, though, as they had been in collusion with the government and military leaders under the military government. Once their partners were overthrown, however, and the door to party politics was opened, many businesspeople entered politics. After the election, Khuekrit Pramot (Kukrit Pramoj), the leader of the small Social Action Party with only eighteen seats, successfully organized a coalition to form government on 17 March 1975. Khuekrit proposed various policies to alleviate poverty in rural areas. When the opposition Democrat Party formed an alliance with leftist parties and began preparations to replace the unstable coalition government, the military pressured the government to dissolve the Parliament in January 1976 (Morell and Chaianan 1981: 262). A general election was held on 4 April 1976 and Seni Pramot of the Democrat Party became Prime Minister.

In this period, Thailand faced drastic changes both at home and abroad. Domestically, movements by students (Murashima 1982), peasants (Murashima 1980) and workers gained momentum and the Communist Party extended its influence. Left-wing parties increased their seats in general elections.[25] Internationally, three countries in Indochina came under the rule of the Communists. In response, the Thai government adopted policies including concessions to peasants and students, reconciliation with Vietnam, normalization of diplomatic relations with China and the withdrawal of US troops (Randolph 1986: chapter 6; Jain 1984: 191–211). The communization of neighboring countries and the rise of the left-wing at home created a strong sense of crisis among conservatives. A series of attacks on leftists by right-wing groups deteriorated social peace and order.

On 6 October 1976, right-wing forces massacred students on the campus of Thammasat University in broad daylight. By that evening, a military group calling themselves the National Administrative Reform Council mounted a coup on the pretext of controlling the chaotic situation.[26] The chairman of the Council was Sangat Chaloyu, former Supreme Commander of the Armed Forces and Commander-in-Chief of the Navy, who had retired several days ago on 30 September. The secretary was Kriangsak Chamanan, who had been promoted to the position of Deputy Supreme Commander on 1 October. It should be noted that neither of them were from the Army's top brass.[27] Two days later on 8 October, Supreme Court Justice Thanin Kraiwichian was appointed Prime Minister.[28] Thanin was a notorious anti-communist and royalist and assumed an uncompromising stance toward left-wing and progressive forces. He also tried to maintain strict legalism and sparked a backlash even among the military and bureaucrats. Although a coup attempt by Chalat Hiransiri[29] on 26 March 1977 failed, the National Administrative Reform Council again staged a successful coup on 20 October 1977. The coup was carried out mainly by Army units of Class 7 graduates[30] of the Royal Military Academy as had been the case in the previous year. Because the Army officers adamantly opposed the appointment of Sangat, a former Navy chief, Council Secretary Kriangsak was appointed Prime Minister instead.

Kriangsak had just been promoted to Supreme Commander in October 1977. He was supported by the Class 7 group because he had served in the Supreme Command for so long that he had little support base within the Army although he was from the Army. Kriangsak's first priority was security, and he worked towards political stability through national reconciliation for that purpose. For example, his government enacted a law granting amnesty for those who had been involved in the March 1977 coup d'état and the 6 October 1976 incident (Matichon 1989: 57–8). More importantly, it enacted the 1978 Constitution which opened the way to a resumption of parliamentary politics. Kriangsak held a general election in 1979. The Class 7 group who had initially supported Kriangsak was unhappy about his inefficient economic management as well as his poor dealings with the Parliament and eventually gave up on him. On 29 February, Kriangsak was presented with the choices of either resignation or coup and chose to resign.

The next prime minister was the Commander-in-Chief of the Army, Prem Tinsulanon. He returned from the northeast region to the capital as the Army's Assistant Commander-in-Chief in 1977 and was promoted to Commander-in-Chief the following year. He had little personal power base among the metropolitan units due to his long provincial assignment and was mainly supported by the Class 7 Group.

The conservative pact

Under Prem, conservative forces were able to make democracy safe for their own interests. This process had two main aspects. The first was the destruction of the left-wing threat. The second was the emergence of a parliamentary democracy which represented capital rather than popular support or ideologies.

The Prem administration lasted for eight years, which can in part be attributed to having successfully dealt with two important issues that it had inherited from the previous administration: the Communist Party and a stagnant economy. Based on his own frontline experience of anti-guerrilla fighting in the northeast region, Prem issued the Order of the Prime Minister's Office No. 66/2523 upon assuming office in 1980. Giving priority to a political instead of militaristic approach, the order addressed various conditions that had fostered the expansion of the Communist Party (e.g. political, administrative, social and economic inequalities) while offering amnesty to any guerrillas who would surrender (Tamada 1988).[31] China and the countries of Indochina stopped providing support to the Communist Party of Thailand following the fallout between China and Vietnam in late 1978. Combined with an effective domestic policy designed to entice the insurgents to return to allegiance, the Communist Party of Thailand was decimated by the early 1980s (Takahashi 1997). All of this took place in times of serious economic turmoil. Thailand had been severely affected by the second oil shock in 1978 and was suffering from a recession and mounting external debt. The government's approach to economic recovery included adopting unpopular measures, such as fiscal tightening and currency devaluation, while appealing to the business community for cooperation.

More importantly, unlike his predecessor Kriangsak, Prem sought support not only from the military but also from the Parliament (i.e. political parties) in his efforts to deal with these issues. By never running for election (and thus not becoming an MP), Prem was better able to maintain equal distances from all political parties, and could thus choose the most suitable parties to form coalition governments according to circumstances.[32] That the Prem administration had the support of both the military and political parties can be seen in the allocation of cabinet posts. The national security-related posts and some economic posts were earmarked for the Prime Minister and allocated to non-MPs. The defense and interior ministers were selected from military personnel. Economic posts were distributed to people who were experienced in administration or business. In particular, the Finance Minister's post was always given to a non-MP. Prem was able to do this precisely because he had a support base in the military as well as in political parties.[33] The remaining posts were allocated to the parties in the ruling coalition according to their number of seats in parliament. Importantly, the number of posts allocated to MPs increased steadily at each cabinet reshuffle. The proportion of MPs in the cabinet was 42% at the time of its formation in 1980, increasing to 56% in 1981 and 73% in 1983, and reaching 87% in 1986. Eighty-seven percent is higher than the figures for the Banhan administration in 1995 and the Chawalit administration in 1996. In addition to his maneuvering of political parties, Prem won the confidence of the monarchy by serving the King faithfully and humbly, unlike Kriangsak who kept some distance from the King.

Prem's administration appeared to continue forever, but its end came in the form of Prem's retirement from politics. One of the triggers for his retirement was a petition signed by ninety-nine people, mostly academics, that was submitted to the King on 26 May 1988. This petition clearly elucidates the power structure on which the Prem administration was built.

> We would like to... inform Your Majesty of the situation in our homeland.
>
> The state of the government is becoming more chaotic every day and the people are losing confidence in our parliamentary democracy. This is because...our political leader, the Prime Minister, does not maintain strict neutrality but stays too close to the monarchy and the military. The military is supposed to exist for the purposes of national defense and developmental support. Yet, the Prime Minister has forced the military to express its support for him in order to preserve his own political status. This has caused factional infighting within the military to escalate to an intolerable level...[W]e request Your Majesty's assistance with this matter to ensure that the political leader in the position of Prime Minister will strictly maintain his neutrality and not move too close to any institution for the sake of protecting his political position. (*Su Anakhot*, 1 June 1988)

The above document clearly indicates that the King and the military were supporting the Prem administration. It also boldly requested the King to withhold his support.[34]

After the general election of 24 July 1988, Prem announced his retirement from politics. There were several factors behind this move.[35] A growing weariness of his government after eight years was one factor. A second factor was that Chat Thai Party became the largest political party in the parliament and, of all the party leaders, its leader, Chatchai Chunhawan, was acceptable to the monarchy, the military and the business community as the next prime minister. Third, Prem had already resolved the two major issues of economic reconstruction and anti-communist measures. The fourth and most important factor was that it seemed to be the King's will. Prem had made the following remark in 1986: 'I'm not the Prime Minister because I want to be. It has been six years already. I don't know how many more years I will continue ... [I]f you want to be happy, do not become a Prime Minister' (Prasong 1989: 65). Shortly after his retirement, on 23 August 1988, Prem was appointed as a Privy Councilor. On 28 August he was awarded the nation's highest decoration, and on the following day was conferred the title of 'Senior Statesman (*ratthaburut*)' (Chatthawa 1995: 691–5).[36] This bestowal of unprecedented honors was no doubt an expression of the King's appreciation for his services. It can be interpreted as recognition for the great efforts made by Prem in the transition from a military government to party politics while increasing the authority of the monarchy, engineering the economic recovery and bringing about the demise of communism in Thailand.

Institutionally managing the left

The conservatives had rejected democracy in 1976 out of concerns about left-wing forces. The key issues were the election of left-wing MPs to the parliament and the government's over-responsiveness to the demands of the electorate. In the 1975 general election, the Socialist Party (*sangkhomniyom haeng prathet thai*) won fifteen seats, the Socialist Front Party (*naeoruam sangkhomniyom*) won ten seats and the progressive New Force Party (*phalang mai*) secured twelve seats.[37] Conversely, the coalition government formed in 1975 incorporated a wide range of demands from students, peasants and workers in its policy. For the conservatives, this was an unwelcome move. 'From the perspective of many members of the Thai elites,' '[t]he demands for reform seemed ...synonymous with a call for a communist government. The concessionary policies of the civilian government appeared to some as heading in the direction of socialism' (Bowie 1997: 107). The conservatives were concerned that the government was giving too much credence to these demands and would feel pressure to make endless concessions as the demands increased. These issues had to be resolved or alleviated to eliminate the conservatives' concerns before parliamentary politics could resume and further consolidate.

Legal provisions were enacted to make it more difficult for left-wing candidates to be elected. The 1978 Constitution incorporated provisions that were designed to restrain left-wing political parties (Murashima 1987: 163–4). Article 94 banned independent MPs. Article 103 stipulated that MPs who lost party membership would be disqualified. To stop the proliferation of small parties, Article 95 stipulated that each party should nominate a number of candidates equal to or greater than one-half of the total number of parliamentary seats.[38] Furthermore, Article 7 of the 1981 political party law provided that the qualification for a political party was a nation-wide membership of 5000. This provision was intended to encourage membership in the large parties supported by businesspeople. With these rules and the development of the vote broker (*huakhanaen*) system, which is to be discussed below, the left-wing MPs of the 1970s were forced to retire from politics or switch to a conservative party. In the 1979 general election, the Socialist Party and the Socialist Front Party merged to form the Democratic Socialist Party (*sangkhom prachathipatai*) but failed to win a seat. Alternatively, the New Force Party won eight seats but broke up after an internal dispute. In the 1983 general election, the Democratic Socialist Party won two seats while the New Force Party won none. In the 1986 general election, the Democratic Socialist Party failed to secure the legally required number of candidates. The New Force Party won one seat but expelled this MP from the party in the following year. The Democratic Socialist Party and the New Force Party merged in 1988 to form the Democratic Socialist Force Party (*phalang sangkhom prachathipatai*) and won one seat. However, none of the incarnations of former socialist-leaning political parties could manage to win a seat in the 1990s (Suthachai 2001: 102–10). The demise of the left-wing parties meant that their MPs had no choice but to join a conservative party if they wanted to remain in politics.

An electoral system based on money
Among the reasons that the elected governments of the 1970s adopted policies that appeared to be overly accommodating in the eyes of the conservatives was that MPs did not have stable connections with their electorates. That is, they were worried about their chances of being re-elected. Having stable support bases would minimize their worries about re-election and would have allowed them to get away with half measures when faced with various demands, since their responsiveness (or lack thereof) to their electorates would have little affect on election results. One measure of the solidity of an MP's support base is the re-election rate, which was only 28% in the 1975 general election and 37% in the 1976 general election. With such unstable support bases, MPs and the government had no choice but to be particularly sensitive to social and economic climates. The re-election rate climbed to over 50% in the 1980s and over 60% in the 1990s (Horikoshi 1997: 52). This increased stability was attributed to changes in the modality of election campaigning.

The 1981 lower house by-election held in Roi Et Province produced a phenomenon that came to be known as 'Roi Et disease' (*rok roi-et*). This refers to the massive vote buying strategy adopted by former Prime Minister Kriangsak, who was plotting his political comeback. Vote buying itself was not a new phenomenon but the case attracted public attention because of its large scale. It soon spread throughout the country, becoming common practice. An intermediary who asks a voter to vote for a particular candidate in exchange for financial reward is a vote broker. A vote broker usually looks after a certain number of voters. Once an election season comes, he or she receives funds and remuneration from a candidate, and then sets about buying votes. In the 1980s, candidates began competing fiercely to win vote brokers rather than voters. Political parties began to focus on recruiting candidates who were capable of commanding sufficient votes to win on their own, rather than on expanding party membership or formulating attractive platforms. What mattered was obviously money, as political parties with more financial resources came to win more seats. These moneyed parties were the conservative ones that were funded by businesspeople. In effect, then, in the 1980s, businesspeople bought political parties, which bought MP candidates, who bought vote brokers, who bought voters. The Prem administration increased the posts for party politicians in the cabinet and distributed the provincial development budget to all MPs, thus contributing to the development and entrenchment of this system.[39] Having access to the cabinet was an incentive for businesspeople to contribute funds, and the development budget increased the ability of MPs to secure vote brokers. With the rising expectations for rewards, the electoral politics became worthy of investment and attracted a substantial influx of funds.[40]

These changes dispelled the conservatives' anxieties. It became impossible for those with no financial resources, left-wing MPs for example, to be elected even if they had eloquence. Those who were elected were primarily conservative businesspeople from the provinces. And since MPs could rely on vote brokers to look after their electorates, they no longer needed to be concerned about their electorates' desires. Having to attract these MPs financially, political parties on the whole continue to be dependent on their businesspeople donors and thus tend to take more heed of the will of financiers than their electorates. Parties cannot neglect their financiers, or they would suffer from deficient funds in the next election and lose seats. Through these processes, party politics became a convenient vehicle for the protection and promotion of the interests of the conservatives rather than a threat to them.

When an elected MP, Chatchai, assumed the premiership in 1988, democratic transition was over and came close to the emergence of the consolidation phase. However, relations between the government and the military became strained. As neither the Prime Minister nor the military was ready to compromise, a military group, identifying itself as the National Peace-Keeping Council, overthrew the government on 23 February 1991. Army Commander-in-Chief Suchinda Khraprayun personally asked Anan Panyarachun to assume the office of Prime Minister (SLN 1992a: 48). The public welcomed the new Anan administration, with its slogan to eradicate 'money politics' (*thanathipatai*). For a start, the cabinet was predominantly bureaucrats. The absence of a popularly elected parliament created a very favorable environment for the government, which managed to enact and amend a vast number of laws. According to the literature summarizing this administration's accomplishments, there were 755 official actions, including 246 laws, 318 government ordinances, one royal decree, 174 ministry ordinances and sixteen regulations of the Prime Minister's Office (SLN 1992b: 182–244).

The National Peace-Keeping Council organized a pro-military party coalition through political maneuvering in preparation for a general election scheduled to be held in March 1992. The pro-military coalition won a majority in the election and Suchinda reneged on his promise, becoming Prime Minister in April 1992. This administration, with support from a parliamentary majority as well as the military, would soon die an unexpected death. In the month after the government was formed, massive protest rallies were organized demanding the resignation of the Prime Minister, and the military began to fire at the crowd on 17 May. In Thailand this incident is popularly called the 'Barbarian May.' The King intervened to bring the situation under control and Suchinda stepped down. Anan was reappointed as the Prime Minister. The second Anan administration was as much a 'bureaucratic government' as before. The greatest challenge for the Anan administration was to deal with the aftermath of the May incident and prepare for the return of party politics. To this end, it dissolved Parliament on 29 June and scheduled a general election on 13 September.

Consolidation phase

Although the 1991 coup caused a disruption, Thai democratization moved into a consolidation phase in the 1990s. On the one hand, the military retreated from politics and it was established that the Prime Minister should be an elected MP, and general elections became more significant than in the previous decade. On the other hand, party politics was not immune from criticism at all. Calls for political reform gained force. The middle class which became politically assertive was an important supporter of arguments for the reform. Thus a new Constitution was drafted in 1997 to ease the criticism. This text will explain the consolidation phase in detail.

In the September 1992 general election, the Democrat Party became the leading party and its leader Chuan Likphai was appointed Prime Minister. The Chuan administration set up the Democracy Development Committee when calls for political reform came forth in 1994. In 1995 this committee made a recommendation that political reform should be implemented by a fully-fledged revision of the 1991 Constitution. However, Chuan dissolved the Parliament on 19 May 1995 as a vote of no confidence was about to be passed. In the July 1995 general election, the Chat Thai Party became the leading party and its leader Banhan became Prime Minister. Banhan decided to fully revise the constitution with the aim of political reform. Before he began this process, however, he came under intense attacks in the Parliament during the debate surrounding a no-confidence motion in September 1996. Having lost the support of the ruling coalition, he dissolved the Parliament. In the November 1996 general election, the New Aspiration Party won 125 seats, two seats more than the Democrat Party, to become the leading party. Its leader, Chawalit Yongchaiyut (Chavalit Yongchaiyudh), became Prime Minister.

The formulation of a new constitution was progressing under the Chawalit administration. The final draft was presented before the Parliament in August 1997. The perception that a new constitution was essential for the nation's recovery from the economic crisis which began in July became entrenched, and the Parliament had no choice but to approve the draft although many MPs were not happy with it. The new constitution came into force on 11 October. Those who had given top priority to drafting a new constitution and holding a general election were now in support of putting the economy first. Parliament was not dissolved until 9 November 2000, just before the end of its full-term, and the general election under the new constitution had to wait until January 2001. There, the new Thai Rak Thai Party, headed by Thaksin, enjoyed a historic landslide victory.

Summary

There are an increasing number of researchers examining the democratization of Thai politics, many sharing two features. First, they limit their scope to the 1990s and do not pay sufficient attention to historical context. Second, they shed light on proponents for democratization. However, the process of democratization did not begin abruptly in the 1990s. We should try to explain the continuity between the 1980s and 1990s. The democratization can be divided into two phases: transition and consolidation. The transition phase started in the late 1970s and ended in the early 1990s. This period was characterized by the appeasement of opponents against democracy rather than the active role of proponents for democracy. As party politics was denied in 1976 due to fear of leftist forces, the conservative forces needed to eradicate the left in order to resume parliamentary democracy. This appeasement resulted in conservative and moderate democracy that was rarely harmful for the opponents.

Against this background, this book will explain the consolidation phase in the 1990s from the same angle. It was a victory of conservative and hesitating forces rather than of ardent proponents for democracy. Participants in the protest rally in May 1992 were people of all classes and kinds, and the rally was led by Chamlong Simueang. However, the dominant explanation is that these people were of the urban middle class and joined the rally voluntarily. Thus, the middle class has monopolized the credit and come to dominate democratization discursively. Due to its discursive power, the middle class became very assertive and influential. In the 1990s, people who showed displeasure with party politics most explicitly belonged to the middle class. Arguments for political reform and the 1997 Constitution which were hostile to elected MPs were measures to accommodate this grumbling class. The successful accommodation resulted in the disappearance of the hesitant force. As the middle class is more moderate and conservative than urban lower class people or rural residents, resultant democracy is not unfavorable to the upper class. Thus there are no politically powerful forces which negate the reformed politics. Democracy has been consolidated in this way.

Part I of this book provides an empirical review of the May 1992 incident. Chapter Two is a discussion of the incident. In seeking to understand how such a large-scale rally, a historical rarity in Thailand, came about and why it came about in May 1992, the relationship between the incident and the middle class will become clearer. Chapter Three considers the effect of the May incident on the military. Traditionally, in Thailand, a post-coup d'état period was really an inter-coup period, just as a postwar period is, in most instances, an interwar period. However, the likelihood of a coup decreased markedly after 1992. This phenomenon will be analyzed by focusing on personnel changes within the military. Part II examines the political reform which began in the mid-1990s and resulted in the enactment of a new constitution. Chapter Four deals with the argument for political reform and the drafting process of the 1997 Constitution. Chapter Five considers the significance of the 2000 Senate election which was the first general election held under the 1997 Constitution. Finally, Chapter Six discusses how Thai politics has changed as a result of political reform following the 2001 general elections.

Part I
The May 1992 Incident

A special edition of *Phuchatkan* reporting on the May 1992 incident

In May 1992, a large-scale protest rally calling for the resignation of Prime Minister Suchinda was held over several days in the capital of Thailand, Bangkok. The government deployed troops to suppress the demonstration in the early morning of 18 May and it developed into a disastrous incident causing many casualties through to the night of 19 May. Suchinda was forced to step down to take responsibility for the bloodshed, and the military, which had supported the government, was driven out of politics. This is the incident referred to as 'Barbarian May' (*phruetsapha thamin*) in Thailand.

There is hardly anyone who disagrees with the view that this incident became the crucial turning point for the consolidation of democracy in Thailand. Nevertheless, not enough research has been carried out on this incident. Why was the large-scale rally held? Why was it held in May? Why did the troops open fire at the crowd? None of these occurrences were inevitable; they demand some sort of explanation. Moreover, what contributions did the incident make to democratization? How did the military withdraw from politics? Why did a political reform movement emerged several years after the incident? There has never been any persuasive explanation addressing these questions.

A major reason for the lack of research on the Barbarian May incident can be found in the predominance of the middle class (*chonchan klang*) leadership theory which has led many researchers to suspend further thinking. This middle class leadership theory fits, too perfectly, the formula of the modernization approach which argues that economic growth expands the middle class and brings about democratization as a consequence. For once, we need to free ourselves from its spell and examine the incident with fresh eyes.

First, in Chapter One I closely examine the large-scale rally. The size of the crowd was the largest in almost twenty years in Thailand. If this massive rally had not occurred, bloodshed and government change would not have happened. Why was it possible to organize such a large-scale rally? The priority is to elucidate the reason why it developed on such a large scale rather than to investigate who the participants were. Then, the aftereffects of the incident will be discussed. This implies shedding light on the reason why the middle class eventually came to be cast in the leading role even though Chamlong Simueang (Srimuang) had been regarded as the key figure by both his supporters and enemies during and immediately after the incident (for example, Prudhisan 1992: 126; Khian 1993: 67; Khian 1997: 33; Pasuk and Baker 1995: 359). The significance of this 'misappropriation of the credit' in the subsequent democratization process will be touched upon as well.

Chapter Three will address the relationship between the incident and the military. The incident precipitated the political withdrawal of the military which had wielded great political power since 1932. This has led political parties to take the center stage of politics. The military was forced to back down because troops fired into the crowd and caused many casualties. Why did they open fire at the demonstrators? What is the causal relationship between the incident or the shooting and the military's withdrawal from politics? The key to answer these questions is likely to be found in factional dynamics within the military. Personnel changes in the military will therefore be the focus of investigation.

1
The Large-Scale Rally: Cause and Effect

The formation of the Suchinda administration

The appointment of Army Commander-in-Chief Suchinda to the Prime Ministership on 7 April 1992 triggered the large-scale rally in May of that year. Why did Suchinda become Prime Minister when his appointment would certainly draw condemnation? It all started with a coup d'état by the National Peace-Keeping Council (NPKC) on 23 February 1991. In order to understand why Suchinda's appointment drew criticism and set off a massive protest rally we must first review the events of the year or so between the coup and his appointment.

The 1991 Constitution
Following a successful coup, the NPKC scrapped the 1978 Constitution and enforced a provisional constitution while embarking on the drafting of a permanent constitution. The contents of the draft prepared by the drafting committee appointed by the government were very similar to the 1978 Constitution. The main features were as follows: active public servants (both civil and military) are not permitted to become cabinet members; the Parliament consists of the House of Representatives which is popularly elected and the Senate which is appointed; active public servants can be appointed to the Senate; the first round of Senate appointments is to be made by the chairman of the NPKC; and cabinet members including the Prime Minister do not have to be members of the House of Representatives.

The drafting process was scrutinized very closely. There were two reasons for this. One was the amendment of the draft by Parliament. The incumbent Parliament consisted entirely of the members who were appointed by the NPKC because the previous Parliament was dissolved in the coup d'état and there were no elected MPs. The draft amendment committee was sensitive to the intentions of the NPKC and tried to make amendments that ran counter to democratization, such as reinforcing the power of the Senate. Another, more important reason was the presence of a deep suspicion that the NPKC might attempt to retain power even after the next general election. The stipulation that the Prime Minister does not have to be an elected MP would have extremely important implications if the military leaders wanted premiership after the general election; it would allow a military official to become Prime Minister without winning a lower house seat in the election as long as he is retired from service. This stipulation presented the possibility of the formation of an administration similar to that of Prem's during the 1980s. If a military official becomes Prime Minister, with more power delegated to the Senators appointed by the military, controlling the government would be very easy.

Such suspicion triggered an upsurge of strong opposition when Parliament began deliberations on the draft. Opposition further intensified in November 1991 as the day of parliamentary vote approached. On 19 November, a gathering to oppose the draft was organized by the Campaign for Popular Democracy (*khanakammakan ronnarong prachathipatai*: Kho. Ro. Po. for short, or CPD), the Student Federation of Thailand (*sun nisit naksueksa haeng prathet thai*: So. No. No. Tho. for short, or SFT) and seven political parties including the Democrat Party, the Phalang Tham Party and the New Aspiration Party at Sanam Luang. The confrontation was ended by the King's annual address which was customarily given on 4 December, the day before his birthday. In 1991, the King declared that 'no rule is unchangeable; you should not fight over a rule as it can be amended; no blood should be spilt over it,' and that 'people are now confused whether to amend or not, whether to promulgate or not, whether to promulgate first, then amend, or whether to amend first, then promulgate... let us try it first, and we keep it if it works and we change it if it doesn't' (Phumiphonadunyadet 1991: 45, 47). It was obvious that the King was referring to the constitutional dispute at that time. People could no longer voice their objections and the draft constitution was promulgated and put in force on 9 December.

Maneuver on political parties

The NPKC, which used a cleanup of politics as a pretext for its action, established a committee under Decree No. 26 issued on 25 February 1991 to investigate the assets of politicians who were suspected of having ill-gotten wealth. The committee was chaired by Sit Chirarot (Sitthi Chirarochana).[1] Sit was a retired Army Chief of Staff and was the Interior Minister from June 1981 to August 1986 in the Prem government. He had a prominent reputation as a person of integrity during and after his time in the Army and was an ideal choice for the chairman of the committee. Sit accepted the appointment because of his connection with Suchinda who was the secretary to the Interior Minister from July 1981 to August 1982. Serving Sit was one of the reasons Suchinda stood out as having the most successful career among the Class 5 officers. In other words, for Suchinda, Sit was the former boss to whom he was greatly indebted. Therefore, this investigation of corrupt politicians could not be launched in order to justify the coup or to maneuver on political parties.

On 27 February, the NPKC announced the names of twenty-two politicians who were going to be investigated. The following day, three more people, including former Prime Minister Chatchai, were added to the list. Most of them were the cabinet members of the Chatchai administration. Since the twenty-five politicians on the list were widely suspected of corruption, the policy to pursue improper moneymaking was applauded. However, there was some disappointment, too, as the committee pared down the list. The committee sorted the suspects based on the results of its investigations and began to make announcements from May as they proceeded. By August, the number of suspects on the list was cut to thirteen, almost half of the original group. The first person cleared of suspicion in May was Narong Wongwan, the leader of the Ekkaphap Party. Among the thirteen, three were cleared, including Banhan Sinlapaacha, the secretary-general of the Chat Thai Party. In the end, only ten people were identified as having engaged in making ill-gotten wealth. In the process of this investigation, the sense of mistrust deepened as people suspected that the NPKC might be using it as a means to control political parties.

The assets of the politicians who were suspected of improper moneymaking were frozen (*Matichon Sutsapda*, 10 March 1991; 17 March 1991). They were unable to operate their political funds until they were cleared, which left them in a state of paralysis. Moreover, those who were found guilty would be branded as corrupt politicians and their political activity would be jeopardized. Consequently, when most of the leading politicians became the target of the investigation, former Army Commander-in-Chief Chawalit was placed in the most advantageous position for the next general election. He formed the New Aspiration Party in October 1990 and launched a political campaign for the general election, which was expected to be held by July 1992 at the latest when the term of the lower house members was due to expire. Chawalit was the former boss of the military leaders, including Suchinda, and had a good relationship with the military.[2] However, the relationship deteriorated when the military began to build its own support bases among political parties as described later.[3] Now that the military leadership had decided to stand against Chawalit in the March 1992 general election, they had to defeat the New Aspiration Party. If Chawalit won the election and became Prime Minister, the military would not be able to escape some sort of reprisal.[4]

Firstly, the NPKC included twelve former lower house MPs in the government-appointed legislative assembly. One of them, Phinit, the deputy leader of the Ekkaphap Party, announced on 21 May 1991 that he was forming a new political party called Sammakkhitham (*Matichon Sutsapda*, 26 May 1991). The party was formally registered on 20 June. Narong, who had just been cleared of the improper moneymaking allegation in May, was appointed as the party leader and Thiti, a retired Air Force Squadron Leader, was appointed as the secretary-general. The party was organized for Air Force Commander-in-Chief Kaset.[5] This is evident in an interview given immediately before the May 1992 incident by Air Chief Marshal Anan Kalintha,[6] who was the closest associate of Kaset and was the Interior Minister in Suchinda's cabinet, in which he commented: 'There is almost no doubt that Kaset will stand for election after his retirement. He will probably lead the Sammakkhitham Party. However, we need to see how the situation develops. If the Sammakkhitham Party maintains strong unity, it will happen' (*Matichon Sutsapda*, 8 May 1992). Secondly, Air Chief Marshal Sombun Rahong, who was the president of the Airport Authority of Thailand (AAT), became the leader of the Chat Thai Party in November 1991. Sombun's association with the party goes back to the 1970s when he was appointed as an *aide-de-camp* to Defense Minister Praman, who was the leader of the Chat Thai Party at the time. Sombun's appointment to the party leadership was realized by the party's secretary-general Banhan, who had just escaped a guilty finding for improper moneymaking.[7] However, Sombun had a much closer relationship with Commander-in-Chief Kaset than with the party executives, evident from the simple fact that he held the position of the AAT president, which was an important, lucrative post for the Air Force top brass besides Thai Airways International. Sombun also made so much financial contribution to the establishment of the Sammakkhitham Party that no one would have been surprised had he become its leader. Thirdly, Samak Sunthorawet, the leader of the Prachakon Thai Party, had a younger brother who was an active Air Chief Marshal as of April 1991. Therefore, Prachakon Thai could be considered to be one of the political parties close to the Air Force. In short, Kaset was making steady progress with his behind-the-scenes maneuvering of political parties.

At the same time, the Army was not sitting idle. Lieutenant-general Khasem Kraisan, who was an old friend of Suchinda's from their secondary school days, retired from the Army and joined the Social Action Party.[8] The then leader of the party, Montri Phongphanit, had been found guilty for improper moneymaking. Khasem entered the weakening party as the secretary-general.[9] However, the strength of the Social Action Party was no match for that of the Sammakkhitham Party or the Chat Thai Party. Chat Thai became the leading party when it won eighty-seven out of 257 seats in the July 1988 general election. Sammakkhitham was a new party but had so many former MPs and highly popular candidates that it was expected to become the leading party in the March 1992 general election. Conversely, the Social Action Party used to be a major party with over 100 seats in the early 1980s, but weakened to fifty-four seats in the 1988 general election. Moreover, it further lost its strength due to another internal dispute during the

Chatchai administration. In fact, the Sammakkhitham Party became the leading party by winning seventy-nine seats in the March 1992 general election, followed by seventy-four seats for the Chat Thai Party, seventy-two for the New Aspiration Party, forty-four for the Democrat Party, forty-one for the Phalang Tham Party, thirty-one for the Social Action Party and seven for the Prachakon Thai Party. The four already pro-military parties secured a parliamentary majority by winning 191 out of 360 seats.

Appointment of Suchinda as Prime Minister

After the March general election, the pro-military parties immediately began talks on the organization of a new cabinet. Initially, Narong, the leader of the leading Sammakkhitham Party, was the agreed candidate for Prime Minister. However, it turned out that Narong was denied an entry visa to the US in July 1991 on suspicion of his involvement in dealing drugs.

Since someone who could not visit the US was considered inappropriate to be a Prime Minister, the parties began looking for a new candidate.[10] This was when Suchinda's name came up. He held the positions of Army Commander-in-Chief and Supreme Commander of the Armed Forces concurrently at the time. He had announced that he would not become Prime Minister when a campaign against the pro-military draft constitution developed in November 1991. Why did Suchinda renege on his promise and accept the Prime Ministership? Did he intend to become Prime Minister from the beginning?[11]

There seems to be a number of factors leading to his appointment,[12] the most important of which was who would become Prime Minister if Suchinda would not accept the appointment. As explained earlier, this pro-military coalition was virtually a pro-Air Force coalition. There was a high likelihood that someone from the Air Force, which had an extensive support base in the House of Representatives, would become Prime Minister. Air Force Commander-in-Chief Kaset was very keen (Watsana 2002b: 292–298). However, the Army could not accept an Air Force chief as their Prime Minister. In Thailand's long history of military rule, the Prime Minister was always appointed from the Army top brass. Among the three forces, the Army enjoyed overwhelming power and prestige. It would be intolerable for the Army to be placed in a subordinate position to a Prime Minister from the Air Force.[13] Secondly, the appointment of Suchinda as Prime Minister would mean his retirement from service. The post of the Army commander-in-chief would become vacant and create a chance of promotion for other generals (Okazaki et al. 1993: 125–126). Deputy Commander-in-Chief Itsaraphong was scheduled to retire in 1994 while Suchinda was scheduled to retire in 1993. If Suchinda stayed until his retirement, Itsaraphong would have only one year as the Commander-in-Chief before his own retirement. If Suchinda retired in 1992, Itsaraphong could stay in the top job for longer. Therefore, it is highly likely that the Army leadership approached Suchinda about the appointment on the pretext of saving the Army's honor, but in actual fact they were motivated by the prospect of their own promotion. In fact, Itsaraphong, who succeeded Suchinda as the Commander-in-Chief, commented that the Suchinda administration fully supported by the military would be '2000%' safe (Watsana 2002b: 304). Alternatively, Kaset, whose Prime Ministerial aspirations were thwarted, was offered the post of the Supreme Commander of the Armed Forces. Because Suchinda retired from service together with his sworn friend, Assistant Commander-in-Chief of Army Chatchom, two of the Army top jobs called the 'five tigers' (Commander-in-Chief, Deputy Commander-in-Chief, Chief of Staff and two Assistant Commander-in-Chiefs; see Chapter Three for the significance of these posts) became vacant and brought about slightly more personnel changes than usual. In other words, Suchinda's accession to the premiership gave the Army leadership a chance to kill two birds with one stone. From Suchinda's point of view, he could become Prime Minister precisely because of the rock-solid support of the military.[14]

In light of his earlier promise, Suchinda's acceptance of the appointment attracted criticism. Adding fuel to the fire was the makeup of the cabinet. With firm support from the military, as was the case with the Prem administration, non-MPs were appointed to some of the cabinet posts such as the Finance Minister, the Interior Minister and the Defense Minister. However, about 80% of the cabinet posts had to be distributed among MPs to ensure support from a parliamentary majority. Those who landed such jobs were usually the party executives. Many of them had been on the NPKC list of politicians who were suspected of improper moneymaking. If they started insisting on cabinet jobs and if the Prime Minister rejected them, they might break away from the coalition. Then, the coalition would lose its majority in the House of Representatives and the survival of the administration would be threatened.[15] After difficult negotiations, the cabinet lineup ended up including several politicians who had been found guilty of improper moneymaking. Suchinda must have been dissatisfied with this situation as he was sure that it would draw heavy criticism. On this point the difference with the Prem administration should be noted, to which the Suchinda administration is often said to be similar. Prem could easily swap his coalition partners because he kept almost equal distances from all political parties. In contrast, Suchinda's coalition partners had been prearranged and he had to agree to their demands if he wanted to maintain the majority in Parliament. The democratic principle of majority rule was working. Suchinda contradicted his own justification of the coup by including these popularly convicted politicians in his cabinet and drew even harsher criticism from the outset of his administration.

Rally demanding the PM's resignation

The large-scale protest rally of May 1992 was held in two rounds: first from 6 to 11 of May and second from 17 to 20 of May. The rally started in front of the Parliament and moved to the square in front of the palace (Sanam Luang) via Ratchadamnoen Avenue on the night of 7 May. The crowd moved out of Sanam Luang and went back up Ratchadamnoen Avenue on the following night. This time the march was blocked at Phan Fa Bridge and the rally continued on the avenue until the morning of 11 May. This was the first round. When the rally was disbanded on 11 May, the participants agreed to resume the rally at Sanam Luang on 17 May. The second round of the rally can be divided into two phases as the atmosphere changed dramatically after Chamlong was arrested on 18 May. On 17 May, the crowd marched out of Sanam Luang and was once again blocked at Phan Fa Bridge. In the early hours of 18 May, troops began firing into the crowd, causing casualties among the protesters. The rally continued on Ratchadamnoen Avenue but Chamlong was arrested on that afternoon. The rally was dispersed briefly but reassembled in the evening. Troops repetitively opened fire at the rally until the morning of 19 May, leaving many protesters dead or injured. The rally and the crackdown finally ended when the King intervened on the night of 20 May.

The first round
There were many grievances against the creation of the Suchinda administration, as described earlier (Khian 1997: 11–23; RT 1992: 4–6 and others). In short, the main issue was that the military leader Suchinda retained the power he seized in the 1991 coup even after a general election. Suchinda declared in November 1991 that he would not become Prime Minister, but after the March 1992 general election he assumed the office of Prime Minister with the backing of the prearranged coalition of pro-military parties. Moreover, although Suchinda used the cleanup of politics as justification for the coup and was applauded for launching an investigation into improper moneymaking by politicians, he included some of the politicians who were implicated in the improper moneymaking allegations in the cabinet. Many people were understandably displeased at the course of events.

The appointment of Suchinda as Prime Minister was confirmed on 7 April and Chalat Worachat[16] began a hunger strike in protest on the next day. Following the inauguration of the cabinet, the Student Federation of Thailand (SFT) and the Campaign for Popular Democracy (CPD) began protests and organized a rally at Royal Plaza near the Parliament on 20 April. They were joined by opposition parties and about 50,000 protesters. Suchinda, however, seemed unmoved by this upsurge of criticism.

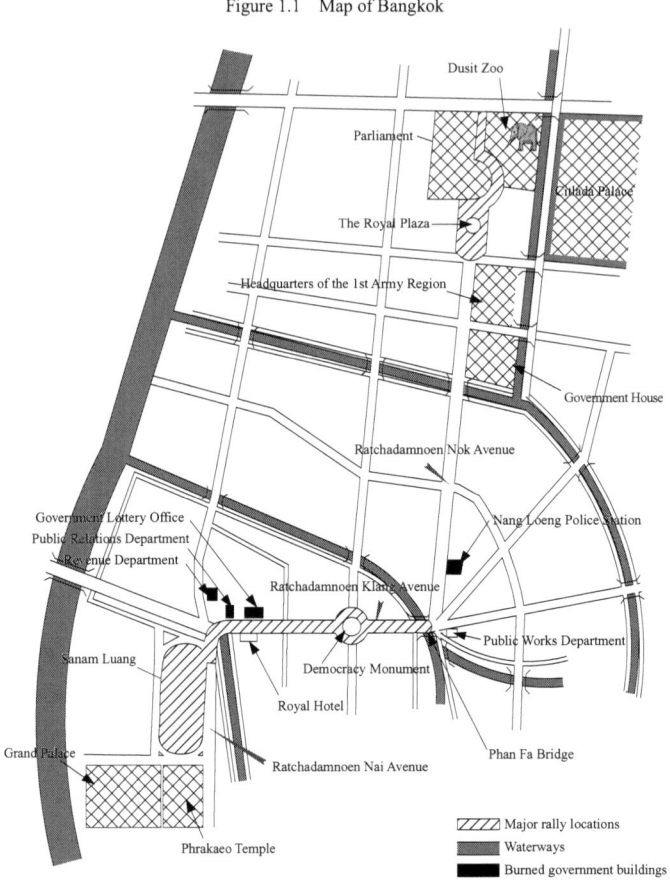

Figure 1.1   Map of Bangkok

As the Prime Minister was scheduled to deliver his policy speech on 6 May, Chamlong, the leader of the opposition Phalang Tham Party, announced that he was going on a hunger strike on the night of 4 May. When he started a sit-in in front of the Parliament, he distributed copies of his farewell letter which was virtually his will. It had a sensational title which read, 'I stake my life. If the protest does not succeed, I will die in seven days.' The main body of the letter stated, 'I will not be able to live much longer than seven days. I will not stop until General Suchinda resigns or I die of starvation,' and appealed to the public to 'take a day off from work and please attend the peaceful rally from 8:00 a.m. on 6 May… See you in front of the Parliament.' It stressed that 'protests will have little impact after 6 May,' and concluded by emphasizing for effect, 'I would like to take this opportunity… to bid farewell to everyone, particularly my supporters' (Tamada 1992b: 376–377).

On the morning of 6 May, while the government used television subtitles to ask viewers not to join the rally since it would cause traffic jams and might develop into a riot (*Matichon*, 7 May 1992), there was a crowd of about 20,000 protesters when the Prime Minister began his policy speech at 9:40 a.m. (*Bangkok Post*, 7 May 1992) which swelled to over 100,000 by the evening.[17] It was the largest rally since the uprising on 14 October 1973.[18]

Despite this massive rally, the Prime Minister did not resign. The Parliament was reconvened at 10:00 a.m. on the next day. Faced with criticism from the opposition inside the Parliament and pressure from the protest rally outside, Suchinda spoke out in Parliament before noon. He cited the following four reasons for his acceptance of the appointment. First, the constitution did not forbid a non-MP from becoming Prime Minister. Second, he was trying to protect the regime from a certain opposition party leader who was scheming to establish a communist regime. Third, he was trying to protect Buddhism from a certain opposition party leader who was supported by a heretic religion. Fourth, he intended to prevent corruption among MPs who had won their seats by bankrolling the last general election. The second and third points were attacks on Chawalit (former Army Commander-in-Chief and the then leader of opposition New Aspiration Party) and Chamlong respectively and the fourth point was a condemnation of all elected MPs on both sides of politics.

The statement amounted to Suchinda's declaration of war. By the afternoon of 7 May, the government began to broadcast joint programs to criticize the protest rally repeatedly. After 3:00 p.m., warnings from the military against the rally were announced frequently and Suchinda's parliamentary speech was also broadcast many times. In the evening, Channel 5 TV station, which was controlled by the Army, broadcast the interview of former Prime Minister Khuekrit Pramot, criticizing Chawalit and Chamlong (*Matichon*, 8 May 1992).

As the Prime Minister made his confrontational stance clear, Chamlong had his aide read his letter at 5:40 p.m. asking more people to join the rally (*Naeona*, 8 May 1992). The crowd kept growing and reached 150,000 before 8:00 p.m.. There is no large space in front of Parliament, only a footpath slightly wider than usual. The crowd filled the road and footpath in front of Parliament and spilled onto the nearby streets and the Royal Plaza. At 8:00 p.m., Chamlong decided to move the rally to Sanam Luang and he himself headed there in a car at 8:30 p.m..

At 9:10 p.m., Chamlong had his aide read another letter asking people to stay with him at Sanam Luang all night because the police might arrest him if the crowd got smaller (*Matichon*, 8 May 1992). Stages were set up in Sanam Luang where the leaders of the opposition, the SFT, and the CPD and TV personalities made speeches. After 6:00 a.m. on 8 May, the crowd at the rally became small. Chamlong wrote his second will reconfirming his determination in defiance of death and had it written in large characters and displayed (*Thai Rat*, 9 May 1992). As the number of protesters decreased further, he had his aide read his letter at 10:45 a.m., reaffirming that he would resolutely continue his hunger strike (*Phuchatkan* 9 May 1992).

Conversely, the government criticized the rally on the Army's radio program from 6:45 a.m., claiming that the rally might get out of control and deteriorate into a dangerous situation since the protesters consisted of such various elements as students, a mobilized mass, professional assassins, and people wearing shabby clothes as if they came out of the jungle (hinting that they were communist insurgents). At 10:30 a.m., a group of thirty people claiming to be the representatives of the Buddhists visited the Prime Minister and presented him a bunch of flowers to express their gratitude to him for his statement in Parliament defending Buddhism (*Matichon*, 9 May 1992). This visit was broadcast on television. In the afternoon, the Interior Minister invited representatives of various newspapers and asked for self-control in their reporting of the rally. The Interior Ministry issued a notice prohibiting the employees of state-owned companies from joining the rally (*Matichon*, 9 May 1992). At 3:45 p.m., Suchinda issued a warning not to obstruct the Buddhist Week ceremonies, scheduled to be held at Sanam Luang from 10 to 16 May (*Matichon*, 9 May 1991). Suchinda went on television at 7:30 p.m. to explain why he accepted the Prime Ministerial appointment and warned that the protest rally might develop into a riot. Then he declared that, although he personally had no qualms about resigning from the post, he could not resign because it would set a bad precedent if he yielded to protests outside the Parliament staged by a parliamentary minority (*Matichon*, 9 May 1991).

As tension had continued to rise since 4 May, a number of scholars petitioned the King on 6 and 7 May to dissolve the Parliament (*Matichon*, 7 and 8 May 1992). Both the ruling and opposition parties opposed the dissolution when they were asked by the royal secretary-general about this matter on 7 May. The speaker of the House of Representatives began to coordinate bipartisan support for the amendment of the constitution in order to resolve the deadlock in the Parliament (*Matichon*, 8 May 1992). Five ruling coalition parties entered into discussions on the amendment from 9:30 a.m. on 8 May and Montri Phongphanit, the leader of the Social Action Party, announced at the press conference at 1:30 p.m. that they had agreed to make five amendments to the constitution (*Matichon*, 9 May 1992). The main issue was whether the Prime Minister should be an elected MP or not.

Chamlong, who insisted on Suchinda's immediate resignation, softened his attitude slightly after meeting the representatives of four opposition parties in the late afternoon on 8 May. However, as mentioned earlier, Suchinda announced on television at 7:30 p.m. that he had no intention of resigning. Afterwards,

Chamlong had his aide read the following message to the crowd of over 150,000 at the rally[19]:

> Do not be deceived by the constitutional amendment... The government will not be able to impose martial law or stage a coup d'état... However, they may try to use the military to disperse the rally when the crowd number becomes small. Do not be afraid of danger at this point. People from the provinces are also coming to join us. There will be more participants on the weekend... The Prime Minister won't be able to stay on... when he is condemned continually for five days. (*Matichon*, 9 May 1992)

Before 9:00 p.m., Chamlong got in a car and led the crowd out of Sanam Luang. They marched on Ratchadamnoen Avenue in the opposite direction from the previous night. At Phan Fa Bridge, they were stopped by the police barricade. After his unsuccessful negotiation with the Central Investigation Bureau Commissioner in charge of the blockade, Chamlong made a speech to the rally participants at 10:40 p.m. to the effect that: even if we are dispersed, we will continue the rally tomorrow and the day after tomorrow; the city traffic will be paralyzed; our only options are to stay here over night or to go forward (*Matichon*, 9 May 1992). The stage was moved from Sanam Luang to the vicinity of the Democracy Monument and Chamlong's two letters were read at 11:30 p.m.. One was addressed to the government which read: 'even if you try to dissolve the rally by arresting all of us, there won't be enough space to accommodate us... if you mount a coup d'état, coup leaders will have to go into exile in a foreign country sooner or later... all that is required to settle this situation is the resignation of the Prime Minister.' The other letter was addressed to the protesters at the rally which read: 'we will definitely win tomorrow... if we occupy Ratchadamnoen Avenue, traffic in the entire area of Bangkok will be paralyzed and the Prime Minister will not be able to stay on' (*Matchon*, 9 May 1992). Both letters were intended to inspire rally participants and urge them to stay on. Another stage was set up and opposition politicians, popular singers and political activists came on stage one after another all night and made speeches to keep the crowd interested.

In fact, Chamlong moved the rally crowd on his own initiative. Only some of the protesters followed Chamlong and the majority remained at Sanam Luang. Three opposition parties other than the Phalang Tham Party decided not to move. Parinya Thewanaruemitkun, the chairman of the SFT, and Khothom Ariya, the vice-chairman of the CPD, both asked the protesters not to move (*Matichon*, 9 May 1992). At 11:08 p.m., Khothom announced to the crowd that the CPD, the SFT and other NGOs[20] would stop playing a leading role and hand over the leadership to the Phalang Tham Party. During Khothom's announcement, Parinya quarreled with MPs of the Phalang Tham Party on the stage (*Thai Rat*, 9 May 1992). When

Chalat, who had insisted on staying, announced at 11:20 p.m. that he was moving, everyone agreed to follow him (*Matichon*, 9 May 1992). By around 11:30 p.m., the last remaining 20,000 or so people began to move out (*The Nation*, 9 May 1992) and Ratchadamnoen Klang Avenue was filled with demonstrators.

Capitalizing on the discord amongst the opposition leadership, the government immediately reported the news on television, praising the secession of the SFT and the CPD from the rally at midnight of 9 May (*Matichon*, 9 May 1992). Half an hour later another television news broadcast claimed that, although the remaining crowd at Sanam Luang went home in response to Khothom's request, Chawalit and Chamlong had set up stages near Phan Fa Bridge and were inciting the people to join the rally (*Matichon*, 9 May 1992). At 1:00 a.m., a statement from the Capital Security Command[21] was broadcast. It declared that the rally at Sanam Luang ended at 12:30 a.m. and the remaining crowd at Phan Fa Bridge consisted of a small number of students (*Matichon*, 9 May 1992). To counteract these government reports attempting to create the false impression that the rally was only supported by a small number of radicals, the CPD and the SFT made an announcement at 12:50 a.m. and 1:30 a.m. denying their secession from the movement (*Matichon*, 9 May 1992).

On the morning of 9 May, Chamlong asked the people at the rally whether he should continue a hunger strike or take a meal to keep fighting. The crowd opted in favor of the latter with thunderous applause (*Matichon*, 10 May 1992). After a meal and a rest, Chamlong gathered the Phalang Tham executives at 10:30 a.m. and advised that he would resign as the party leader (*The Nation*, 10 May 1992). He appeared on the stage near the Democracy Monument at 10:45 a.m. and announced that he had resigned as the party leader because the government had accused him of leading the movement for his personal interest for power and this accusation had been discouraging the people from joining the rally. He also expressed his disappointment that many of the protesters went home in the morning despite his plea for them to stay and the rally organizers had to try to regroup themselves because they were surrounded by government forces now that the scale of the rally became small (*Matichon*, 10 May 1992).[22]

Chamlong was busy and energetic during the daytime on 9 May after he discontinued fasting. He made several speeches in the morning and gave many interviews to domestic and foreign reporters from midday through the afternoon (*Matichon*, 10 May 1992). In his 3:00 p.m. speech, he appealed as follows: the government was reinforcing troops around Phan Fa Bridge and he hoped more people would come to the rally so that the government could not use force to break it up. 'Please do not think that you no longer need to come out to help just because I have stopped a hunger strike and will not die any more. I hope more people will come to help us bring democracy to this country' (*Matichon*, 10 May 1992).

Conversely, the government was applying certain tactics to dissolve the rally. At 10:08 a.m., Channel 5 broadcast the news welcoming Chamlong's decision to call off a hunger strike, giving the impression that the rally was over (*Matichon*, 10 May 1992). At 10:23 a.m., the government broadcast a statement severely criticizing Chamlong and Chawalit for trying to turn the rally into a violent demonstration for their own ambition for power by moving it to the Chitlada Palace (the King's residence) (*Matichon*, 10 May 1992). At 10:35 a.m., the military criticized Chamlong and Chawalit for inciting a riot which might result in a terrible disaster (*The Nation*, 10 May 1992). At around noon, Prime Minister Suchinda stated in an interview that the police had set up roadblocks the previous night because some of the protesters were inciting the crowd to surround the Chitlada Palace and petition the King for intervention and that the government would never allow such an action because the King should not be bothered (*Naeona*, 10 May 1992; *Thai Rat*, 11 May 1992; *Matichon*, 10 May 1992). In the evening when the number of participants tended to rise, the Capital Security Command issued statements at 6:30 p.m. and 6:45 p.m. urging the public to not participate in the rally (*Matichon*, 10 May 1992). After 9:30 p.m., the military broadcast a false report that Suchinda had agreed to the constitutional amendment and urged the protesters to go home (*Matichon*, 10 May 1992).

By 7:30 p.m. on Saturday 9 May, the crowd at the rally had swelled to about 100,000.[23] Earlier in that afternoon, the Speaker of the House of Representatives had gathered the delegates from each party and discussed the constitutional amendment for two hours. According to the speaker, parties agreed to narrow down the amendment to four points but the government parties needed more time to examine the points in detail. He expected that the opinion of each party would be finalized by 15 May (*Matichon*, 10 May 1992; *Naeona*, 10 May 1992; *Daily News*, 11 May 1992). The Speaker stated on television at 12:10 a.m. 10 May that both the government and the opposition parties agreed on the constitutional amendment in principle (*Thai Rat*, 11 May 1992; *Matichon*, 15 May 1992). In response to this development, the delegates of four opposition parties, the CPD and the SFT deliberated on the dissolution of the rally. They were unable to announce the dissolution,[24] however, and they continued the rally on 10 May.

In any case, the rally had to be disbanded or moved elsewhere because the King was scheduled to pass through Ratchadamnoen Avenue on 14 May. The rally organizers, including Chamlong, had a meeting from 6:00 p.m. on 10 May. Their decision was not announced to the crowd even after midnight (*Matichon*, 11 May 1992). Finally, at 4:15 a.m. 11 May, Chamlong appeared on the stage to announce the dissolution of the rally and asked the people to observe the development on the constitutional amendment carefully and gather at Sanam Luang again at 5:00 p.m. on 17 May (*Krungthep Thurakit Sutsapda*, 16–22 May 1992). In order to avoid chaos they had waited until Monday morning when many people would go home and the crowd would become more manageable.

The first phase of the second round

On 14 May, the Confederation for Democracy (*samaphan prachathipatai*: CFD) was formed in preparation for the resumption of the rally on 17 May. Its committee consisted of seven members, including Chamlong, Prathip representing a slum NGO, San and Weng who were medical doctors representing a medical NGO, Somsak representing the state-owned company labor union, Parinya representing students, and Chalat's daughter representing her father who was on a hunger strike. It was chaired by San.

In the lead up to 17 May, the government took various measures to obstruct the rally. Prime Minister Suchinda indicated on 13 May that the governor of the Bangkok Metropolitan Authority (BMA) might be fired or the BMA assembly dissolved should the BMA lend its mobile toilets for the rally on 17 May (*Bangkok Post*, 14 may 1992). This remark drew heavy criticism and the Interior Minister announced on 14 May that the BMA could lend mobile toilets (*The Nation*, 15 May 1992). In fact, however, the military had already booked to hire them even though it did not need them at all (*The Nation*, 17 May 1992; *Matichon*, 17 May 1992).[25] On 15 May, the military tried to have the Buddhist Week ceremonies at Sanam Luang extended to 20 May (*Matichon*, 15 May 1992). On the morning of 16 May, the Department of Labor requested labor unions in writing not to attend the rally on 17 May (*Matichon*, 17 May 1992). From 14 May, two state-owned banks (Krung Thai Bank and Government Saving Bank) began to warn the staff not to attend the rally over the in-house PA system (*Bangkok Post*, 16 May 1992). State radio stations banned the broadcasting of the songs of the four singers who had taken part in the first round of the rally in order to put pressure on the entertainers (*The Nation*, 16 May 1992).

On 15 May, the government organized pro-Suchinda rallies in many provinces simultaneously. Each rally was held in front of a provincial government building. Participants were welcomed by the provincial governor and provided with soft drinks by the provincial authorities. Even food was served in some provinces. Some rallies were attended by government MPs and soldiers. Most were attended by several thousand people and some only attracted less than a thousand. All were mobilized by the Interior Ministry through its chain of command in the provincial governments (*Matichon*, 15, 16 and 17 May 1992; *The Nation*, 16 May 1992).[26] On 16 May, former Prime Minister Khuekrit expressed his support for Suchinda at a press conference and boasted that he would be able to mobilize as many as 100,000 people if he made a speech at Sanam Luang (*Matichon*, 17 May 1992).

On the evening of 17 May, the government organized free concerts for 'drought relief' at two locations in Bangkok (at the Army sports stadium and the Wongwianyai rotary plaza[27]) to counteract the protest rally at Sanam Luang. The concerts were well publicized in advance. Many of the audience members at the Army stadium were brought in from provinces near Bangkok on chartered buses, mobilized by village chiefs. The crowd at the stadium numbered around 10,000 people mainly of middle to advanced age (*Daily News*, 18 May 1992; *Thai Rat*, 18 May 1992).[28] At Wongwianyai, there were several thousand of mostly young people. This concert was televised live nationally on Channel 11, which was controlled by the Public Relations Department (*Matichon*, 18 May 1992; *Khao Sot*, 18 May 1992; *Thai Rat*, 18 May 1992; *Daily Mirror*, 18 May 1992). Although the concerts were meant to raise funds for drought relief, the amount of contributions collected was very small.

Conversely, the attempt to amend the constitution, which prompted the dissolution of the first round rally, was reaching an impasse. On 11 May, five government parties discussed the constitutional amendment and agreed to meet again on 18 May to discuss the result of each party's deliberations. Discussions were held at the party level on 13 May that were dominated by cautious opinions. On 14 May, Speaker of the Senate, acting as the Parliamentary President, said that the government parties would submit their bill on 18 May and the Parliament would begin deliberations on 22 May (*Matichon*, 16 May 1992). On 17 May, the secretary-general of the Chat Thai Party in the ruling coalition said that the party's review committee would not be able to reach a conclusion in time and they would only consider the bill from the opposition parties on 22 May. At the same time, he remonstrated that politics should be conducted inside the Parliament, not on the streets (*Thai Rat*, 18 May 1992). The government parties insisted that the Speaker of the House of Representatives had made a hasty announcement on 9 May and that they had informed the King that they actually had not agreed to amend the constitution.

On 17 May, people began to gather in small groups at Sanam Luang. There were 20,000–30,000 people by the time speeches started at 4:00 p.m. (*Matichon*, 18 May 1992; *Phuchatkan*, 18 May 1992; *Dao Sayam*, 18 May 1992). According to the police estimation, the crowd number was 50,000 at 5:45 p.m., 80,000 at 6:30 p.m. (*Khao Sot*, 18 May 1992), and continued to rise quickly. By 8:00 p.m., the number exceeded 200,000 and the crowd spread beyond the central passage in the square.[29]

The rally organizers of the CFD held a meeting from 5:00 p.m. and all the key leaders gathered backstage by 6:30 p.m.. Music and plays were performed and speeches were made on the stage but none of the key CFD members had spoken by 8:00 p.m. (*Sayam Rat*, 18 May 1992). In order to stop people from going home because they could not hear the events from the main stage on the north end of Sanam Luang, a smaller stage was set up in front of the Justice Ministry on the northeast side shortly past 8:00 p.m. (*Phuchatkan*, 18 May 1992; *Matichon* 18

May 1992). At 9:00 p.m., the CFD committee members finally appeared on the main stage. Chamlong spoke first, then committee member Weng announced that they would move the rally to the Government House. Demonstrators on the north side of Sanam Luang departed first, followed by those on the south side led by Chamlong (*Thai Rat*, 18 May 1992; *Phuchatkan*, 18 May 1992; *Naeona*, 18 May 1992).

The first group of demonstrators reached Phan Fa Bridge at 9:40 p.m.. The police had already barricaded the area with barbed wire. The situation was the same as that on 8 May, except that this time some of the demonstrators clashed with police. The police sprayed the demonstrators trying to break through the barricade with water cannons from fire trucks. Demonstrators threw rocks, bottles and wood pieces at the police. At 10:05 p.m., Chamlong caught up with the first group and repeatedly asked them to sit down calmly on the street in front of the bridge to no avail. The crowd on the other side of the bridge also clashed with the police and some demonstrators threw firebombs. Police officers beat the demonstrators with truncheons and destroyed motorbikes and vehicles parked nearby. A group of people seized a fire station near the bridge and destroyed fire trucks inside at around midnight (*Naeona*, 18 May 1992). At 12:00 midnight, Chamlong told the demonstrators that the mob who threw firebombs and torched cars had been hired by the government to provoke disorder and they should not believe these instigators. At the same time, he placed a human barrier between the police and the crowd to prevent further clashes (*Thai Rat*, 18 May 1992).

At 12:30 a.m. 18 May, the government declared a state of emergency in the Bangkok metropolitan area on the grounds of subversive and violent activities. At around 12:35 a.m., a group of people forced their way through the police barricade at Phan Fa Bridge into Ratchadamnoen Nok Avenue and destroyed police vehicles (*Naeona*, 18 May 1992; *Thai Rat*, 18 May 1992; *Matichon*, 18 May 1992).[30] The Interior Ministry issued an order at 1:30 a.m. prohibiting gatherings of more than ten people, and another order at 1:35 a.m. prohibiting the publication of anything which might threaten security and order (*Matichon*, 18 May 1992).[31] At 1:45 a.m., the Capital Security Command warned that it would use force to suppress the rally unless it was disbanded promptly (*Naeona*, 18 May 1992). Several hundred people on Ratchadamnoen Nok Avenue broke into the Police Division of Child and Youth Welfare and the Nang Loeng police station, damaged property, and set fire to the buildings shortly after 2:00 a.m.. At 3:00 a.m. from the Capital Security Command, the television news broadcast a warning that military troops were going to be deployed as there was no sign of the riot calming down. News of destructive activities was reported again at 3:15 a.m. and 3:20 a.m.. At 3:30 a.m., troops began to advance along Ratchadamnoen Nok Avenue and suddenly opened fire near the Nang Loeng police station, causing fatalities. A newspaper reporter who was covering this incident had his camera confiscated (*Thai Rat*, 19

May 1992). Immediately after this, the government warned on television again that troops were being deployed (*Thai Rat*, 19 May 1992; *Naeona*, 19 May 1992; *Daily News*, 19 May 1992). Shortly after 4:00 a.m., troops began an operation to push back the crowd on Ratchadamnoen Nok Avenue to Phan Fa Bridge by firing warning shots. This resulted in numerous deaths and injuries (*Thai Rat*, 19 May 1992). An officer at the scene shouted, 'Who told you to shoot people; I ordered you to fire into the air' (*The Nation*, 19 May 1992). Some soldiers had shot fleeing protesters in their backs. The television news reported that the military had already suppressed the riot (*Krungthep Thurakit*, 19 May 1992), however troops continued a mopping-up operation intermittently. Following a warning at around 5:30 a.m., troops sprayed the protesters with water cannons and fired shots into the air for twenty minutes at Phan Fa Bridge (*Krungthep Thurakit*, 19 May 1992). The government released a statement on television at 5:45 a.m., explaining why military troops had been deployed (*Krungthep Thurakit*, 19 May 1992), and announced at 6:00 a.m. that the riot was suppressed without bloodshed (*Naeona*, 19 May 1992).[32] By this time, the mopping-up operation was suspended and there was a temporary lull.

Prime Minister Suchinda convened an urgent cabinet meeting at 10:00 a.m. 18 May and explained the reason for declaring a state of emergency. Then he went to the headquarters of the first Army region and released a statement on television at 2:00p.m.:

> Chamlong... repeatedly organized the protest rally to realize his political ambition and incited the participants to violence; Since they had been stopped from moving the rally on 8 May, the organizers should have known that the government would not allow them to move on Ratchadamnoen Avenue; This clearly indicates that major-general Chamlong was hoping for acts of violence; (Due to recurrent subversive acts) I had to declare a state of emergency. (*Phuchatkan*, 19 May 1992; *Matichon*, 19 May 1992)

The military reinforced troops from around 2:30 p.m. and began to close in on the demonstrators from both Phan Fa Bridge and the Democracy Monument with guns firing into the air at 3:00 p.m.. They finally arrested Chamlong. The remaining 700 or so demonstrators were also arrested and transferred to the police school which was used as a temporary detention center (*Matichon*, 19 May 1992).[33] Once the mopping-up operation was completed, the government replaced the capital-based police units with units from the outer metropolitan areas (*Thai Rat*, 20 May 1992). Although the government announced on television at 4:00 p.m. that it had dissolved the rally without bloodshed, this round of mopping-up had also caused many casualties (*Krungthep Thurakit*, 19 May 1992).

The second phase of the second round

The protest rally had been dispersed but the protesters began to gather in small groups and congregated in many places between Sanam Luang and Phan Fa Bridge on the evening of 18 May. Troops repeatedly fired warning shots. The biggest crowd gathered in front of the Public Relations Department and the Government Lottery Office. The protesters confronted the troops, repeatedly charged at them only to retreat when shots were fired by the soldiers. There were a number of casualties there. Some of the protesters raided the Public Relations Department and the Lottery Bureau, damaged property inside and set fire to the buildings. Others set fire to the Revenue Department. Some even hijacked petroleum and gas tankers and set fire to them, but they stopped short of turning it into a major disaster. From 5:00 a.m. 19 May, troops began a full-scale mopping-up operation on Ratchadamnoen Avenue and captured protesters who had failed to escape or taken refuge in the Royal Hotel which had turned into a temporary field hospital (*Daily News*, 20 May 1992; *Matichon*, 20 May 1992). The television news at 6:15 a.m. reported that the military had suppressed a riot on Ratchadamnoen Avenue and arrested about 700 rioters (*Thai Rat*, 20 May 1992).

Apart from Ratchadamnoen Avenue, motorcycle gangs had been rampaging throughout the city since about 10 p.m. on 18 May.[34] They mainly vandalized traffic lights and police booths. Some attacked the railway central station and others hijacked commuter buses and gasoline tankers. The elusive gangs moved around swiftly, leaving a trail of destruction. Police had to resort to a crackdown on motorcycle gangs and the government also shifted their attention from Ratchadamnoen Avenue to these gangs.

Between 3:55 a.m. and 7:30 a.m. on 19 May, the Capital Security Command issued four statements on television, one after another, and tried to blame a communist conspiracy for the military's violent suppression operation. They explained that a new mastermind appeared the previous night and the tone of the rally changed completely; communist insurgents slipped in amongst the crowd and incited violence; they used motorcycle gangs to 'steal gasoline tankers and set the capital ablaze;' this was a conspiracy to 'seize power' in the midst of 'escalating confusion and chaos' 'based on a violence-oriented ideology' (*Thai Rat*, 20 May 1992; *Matichon*, 20 May 1992). Channel 5 showed two of the arrested motorcycle gang members at 9:30 a.m. who testified that they had been hired by a figure suggestive of a New Aspiration Party executive (*Matichon*, 20 May 1992). At 2:45 p.m., the Prime Minister released a statement along the same line on television, saying that the government had to use force to suppress the riot in order to stop a communist revolution attempt by an opposition leader who was a communist sympathizer (*Matichon*, 20 May 1992). In other words, the government claimed that it was a conspiracy by the New Aspiration Party leader Chawalit.

From the morning of 19 May, small rallies were held at various locations throughout the city. In particular, about 30,000 protesters gathered at Ramkhamhaeng University in a suburb of Bangkok from the evening and the rally continued on 20 May. Protesters were back on Ratchadamnoen Avenue too. Anti-government rallies were also held in provinces, especially in university towns such as Chiang Mai, Songkhla and Khon Kaen, which gathered strength fuelled by strong anger at the bloodshed that had occurred in the capital. However, there was a sense of powerlessness among the protesters as they knew they were no match for armed troops. It seemed that only the King could defeat the gun.[35] Since 18 May, the protesters hoped increasingly desperately that the King would intervene and punish the Prime Minister for causing so many casualties by the use of excessive force. The King finally stepped in to control the situation on the night of 20 May.

Confrontation between good and evil

Chamlong Simueang (Chamlong Srimuang)
Chamlong was one of the Class 7 officers who graduated from the Army Academy (Chunlachomklao Royal Military Academy) in 1960. He was selected to be Secretary to the Prime Minister when Prem formed government in 1980. When the popular election system for the post of Bangkok Governor was reintroduced in 1985, he resigned from the Army and stood as an independent candidate. He won the election and later formed the Phalang Tham Party. He was a follower of a new Buddhist sect called Santi Asok and practiced an exceptionally strict discipline for a lay person, as illustrated by his diet regime of one vegetarian meal a day. He was highly regarded for his integrity and initiative during his time as Governor. This is why he was re-elected as Governor in 1990 by winning 64% of votes, and why his party won an overwhelming victory by claiming fifty of fifty-six metropolitan assembly seats and 184 of 220 district council seats. He stepped down from the governorship to stand as a candidate for the March 1992 general election. He and his party won decisively by securing thirty-two of thirty-five seats in the capital (McCargo 1997). He steadily expanded his support base in Bangkok and enjoyed immense popularity.

A large-scale rally assembled in response to his appeal. He was able to mobilize a large number of people for the following reasons.
1. He was highly popular and well-known due to his good performance as Governor for two terms and his clean, modest and stoic lifestyle.
2. However, since he felt his reputation was not strong enough to mobilize people, he went on a strict hunger strike.

3. He used what could amount to emotional blackmail by releasing a statement in the form of a will claiming he would die if the people did not come to the rally. On this point, Chamlong himself made the following admission at 10:45 a.m. on 9 May after suspending his hunger strike: 'I needed a large number of people. People would not respond to my appeal and come to the rally if I was living in comfort. That is why I had to resort to a dangerous means and threaten to die if people did not come to the rally' (*Matichon*, 10 May 1992). This shows that it was not easy even for a person as famous as Chamlong to organize a large-scale rally.

During the first round of the rally from 6 to 11 May, Chamlong had the support of opposition parties, the CPD, the SFT and NGOs. It was a form of a joint campaign. On the morning of 9 May shortly before he stopped his hunger strike, he was asked by a reporter whether he had been leading the rally single-handedly. He explained his role in the campaign by writing as follows:

> Yes. The rally has been under my total leadership. This is because: (1) On 7 May, the street in front of Parliament was packed full and there was not an inch of space left. I could not stand any more and proposed to the committee to move. The committee was indecisive. Professor Khothom said… we couldn't do this and couldn't do that. So I had to give them an ultimatum and told them I did not care if the committee would not move, I would lead the people. Then the people managed to move quite smoothly…; (2) Such a massive task requires willpower and experience. I looked around and realized I was the best qualified for the task; (3) The people who come to the rally do so because they either like me or pity me. They believe in what I say. To lead people, a leader must earn their trust; (4) Judging from the result, I have led the people correctly. Last night (8 May), I took the same action. I led the people out of Sanam Luang. Many of the committee members opposed me. Almost all the people followed me…; (5) A person who was interested in politics told me three or four days ago that if I should leave leadership in the hands of the committee, this campaign would not succeed because the committee had no determination, no high profile and no experience. (*Matichon*, 10 May 1992)

This last comment is very indicative of his almost arrogant confidence and pride that it was he who mobilized and led the people.

On 14 May, rally organizers formed the Confederation for Democracy (CFD) and elected seven committee members, including Chamlong, in preparation for the second round of rallying on 17 May. It was intended to give more prominent roles to those who worked behind the scenes during the first round and to attract more participants. However, it should be noted that the representatives of opposition parties and the CPD were not in the committee. Chamlong explained as follows: Political parties take too much time to coordinate party opinions and were not suitable for the CFD which needed to make decisions promptly; and Professor Khothom of the CPD was too busy with his university duties and unable to concentrate on the CFD[36] (*Matichon*, 15 May 1992). As a result, the rest of the committee members were either Chamlong's close associates or persons with little leadership capabilities. Thus Chamlong continued to be the 'Commander-in-Chief' in the second round of the rally[37] (*Thai Rat*, 18 May 1992).

Suchinda Khraprayun

It was not only the opposition parties, the CPD, the SFT and NGOs that helped Chamlong. On 16 May, Chamlong was asked if the obstructive actions of the government had helped intensify the protest movement. He replied, 'That is correct. The government has been helping us all along' (*Matichon*, 17 May 1992). The desperate measures taken by the government to obstruct the rally were often counterproductive. They only intensified a sense of distrust or dissatisfaction towards the government and helped increase the number of participants in the rally.

The government's biggest mistake was strict censorship of the television and radio news programs. The government began to tighten control on the broadcast media on the afternoon of 7 May. All five television stations began broadcasting joint news programs led by Army-operated Channel 5. There was hardly any reporting on the protest rally and any news related to the rally was always distorted. The government tried hard to discourage people from attending the rally by using negative language such as rioters, violence and agitation, or reporting misinformation such as: the rally was over; the demonstrators were a small number of radicals; the rally would benefit communists; and the rally was an act of irreverence to the royal family. For instance on 9 May, television news repeatedly reported from midnight that the CPD and the SFT had broken away from the protest rally. In the morning, it reported without explanation that Chamlong had stopped a hunger strike and resigned as the party leader. This was intended to mislead the viewers into believing that Chamlong had lost and ended the rally. In the evening, television news warned not to obstruct the passage of Princess Sirinthon which was scheduled for the following day (*Naeona*, 12 May 1992).

The government censorship was limited to the broadcast media.[38] The print media reported on the protest rally in detail every day.[39] It was obvious to the people that the government was forcing television and radio stations to broadcast deceptive news reports. For instance, the television repeatedly reported on 10 May that the Princess was forced to take an alternative route because the protesters were blocking her passage. However, newspapers on 11 May reported with photos on the front page that many people on Ratchadamnoen Avenue waited for the Princess to pass in an orderly fashion and exposed the government's lie (*Matichon*, 11 May 1992; *The Nation*, 11 May 1992). The broadcast media lost its credibility day by day. When the Prime Minister announced that the number of dead was forty on the afternoon of 20 May, few believed it. One opposition politician stated at the rally at 2:00 p.m. on 10 May 'I would like to thank the government-controlled mass media which does not report the facts of the rally and collectively lies to the people' (*Daily News*, 11 May 1992). As the one-sided reports from the government continued, more and more people joined the rally out of anger or curiosity.

Starved for information, people had rushed to buy newspapers and magazines since 8 May. At newsstands, newspapers containing multiple reports on the rally and criticisms aimed at the government sold out first. Even normally unpopular ruling party-affiliated newspapers sold well. Newspaper companies received telephone calls constantly from many readers who wanted to know the latest information on the rally or wanted to complain about the government. Now, the newspapers were the enemy of the government. The more hostile a newspaper was to the government, the better it sold. As the newspapers sensationalized the dirty and brutal actions of the government and inflated the scale of the rally to 500,000 and even 1,000,000, more people were drawn to the rally. Chamlong himself commented to reporters when he stopped his hunger strike on 9 May, 'I am very grateful to the newspapers. I sincerely hope that they will report on the rally. Otherwise not many people will turn up' (*Matichon*, 10 May 1992). Censorship of the broadcast media increased the demand for newspapers and the newspapers fuelled the public's anger at the Prime Minister and increased the scale of the rally.

The government attempted to control the print media after it declared a state of emergency on 18 May, but most of the newspapers ignored it and continued to report on the protest rally. Once the broadcast media had turned into a virtual information apparatus run by the military headquarters, the metropolitan residents, at least, stopped believing in the broadcast media and relied solely on the newspapers for information. The newspapers did not always report the truth. As the scale of the rally expanded, it became more difficult for reporters to fully grasp the whole picture. There were substantial discrepancies in the facts reported by different newspapers. Still, the public had far more trust in the newspapers than in the broadcast media. If some newspapers reported that some corpses were sighted somewhere and soldiers carried them elsewhere, many people believed it. Even more credibility was attached to any report attributed to prominent persons, as in the case of a report claiming that former MP (who won the 1996 gubernatorial election) Phichit Rattakun came out of the Royal Hotel at 12:55 a.m. on 19 May and said there were about 100 dead bodies in the hotel lobby (*Matichon*, 19 May 1992). The actual number of the dead was not important. No one knew the actual number of casualties in the midst of the turmoil. The important thing was that the readers believed that many people had been killed.

In addition to news censorship, the government resorted to all sorts of measures in order to obstruct the rally. One example was its attempt to stop the lending of mobile toilets to the rally on 17 May. The rally organizers ridiculed the government's action by saying that it was trying to shut down their buttocks as well as their eyes and ears. Holding a couple of free concerts at the same time as the rally on 17 May was another example.

Obstruction was not the only factor that intensified people's anger. The government parties drew criticism when they changed their attitude toward the constitutional amendment once the rally was dissolved, although they had agreed to it earlier. Remarks made by the government and military leadership including the Prime Minister had the same effect. Prime Minister Suchinda repeatedly made provocative comments in the wake of his parliamentary speech on 7 May. The Deputy Minister of Agriculture told reporters on 9 May that rally participants were followers of Santi Asok and slum residents who were hired for 300 baht per day (*Matichon*, 19 May 1992). Such obstructive measures and offensive remarks did nothing but convince the people that Prime Minister Suchinda was an evil man and had to resign.

The contrast between good and evil became clearer as the government tried to obstruct the rally. Chamlong, who had been famous for his religious discipline and integrity, had the image of a man of justice (*tham*) from the beginning. Suchinda's words and deeds made Chamlong look even better. Few people criticized Chamlong when he stopped his hunger strike on 9 May. In contrast, Suchinda, who had been criticized since the beginning of his Prime Ministerial appointment, further lost credibility and gained a bad image as he tried to resort to wiles to obstruct the rally. As his image changed from grey to black, the situation became as clear as black and white in people's minds. The simplified perception of the protest rally as a fight for justice in addition to democracy played a major role in increasing the number of participants in the rally. No one else could better symbolize the struggle between good and evil than Chamlong. He played a vital role in the May protest rally.

How the credit was misappropriated

Chamlong was supposed to have been the central figure in the May protest rally. However, he eventually slipped off center stage in the discourse surrounding the incident. The view that gives the credit to the middle class has now become dominant. There seems to be three major reasons for this: the King's intervention, blame for the bloodshed, and the role of the mass media.

The King's intervention
When the government demonstrated its determination to suppress the rally by deploying troops, it seemed that the protesters had no option but to ask the King for help. On the morning of 18 May, the day after the first bloodshed, Chamlong

telephoned Privy Councilor and former Prime Minister Prem and the daughter of the royal *aide-de-camp* (*samuharatchaongkharak*) (*Matichon*, 19 May 1992). He pleaded with Prem to 'take an appropriate step' (*Krungthep Thurakit*, 19 May 1992). Not only Chamlong but most people felt sad and powerless and hoped for an intervention by the King.[40]

Such over-reliance on the King stems from an absolute respect and loyalty for the King's authority. The present King has consolidated his authority steadily since the 1960s. He ordered the leaders of the military junta to step down in 1973 and established a solid position for himself in the 1980s. Many believed that the King should be able to punish the Prime Minister. Despite his people's longing for his intervention after 18 May, however, the King did not make a move immediately. There are two conceivable reasons. One possibility is that he was unable to make a move. A lot of behind-the-scenes maneuvering is required for the King to take action, as an intervention by the King should never end in failure. The King can step in solemnly only when all preparations have been carried out. It is possible that it took some time to make such preparations.[41] Another possibility is that the King might not have been sympathetic to the protest rally.[42]

It was not until the night of 20 May that the King stepped in to control the situation. There had been some signs pointing to this intervention since the morning of that day. An interview with Princess Sirinthon staying in France at the time was broadcast on television at 6:00 a.m.. She said, 'What I desire most sincerely is that those killing the people will stop using violence. They are all Thais even though they may have different opinions... I hope they will talk over and solve their differences in another way.' This was the first criticism against the government that was broadcast on television since 7 May (SKT 1992: 9). At 8:00 p.m. on the same day, an interview with the Crown Prince visiting South Korea at the time was broadcast. He urged everyone to cooperate with each other to solve the problems (SKT 1992: 8). The two stations owned by the Mass Communication Organization of Thailand and the Public Relations Department respectively reported the details of clashes on 17 and 18 May for the first time. Scenes of troops using excess force to suppress the protesters were also broadcast. At 7:30 p.m., a picture of Chamlong detained in a police cell was televised. The broadcast media blackout began to crumble. More importantly, privy councilors had a meeting at Prem's official residence from 9:00 a.m. to 11:45 a.m. on 20 May. They reportedly decided then to recommend that the King dismiss Suchinda (*Krungthep Thurakit*, 21 May 1992). They did not choose to meet at the palace, which suggests they expected reporters to find out about it.

At 9:30 p.m. on 20 May, the King summoned Suchinda and Chamlong to the palace and, in the presence of the President of the Privy Council and Prem, reprimanded them for causing bloodshed and urged them to resolve the conflict peacefully (SKT 1992:7). This scene was televised at midnight of 21 May. The outcome was not the immediate dismissal of the guilty party Suchinda, which many were hoping for, but both parties were equally blamed for the incident. Although the King's intervention ended the violence, the protesters were not fully satisfied with the outcome. The next morning, newspapers praised the King's decision in big front page headlines. Only *Phuchatkan* conveyed the sense of discontent in its headline, 'Dream was shattered, Suchinda remains Prime Minister' (*Phuchatkan*, 21 May 1992).[43] If the King had taken sides with Chamlong and punished only Suchinda, Chamlong would have been able to come out from the detention cell triumphantly as a hero. The King's decision to the contrary foreshadowed subsequent criticisms of Chamlong.

Blame for bloodshed

Following the incident, some people began trying to locate the responsibility for the bloodshed. Although most of them accused the military, there were some who leveled their criticisms at Chamlong. A typical example was an attack by pro-military forces accusing Chamlong of 'leading the people to death.' In addition to the hostile forces, critical voices were also raised by some newspapers which had been sympathetic to the rally. English-language paper *The Nation* commented on 19 May, 'moving (the rally)…was designed to provoke confrontation…(H)asty action could invite a tragedy (T)he violence ended up alienating many people from the rally' (*The Nation*, 19 May 1992).

Why did Chamlong move the rally? His primary aim was to oust Suchinda as the Prime Minister. He tried to hold a large-scale protest rally in order to achieve it. If it did not have the intended effect, he would have to apply more pressure. A demonstration march was one of the means to achieve it. Chamlong was asked by a reporter shortly after 6:00 a.m. on 9 May why he moved the rally out of Sanam Luang, and he replied by writing as follows:

> I moved because the people would lose interest if they stayed at Sanam Luang all the time. They would become tired of listening to speeches all day. We should take a demonstrative action by marching. Otherwise we cannot make progress in our struggle. Secondly, the government is planning to hold the ceremony of first plowing (*phuetmongkhon*) in Sanam Luang tomorrow, 10 May. Thirdly, the crowd moved in an orderly manner when I first tried it on 7 May and I was confident that they would move smoothly again this time. (*Matichon*, 10 May 1992)

The march was designed partly to lift the morale of the protesters.

Having declared a hunger strike and appealed to the public to attend the protest rally on 6 May, Chamlong was envisaging a short decisive battle. Once he was on a hunger strike, he had no time to wait and see. If the standoff were to continue for many days, Chamlong would be in trouble. Further, the larger the scale of the march, the more effective it would be as a pressurizing tactic. Consequently, Chamlong moved the rally on 7 May during a time period when the number of participants increased. Once the rally moved to Sanam Luang and attracted an even larger crowd than on the previous night, Chamlong moved it again, just before 9:00 p.m. on 8 May. Faced with this pressure, the speaker of the House of Representatives scrambled to make some progress on the constitutional amendment but Prime Minister Suchinda appeared unmoved.

The march was expected to generate more than a demonstrative effect. If the march moving out of Sanam Luang on 8 May was not blocked by the police, the protesters could proceed to Government House, the Prime Minister's official residence, and the Chitlada Palace. If they managed to march to the Palace, as was the case in October 1973, they could petition to the King to dismiss the Prime Minister.[44] The fact that the destination of the march was not disclosed to the participants strongly suggests that Chamlong was most likely heading toward the Palace on that day. Conversely, if the police blocked the march, Ratchadamnoen Avenue would become impassable and Bangkok's notorious traffic jam would become even worse. If the public's anger over traffic congestion was directed towards the government, pressure on the Prime Minister should increase.

At the time of the march on 17 May, the participants were told that they were going to Government House to put direct pressure on the Prime Minister. However, the Prime Minister was away on a tour of the northern region at the time and it was doubtful that the march would have had such an effect. It was also obvious to everyone, as Suchinda pointed out in his statement on 18 May, that the government would certainly block the movement of the rally. The police and the military had set up barricades on all the roads leading to Government House and the Palace. The protesters had already learned that if the march was blocked and they had to hold a rally on the street, it would not be able to create sufficient pressure to force the Prime Minister to resign.

Following a large-scale rally, demonstration marches, and street rallies, the next means available to the protesters was bloodshed. *Daily News* reported that it had received information about a decision made at a CFD meeting on the evening of 17 May. It alleged that the rally leaders decided to move the crowd out of Sanam Luang in order to provoke the government to use force because it was becoming difficult to gather several hundred thousand people to the rally and they needed to bring the battle to an end on that day (*Daily News*, 18 May 1992).[45] It is reasonable to surmise that the rally leaders were trying to induce bloodshed because the street rallies since 8 May had failed to force the resignation of Prime Minister Suchinda (Khian 1997: 39).

Bloodshed would cause a storm of criticism. It goes without saying that the number of casualties should be kept to a minimum. Most importantly, the blame should be laid at the feet of Suchinda. For this purpose, the protesters should avoid the stigma of rioters. Demonstrators should give the impression that the government unilaterally used violence to suppress a peaceful rally so that the government would lose legitimacy and all the blame would be directed at the Prime Minister. In fact, the Prime Minister came under harsh criticism from the international community as soon as the scenes of brutal crackdown were broadcast all over the world. If the Prime Minister should decide to stay and weather a storm of criticism at home and overseas, the rally leaders would have to appeal to the King's benevolence.

The government also should have anticipated that the use of firearms would draw criticism. Violence erupted at around midnight of 17 May prior to the shooting of protesters by troops. It remains a mystery as to whether the attacks on police buildings were carried out by the CFD operatives, the government operatives or some unrelated vandals. However, in the case of attacks on the Nang Loeng Police Station which triggered the deployment of troops, the police had abandoned the emergency headquarters and vacated the building earlier. Despite the presence of 5000 heavily armed troops nearby (*Naeona*, 18 May 1992), the government did nothing to stop about 1000 rioters from looting, destroying and burning the building (*Krungthep Thurakit*, 19 May 1992). It was reported that the troops on Ratchadamnoen Avenue turned a blind eye to the looting and burning of nearby government facilities from the night of 18 May to the morning of 19 May (*Daily News*, 20 May 1992). It is likely that the government intentionally held back a crackdown on these occasions.

Chamlong is partly responsible for many casualties. If he had continued the rally at Sanam Luang, the military would not have fired at protesters. Then, the rally would have petered out and the Prime Minister could not have been removed. Bloodshed and Suchinda's resignation were inseparable. Those who recognize the May incident as a victory for the democratic movement are not in the position to criticize Chamlong for moving the rally. Criticizing bloodshed is no different from saying that Suchinda's resignation was not necessary, that is to say, holding a large-scale, morale-boosting rally was sufficient. Nevertheless, some of the pro-democracy forces disregarded this obvious fact and began to criticize Chamlong after the incident.

The middle class leadership theory
Who were the participants of the rally? Why did they participate? These are two separate questions. In a telephone interview with a Thai living in the US on 25 May, Chamlong commented as follows. 'People from many provinces came to at-

tend the rally and their occupations were diverse. It was not a group of a particular type of people, such as students and teachers only or workers only, as had been the case in the past. It was hard to believe but all types of people participated... Even the middle class living in comfort couldn't help but participate' (*Matichon*, 31 May 1992). Many of the researchers, who cast NGOs in the leading role rather than Chamlong, insist that people from all social classes gathered at the rally. From the rally organizers' point of view, it did not matter very much who came to the rally and it was meaningless to place an emphasis on a particular class of people. This view was shared by the government, which criticized the rally as a mobilized, organized event.

Nevertheless, the print media and researchers increasingly focused their interest on who the participants were. More than a few observers pointed out immediately after the start of the rally that many of the participants were middle class people.[46] As early as 7 May, *The Nation* called the crowd the 'yuppie mob' (Callahan 1998: 46). Others reported that the participants on 8 May were mostly of the middle class because many of them had a cellular phone[47] and were dressed neatly, and some even drove their cars to the rally (*Thai Rat*, 9 May 1992; *Ban Mueang*, 9 May 1992). A newspaper, quoting Associated Press, reported that since most Thai people were not interested in politics, those who were participating in the rally were middle class people whose number had increased due to economic growth in recent years (*Matichon*, 10 May 1992).[48] The participants in the rally on 17 May were observed to be 'mostly middle class people and businesspeople' or 'well-educated and well-off people' (*Khao Sot*, 18 May 1992; *Naeona*, 18 May 1992).

Krungthep Thurakit Sutsapda, a business weekly, provided a more detailed explanation with an analytical appearance. Its 16 May issue, which was published before the second round rally on 17 May, had a thirteen-page feature article on the first round rally with a headline on the front cover proclaiming 'a rally of historical significance.' It reported that about 30% of the rally participants were middle class people who carried a cellular phone. They were punctual (turning up in the evening, going home at night or in the morning, and coming again in the evening), neatly dressed, well-disciplined, intelligent enough to criticize speakers, and some of them drove to the rally. Then it grouped 'the middle class as the main actor' into four subcategories: (1) the middle class including private sector employees, self-employed people and businesspeople who were well-off and interested in politics and social issues; (2) members of Santi Asok who also helped as the support staff at the rally; (3) the middle class in Bangkok who had personally supported Chamlong since his time as the governor; and (4) highly-educated people (including those came from provinces) who had been involved in various forms of social activism including NGOs since the October 1973 uprising

(*Krungthep Thurakit Sutsapda*, 16–22 May 1992). This article was significant in that it forced various types of participants into a single category called the middle class and placed it in the foreground of the debate.

An article published in *Phuchatkan*, a business newspaper, on 19 May in the midst of the incident gave a sort of scientific authenticity to this impressionistic argument. It reported on the results of a survey carried out at the rally on the evening of 17 May through about 2,000 copies of a questionnaire form distributed by the Social Science Association of Thailand. It was an exclusive report to *Phuchatkan*.[49] According to the color-printed article on the front page carrying the headline, 'Survey found 50% of participants as private company employees,' the survey was conducted to 'ascertain whether a considerable proportion of the rally participants were middle class people as it was often alleged.' The results showed that 52.0% of the respondents were university graduates and 14.5% had a master's or higher degree, hence two thirds of the respondents at least had a university education. An overwhelming majority were young people in their twenties and thirties, with 2.0% under the age of twenty, 39.4% in their twenties, 36.5% in their thirties, 14.2% in their forties and 6.7% over the age of fifty. Only 8.4% were students, 14.8% were public servants, 6.2% were state-owned company employees, 45.7% were private company employees and 13.7% were self-employed. Fourteen-point-one percent earned a monthly income below 5,000 baht, 28.5% earned between 5,000 and 10,000 baht, 30.0% earned between 10,000 and 20,000 baht, 15.5% earned between 20,000 and 50,000 baht and 6.2% earned 50,000 or more (*Phuchatkan*, 19 May 1992).[50] These findings indicated that the main constituent of the rally was the middle class, as expected.

There are serious doubts regarding the accuracy of this survey. It is true that the composition of protesters changed dramatically compared to the student-led October 1973 uprising. The number of students was small this time because campus activism had declined by the 1980s and also May was in the middle of a long, year-end summer vacation for university students. The middle class accounted for over 20% of the workforce based on a broader classification by occupation (Girling 1996: 43),[51] and the proportion was higher in the capital. It was therefore quite natural that many of the participants were middle class people, and it would have been rather odd if this group did not join the rally. It was possible that they represented 30% or so of the total participants. However, it is highly doubtful that they exceeded one half of the participants. For example, the total number of university graduates in Bangkok was 920,000 in 1990. If the number of rally participants on 17 May was 500,000 and two thirds of them were university graduates, as reported by *Phuchatkan*, the number of university graduates at the rally would be almost 350,000. This would mean that more than one third of the university-educated population in Bangkok attended the rally. This is beyond the realm of possibility because the university-educated population includes graduates of military and police academies, people of middle age or older, and conservative people. It was found at a later date that forty-four people were killed during the incident, and 85% of them were single, 86% had an education lower than high school level and 80% were below the age of twenty (Khanakammakan Yat Wirachon Phruetsapha 35 n. d.: 118; OcKey 1999: 244). These individuals do not fit the image of the middle class with a stable life. It is also evident from various video tapes on the rally released for sale after the incident that the middle class was not the majority among the demonstrators.[52] Perhaps, although the rally was attended by people of diverse occupations and social classes, the middle class simply stood out because of the way they dressed and the personal belongings they carried (*Thai Rat*, 11 May 1992).

Nevertheless, simply because this survey conducted by the Social Science Association of Thailand was the only survey carried out on rally participants, and also because it appeared a 'scientific' investigation, the middle class majority theory became undeniable. It is significant to note that this theory was enthusiastically reported by two leading business papers in Thailand, *Krungthep Thurakit* and *Phuchatkan*. Phuchatkan Co., Ltd. in particular published a book on the May incident immediately after it and commented in the postscript that the incident was 'the middle class movement that will go down in history.' It was 'the success of the middle class' that 'the middle class woke up, participated in a political movement in various ways and took us to the entrance of the last corner leading to full democracy' (Phuchatkan 1992: 176). It declares that the incident was a democracy movement led by the middle class. The chief editor of the daily edition of *Phuchatkan* wrote that the central force of the movement was the 'new bourgeoisie' and that 'a majority of the readers of this newspaper belong to this class' (Vishnu 1992: 10–11).

The readership of the 'quality papers,'[53] including these business papers, are mostly middle class people. Readers would certainly be pleased to read reports praising the middle class for leading the democracy movement. And, by using the collective term 'the middle class,' the papers praised the entire middle class, including those who had nothing to do with the protest rally. Surely this must have resulted in increased sales. In fact, business was brisk for the print media after the May incident. In June, the business weekly *Krungthep Thurakit Sutsapda* was turned into a general weekly, *Nation Sutsapda*.[54] In August, English-language paper *Bangkok Post* launched Thai-language daily *Sayam Post*. Watthachak Co., Ltd., a publisher of various daily newspapers and weekly magazines, launched a new political weekly in May. Another weekly political magazine, *Khao Thai*, was born also in May, and business paper *Prachachat Thurakit* began to include a supplementary edition on politics. This increase in publication activity occurred because of the increased demand for political news. The proliferation of these publications after the incident suggests that the interest of the mostly middle class readership in politics was not necessarily strong before the incident but clearly increased in its wake.

Influenced by the middle class majority theory written up in the newspapers, researchers began to take an interest in the study of the middle class. Little research had been carried out previously on the subject of the middle class in Thailand precisely because they had never played a prominent role in politics. However, a seminar entitled 'The middle class and the democratization of Thailand' was held at Chulalongkorn University in November 1992. The contents of the seminar was compiled into a book and published in May 1993 (Sangsit and Phasuk 1993). The seminar and the book stimulated further research on the middle class and considerably helped the middle class majority theory find acceptance among researchers.

The original observation that there were many middle class people participating the rally would soon make a twist in logic and turn into the argument that the people attended the rally because they belonged to the middle class. The middle class majority theory was transformed into the middle class leadership theory. It argued that the middle class had always desired democracy and many of them voluntarily participated in the protest rally in May 1992. One researcher insists that the middle class has been pro-democracy consistently because it consists of the 'October 14th generation' who played the leading role in the 1973 student uprising (Thirayut 1994). This is rather far-fetched because the middle class, apart from a very small minority, had never been involved in political activism. There is hardly any evidence other than the May 1992 incident that the middle class had been pro-democracy. The only explanation is that the sleeping middle class suddenly woke up.[55] They participated in the rally at the urging of Chamlong. At best, they merely did not reject Chamlong's attempt to mobilize them. Those who participated in a truly voluntary manner would be the people who joined after the evening of 18 May when Chamlong was arrested and the rally had no leader/organizer. If bloodshed alienated 'many people,' i.e. many middle class people, from the rally as alleged by *The Nation* (19 May 1992), these voluntary participants must have been other than middle class. Nonetheless, what has become an accepted theory is the view that the pro-democracy middle class was not mobilized by someone but voluntarily participated in the protest rally. It was therefore only a matter of time before the leaders and organizers of the rally, including Chamlong, would lose significance in the explanation of the May incident.

Impacts on democratization

What impacts did the May 1992 incident and the middle class leadership theory have on the subsequent democratization of Thai politics? Two major impacts were notable. One was Chamlong's downfall and the other was the growing calls for political reform in favor of the middle class.

Chamlong's downfall

While Chamlong expressed his regret over the casualties after the incident, he insisted that the blame belonged with the government alone. Chamlong sounded very confident in his memoirs of the protests published in June 1992 (Chamlong 1993). He declared his faith in his mobilization tactics by saying that he could counter a coup d'état with a wall of people.

Mass political mobilization has rarely been witnessed in Thailand, a nation which has no experience of an independence movement. Attendance at political gatherings was mostly limited to students, laborers and farmers. Chamlong was the first parliamentary politician who mobilized an unlimited number of people to a rally against this tradition. Politics by mass mobilization is highly dangerous. It may result in bloodshed and casualties, or the crowd may become uncontrollable or begin to make radical demands. Worse still, they may rebel against the monarchy. In terms of democracy, it is difficult to establish a stable parliamentary system if opposition parties resort to mass mobilization outside the Parliament every time they want something, as argued by Suchinda. Chamlong was prepared to exploit street politics as well as parliamentary politics if necessary. His downfall amounted to the removal of a dangerous element from politics and a lesson to those who were to follow him. Mass mobilization against the tradition once again became a taboo. Consequently, Chamlong's downfall greatly contributed to the consolidation of stable parliamentary democracy.

Chamlong's downfall was closely tied to criticisms over the bloodshed. Following the incident, the Parliament was dissolved in June and a general election was scheduled to be held in September. During the election campaign, the media divided political parties into two groups. The government parties in the Suchinda administration were the 'evil parties' and the four opposition parties were the 'angel parties' supported by the media. Among the opposition camp, Chamlong's Phalang Tham Party was most conspicuous in the May incident and Chawalit's New Aspiration Party also supported the rally. In contrast, the Democrat Party kept a low profile. Some of its MPs attended the rally and made speeches. However, because it only played a small role in the rally, no MPs of the Democrat Party were arrested or barred from leaving the country, unlike the MPs of Phalang Tham, New Aspiration and Ekkaphap. When all the opposition parties were bundled into the 'angel camp,' the contribution made by each party was averaged out to the advantage of the Democrat Party.

While the Democrat Party had enjoyed a solid support base in the southern region since the 1980s, its fortune was largely decided by the results of elections in Bangkok. It competed fiercely with the Phalang Tham Party which was based mainly in Bangkok. Since the Democrat Party suffered a disastrous loss in the March 1992 general election, it adopted the strategy of criticizing Chamlong in its campaign to regain seats in the capital in the September election. It used slogans such as 'We uphold parliamentary politics' and 'No tears if you elect (party leader) Chuan.' These were designed to emphasize the contrast between Chamlong's radicalism and the moderatism of the Democrat Party. Its campaign took the same line as that of the pro-military camp with the slogan 'Chamlong led the people to death.'[56]

At the same time, there were some developments which resembled the unsettled and threatening conditions after the October 1973 uprising—frequent terror attacks perpetrated by pro-military forces as part of their comeback strategy. Right-wing organizations with links to the military continued their campaign to criticize Chamlong, Chawalit and the CFD and held a rally of about 1000 people at Sanam Luang on 22 July (*Khao Thai*, 27 July 1992). There were several bomb explosions. Firstly, the headquarters of the Social Action Party was bombed on 30 May due to discord among ruling parties (*Matichon Sutsapda*, 5 June 1992). On 13 August, an explosion at Hat Yai railway station in the south left three dead and seventy-four injured (*Matichon Sutsapda*, 28 August 1992). A car owned by the chief editor of *Watthachak* was vandalized on 18 August, then a fire bomb was thrown into the home of the host of a television debate program two days later (*Matichon Sutsapda*, 28 August 1992). The president of a medical university, who was a member of the government committee of investigation into the May incident, resigned from the committee on 23 June after receiving many threatening telephone calls to his home (*Matichon*, 24 June 1992). Chamlong also was under constant threat of violence and hired a private security company to guard him during the election campaign. Bomb explosions continued even after the general election. An explosion at the Interior Ministry on 9 October left three people injured. The Embassy of Myanmar was bombed on 18 October. There were telephone calls threatening the bombing of Thai Airways on 19 October and the Parliament on 20 October. An explosion at a concert of Arisaman Phongrueangrong, a popular singer, in Ratburi Province on the night of 30 October caused two deaths and ten injuries. Arisaman was one of the popular entertainers who had actively participated in the May rally. On 23 December, a bomb exploded at Thon Buri bus terminal in Bangkok, leaving four dead and three seriously injured (*Matichon Sutsapda*, 8 January 1993).

Explosions continued into 1993. Chanthaburi telephone exchange station was bombed on 13 January. A letter bomb exploded at a Bangkok post office on 10 February, causing five deaths and six injuries. Three explosions in Lop Buri on 11 and 12 February left six people injured (SC 1999). The security police believed that many of these bombings had been carried out by the pro-Suchinda faction in the military partly because a serving soldier was arrested as a suspect in the Interior Ministry and Lop Buri bombings. Many people regarded these attacks as reprisal or harassment against Chawalit who was appointed as the Interior Minister responsible for the maintenance of public order. In these circumstances, the people felt increasingly apprehensive about security and gradually became more conservative in favor of order.

English-language paper *The Nation* appealed to the public to vote for the Democrat Party on the front page on the day before the 13 September voting, declaring that '(Democrat leader) Chuan offers the only clear choice as PM' on the grounds that 'this is not the time for political mavericks, "heroes of democracy" or one-man ad hoc parties' and 'with Chuan as Prime Minister, Thailand can regain confidence in the Parliamentary system and face the democratic world with pride' (*The Nation*, 12 September 1992). Affected by severe criticisms from pro-military parties and the Democrat Party, the number of seats in the capital won by the Phalang Tham Party diminished from thirty-two down to twenty-three.[57] In contrast, the moderate Democrat Party increased its seats in the capital from just one to nine, thanks to the goodwill associated with the angel parties. Its expansion in the capital electorate boosted it to the position of leading party and its leader Chuan became the Prime Minister.[58] It was effectively a defeat for Chamlong, whose political fortune continued to decline from then on.

Calls for political reform

The middle class leadership theory praised the middle class as the main actor in democratization and bred arrogance among middle class people. They tended to look down on the masses (*chaoban*) such as the urban lower class and rural people. A student who went to Phan Fa Bridge on the morning of 18 May commented on the situation. There was a cease-fire at the time and some of the protesters went to chat with soldiers or offer them some food. The soldiers came from provinces near Bangkok. The student wrote that there were some among the rally participants who

> insulted soldiers by saying that rural people were ignorant and no good to talk with. Some asked soldiers if they knew the meaning of democracy with a straight

face. If you were a youth who came to Bangkok from the countryside for the first time, found that urban people were a lot better-off than rural people, young people wore expensive and fashionable clothes, shopkeepers carried cellular phones and drove expensive cars such as Mercedes and BMWs, and they called you ignorant with contempt, it is quite natural that you get angry. (*Sayam Rat Sapdawichan*, 19–26 July 1992)

For most of the middle class people who wanted to draw a clear line between themselves and the 'ignorant, poor and vulgar' masses, the middle class leadership theory was very agreeable because it attested that the middle class were different from the masses by elevating the former to the leadership position in the democracy movement of May 1992.

The middle class leadership theory has always argued that the majority of the rally participants were middle class. This amounts to the exclusion of non-middle class participants, particularly those of the lower class who were killed or injured in the incident, from the democratization forces (Callahan 1998: 72). Slum dwellers and Santi Asok members who supported the rally behind the scenes were given no credit whatsoever for their contribution to democratization. This leadership theory not only robbed Chamlong of the leading role but also treated non-middle class participants as insignificant players.[59]

Furthermore, the argument that only the middle class voluntarily and independently participated in the rally has led to the view that other people did not act voluntarily or independently. What followed was the conclusion that the masses which represented over 70% of the population could not take any political action unless mobilized (*radom* or *ken*) or organized (*chattang*) by politicians, bureaucrats or intellectuals, and that this type of passive political movement had no legitimacy (Callahan 1998: 71). Suchinda complained in May 1992 that he wondered why the newspapers 'claimed that my supporters were mobilized and the opposition supporters were voluntary participants' despite the fact that there were many participants at the 17 May rally who were hired or mobilized by religious organizations and political parties (*Khao Sot*, 18 May 1992). There have been several rallies in Bangkok since 1992 although they were far smaller than the May rally. Participants were usually laborers in the Bangkok metropolitan area or farmers from the provinces. These rallies were criticized as organized events. Participants were often asked how much and by whom they were paid. Conversely, a demonstration held in the business district after the 1997 currency crisis was applauded as a voluntary, non-organized action. Apart from the rallies attended by people who are mobilized in exchange for payment or coerced by authority, any orderly rally or demonstration of a certain scale always needs leaders and organizers, and participants join the action with their livelihood or interests at stake. It is quite unfair to ignore these obvious facts and criticize mass political actions.

The media and the middle class are interrelated. The media gave the middle class a sense of self-importance by praising this sector of the populace as the leader of democratization, and the views and opinions of the over-confident middle class were expressed through the media. By acting as the mouthpiece of the middle class, the media could strengthen its own position and influence.[60] This was a self-serving arrangement because the media bestowed power on the middle class and benefited from it with its own increased authority. Signs of change in journalism, from that directed at all readers and viewers to that catering to middle class opinions only, became apparent. For example, Prathip and San of the CFD together with the representatives of slum district residents visited Chawalit on 16 September 1997 in order to express their support for the Prime Minister who was under attack for causing the currency crisis. According to Prathip, this was because 'this government has provided the most benefits to the poor in comparison with the last seven or eight governments.' However, an editorial in *Matichon* accused Prathip of 'giving up an ideal,' and an editorial in *Phuchatkan* harshly criticized the visit stating that 'slum dwellers... visited a graveyard to cheer up a ghost (referring to the Prime Minister on the verge of resignation)... it seems odd' (*Athit*, 26 September 1997). This suggests that the middle class had developed into a large enough market for the media. Although still a minority in number, the voices of the middle class expressed via the media came to be treated as public opinion and dominated political discourse, creating a situation where 'urban residents had "a strong voice" but "few votes" and rural residents had "a weak voice" but "many votes"' (Kho. Pho. Po. 1995: 61). Therein lies the significance of the view which regards the middle class as the 'real victor of the May incident' (Girling 1996: 20). Because the middle class was small in number, intellectuals, businesspeople and NGOs were added to the core middle class and lumped together under the names of 'civil society (*prachasangkhom*),' 'the public (*satharanachon*)' and 'the citizenry (*phonlamueang*),' to the exclusion of the masses. Then, their opinions expressed through the media were dressed up as public opinion. This situation later evolved into their objection against parliamentary politics, calls for political reform and the enactment of the 1997 Constitution. These aspects will be addressed in Part II of this book.

2
Political Decline of the Military: Reasons and Processes

Why personnel changes?

The 'Barbarian May' incident seriously affected Thai politics. The military, which had consistently been the most powerful political force in the country since the 24 June 1932 revolution which sparked the transition to a constitutional monarchy, suffered a particularly severe setback and was rapidly displaced from the political center stage. Despite adopting a parliamentary government system after the 1932 coup, the cycle of one military junta overthrowing another via a military coup was repeated many times throughout the remainder of the twentieth century. There have been ten successful coups since 1932, eight of which involved a change of government. In contrast, there were fifteen general elections between 1932 and 1991, but only four of them resulted in a change of government, and a direct changeover from one popularly elected government to another popularly elected government occurred only once, in 1976. Hence, it is no exaggeration to say that coup d'état was effectively the normal procedure for a change of government in Thailand. During the sixty years from June 1932 to June 1992, nineteen people held the office of prime minister. All were former public servants—either civil or military—and of those who enjoyed relatively long tenures, the majority were ex-military prime ministers.[1] During the six decades, the prime minister's office was occupied by serving military chiefs who had side-stepped into the premiership for a total of forty-seven years.[2] Suchinda was the last serving military chief to assume the premiership, but as discussed in Chapter One, he was forced to step down in the following month. It appeared that the military had lost not only the premiership, but also its political influence. This was not simply a matter of political influence; the military also became less assertive in both words and deeds. How did this change come about?

In contrast to the long and well-documented history of military involvement in politics, civil-military relations remains one of the least researched areas in Thai politics. Further, there has been even less research concerning the military's withdrawal from politics than that focusing on its interventions.[3] Surachat, one of the few scholars to have studied civil-military relations in-depth, states:

'The military's political power declined dramatically after the political crisis of 1992. The crisis confirmed that the tradition of military officers playing a role and intervening in politics had become "outdated" and destroyed the military's political influence' (1998a: 210). Elsewhere he claims that the May incident was a political defeat for the military and became a turning point in civil-military relations (1998b: 193–4): 'the military truly returned to its barracks' for the first time after the incident, and 'the era of military interventions in politics came to an end' (Surachat 2001: 77). There seems to be little room for objections to the view that the May incident was the decisive event that triggered the political withdrawal of the military.[4]

However, what is the causal relationship between the incident and the military's withdrawal? Surachat provides a rather sketchy answer to this which can be summarized in three points. First, the military no longer had a role to play because the political system had been democratized. Second, the military was unable to continue to intervene in politics after its brutal suppression of the demonstrations was harshly criticized and the public's confidence and support clearly diminished (Surachat 2000: 40; 2001: 84). Third, the attitudes of military officers have changed such that they no longer consider it appropriate to intervene in politics (Surachat 1998a: 112–13, 118–19; 1998b: 195). Let us consider these points in more detail.

First, increasing democratization and the military's withdrawal are two sides of the same coin, and thus we cannot explain one in terms of the other. Furthermore, although democracy had already been realized in 1988—in the sense that an election-based political system was put in place, including the appointment of an elected MP as prime minister—growing scandals about financial corruption sparked the 1991 coup d'état. Although in the aftermath of this coup democracy was once again put into practice, not everyone was satisfied with it. Campaigns for political reform gathered pace in the mid-1990s, leading to the adoption of a new constitution in 1997. It is thus not entirely correct to suggest that democracy had taken such a firm hold during the 1990s that it would no longer allow military interventions. It would be more correct to say that the military did not intervene during this period even though it had opportunities to do so. From this perspective then, the more correct question is why did the military not intervene again? To answer that democratization stopped the military from intervening in politics is to put the cart before the horse.

The second explanation, that public confidence and support had enabled the military to intervene in politics, is equally inadequate, for it rests on the supposition that the military's coups and interventions had been in response to the public's needs or desires. This is patently not the case. Although public support and expectations may make interventions easier, they do not prompt them. For example, Prime Minister Thanom Kittikhachon mounted a coup in order to abolish a popularly elected parliament and return to military rule in 1971. This was hardly a response to public expectations. Conversely, there were growing expectations of a coup immediately after the currency crisis in 1997, yet the military did nothing. The military acts for its own reasons; its actions are rarely determined entirely by external factors or events, as if it were a puppet on a string. Furthermore, the claim that the May incident triggered an upsurge in anti-military sentiment and increased pressure on the military to withdraw is unsubstantiated. In fact, a public opinion survey conducted by Funatsu and others in Thailand in September 1994 suggests the opposite. One survey question asked respondents whether or not they agreed to the statement, 'The military taking power is a good thing.' Note that this was not a broadly worded hypothetical or abstract question such as 'a coup d'état may be inevitable in some cases.' Instead, it directly asked whether respondents would support a coup d'état. Although the percentage of respondents who agreed in the Bangkok metropolitan area was only 13% (80% disagreed), figures were substantially higher in rural areas, where approximately 70% of the population lived. Here, the figures were 24% in agreement (70% disagreed) in the central region, 40% (45%) in the northern region, 38% (57%) in the northeastern region and 25% (71%) in the southern region (IDE 1995: 71). In the north and northeastern regions in particular, nearly 40% of respondents supported a coup. Although it might seem reasonable to assume that public support and confidence in the military must have decreased rather than increased after the May incident, considering that the survey was conducted only two years after the incident and during an unprecedented economic boom, it seems surprising that such a large number of respondents agreed to the statement, even in Bangkok. It thus seems that although the military was harshly criticized by the print media, it retained its popularity in the rural areas where the majority of the population lives. The military's popularity did not fall so low as to make the people any less prepared to accept more coups or political interventions.[5]

This was also demonstrated in the first senate election in the history of Thailand, held in 2000. Thirty Army generals stood as candidates and ten were successful. Yet the seven who stood as candidates in Bangkok all failed, which means that, despite their unpopularity in the capital, ten out of twenty-three candidates were successful in other electorates—an outcome consistent with the abovementioned survey results. In this election, about 1500 candidates competed for 200 senate seats, which translated into a success rate of about 13%. In comparison, the generals' success rates of 33% nationally and 43% outside of Bangkok were considerably high (see Chapter Five). This popularity is not necessarily a direct indication of public support for military coups and interventions, but it does serve to undermine claims that the military was no longer able to intervene in politics as a result of its loss of public support and confidence.

The third and last explanation was a change in the attitudes of military officers—was this then the crucial factor in its withdrawal from political intervention? Did a transformation from politicized soldiers into 'professional soldiers (*thahan mueachip*)' actually occur? Since the 1980s, it has been argued that military men should concentrate on military matters. From this perspective, military officers who had expert knowledge of politics and were deeply engaged in political activity came to be referred to with contempt as 'politicized soldiers'. A typical example was Army Commander-in-Chief Chawalit, who was deeply involved in political maneuvering to influence the cabinet and political parties. In contrast to Chawalit, hot-blooded militarists who disparaged political backroom wheeling and dealing in favor of guns and swords were sometimes called 'professional soldiers.' Yet, most of the officers who carried out the coups of 1981, 1985 and 1991 and caused bloodshed in 1992 were the latter type of officers; there were practically no officers in the inner circle of the military who had not dabbled in politics. It is practically impossible for such politically-minded military men to change their attitudes in the short time available after the May incident to become 'professional soldiers' concentrated solely on the military objective of maintaining national security. Such a change would require a comprehensive shake-up of the upper-echelons of the military, but there has been no such shake-up as discussed below. Consequently, it does not seem appropriate to place much emphasis on such a change in attitude.

So where does this leave us in understanding how the May incident relates to the military's withdrawal from politics? What are the conditions which once facilitated its involvement in politics that have been lost? Why was the military able to intervene in politics until the early 1990s, and what changed after the May incident?

The most important source of the military's political power has been its potential to mount a successful coup. A coup need not be staged as the exercise of this power. All that is necessary is that people believe that a coup is a possibility and that it will succeed if mounted. When government leaders foresee the possibility of a coup, they satisfy the military's demands—at least to some extent—unless they are prepared to be overthrown. That is, the possibility of a coup alone is sufficient to add weight to the opinions of military leaders. Conversely, if the possibility of a coup being mounted or successful has disappeared or significantly diminished, the military's capacity to pressure the government is equally reduced. Government leaders need no longer pay attention to the demands or opinions of the military leadership. Once its ability to execute a successful coup is significantly in doubt, the military is no longer a prominent institution but just another administrative organ of the government.[6]

Before a coup d'état is attempted, there must be a good chance of success. Yet a coup always involves some risk of failure, as can be seen in Thailand's contemporary history. A comparison of the circumstances surrounding the three coups (two failures and one success) since 1980 (1981, 1985 and 1991) reveals that the incidence of a coup largely depends on whether there is an intense conflict either within the military or between the military and the government or not. At the same time, the military's internal relationships—whether conflictual or harmonious—are important factors in determining the outcome of a coup (Tamada 1992a: 415–19).[7] There must be strong unity within the military if a coup is to be successful. If complete unity is impossible, it is desirable to limit division to two major factions at most. Without such unity or cohesion, it is very difficult to mount a successful coup. In the normal course of events it is not difficult for people outside of the military to ascertain how united the military leaders are in opinion and purpose, and thus to gauge with considerable accuracy the chance of a coup succeeding, should it occur. Needless to say, a high probability of success does not necessarily imply that a coup d'état is inevitable, or even highly likely. Most of the time, the military leadership sees no need for a coup, and even when it does see a need, it must take into account the potential implications for international political and economic relations. Nevertheless, internal unity is a crucial factor for military leaders to consider when deciding whether to launch a coup or not.

The most important requirement for the successful execution of a coup is a strong military leader. The most powerful man in the Thai military is the Commander-in-Chief of the Army. Whether or not he is a strong enough leader is the key factor. For the Army Commander-in-Chief to be able to assert his leadership, he must have a stable support base within the military. One way to build such a support base is through personnel shuffling. Conversely, if the Army Commander-in-Chief is not a strong leader and does not enjoy strong unity among the military leadership, there is little chance of a coup d'état being mounted and the military's political power is diminished. In short, there are various ways to reduce the chances of military leaders intervening even when they want to, and thus to reduce the significance of their opinions.[8] Accordingly, it is not unreasonable to hypothesize that continuous personnel changes since the May incident have prevented the emergence of any leader with sufficiently strong leadership and ensured that there is no overriding unity among the military's upper-echelons. The absence of any leader who could successfully mount a coup has significantly reduced the military's political power. By thus undermining the military's capacity to mount a coup, the frequency and significance of the military's interventions in politics should decrease.

Before examining this hypothesis, however, there is another question to answer. Since it seems likely that the military's political demise was precipitated by the troops shooting demonstrators during the May incident, we must try to ascertain why the troops opened fire. A simple explanation that the military naturally defends a military government is hardly sufficient. Even at the time of the incident, not to mention with the benefit of hindsight, any cool-headed analysis would have easily predicted that brutal suppression of a civil demonstration would draw harsh condemnation, both at home and abroad. The massacre that immediately preceded the October 1976 coup d'état in Thailand had also been harshly reviewed, both at home and abroad. Conversely, the military refused to support clearly defunct political government leaders, opting instead to protect itself. Similar events occurred in Thailand in 1957 and 1973. In neither case did the mainstream faction of the military stand up to defend the government. Nevertheless, in May 1992, the troops opened fire at demonstrators. What led them to resort to this reckless act of shooting which caused so many casualties? The answer to this question seems to be related to personnel changes.

Before we can discuss the relationship between politics and military personnel changes, though, I need to explain the military personnel system, which has been neither widely studied nor understood.[9]

Personnel changes and political power

The organizational structure of the military is headed by the Minister of Defense, assisted by the Permanent Secretary of Defense. The latter is required to be a serving military officer. Immediately beneath them is the Supreme Commander of the Armed Forces who oversees the Army, Navy and Air Force. Each force is headed by its own Commander-in-Chief. The legal authority to order posting changes and promotions for personnel with the rank of general or above is vested in the Defense Minister. This authority is vested in the Commander-in-Chief for field officers (with the rank of colonel, lieutenant colonel, or major), in division commanders for company officers (with the rank of captain, first lieutenant, or second lieutenant), and in battalion commanders for noncommissioned officers. There is a large-scale reshuffle of the generals on 1 October every year.[10] A more moderate reshuffle takes place on 1 April. Significant numbers of officers are affected by these periodic personnel changes.[11] For example, the October 1996 reshuffle transferred a total of 565 generals for three forces, of which 156 were Army generals, and the October 1998 reshuffle transferred a total of 522 generals for the three forces, of which 169 were Army generals. Since most generals hold some sort of office, it is not only their placement but also their appointment that must be considered in each reshuffle. It is difficult, of course, for a defense minister to fully understand the situation when there are so many generals. Hence, the schedule of transfers for the generals is actually prepared by the Commander-in-Chief, then checked by the Supreme Commander, the Permanent Secretary of Defense and the Minister of Defense, before it is passed to the Prime Minister who submits it to the King for royal sanction (refer to Table 2.1 for a list of office holders since the 1980s). Thus, in effect, the Commander-in-Chief can in most cases affect personnel changes among both the generals and the field officers at his convenience. Most commanders-in-chief take advantage of this power in their attempts to solidify their own personal support bases within the military.

However, this does not mean that the Commander-in-Chief can arbitrarily make changes to personnel postings. There are some clear rules of personnel management in place which function to safeguard against the over-concentration of power in the hands of the Commander-in-Chief. First is the ever-present possibility of intervention from above, which usually occurs during the drafting of the transfer list. All personnel transfers must be coordinated with the Supreme Commander and the Defense Permanent Secretary.[12] The Prime Minister and the Defense Minister may also have a say. The Defense Minister occasionally changes appointments to important posts upon reviewing the Commander-in-Chief's first draft list. Intervention at such a late stage is rare, however, and thus, when it does occur, it is sensationally reported in the media. Nevertheless (i.e., despite these formal checks and balances), the extent of intervention that any minister can make at any stage is largely dependent upon the power relationship between him and the Commander-in-Chief. If, for example, the minister is a prominent retired general with many supporters in the military, as was the case with Prem and Chawalit, he has more room to intervene.

Second, seniority is highly valued. It is almost impossible to skip ranks, say, from lieutenant-colonel to major-general. Any promotion that breaches this seniority rule causes deep resentment in the military. Third, personnel changes must be balanced such that internal conflict is not intensified. Various factions in the military are in perpetual competition for important posts. Promotions and postings are the military's most keenly fought internal political issues. When some factions are favored in personnel changes, others may feel aggrieved and inter-factional disputes can intensify. Fourth, the mandatory retirement age of sixty is strictly observed. Those who are appointed Commander-in-Chief are invariably close to retirement, and thus there are rarely many personnel reshuffles during their short tenures. Hence, in reality, they have rather limited opportunities to manipulate their support bases. It is important to note that, unlike some other countries, it is virtually impossible for Thai military leaders to hold on to power by extending the age limit[13] or to retain de facto command

Table 2.1 Prime ministers, defense ministers, supreme commanders and commanders-in-chief of the Army (since 1980)

	Prime Minister	Defense Minister	Supreme Commander of the Armed Forces	Commander-in-Chief of the Army
1 Oct 1978			Gen. Soem	Gen. Prem
22 May 1979		Gen. Prem		
3 Mar 1980	Gen. Prem			
1 Oct 1980			Gen. Saiyut	
26 Aug 1981				Gen. Prayut
1 Oct 1982				Gen. Athit
1 Oct 1983			Gen. Athit	
27 May 1986				Gen. Chawalit
5 Aug 1986		ACM Phanian		
1 Oct 1986			ADM Supha	
1 Oct 1987			Gen. Chawalit	
9 Aug 1988	Gen. Chatchai	Gen. Chatchai		
29 Mar 1990		Gen. Chawalit	Gen. Sunthon	Gen. Suchinda
22 June 1990		Gen. Chatchai		
2 Mar 1991	Anan	ADM Praphat		
1 Oct 1991			Gen. Suchinda	
7 Apr 1992	Gen. Suchinda	Gen. Suchinda	ACM Kaset	Gen. Itsaraphong
10 June 1992	Anan	Gen. Banchop		
1 Aug 1992			ACM Woranat	Gen. Wimon
23 Sept 1992	Chuan	Gen. Wichit		
1 Oct 1994			Gen. Watthanachai	
18 Jul 1995	Banhan	Gen. Chawalit		
1 Oct 1995			Gen. Wirot	Gen. Pramon
1 Oct 1996			Gen. Mongkhon	Gen. Chettha
25 Nov 1996	Gen. Chawalit	Gen. Chawalit		
14 Nov 1997	Chuan	Chuan		
1 Oct 1998				Gen. Surayut
1 Oct 2000			Gen. Samphao	
9 Feb 2001	Thaksin	Gen. Chawalit		
1 Oct 2001			ADM Narong	
1 Oct 2002		Gen. Thammarak	Gen. Surayut	Gen. Somthat

Note: The appointment of prime minister is made several days prior to the appointment of cabinet ministers. The appointment dates of defense ministers are used in the above table for simplicity.

after retirement.[14] On the broader political stage, this means that a retired military officer's entry into politics is usually a personal matter that has little to do with the military organization or its power structures, and hence should not be interpreted as political intervention by the military.

In the competition for good posts, personal connections are as important as ability[15] and performance. There are various ways to foster personal connections in the military. One of the most important is the horizontal relationships among classmates at a military academy. Each of the three forces has its own military academy. Since most commissioned officers in each force are the graduates of the same military academy, there are no alma mater-based factions.[16] What differentiates graduates of the same academy is Class. The Army Academy (currently Chunlachomklao Royal Military Academy) was reorganized after the Second World War and began to grant Bachelor of Science degrees to its graduates in 1954. Officers who graduated in that year are called Class 1 graduates. The Academy fosters collegiality among classmates to strengthen unity, and in the process forms a clique that, in later years, benefits each member in the competition for promotion and postings. Classmates work to ensure that the most successful of them gets further ahead, because as he rises to higher positions he will provide reciprocal favors to his classmates.

Another important means of fostering strong personal connections is through the vertical relationship between commanding and subordinate officers at every level of the hierarchy. Commanders appreciate and reward loyalty from their subordinates. Such relationships, nurtured while they are serving in the same unit, often continue to bear fruit for both parties long after their official relationship has ended. This can be observed in the commissariat as well as in fighting units.

A third source of collegial bonds arises among members of the different units of the service such as the infantry, artillery, cavalry, engineering, etc. Officers in smaller units such as the cavalry[17] and artillery[18] tend to form stronger bonds than is the case in, for example, large infantry units. Family,[19] hometown and secondary school relations can also be significant, but to a lesser extent. Family ties, especially, are not typically extensive, but are very strong (see Figure 2.1).

Of the three military forces, the Army plays the most important role in both national politics and the military's internal politics. Only the Army can successfully mount a coup d'état in Thailand, and thus it has enjoyed unrivalled political power. Accordingly, personnel changes in the Army will be discussed in this section. The highest echelon in the Army is comprised of a commander-in-chief, a deputy commander-in-chief, a chief of staff and two assistant commanders-in-chief. These five posts are called the 'Five Tigers' (*ha suea*). In terms of ranking, the commander-in-chief is the highest, followed by the others in the order presented above. Although it is possible for an assistant commander-in-chief to jump over the deputy's posting and straight into the post of commander-in-chief, downgrading from this exalted position to a lower post is an extremely rare occurrence.

Naturally, throughout the Army, the most coveted posts are those which can be a stepping stone on the way to higher ranks, especially those which can provide a route to the Five Tigers. Examining the history of promoting Army

Figure 2.1 An example of matrimonial relations of Army leaders (The Sasiprapha family)

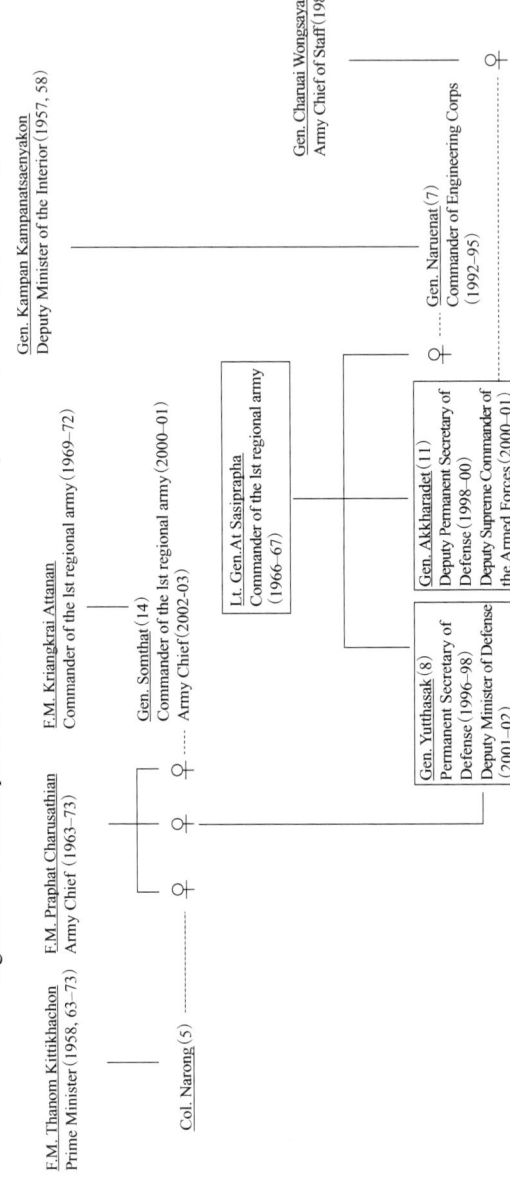

Source: Prepared by the author based on information mainly from cremation volumes (Praphat C 1998; At 1972; Kriangkrai 1973).
Note: The numbers in parentheses refers to the Army Academy classes.

chiefs since the 1980s, two distinct courses are discernible. One course follows a succession of fighting unit command posts, beginning as a battalion commander (lieutenant-colonel), then moving to a regimental commander (colonel), a divisional commander (major-general), a regional commander (*mae thap phak*) (lieutenant-general) and then one of the Five Tigers. The other is the General Staff course. One becomes a major-general in a post such as the Director of Army Operations, then rises to a lieutenant-general as either the Assistant Chief-of-Staff or the Deputy Chief-of-Staff and on to one of the Five Tigers.

There are six regional commanders or equivalent posts in the Thai Army. Thailand is divided into four regions—Central, Northeastern, Northern and Southern—which are numbered from the First to Fourth respectively, and each has a regional commander.[20] The Special Warfare Unit and the Air Defense Unit are sometimes called the Fifth and Sixth Regions, and each of them has its own commander. Of the six, the Commander of the First Army Region, stationed in Bangkok, is the most important. There are four divisions in the First Region—the First Division[21] and the Second Cavalry Division are stationed in Bangkok, the Second Infantry Division in Prachin Buri and the Ninth Infantry Division in Kanchana Buri. The Third and Sixth Infantry Divisions are part of the Second Region, the Fourth Infantry Division and the First Cavalry Division are assigned to the Third Region, and the Fifth Infantry Division is in the Fourth Region. The Special Warfare Unit was developed from the Paratroops Unit and now comprises the First Special Warfare Division in Lop Buri and the Second Special Warfare Division in Chiang Mai in the North.[22] The Air Defense Unit was established in April 1992 and consists of the Anti-Aircraft Division in Bangkok and the Artillery Division in Lop Buri (Figure 2.2). Again, the divisions stationed in or near Bangkok are more important than others and, hence, the First Divisional Commander is typically regarded as the most likely candidate for a future top posting.[23]

The Commander-in-Chief tries to appoint trustworthy officers to these important posts in order to reinforce his support base. He typically looks first to his classmates. Since it is impossible to fill all of the key positions with his classmates, he tries to assign trustworthy juniors to the regional commander and divisional commander posts. Choosing juniors who have extensive personal connections can help to further strengthen his own support base, because when he appoints one person, that appointee's associates are likely to also be brought into the support group. Officers of a closely united Class are the most expedient choices.[24] If all goes well, the Army leadership will be succeeded by the generation of lieutenant-generals who most strongly support the commander-in-chief, and they, in turn, will be succeeded by the divisional commanders in the next generation who are most loyal to them.

Figure 2.2 Royal Thai Army unit organization chart (major units only)

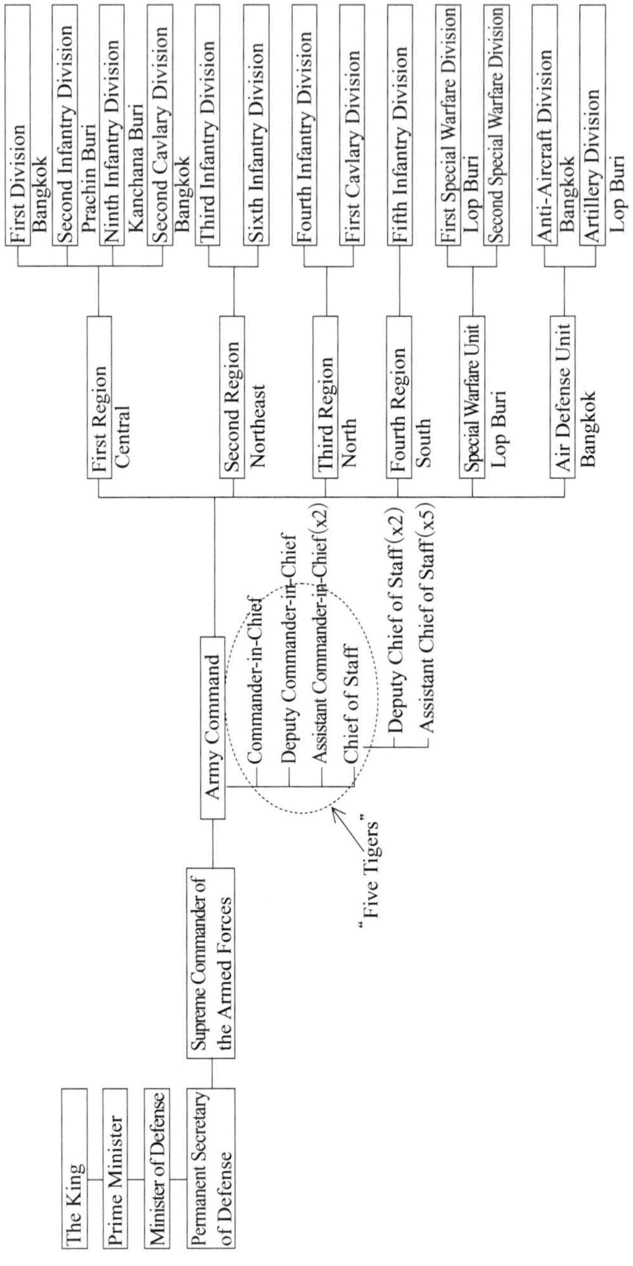

Source: Prepared by the author.
Note: Only division locations in Bangkok and its vicinity are indicated.

As with any pyramid-shaped organization, the number of posts decreases towards the top. For example, there are five places for the post of assistant chief-of-staff but only two places are available for the office of deputy chief-of-staff above them. These two deputy chiefs-of-staff and six regional commanders compete for the Five Tiger posts. Other contenders sometimes join the race as well. Of course, most of them must miss out. The losers must be placed in nominal posts such as deputy, assistant, attaché to a commander, attaché to a command, attaché to the office of a commander, advisor and expert. They retain some chance of returning to the right career track as long as they are assigned to posts within the Army. Transfer to outside departments, however, such as the Supreme Command and the Office of Permanent Secretary is virtually a dead-end for most careers since there is little prospect of returning to the Army. Those who have beaten tough competitors to 'win' one of the more lucrative posts typically try to 'sideline' them to an 'outside' posting discreetly. Hence, the key posts at the Supreme Command and the Office of Permanent Secretary have been available for parachuting 'losers' in the respective promotion contests of the three forces.[25] They have no other choice but to seek distinction within these 'outside' departments. Thus it is extremely difficult for officers who are assigned to the Supreme Command of the Armed Forces or the Office of Permanent Secretary early in their careers to achieve internal promotion to the top jobs. Hence officers in all three forces generally dread being transferred to these 'outside' departments—such postings are regarded as demotions. Nevertheless, key posts at the Supreme Command and the Office of Permanent Secretary are undeniably far more attractive than many other marginalizing posts within the three forces.

Class 5 and the shooting in May 1992

The rise of Class 5

The players of the February 1991 coup d'état and the May 1992 incident were Class 5 officers who had graduated from the Army Academy in 1958. They included the son of a former prime minister from the 1960s and the younger brother of a military strongman from the mid-1970s. In the late 1970s, however, Class 5 officers were eclipsed by Class 7 officers who, although two years their junior, dominated the field ranks and wielded great power. Class 5 came to the fore only after the downfall of Class 7 in 1981.

When Class 7 officers, who formed Prime Minister Prem's principal support base, failed in their coup attempt of April 1981 they lost power. Athit Kamlangek, a member of Preparatory Class 5,[26] which had played a lead role in suppressing the attempted coup, rose to prominence. Athit provided a new support base to

Table 2.2 Personnel changes in the Army leadership (1), 1980–1991

	1 Oct 1980	1 Oct 1981	1 Oct 1982	1 Oct 1983	1 Oct 1984	1 Oct 1985
Commander-in-Chief	Prem38[81*]	Prayut C.(P1)	Athit K.(P5)	Athit K. (P5)	Athit K. (P5)	Athit K. (P5)[86*]
Deputy Commander-in-Chief	San C.39[81]	Sak39[82]	Suep (P3)[84]	Suep (P3)	Thianchai (P5)	Chuthai(P5)[86
Chief of Staff	Prayut C.(P1)[82]	Pamot(P3)[83]	Pamot (P3)	Banchop (P4)[86]	Banchop (P4)[86]	Chawalit(1)[92]
Assistant Commander-in-Chief	Amnat D.(P1)[83]	Athit(P5)[85]	Thianchai(P5)[85]	Thianchai (P5)	Mana R. (P5)[85]	Kamhaeng(P5)
Assistant Commander-in-Chief	Pin39[81]	Phaichit39[82]	Pathom(P4)[85]	Pathom (P4)	Ongat(P5)[85]	Akkharaphon(P5)[86]
Deputy Chief of Staff	Chamnan(P5)	Suep(P3)	Prayun(P5)	Mana R.(P5)	Chuthai(P5)	Wanchai R.(1)
Deputy Chief of Staff	Chaloem(P1)	Pathom(P4)	Banchop(P4)	Chawalit(1)	Chawalit(1)	Charat(P7)
First Regional Commander	Wasin(P3)	Athit (P5)	Phat(P4)	Phat (P4)	Phichit(2)	Phichit(2)
Second Regional Commander	Lak39	Phak(P5)	Phak (P5)	Phak (P5)	Phisit (P6)	Phisit (P6)
Third Regional Commander	Sima(P1)	Phrom (P1)	Phrom (P1)	Thiap(P5)	Thiap (P5)	Ruamsak(P7)
Fourth Regional Commander	Chuan(P1)	Han L.(P5)	Han L. (P5)	Wanchai C.(P5)	Wanchai C.(P5)	Wanchai C.(P5)
Special Warfare Unit Commander	-	-	-	Anek(P4)	Sunthon(1)	Sunthon(1)
Anti-aircraft Unit Commander	-	-	-	-	-	-
First Divisional Commander	Suchin(P5)	Phichit(2)	Phichit(2)	Phichit(2)	Itsaraphong(5)	Wimon(5)
Second Infantry Divisional Commander	Aram(P6)	Prachum(P7)	Prachum (P7)	Prachum (P7)	San S.(5)	San S.(5)
Ninth Infantry Divisional Commander	Sin(P5)	Somkhit(1)	Somkhit(1)	Somkhit(1)	Choetchai(5)	Choetchai(5)
Third Infantry Divisional Commander	Suwan(P4)	Bunchai(P7)	Bunchai (P7)	Bunchai (P7)	Somphon(5)	Somphon(5)
Sixth Infantry Divisional Commander	Phisit(P6)	Phisit (P6)	Itsaraphong(5)	Itsaraphong(5)	Bunthaen(6)	Bunthaen(6)
Fourth Infantry Divisional Commander	Phrom(P1)	Ruamsak(P7)	Siri(4)	Siri(4)	Siri(4)	Choe(5)
First Cavalry Divisional Commander	Prayat(P6)	Chaichana(1)	Chaichana(1)	Sathon(4)	Sathon(4)	Phairot(5)
Fifth Infantry Divisional Commander	Pricha(P5)	Panya(1)	Panya(1)	Chap(4)	Chap(4)	Kitti R.(8)
Anti-aircraft Divisional Commander	Prasat(P4)	Prasat (P4)	Watthanachai W.(4)	Watthanachai W.(4)	Wirot(5)	Wirot(5)
Artillery Divisional Commander	-	-	-	Wirot(5)	Phuchong(5)	Phuchong(5)
Second Cavalry Divisional Commander	Chaichana(1)	Wichat(2)	Wichat(2)	Wichat(2)	Ariya(5)	Ariya(5)
First Special Warfare Divisional Commander	-	-	Wimon(5)	Wimon(5)	Wimon(5)	Watthana S.(8)
Second Special Warfare Divisional Commander	-	-	-	Khachon(5)	Khachon(5)	Khachon(5)

Prime Minister Prem and was rewarded by promotion to the position of the Army Commander-in-Chief in October 1982. From there, he steadily built up his own support base within the Army. Athit ousted all potential rivals from the upper echelons of the Army, promoting his Preparatory Class 5 friends to the Five Tiger posts. They were supported, in turn, by their junior Class 1, Class 2 and Class 5 officers (see Table 2.2).

However, as his political ambition to take over the prime ministership from Prem became apparent, the Athit faction split into two. This split was directly related to the maneuvering to be Athit's successor, since he was due to retire in 1985. The two prime candidates for the succession, Chawalit, from Class 1, and Phichit, from Class 2, declared their allegiances to Prem and Athit respectively. In this struggle, Class 5 aligned itself with the Prem-Chawalit faction via Suchinda.[27] The conflict escalated to a coup on 9 September 1985. Athit was dismissed the following May and Chawalit was appointed Commander-in-Chief at the relatively young age of fifty-four.[28] Chawalit's dream was to become prime minister with the support of the military but without resorting to a coup d'état. He made personnel

1 Oct 1986	1 Oct 1987	1 Oct 1988	1 Oct 1989	1 Apr 1990	1 Oct 1990	1 Apr 1991	1 Oct 1991
Chawalit(1)	Chawalit(1)	Chawalit(1)	Chawalit(1)	Suchinda(5)	Suchinda(5)	Suchinda(5)	Suchinda(5)
Phisit (P6)[87]	Wanchai R.(1)]	Wanchai R.(1)	Suchinda(5)	Itsaraphong(5)	Itsaraphong(5)	Itsaraphong(5)	Itsaraphong(5)
Wanchai R.(1)[92]	Charuai(1)[90]	Charuai(1)	Charuai(1)	Wirot(5)[96]	Wirot(5)	Chatchom(5)[93]	Chatchom(5)
Phichit(2)[92]	Phichit(2)	Phichit(2)	Itsaraphong(5)[94]	Arun(3)	Arun(3)	Wirot(5)	Wirot(5)
Sunthon(1)[91]	Suchinda(5)[93]	Suchinda(5)	Arun(3)[92]	Wimon(5)[95]	Wimon(5)	Wimon(5)	San S.(5)[94]
Charuai(1)	Ngamphon(1)	Arun(3)	Wirot(5)	Pramon(6)	Pramon(6)	Pramon(6)	Pramon(6)
Suchinda(5)	Kasem(1)	Saphrang(1)	Chatchom(5)	Chatchom(5)	Thawon(5)	Choetchai(5)	Choetchai(5)
Watthanachai W.(4)	Watthanachai W.(4)	Watthanachai W.(4)	San S.(5)	San S.(5)	San S.(5)	San S.(5)	Phaibun H.(5)
Itsaraphong(5)	Itsaraphong(5)	Itsaraphong(5)	Wimon(5)	Phaibun H.(5)	Phaibun H.(5)	Phaibun H.(5)	Ariya(5)
Chaichana(1)	Siri(4)	Siri(4)	Siri(4)	Siri(4)	Phairot(5)	Phairot(5)	Phairot(5)
Wisit(2)	Wisit(2)	Wisit(2)	Yutthana Y.(4)	Yutthana Y.(4)	Yutthana Y.(4)	Kitti(8)	Kitti(8)
Wimon(5)	Wimon(5)	Wimon(5)	Khachon(5)	Khachon(5)	Khachon(5)	Khachon(5)	Khachon(5)
-	-	-	-	-	-	-	-
San S.(5)	San S.(5)	Mongkhon(9)	Watthana S.(8)	Watthana S.(8)	Chainarong(11)	Chainarong(11)	Thitiphong(11)
Manat(8)	Manat(8)	Manat(8)	Chainarong(11)	Chainarong(11)	Thitiphong(11)	Thitiphong(11)	Phanom(11)
Mongkhon(9)	Mongkhon(9)	Watthana S.(8)	Watthana B.(8)	Watthana B.(8)	Watthana B.(8)	Watthana B.(8)	Suwinai(11)
Bunthaen(6)	Bunthaen(6)	Banthao(8)	Banthao(8)	Banthao(8)	Samphan(10)	Samphan(10)	Samphan(10)
Banthao(8)	Banthao(8)	Chettha(9)	Chettha(9)	Chettha(9)	Prasoet(11)	Prasoet(11)	Prasoet(11)
Choe(5)	Choe(5)	Chamkat(8)	Chamkat(8)	Chamkat(8)	Sommai(11)	Sommai(11)	Sommai(11)
Phairot(5)	Phairot(5)	Lithai(8)	Lithai(8)	Lithai(8)	Lithai(8)	Lithai(8)	Kamon(9)
Kitti R.(8)	Kitti R.(8)	Somchet(9)	Panthep(9)	Panthep(9)	Panthep(9)	Winit(9)	Winit(9)
Wirot(5)	Phaeo(5)	Phaeo(5)	Phaeo(5)	Phaeo(5)	Samphao(12)	Samphao(12)	Samphao(12)
Phuchong(5)	Phuchong(5)	Suwit(6)	Suwit(6)	Suwit(6)	Suwit(6)	Suwit(6)	Udom H.(12)
Ariya(5)	Ariya(5)	Thotsaphon(6)	Thotsaphon(6)	Thotsaphon(6)	Thotsaphon(6)	Thotsaphon(6)	Yutthaphan(5)
Watthana S.(8)	Oraphan(8)	Oraphan(8)	Surayut(12)	Surayut(12)	Somsak(12)	Somsak(12)	Somsak(12)
Oraphan(8)	Surachet(8)	Surachet(8)	Han P.(11)	Han P.(11)	Han P.(11)	Han P.(11)	Han P.(11)

Notes:

1 <n>, (Pn) and (n) next to each name indicate the year or Class at Army Academy (Chulachomklao Royal Military Academy). For example, <38> denotes the admission in 1938. (Pn) denotes a preparatory class at the army preparatory school before it was reorganized into the present Army Academy. It starts with P1 which was admitted in 1940 and ends with P7. (1) denotes Class 1 of the present Army Academy which corresponds to P8.

2 [xx] next to the Five Tiger posts denotes a retirement year. [85] means the mandatory age retirement in September 1985. [*] indicates that the retirement was postponed.

3 Family names have been omitted for simplicity. Where there are more than one person with the same first name, the initial letter of the family name is added. For example, San C. means San Citpathima and San S. means San Siphen.

4 Horizontal broken lines in the table denote the distinction between the ranks of general, lieutenant-general and major-general. '-' means that the post did not exist at the time.

changes with a view to forming a support base. Chawalit promoted his Class 1 classmates to the Five Tiger posts, then gradually promoted Class 5 officers to the regional commands and eventually the Five Tigers. He promoted Class 8 and 9 officers to the divisional command posts vacated by Class 5 officers. Chawalit stepped down in March 1990, well before his mandatory retirement was due in September 1992, to join the cabinet of Prime Minister Chatchai.

Class 5 provided Chawalit's support base and gradually occupied almost all of the key posts in the Army. Upon Chawalit's resignation in 1990, Suchinda, the leader of Class 5, was promoted to Commander-in-Chief. This move further consolidated the Class 5 monopoly on the key posts, preserving the Chawalit faction in the upper echelon postings while 'ejecting' the 'obstacles'—mainly of Class 8—to the Supreme Command. Particularly notable among the members of Suchinda's group were Itsaraphong Nunphakdi, a Class 5 classmate and an older brother of Suchinda's wife, and the head of the alumni society of Class 11, Chainarong Nunphakdi, a relative of Itsaraphong's.[29] Through this combination of Class allegiances and family ties, the Army leadership at that time was more closely united than it had been since the death of Sarit in December 1963.

The Class 5 Army officers also formed a fellowship with the Air Force and Navy officers who had graduated from their respective academies at the same time, in 1958. In the Air Force, a Class 1 (1958) graduate became the Commander-in-Chief in October 1987. In the Navy, a 1958 graduate was expected to become the Commander-in-Chief in October 1991. Furthermore, they cultivated friendships with the Army Academy graduates of 1958 who had joined the police force. This fellowship extending over the four forces was called the '0143 club.'[30] The formation of such a broad cross-sectional group is uncommon—virtually unprecedented—and the military leadership enjoyed a strength of unity after the voluntary retirement of Chawalit.

When Chawalit resigned from the cabinet after a dispute with another minister, the military demanded that Prime Minister Chatchai dismiss the other minister from the cabinet. Chatchai promised to comply but never acted. Having been treated lightly and lost face, the military leaders gradually began to challenge the Prime Minister. The Prime Minister stood firm, perhaps not believing that the military would resort to a coup. He tried to suppress the conflict by dismissing certain military leaders, but this turned out to be a dangerous provocation. The military's anger finally erupted in the form of a coup d'état by the National Peace-Keeping Council on 23 February 1991.[31] The fact that it was the Air Force rather than the Army that carried out the most important task of detaining the Prime Minister had significant implications for subsequent political events. It should also be noted that the coup was generally welcomed in Thailand, receiving very little in the way of negative reaction,[32] despite the fact that the rest of the world was becoming more uniformly opposed to political intervention by the military after the end of the Cold War in Europe.

The heyday of Class 5

Class 5 finally secured all Five Tiger posts in the post-coup periodic reshuffle on 1 April 1991. Equally important was Class 11. The number of Class 11 officers in fighting division command posts leapt from two to five in the October 1990 reshuffle, and increased to six in October 1991. All three infantry divisions stationed in the First Region were then under the command of Class 11 officers. Chainarong, the leader of Class 11, was promoted from First Division

Commander to First Brigade Commander in October 1991. The next most prevalent group at the divisional command level was Class 12. Class 12 officers secured three divisional command posts in October 1991 and the post of Special Warfare Unit Commander as well as the newly-established post of Air Defense Unit Commander on 1 April 1992.

When Suchinda left the Army on 7 April 1992 to assume the premiership, one of the assistant commanders-in-chief resigned to join his cabinet. These two vacancies in the Five Tiger posts triggered a relatively large-scale personnel reshuffle. Deputy Commander-in-Chief Itsaraphong was promoted to Commander-in-Chief. Three of the remaining four Tiger posts were given to Class 5 officers. First Brigade Commander Chainarong was promoted to First Regional Commander. Of thirteen divisional command posts, five were taken by Class 11 officers and four by Class 12 officers.

So what did this lineup mean? The timing of their age of retirement was important for Class 5. Itsaraphong was due to retire in 1994. Two of the Five Tigers, Deputy Commander-in-Chief Wirot Saengsanit and Chief of Staff Pramon Phalasin, were both younger and not due to retire until 1996. In regular order, Wirot would most likely succeed Itsaraphong.[33] As Wirot was one of the youngest of the Class 5 officers, his successor would be someone from a younger generation. The most likely candidates were the regional commanders and the deputy chiefs of staff. As of 7 April 1992, both deputy chiefs of staff were due to retire before 1996. Two of the six regional commanders were Class 5 officers and were also due to retire before 1996. That left four possible candidates. The Fourth Regional Commander at the time was a Class 8 officer who had little prospect of rising to the top position since none of his classmates held powerful posts. The remaining three regional commanders were thus the most probable candidates. They were all from Class 11 and 12 and thus had many classmates at the level of division commander.

The leading contender was Chainarong Nunphakdi, who had family relations with both Prime Minister Suchinda and Army Commander-in-Chief Itsaraphong, as well as many classmates in powerful Army positions. To put this another way, his meteoric rise was most likely due to his family relations with the military and political chiefs, and Class 11 officers were being promoted to important positions to consolidate support for the future commander-in-chief.

For Wirot, who was hoping to retire as the Commander-in-Chief in 1996, it would be difficult to reach the top position and keep it until his retirement without the support of the Nunphakdi clan. His Class 5 classmates would begin reaching retirement age in 1993 and their support would certainly peter out soon thereafter. Once his classmates were gone, he would have no-one else to provide support except for his junior officers. Class 11 and 12 officers were supposed to form his support base. Class 11 was led by Chainarong. Class 12 was headed by Air Defense Unit Commander Samphao Chusi and Special Warfare Unit Commander Surayut Chulanon. Samphao would be the most likely source of support for Wirot as they were both artillery officers. It would be difficult, but also unnecessary, for Samphao to overtake Chainarong to become the commander-in-chief. Chainarong was due to retire in 1999, Samphao in 2001 and Surayut in 2003. So, even if Samphao became the commander-in-chief after Chainarong, he would still have two years to hold the office himself before retirement. Predicting who would be appointed commander-in-chief that far into the future was fraught with uncertainties, yet it was almost certain that, with the main infantry divisions under the command of his classmates, Chainarong would be appointed to the post. The reason that many Class 11 and 12 officers were promoted to divisional command posts in the early 1990s was to establish a line of succession from Suchinda to Itsaraphong, Wirot, Chainarong and then to Samphao. The process whereby the Class 5 officers had established power in the 1980s was about to be repeated in the 1990s, primarily by the officers of Classes 11 and 12 (see Figure 2.3). If successful, this would decide the line of succession within the Army leadership for the next ten years or so. All of this is the background to the creation of the Suchinda administration and the troops shooting protesters at the rally that demanded Suchinda's resignation.

Why did the troops fire?

After becoming Prime Minister in April 1992, Suchinda appeared unmoved by a storm of criticism. It seemed impossible that Suchinda's administration might soon break down, considering the strength of support it enjoyed from both the military and the Parliament. Yet, as discussed in the previous chapter, Chamlong mobilized a mass protest rally in May. Chamlong was an Army officer-turned-politician who had been elected Governor of Bangkok in 1985 and won his first parliamentary election in March 1992.[34] The overwhelming support Chamlong enjoyed in Bangkok was demonstrated by his re-election as Governor in 1990, and by the fact that the Phalang Tham Party—which he had founded in 1988 and continued to lead—won fifty of fifty-six seats in the Bangkok Metropolitan Assembly and 184 of 220 seats in district councils in 1990 and thirty-two of thirty-five seats in the Bangkok electorate in the House of Representatives election in March 1992.

The Army leadership's line of succession designed for the next ten years was probably a significant factor contributing to Chamlong's decision to take strong action. Since the Suchinda administration had very strong military support, it was quite likely that it would remain in power for a very long time, as had Prem's

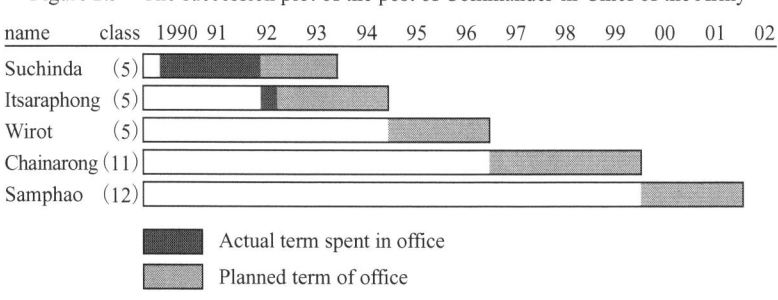

Figure 2.3 The succession plot of the post of Commander-in-Chief of the Army

administration. However, with the strong support base Chamlong had developed in Bangkok as its Governor, it is highly likely that he entered national politics in March 1992 already aiming at the premiership. Since there was no reason to believe that the Phalang Tham Party would not continue to gather strength, Chamlong's chance of realizing his dream did not seem remote. This would not occur, however, if the prime minister did not have to be an MP, or if having a strong support base within the military was essential. Hence, Chamlong chose to apply pressure on the government by way of a mass protest rally.

Chawalit shared Chamlong's desire to drive Suchinda from office as soon as possible.[35] Chawalit, who had already professed his desire to become prime minister while he was the Army's Commander-in-Chief, was perhaps even more eager than Chamlong, which is why he actively supported the rally. As described in the previous chapter, all of the government's attempts to stop the rally proved to be counterproductive, serving only to intensify the calls for Suchinda's resignation. As both Chamlong and Chawalit appeared to stay with the struggle to the end, it was probable that Suchinda was tempted into taking a more hard-lined approach.

However, it is too simplistic to argue that the military is expected to shoot those who rise against the government. To cite just one pertinent example, in Thailand in 1973, a military government was overthrown by an anti-government rally led primarily by students (the 14 October uprising). The fate of the government was sealed when the Army's Commander-in-Chief refused to obey orders to suppress the rally. In the May 1992 incident, in contrast, the military opened fire on the rally due to the mutually interdependent relationship between the military leadership and the Prime Minister. When the mass rally began on 6 May, the military located its countermeasures headquarters at the Capital Security Command, which had been established within the First Army Region Command in August 1981 for anti-communist operations. The Capital Security Command was under the direct command of the Army Commander-in-Chief, who had authority over all the units assigned by the three military forces as well as the metropolitan police force. The local Army unit was under the command of the First Army Regional Commander. In other words, Itsaraphong and Chainarong were in charge of the countermeasure operations during the May incident. Neither could abandon Suchinda, to whom both were related by marriage. Suchinda himself spent more time at the Capital Security Command center than at Government House during this crisis, to help the military leaders deal with the situation. This deep entanglement between the government and military leadership is probably the ultimate reason for the military finally resorting to the autocratic act of shooting the protesters.

Repercussions from the government's collapse would not be restricted to Suchinda's family members within the military, but would affect the entirety of the military leadership. If Suchinda was ousted through this protest action, his most likely successor would be Chawalit, the leader of the main opposition party. When the Suchinda faction of military officers seized power, they had done so at the expense of their former commander, Chawalit. If Chawalit assumed power, he would be likely to dismiss the military leaders allied with the Suchinda faction sooner or later. This included Class 5 leaders such as Wirot, as well as Chainarong's associates among the Class 11 divisional commanders. In short, if the military leaders had abandoned the Prime Minister they might have protected the military organization, but they could not save their own positions because they were too close to the Prime Minister. Moreover, as mentioned earlier, Suchinda had only accepted the prime ministership in response to the Army leaders' request. They would thus be guilty of committing an act of gross disloyalty if they withdrew support from the administration only a month later.

Personnel changes after May 1992

Controlling the situation

Criticisms were voiced from within the military after the shooting incident, but these critics were powerless against the Suchinda faction, with its monopoly of all key command posts. It seemed that even the King was unable to move immediately to control the situation. On the afternoon of 20 May, it was rumored that anti-Suchinda troops from the Second Army Region, the Fourth Army Region and the Special Warfare Unit were advancing toward Bangkok in order to 'liberate' the capital.[36] Rumors flew around that some anti-mainstream troops from somewhere were coming to recapture the capital because it was clear to everyone that only armed force could fight back against armed force. Despite the rumors, though, there was absolutely no chance of such an uprising of anti-mainstream factions occurring under the circumstances, with the military leadership so strongly united.[37] It was not until a network of anti-mainstream officers was formed within the military that the King was able to intervene. As discussed in the previous chapter, on the night of 20 May, the King summoned Suchinda and Chamlong to the palace and reprimanded both of them. His intervention resulted in a draw, of sorts, for the Prime Minister and the rally organizer. In addition, a royal decree was issued on 23 May providing immunity to Suchinda and the military leaders from any criminal liability for the shooting.[38] Suchinda's resignation as Prime Minister was announced on the evening of 24 May.[39]

Soon after Suchinda's resignation, moves began towards a constitutional amendment that would require that the Prime Minister always be an elected Member of Parliament. As the ruling coalition had dropped their opposition to such an amendment, it was passed by the Parliament unanimously on 10 June. Under the new requirements, the ruling coalition parties decided to nominate Sombun Rahong, the leader of the Chat Thai Party, for the position while retaining the composition of the coalition at the time. This choice would have also suited the military leadership, which was hoping to avoid any repercussions for the incident if it possibly could.[40] It appeared as if the military would avoid all criminal charges, despite the many casualties, and that someone from the ruling coalition parties would be the next prime minister. Clearly, neither of these outcomes suited the rally leaders, organizers and participants. Hence they were relieved and overjoyed when the former Prime Minister Anan was appointed as the new prime minister on 10 June by the King's discreet but bold decision.[41]

The Minister of Defense and personnel changes

Two aspects must be considered when examining personnel changes in the Army after May 1992. The first is a broad picture of factional changes within the Army since the 1980s. The Suchinda faction, which was dominant in the early 1990s, had developed from a faction controlled by Chawalit, the Commander-in-Chief in the late 1980s. The Chawalit faction had developed from a faction that had supported Prime Minister Prem in the early 1980s. The pro-Prem faction included a faction led by the then Commander-in-Chief Athit in the early 1980s. The Chawalit faction included a non-Suchinda faction and the Prem faction included non-Chawalit factions. The Athit faction was against both the Chawalit and Suchinda factions. To the Suchinda faction, after Anan's temporary appointment as Prime Minister, the appointment of officers to the military leadership from its rival factions would amount to a purge.

The second aspect is the changes in the government, particularly Ministers of Defense, after May 1992. As mentioned earlier, Defense Ministers had some direct influence regarding the military's personnel assignments. The extent of a Minister's influence depended on his political power and, more particularly, on the power relations between him and the military leaders. All of the Defense Ministers and Deputy Defense Ministers from May 1992 have been retired military officers, with the exception of Chuan (November 1997 to February 2001). Among these ex-military ministers, Chawalit had outstanding influence because he had been an Army chief in the 1980s as well as the Minister of Defense several times in the 1990s, when he was the leader of a political party.

Punitive personnel reshuffle

The Anan administration, which was formed in June 1992, carried out punitive personnel changes on 1 August to hold the relevant military leaders responsible for the May incident. In the Army, the Commander-in-Chief, the Deputy Commander-in-Chief, the First Regional Commander and the Assistant Chief of Staff in charge of Intelligence were all transferred. This meant that not only the incumbent Commander-in-Chief (Itsaraphong) but also the 'anointed' candidates for the next Commander-in-Chief and one after that (Wirot and Chainarong) were also removed from the line of succession. In the process of this reshuffle, various figures were identified as possible successors. Considered candidates for Commander-in-Chief included officers who were remote from the Suchinda faction, while all those suggested for the First Regional Commander were close to either Prem or Chawalit. Itsaraphong and others strongly opposed these candidates (*Khao Thai*, 10 August 1992).

In the light of such resistance, Wimon Wongwanit, the Deputy Supreme Commander of the Armed Forces, was appointed to the post of Army Commander-in-Chief.[42] Although Wimon had been side-lined from the Army to the Supreme Command in October 1991, he was nevertheless one of the key members of Class 5. He commented on 6 November 1992, 'I became the Army Commander-in-Chief amid all sorts of trials and tribulations... What was most painful for me was that my success was founded on the unfortunate circumstances of my friends' (*Khao Thai*, 16 November 1992), clearly referring to Suchinda and Itsaraphong. At the same time, the Second Brigade Commander, Class 9 officer Chettha Thanacharo, was promoted to First Regional Command. He was an old friend of Itsaraphong's and Chaiarong's (*Khao Thai*, 17 August 1992) and his appointment could thus placate the Suchinda faction.[43] In other words, the supposedly 'punitive' reshuffle of August 1992 was full of compromise.

All the same, there were a significant number of people in the military's upper echelon who were replaced in this reshuffle (see Table 2.3). Noteworthy is the transfer of two Class 2 officers from the posts of Deputy Permanent Secretary of Defense to Deputy Supreme Commander of the Armed Forces. Of the two,

Table 2.3 Punitive personnel reshuffle, 1 August 1992

Name	Previous Post	New Post
Kaset Rotchananin(A1)	Supreme Commander of the Armed Forces & Commander-in-Chief of the Air Force	Superintendent-General of the Armed Forces
Itsaraphong Nunphakdi(5)	Commander-in-Chief of the Army	Deputy Permanent Secretary of Defense
Wirot Saengsanit(5)	Deputy Commander-in-Chief of the Army	Deputy Permanent Secretary of Defense
Woranat Aphichari(A1)	Superintendent-General of the Armed Forces (former Commander-in-Chief of the Air Force)	Supreme Commander of the Armed Forces
Phichit Kunlawanit(2)	Deputy Permanent Secretary of Defense	Deputy Supreme Commander of the Armed Forces
Wisit Atkhumwong(2)	Deputy Permanent Secretary of Defense	Deputy Supreme Commander of the Armed Forces
Wimon Wongwanit(5)	Deputy Supreme Commander of the Armed Forces	Commander-in-Chief of the Army
San Siphen(5)	Assistant Commander-in-Chief of the Army	Deputy Commander-in-Chief of the Army
Yutthana Yaemphan(4)	Officer attached to the Army Command	Assistant Commander-in-Chief of the Army
Ueam Manorat(5)	Assistant Chief of Staff of the Army for Intelligence	Advisor to the Army
Chainarong Nunphakdi(11)	First Regional Commander	Commander of the Army Advanced Training Institute
Chettha Thanacharo(9)	Second Brigade Commander	First Regional Commander
Somphong Phimonphan(6)	Commander of the Army Advanced Training Institute	Assistant Chief of Staff of the Army for Intelligence
Prayun Midet(8)	Deputy First Regional Commander	Second Brigade Commander
Kan Phimanthip(A1)	Deputy Supreme Commander of the Armed Forces	Commander-in-Chief of the Air Force

Note: The names of the officers who were subject of this punitive reshuffle are in bold letters. Regarding the number in brackets after each name, (n) is the Army Academy class and (An) is the Air Force Academy class.

Phichit Kunlawanit's posting was particularly important. Phichit had competed with Chawalit for the post of Army Commander-in-Chief in the mid-1980s. As the Class 5 group rose to power in the late 1980s, though, he was demoted from Assistant Commander-in-Chief of the Army to Deputy Supreme Commander of the Armed Forces in October 1989 and then to Deputy Permanent Secretary of Defense in October 1991. Having suffered such ignominious transfers, Phichit was a staunch opponent of the Suchinda faction. He was also the Chairman of the Defense Ministry Committee investigating the May incident and was appointed Privy Councilor following his age-governed retirement in September 1992.[44]

Phichit had formed quite a powerful faction of his own within the Army and to some extent came to wield influence over personnel changes after October 1992.

In short, following the punitive reshuffle, numerous anti-Suchinda officers were promoted while many pro-Suchinda officers remained in place. At the same time, interference from the Defense Ministers increased. In the process the Army Commander-in-Chief's position became incomparably weaker than it had been under Athit, Chawalit and Suchinda. It is worth briefly examining each of the post-August 1992 commanders-in-chief on this point to more fully understand the withdrawal of the military from Thai politics.

Weak Commanders-in-Chief of the Army

Wimon Wongwanit

Following the replacement of the First Regional Commander in August, the commanders of the Second and Third Regions were replaced in the periodic reshuffle of October 1992, which had been decided by the interim Anan administration. More importantly, the commanders of all three infantry divisions stationed in the First Army Region were demoted. They were Class 11 affiliates of Chainarong's and had played central roles in the violent suppression of the May rally. Where there had previously been six Class 11 divisional commanders, who formed the backbone of the Suchinda faction, after the October 1993 reshuffle, there were none. They were replaced by officers from Classes 12, 13 and 14. Class 14 officers, in particular, were given the First Divisional Command and the Second Infantry Divisional Command in October 1992.

Wimon's appointment as Commander-in-Chief was a windfall for him, as he had no significant support base of his own beyond his Class 5 classmates. The Five Tigers as at August 1992 comprised one Class 4 officer, three from Class 5 and one from Class 6. In October 1993, a year after the punitive reshuffle, there were four Class 5 officers and one from Class 6. The untimely increase of the Class 5 officers was nothing but proof of Wimon's limited support base. Only two of the Five Tigers were younger than Wimon—Phaibun Emphan of Class 5 and Pramon Phalasin of Class 6, both due to retire in 1996. Wimon decided that Phaibun should be his successor and appointed him Deputy Commander-in-Chief in October 1994. He demoted Pramon, Phaibun's rival, from Chief of Staff to Assistant Commander-in-Chief in October 1993, then side-lined him to the Supreme Command in October 1994. Three new officers joined the Five Tigers in October 1994. Two of them were Class 5 officers (see Table 2.4).

Wimon's action to fill any vacant Tiger posts with Class 5 classmates, many of whom had already retired and whose membership was therefore shrinking rapidly, indicates the weakness of his support base.

Another noteworthy point about the October 1994 reshuffle is that Class 9 officer Chettha became one of the Five Tigers. He, as mentioned earlier, maintained relatively close ties with Itsaraphong and Chainarong. In this same reshuffle, Chainarong, a Class 11 officer who had been demoted in the aftermath of the May incident, was appointed Deputy Chief of Staff, returning him to the direct path of ascendancy to the Five Tigers and thus providing a possible foothold for his resurgence. Once again, these transfers suggest that Wimon had no support base beyond Class 5 and the Suchinda faction.

Before retiring in 1995, Wimon nominated Phaibun to be his successor. The nomination was overruled by the Defense Minister, however, and Pramon was recalled to the Army from the post of Chief of Staff of the Armed Forces and appointed Commander-in-Chief. There were two reasons for this. First, Phaibun was considered to be under-qualified for the job due to lack of experience; the highest post he had held before joining the Five Tigers had been the Director of the Army Weapons Production Control Center. In contrast, Pramon was adequately qualified, having spent many years in the Army command and held important positions such as Chief of Staff and Assistant Commander-in-Chief.[45] Second, former Commander-in-Chief Chawalit became the Minister of Defense after the general election in July 1995, and Wimon did not have a strong enough position from which to defy Chawalit.

Pramon Phalasin

Pramon was to spend only one year in the office and had no powerful officers among his Class 6 classmates who could support him. He was thus an even weaker Commander-in-Chief than Wimon. His Deputy Commander-in-Chief was a Class 9 officer, the Chief of Staff was a Class 5 officer and the Assistant Commanders-in-Chief were one Class 7 officer and one Class 8 officer at the time (see Table 2.4). The leading candidate to succeed Pramon as Commander-in-Chief was Deputy Commander-in-Chief Chettha of Class 9 (Class 9 had also secured commands in the First and Third Regions).

Chettha Thanacharo

As expected, Chettha was appointed Commander-in-Chief in October 1996. The other Tigers included a Class 7 officer as Deputy Commander-in-Chief, a Class 11 officer as Chief of Staff and one Class 8 officer and one Class 12 officer as the Assistant Commanders-in-Chief. Only two of these officers—Chan Bunprasoet of Class 11 and Samphao Chusi of Class 12—would not retire before Chettha

Table 2.4 Personnel changes in the army leadership (2), 1992–2002

	7 Apr 1992	1 Aug 1992	1 Oct 1992	1 Oct 1993	1 Oct 1994	1 Oct 1995
Commander-in-Chief	Itsaraphong(5)[94]	Wimon(5)[95]	Wimon(5)	Wimon(5)	Wimon(5)	Pramon(6)
Deputy Commander-in-Chief	Wirot(5)[96]	San S.(5)	San S.(5)	San S.(5)	Phaibun E.(5)	Chettha(9)
Chief of Staff	Pramon(6)[96]	Pramon(6)	Pramon(6)	Phaibun E.(5)[96]	Suthep(5)[96]	Suthep(5)
Assistant Commander-in-Chief	San S.(5)[94]	Yutthana Y.(4)[93]	Yutthana Y.(4)	Pramon(6)	Anuphap(5)[95]	Thawan(7)[98]
Assistant Commander-in-Chief	Phaibun H.(5)[94]	Phaibun H.(5)	Choetchai(5)[94]	Choetchai(5)	Chettha(9)[98]	Bandit(8)[98]
Deputy Chief of Staff	Wachira(6)	Wachira(6)	Wachira(6)	Thawan(7)	Thawan(7)	Phadet(8)
Deputy Chief of Staff	Yutthana K.(5)	Yutthana K.(5)	Yutthana K.(5)	Chaiyawut(6)	Chainarong(11)	Paeng(9)
First Regional Commander	Chainarong(11)	Chettha(9)	Chettha(9)	Chettha(9)	Bandit(8)	Winit(9)
Second Regional Commander	Ariya(5)	Ariya(5)	Anuphap(5)	Anuphap(5)	Surayut(12)	Surayut(12)
Third Regional Commander	Phairot(5)	Phairot(5)	Yingyot(6)	Yingyot(6)	Surachet(8)	Thanom(9)
Fourth Regional Commander	Kitti R.(8)	Kitti R.(8)	Kitti R.(8)	Kitti R.(8)	Panthep(9)	Panthep(9)
Special Warfare Unit Commander	Surayut(12)	Surayut(12)	Surayut(12)	Surayut(12)	Chalongchai(10)	Chalongchai(10)
Anti-Aircraft Unit Commander	Samphao(12)	Samphao(12)	Samphao(12)	Samphao(12)	Samphao(12)	Samphao(12)
First Brigade Commander	Yutthaphan(5)	Yutthaphan(5)	Bandit(8)	Phadet(8)	Phadet(8)	Amphon(8)
Second Brigade Commander	Chettha(9)	Prayun M.(8)	Prayun M.(8)	Thanit Wa.(7)	Chusak(8)	Somphan(10)
Third Brigade Commander	Yingyot(6)	Yingyot(6)	Suwit(7)	Panthep(9)	Thanom(9)	Saimit(10)
First Divisional Commander	Thitiphong(11)	Thitiphong(11)	Somphop(14)	Somphop(14)	Somphop(14)	Somphop(14)
Second Infantry Divisional Commander	Phanom(11)	Phanom(11)	Niphon P.(14)	Niphon P.(14)	Niphon P.(14)	Achawin(15)
Ninth Infantry Divisional Commander	Suwinai(11)	Suwinai(11)	Winit(9)	Winit(9)	Chalong(13)	Thawip(14)
Third Infantry Divisional Commander	Rewat(13)	Rewat(13)	Rewat(13)	Rewat(13)	Rewat(13)	Kitti U.(14)
Sixth Infantry Divisional Commander	Prasoet(11)	Prasoet(11)	Prasoet(11)	Sanan(14)	Sanan(14)	Sanan(14)
Fourth Cavalry Divisional Commander	Sommai(11)	Sommai(11)	Sommai(11)	Prayut T.(12)	Prayut T.(12)	Prayut T.(12)
First Cavalry Divisional Commander	Watthanachai C.(12)	Watthanachai C.(12)	Watthanachai C.(12)	Watthanachai C.(12)	Udomchai(13)	Udomchai(13)
Fifth Infantry Divisional Commander	Winit(9)	Winit(9)	Suwinai(11)	Suraphon(13)	Suraphon(13)	Suraphon(13)
Anti-Aircraft Divisional Commander	Thakoeng M.(13)	Thakoeng M.(13)	Thakoeng M.M(13)	Thanit Wo.(12)	Thanit Wo.(12)	Thanit Wo.(12)
Artillery Divisional Commander	Udom H.(12)	Udom H.(12)	Udom H.(12)	Udom H.(12)	Udom H.(12)	Uea(14)
Second Cavalry Divisional Commander	Kamon(9)	Kamon(9)	Kamon(9)	Chamlong(12)	Chamlong(12)	Chamlong(12)
First Special Warfare Divisional Commander	Somsak(12)	Somsak(12)	Somsak(12)	Prasong(14)	Prasong(14)	Prasong(14)
Second Special Warfare Divisional Commander	Bunrot(12)	Bunrot(12)	Bunrot(12)	Tharin(13)	Tharin(13)	Tharin(13)

in 1998; Chan and Samphao were due to retire in 1999 and 2001 respectively. Their potential rival, Surayut of Class 12, was transferred to the insignificant post of Special Advisor of the Army at this time (see Table 2.4).

Speculation about who would replace Chettha as Commander-in-Chief after his retirement in September 1998 was rife (*Sayamrat Sapdawichan*, 31 January 1998, 21 February 1998; *Bangkok Post*, 5 February 1998). Of the twenty Commanders-in-Chief from June 1932 up to Chettha, only two had managed to attain the position without having first held one of the Five Tiger posts. It was extremely difficult for someone with no experience in a Tiger post to become the Commander-in-Chief. Hence, according to precedent, the only strong contenders to succeed Chettha were Samphao and Chan. Samphao belonged to the Suchinda faction and had played a very important role among the Army officers in the 1991 coup. Although he had no part in the 1992 bloodshed, when Suchinda's administration was being formed, it was widely assumed that Samphao would likely be promoted

1 Oct 1996	1 Oct 1997	1 Oct 1998	1 Oct 1999	1 Oct 2000	1 Oct 2001	1 Oct 2002
Chettha(9)	Chettha(9)	Surayut(12)[03]	Surayut(12)	Surayut(12)	Surayut(12)	Somthat(14)
Thawan(7)	Thawan(7)	Samphao(12)	Phatthana(11)[01]	Phatthana(11)	Niphon P.(14)	Watthanachai C.(12)
Chan(11)[99]	Chan(11)	Chan(11)	Montrisak(12)[00]	Bunrot(12)[02]	Somthat(14)[04]	Wirachai(14)[05]
Samphao(12)[01]	Samphao(12)	Niphon P.(14)[02]	Niphon P.(14)	Niphon P.(14)	Sanan(14)[02]	Chaiyasit(16)[05]
Bandit(8)	Bandit(8)	Rewat(13)[01]	Rewat(13)	Rewat(13)	Watthanachai C.(12)[03]	Sirichai(15)[06]
Chokchai(10)	Chaturit(11)	Anan(9)	Bunrot(12)	Kanit(12)	Phongthep(15)	Thakoen N.(13)
Phatthana(11)	Phatthana(11)	Phatthana(11)	Sinat(12)	Buri(13)	Sirichai(15)	Loetrat(18)
Winit(9)	Niphon P.(14)	Thawip(14)	Thawip(14)	Somthat(14)[1]	Phonchai D.(14)	Prawit(17)
Surayut(12)	Rewat(13)	Sanan(14)	Sanan(14)	Sanan(14)	Chirasak(14)	Chirasak(14)
Thanom(9)	Thanom(9)	Sommai(11)	Watthanachai C.(12)	Watthanachai C.(12)	Udomchai(13)	Udomchai(13)
Pricha S.(11)	Pricha S.(11)	Pricha S.(11)	Narong D.(12)	Narong D.(12)	Wichai(14)	Wichai(14)
Hom(11)	Hom(11)	Hom(11)	Sathon S.(12)	Tharin(13)	Tharin(13)	Sonthi(17)
Thakoeng M.(13)	Thakoeng M.(13)	Thakoeng M.(13)	Thakoeng M.(13)	Thongchai(13)	Thongchai(13)	Athit S.(15)
Chamnan(12)	Somphop(14)	Prawit(17)	Prawit(17)	Phonchai D.(14)	Achawin(15)	Yutthasak R.(17)
Somphan(10)	Sanan(14)	Chirasak(14)	Chirasak(14)	Kitkun(14)[2]	Kitkun(14)	Thanu(16)
Saimit(10)	Prawat(9)	Watthanachai C.(12)	Udomchai(13)	Udomchai(13)	Sombunkiat(14)	Sombunkiat(14)
Achawin(15)	Achawin(15)	Nopphadon(17)	Wanchai T.(17)	Phaisan(18)	Phaisan(18)	Chirasit(21)
Prawit(17)	Wanchai T.(17)	Wanchai T.(17)	Udom P.(18)	Udom P.(18)	Udom P.(18)	Anuphong(21)
Thawip(14)	Phonchai D.(14)	Sanchai(16)	Sanchai(16)	Mana P.(18)	Mana P.(18)	Mana P.(18)
Kitti U.(14)	Kitti U.(14)	Phanu(15)	Phanu(15)	Hoen(17)	Hoen(17)	Suchit(19)
Chirasak(14)	Wiwat(15)	Wiwat(15)	Wiwat(15)	Wiwat(15)	Wibunsak(19)	Wibunsak(19)
Prayut T.(12)	Chalo(13)	Chalo(13)	Tomon(17)	Tomon(17)	Tomon(17)	Suthep P.(19)
Udomchai(13)	Udomchai(13)	Sombunkiat(14)	Sombunkiat(14)	Sombunkiat(14)	Nakhon(17)	Nakhon(17)
Suraphon(13)	Phongsak(18)	Phongsak(18)	Phongsak(18)	Phongsak(18)	Phongsak(18)	Wirot B.(20)
Athit S.(15)	Athit S.(15)	Athit S.(15)	Niphon T.(16)	Niphon T.(16)	Niphon T.(16)	Luerit(20)
Uea(14)	Uea(14)	Uea(14)	Chatri(16)	Chatri(16)	Chatri(16)	Wibun N.(18)
Chamlong(12)	Chaloemphon(15)	Chaloemphon(15)	Chaloemphon(15)	Chaloemphon(15)	Sahachai(16)	Sahachai(16)
Chawanit(13)	Chawanit(13)	Chawanit(13)	Sonthi(17)	Sonthi(17)	Sonthi(17)	Banthun(19)
Tharin(13)	Chatchawan(14)	Chatchawan(14)	Amonrit(17)	Amonrit(17)	-[3]	-

Notes: See notes on Table 2.2.
1 Somthat is the same person as First Divisional Commander Somphop.
2 Kitkun is the same person as Third Infantry Divisional Commander Kitti U.
3 The Second Special Warfare Division was abolished as of 30 September 2001.

to Commander-in-Chief in 1999. After May 1992, this was an almost indelible stigma. He was promoted to Assistant Commander-in-Chief in October 1996 with the help of the former Deputy Commander-in-Chief Wirot, who became the Supreme Commander of the Armed Forces in October 1995. Both were originally from the Artillery Unit.[46] In contrast, Chan had no such stigma but was seen to be too close to Prime Minister Chawalit and was not very popular within the Army. Working against both of these contenders was the fact that they had each gone abroad to study and therefore did not graduate from the academy. The position of commander-in chief had always been occupied by a graduate from the academy.

There is little doubt that Chan would have become Commander-in-Chief if Chawalit had still been the Defense Minister when the personnel reshuffle list for October 1998 was being prepared. In the previous October reshuffle, two Deputy

Chiefs of Staff and two Regional Commanders had been selected from Class 11 to support Chan. However, Prime Minister Chawalit stepped down in November 1997, thus taking responsibility for the economic crisis. The Democrat Party came into office and, like his predecessor, Prime Minister Chuan Likphai served also as the Defense Minister. There was no chance Chuan would agree to appoint Chan, because of the latter's close alliance with Chuan's political rival Chawalit. Chettha and Mongkhon Amphonphisit, the Supreme Commander of the Armed Forces, recommended Chainarong of Class 11. Competent and popular in the Army, Chainarong was considered to be the best candidate to reunite the Army, which had lost its unity and autonomy since the May 1992 incident (*Nation Sutsapda*, 6 August 1998). Yet he was the officer most directly responsible for the violent suppression of the May 1992 rally. His appointment as Deputy Chief of Staff of the Army in October 1994 had been met with such harsh criticism that he was side-lined from the Army and sent to the Supreme Command of the Armed Forces in April 1995. With this dark blemish on his record, and his lack of experience in any of the Five Tiger posts, it was preposterous to nominate Chainarong. Hence, after consulting Prem, Chuan brought Surayut back from his nominal post and appointed him Commander-in-Chief.[47] It was an extremely unusual appointment in that Surayut, like Chainarong, had never before joined the Five Tigers.[48]

Surayut Chulanon

Surayut was a Class 12 officer who was due to retire in 2003. His possible tenure of five years would be the second longest term after Chawalit's since the 1970s.[49] Surayut was known to be sharp, and was directly associated with Prem and thus had been considered to be a potential Commander-in-Chief since the 1980s. Upon assuming the position of Commander-in-Chief, Surayut announced to the media that he would not comment on non-military matters and stepped down from all other posts and offices, including that of Senator, Director of the Mass Communication Organization of Thailand (MCOT) and president of his home provincial association (*Matichon Sutsapda*, 6 October 1998). Unlike predecessors who had hinted at their political ambitions by repeatedly stating their commitment to not interfere in politics and not to mount a coup d'état, Surayut avoided making such statements. He was not just paying lip service to noble principles, but was in fact truly an apolitical military man.[50]

Surayut only promoted one of his Class 12 classmates to the Five Tiger posts each year. However, he promoted many of his classmates to the rank of general, often appointing them to honorary posts when nothing else was available. As for the posts of lieutenant-general, his classmates were promoted to the Fourth Regional Command in April 1999 and the Third Regional Command and the Special Warfare Unit Command in October 1999. Four of his classmates have filled the post of Deputy Chief of Staff since 1999 (see Table 2.4). Therefore he consistently extended these favors to his classmates, but he only appointed them to these second best posts rather than the more desirable Five Tiger posts. There seems to be three possible reasons for this course of action. First, Surayut was far more restrained than his predecessors in terms of building his power base, despite his long tenure. Second, he was appointed as Commander-in-Chief with a weak support base and a long tenure. He was perhaps trying to build his support base by maneuvering these second best posts, which would cause less friction than would shuffling the Five Tiger posts. Finally, Surayut did not have a power base within the Army adequate to allow him to thwart interventions by the Prime Minister, the ruling party, the Defense Minister or the Supreme Commander of the Armed Forces.

For the first years of Surayut's command, the lineup of the Five Tiger posts remained virtually unchanged, with two Class 12 officers and one officer each from Classes 11, 13 and 14. The October 2001 reshuffle altered this lineup, however, such that there were now two Class 12 officers and three Class 14 officers. It was also the first time under his command that an officer younger than Surayut joined the Five Tigers—Chief of Staff Somthat Attanan of Class 14. This reshuffle also increased by one the number of Class 14 members assigned regional commands to form a total of three (see Table 2.4). More particularly, a Class 14 officer was posted to the First Regional Command for four successive terms. Even though each term was short, four successive appointments of officers from the same class to the First Regional Command was an unprecedented development. At the same time, two of the three brigade commanders, who were typically the most likely candidates for regional command posts, were also Class 14 officers. In short, through Surayut's appointments, Class 14 acquired the majority of the Five Tiger positions and became the dominant force among the fighting unit commanders of the rank of lieutenant-general. These maneuvers made Somthat the leading candidate to succeed Surayut, who was due to retire in 2003. In fact, Somthat was indeed appointed Commander-in-Chief of the Army, but in October 2002, a year earlier than scheduled. It is worth mentioning here, however, that this early promotion was not entirely unrelated to the fact that Somthat was a brother-in-law of the Deputy Defense Minister Yutthasak Sasiprapha.

Divisive personnel strategy and declining political power

The most important factor in the military's declining political power was not an external factor such as the end of the Cold War, a global trend towards democratization, the rapid growth and collapse of the economy, pressure from the urban middle class, or elusive attitudinal change among military officers. The central factor was the changes in military personnel assignments. All personnel changes after May 1992 served to obstruct the emergence of a Commander-in-Chief of the Army with the personal power to wield strong leadership. Let us review the commanders-in-chief who were appointed after the May incident once again. Wimon had a three year tenure, but he was dependent on the support of the Suchinda faction which was severely weakened in the aftermath of the May incident. Wimon thus could not develop a strong leadership position. His weakness was clearly illustrated when his nomination of a successor was overruled. Pramon, who succeeded Wimon, had only one year in office and thus had no chance of building up a personal support base via personnel changes. The next chief, Chettha, also had a troubled appointment. He had been one of two candidates nominated by Pramon, who could not make up his mind between the two. Chettha's rival, Thawan Sawaengphan, was a member of Class 7, which had lost its power as a result of the 1981 coup. Thawan had left the academy and gone abroad to study, and thus did not graduate from the academy. As mentioned earlier, there was no precedent for appointing a non-academy graduate to the post of commander-in-chief. Hence, Thawan was clearly not a strong contender. Chettha's inability to clearly outclass his rival in the eyes of his predecessor suggests that his support base was not very strong either. His relatively weak position was among the reasons behind why Chettha took a long time to select his successor.

Surayut had no experience in any of the Five Tiger posts and had to begin to build a personal support base after his appointment. He also had to tread cautiously, since quite a few of the key military figures were disgruntled by his extraordinary promotion. Furthermore, he had to deal with interference by the ruling Democrat Party, which expected gratitude in return for his appointment. Hence, although the Commander-in-Chief ostensibly had the power to reassign Army personnel, having such a weak support base made it difficult to exercise strong leadership, which significantly reduced the possibility of a coup. Further, as mentioned, if the military was incapable of mounting a coup, its political power was starkly diminished.

The personnel changes that effectively curtailed the power of the Army Commanders-in-Chief began with the punitive reshuffle that followed the May incident. The initial reshuffle was, however, a compromise rather than a thorough purge of the Suchinda faction. Although the core group of the Suchinda faction, including Itsaraphong, Wirot and Chainarong, were driven out of the Army's key posts along with many of their Class 5 and Class 11 classmates, most of these were gradually reinstated, at least to some extent. Thus, while Itsaraphong quietly awaited retirement in the post of Deputy Permanent Secretary of Defense,

Wirot became the Supreme Commander of the Armed Forces and Chainarong became the Army Deputy Chief of Staff, the Chief of Staff of the Armed Forces, then the Deputy Supreme Commander of the Armed Forces.[51] At the same time, several officers of rival factions who had been sidelined to nominal posts when Chawalit and then Suchinda were Commanders-in-Chief were reinstated and assigned to more significant posts. Typical examples were associates of Phichit (Class 2), who had wielded significant influence in the First Division and the First Region in the mid-1980s. Watthanachai of Class 4 was appointed Supreme Commander of the Armed Forces in October 1992. Bandit Malaiarisun (Class 8)[52] was quickly promoted to the First Brigade Command in October 1992, First Regional Command in October 1994 and then Assistant Commander-in-Chief in October 1995.

The strategy of retaining a few pro-Suchinda officers while promoting new factions was primarily intended to divide and thus weaken the academy class-based factions. This was the hard-learned lesson from the 1981 coup, which was mounted and carried out by the Class 7 faction, and the 1991 coup and the 1992 bloodshed which were orchestrated by the Class 5 faction. The strategy originated from the recognition that when a particular Class dominated key positions (regimental commander and battalion commander in the case of Class 7, and leadership posts in the case of Class 5), the absence of any effective counterforce within the military enabled the dominant group to more readily take reckless action such as mounting a coup. This understanding seemed to be shared in common by the political elite including the King, Privy Councilor Prem, the Prime Minister and the Defense Minister, which is why they deliberately made personnel assignments that would divide factions. They therefore not only avoided concentrating power among the officers of a particular Class, but also distributed key posts to members of various units of the service, of different regions and diversified factions, including Suchinda's, Prem's and Chawalit's. Furthermore, due to their weak personal support bases, commanders-in-chief in the 1990's could not override or avoid interventions by the Defense Minister and others, and therefore had to make various concessions which contributed to undermining the factions.

Another important point to note is that after 1992, the military no longer provided a crucial support base for the prime ministers. The military had provided the sole support base for all of the ex-military prime ministers until the end of the 1970s. During and after the 1980s Prem and Suchinda had each sought support from both the military and the Parliament. These ex-military prime ministers therefore intervened in the military's personnel reshuffles in order to keep their personal and factional supporters in power and thus secure the continuing support of the military. For these prime ministers, it was necessary to foster a pro-prime minister faction that was strong enough to deter the emergence of any anti-prime minister factions within the military while at the same time constraining other forces such as the bureaucracy, political parties, the media and students which might oppose the government. Their direct interventions in military personnel matters helped their respective commanders-in-chief to develop strong support for their leadership, which was nevertheless not strong enough to threaten the government of the day. In contrast, none of the post-1992 administrations were heavily reliant on military support. After 1992, the survival of an administration came to depend solely on securing a parliamentary majority, not the support of the military. A prime minister in a time of democracy does not need to actively interfere with personnel assignments in the military. He/she is more interested in preventing a military leader from growing too powerful. It would be extremely difficult for a commander-in-chief to build a strong faction in the few years he is in office without significant help from the external powers such as the prime minister and the defense minister; and such external help hardly exists. This is one of the key respects in which the military's political power was severely restricted by the consolidation of democratic politics.

A good example of this is Chawalit, who joined the coalition government in September 1992. Chawalit held the post of Defense Minister from July 1995 to November 1997 and again from February 2001 to October 2002. With his background as a former Commander-in-Chief of the Army, he was the only party politician of the time who had strong connections within the military, and was thus capable of being deeply involved in the military's personnel matters. Consequently, other politicians were concerned that Chawalit might join forces with a powerful Army chief. For example, Prime Minister Banhan Sinlapaacha appointed Supreme Commander Wirot (Class 5) as Deputy Defense Minister in 1996, towards the end of his administration, precisely for the purpose of keeping tabs on the formidable Chawalit. Under these constraints, Chawalit tried to recruit the military commanders to his political support base. Nevertheless, he had no intention of either getting the military to mount a coup or of fostering a strong and independent military leader. The ideal military leader for Chawalit would be one who was obedient to Chawalit and not too powerful. This leader would be useless if he was too weak but dangerous if he was too strong. The officers whom Chawalit most trusted were the main divisional commanders who he had appointed when he was the Commander-in-Chief and who were also popular within the military. Because they were competent officers, they had all been sidelined from the Army when Class 5 became dominant. When Chawalit became Defense Minister, he did not return them to the Army chain of command, even though he had authority to influence military personnel assignments. If, for example, he had have reinstated Mongkhon Amphonphisit to the Army chain of command after July 1995, who was due to retire in 2000, it was highly likely that Mongkhon would have been appointed Commander-in-Chief. Since Mongkhon had a large network of strong political and business contacts that he had developed in the 1980s, he would likely be a powerful Army chief. As this was unfavorable for Chawalit, he kept Mongkhon in the Supreme Command and the Defense Permanent Secretary's office.[53] Instead, Chawalit tried to develop leaders out of less prominent officers, such as Chief of Staff Chan Bunprasoet. Despite his personal maneuverings, from the military's point of view Chawalit was not the worst Defense Minister. Many of the important military posts were held by officers of the former Suchinda faction and its umbrella group, the Chawalit faction, since 1992. What would have been troublesome for these military leaders would have been the appointment of a Defense Minister from a non-Chawalit faction. Hence, when the Democrat Party came to power in November 1997 and had the idea to nominate its MP and former Supreme Commander of the Armed Forces, Watthanachai, for Defense Minister, Supreme Commander Mongkhon and Army Commander-in-Chief Chettha negotiated directly with Prime Minister Chuan to serve concurrently as Defense Minister.

A comparison with personnel changes during the 1980s will highlight the contrasting nature of the reshuffles after May 1992. The periodic reshuffles effected on 1 October each year are analyzed below by determining the number of officers and their academy classes in each of the following posts—the Five Tigers, the lieutenant-general-level posts immediately below the Five Tigers (four to six regional commanders and two deputy chiefs of staff), and the divisional commanders of the fighting units (ten to thirteen) which are the most politically important major-general-level posts in the Army.[54]

Firstly, when the Commander-in-Chief's post was held by the likes of Athit (Preparatory Class 5), Chawalit (Class 1), Suchinda, Itsaraphong and Wimon (Class 5), between three and five of the Tiger posts were held by their classmates. In contrast, when Pramon (Class 6) and Chettha (Class 9) were in power in the 1990s, all Five Tiger posts were held by officers from different Classes and none of them was their classmate. Surayut (Class 12) had only two classmates in these key posts (see Table 2.5). The number of classmates in the Five Tiger posts does not always reflect the strength of the Commander-in-Chief's leadership, but as a general rule, it is clear that the Commander-in-Chief can exercise greater power when these posts are held by his classmates rather than by officers from many different Classes.

Of the posts immediately below the Five Tigers, many were held by the officers of Classes which were expected to produce a commander-in-chief in the near future—Preparatory Class 5 in the early 1980s and Class 5 in the late 1980s, for example. These officers were not only numerous, but also stayed in their posts for several years. The longer their term of office, the easier it was to develop a strong support base among officers under their immediate control, such as divisional commanders and assistant chiefs of staff. By contrast, although particular classes did dominate these posts at various times during the 1990s, including Class 9 in 1995 and Class 12 in 1999, their dominance only lasted for one year (Table 2.5). It is difficult to establish a strong support base in such a short time while angling for a promotion to a Five Tiger post.

The numbers of divisional commanders clearly show large variations between different Classes, although the smaller numbers of Class 1 to Class 4 graduates defies direct comparison (see Figure 2.4). Looking at the accumulating total of divisional commanders produced by each Class as of 1 October, Class 7 had none while Classes 3 and 10 had only a few each. In contrast, the number of Class 5 officers was markedly higher than others. Among the classes (up to Class 10) that produced divisional commanders in the 1980s, high concentrations of Class 5 and Class 8 officers are notable. From Class 11 to Class 15, which were classes unlikely to produce any more divisional commanders at the time of this analysis, it is obvious that posts are more evenly distributed between classes than previously, although Classes 11 and 15 had slightly reduced numbers. In addition to the accumulating total that each class has produced, the degree of concentration at any given point in time is also important. For example, more than 70% of the divisional command posts were held by Class 5 in 1985. Class 8 held more than 50% in 1988 and Class 11 held close to 50% in 1991. However, from 1993, such extreme concentrations disappeared as the posts were generally allocated to at least three different classes (Table 2.5). This three-cornered competition worked to check each faction and thus maintain a balance of power. This is but one example of the division of power that occurred in the 1990s.

Examining each Class's process of promotion from divisional commanders to Five Tiger posts from the perspective of building a support base for the future commander-in-chief, an important difference between the 1980s and the 1990s becomes apparent. In the 1980s, a class typically functioned to secure many divisional command posts to nurture its power, used these positions as steppingstones to as many lieutenant-general-level posts as possible, and finally took the post of commander-in-chief. The Classes which succeeded in this process built their power bases from the bottom up and ultimately won the top post. Preparatory Class 5, Class 1 and Class 5 followed this pattern. In such cases, each class had a long time to prepare its support base in the lead-up to its appointment of a commander-in-chief, who was thus capable of exercising relatively strong power immediately after the appointment. Class 5, which had held many divisional command posts over a long period, produced three commanders-in-chief in the space of six and a half years. Following this

Figure 2.4 The number of graduates and the number of divisional commanders by Academy class, 1980-2002

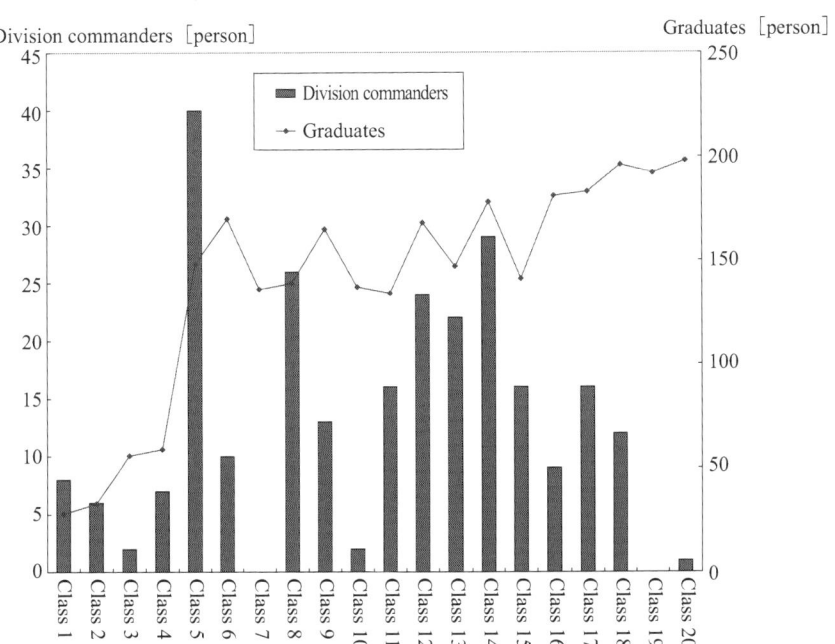

Source: The numbers of divisional commanders were calculated based on the personnel reshuffle list for each year. The numbers of Academy graduates were taken from the list of graduates in the academy's 111th year commemorative publication. (CPR 1998: 184-222)

pattern, Class 8 and Class 11 ought to have each produced a commander-in-chief. However, Class 8 missed its chance as its officers had been sidelined from the mainstream career track by the early 1990s. Class 11, which replaced Class 8, also suffered because of its involvement in the May incident. During Commander-in-Chief Wimon's term in office, no single class dominated the divisional command posts as had Classes 5, 8 and 11. It was evident that these posts were being distributed to multiple classes, as mentioned above. Pramon (Class 6) and Chettha (Class 9) each became Commander-in-Chief before their power bases were adequately prepared, and each reached the mandatory retirement age before they could form a sufficient power base while in office. Chettha's successor was expected to come from Class 11, which had held half of the posts immediately below the Five Tigers. However, the Chief of Staff at the time, who was the leading candidate, was considered to be too close to opposition leader Chawalit. Surayut (Class 12), a dark horse, was therefore appointed to the position instead. Surayut had no experience in the Five Tiger posts and his

Table 2.5 The number of officers in key posts by Academy class, 1980–2001

		1980	1981	1982	1983	1984	1985	1986	1987	1988	1989	1990	1991	1992	1993	1994	1995	1996	1997	1998	1999	2000	2001
P5	General	1	(2)	(2)	(4)	(4)																	
P5	Lt. General	1	(3)	(4)	(4)	(3)	1																
P5	Maj. General	[3]																					
P6	General							1															
P6	Lt. General						1	1															
P6	Maj. General	[3]	1																				
P7	General																						
P7	Lt. General									2													
P7	Maj. General			[3]	2	2																	
Class 1	General							1	(3)	(3)	(3)	(2)											
Class 1	Lt. General					1	2	(2)	2	(2)	1												
Class 1	Maj. General	1	[3]	[3]	1																		
Class 2	General							1	1	1													
Class 2	Lt. General					1	1	1	1	1													
Class 2	Maj. General		2	2	2																		
Class 3	General									1	1												
Class 3	Lt. General								1														
Class 3	Maj. General				1	1																	
Class 4	General													1									
Class 4	Lt. General							1	(2)	(2)	2	2											
Class 4	Maj. General			2	3	2																	
Class 5	General							1	1	2	(4)	(5)	(3)	(4)	(4)	1							
Class 5	Lt. General							(3)	(2)	(2)	(5)	(4)	(5)	(2)	1								
Class 5	Maj. General			2	[4]	[9]	[10]	[6]	[6]	1	1		1										
Class 6	General												1	1	_1_								
Class 6	Lt. General										1	1	(2)	(2)	(2)								
Class 6	Maj. General				1	1	1	1	2	2	2	2											
Class 7	General														1	1	1						
Class 7	Lt. General											1											
Class 7	Maj. General																						
Class 8	General														1	1	1						
Class 8	Lt. General										1	1	1	(2)	1								
Class 8	Maj. General					2	5	5	[7]	[5]	2												
Class 9	General													1	1	_1_	_1_						
Class 9	Lt. General										1	1	1	(4)	2	1	1						
Class 9	Maj. General						1	1	3	2	1	2	2	1									

only classmate in these posts or the posts immediately below them was his rival Samphao. It is thus no exaggeration to say that he was friendless and isolated.

All of the post-1992 Commanders-in-Chief except for Wimon, who inherited an existing support base, assumed the post without a stable support base. This lack of stability led to disputes over personnel changes and internal conflicts within the Army. These were conflicts between small and weak factions, rather than between major factions. Some sought support from outside forces such

		1981	1982	1983	1984	1985	1986	1987	1988	1989	1990	1991	1992	1993	1994	1995	1996	1997	1998	1999	2000	2001	2002
Class 10	General																						
	Lt. General												1	1	1								
	Maj. General								1	1													
Class 11	General																1	1	1	1	1		
	Lt. General																③	④	④				
	Maj. General											2	⑤	⑥	3								
Class 12	General																1	1	②̂	②̂	②̂	②̂	1
	Lt. General										②	②	②	2	1					⑤	③		
	Maj. General									1	2	3	④	⑤	4	3	2						
Class 13	General																	1	1	1			
	Lt. General															1	2	1	1	③	③	2	
	Maj. General											2	3	⑤	3	④	3	2					
Class 14	General																	1	1	1	③̂	②̂	
	Lt. General															1	2	2	2	2	③	③	
	Maj. General											2	4	4	⑥	④	④	3	1	1			
Class 15	General																						1
	Lt. General																					2	1
	Maj. General															1	2	④	④	3	2		
Class 16	General																						1
	Lt. General																						
	Maj. General																	1	3	2	3	1	
Class 17	General																						
	Lt. General																						1
	Maj. General																1	1	2	④	④	④	1
Class 18	General																						
	Lt. General																						1
	Maj. General																	1	1	2	④	④	2
Class 19	General																						
	Lt. General																						
	Maj. General																						③
Class 20	General																						
	Lt. General																						
	Maj. General																					1	③
Class 21	General																						
	Lt. General																						
	Maj. General																						2

Notes:
1. Key posts here means Five Tigers for the rank of General; for the rank of Lieutenant-General, the posts immediately below the Five Tigers (Regional Commanders and Deputy Chiefs of Staff); and for the rank of Major-General, Divisional Commanders.
2. The numbers in the above table represent the numbers of officers in these posts as of 1 October each year. Data for P4 and earlier Classes have been omitted here.
3. ⓝ̂, ⓝ and ⃞n denote the largest group in the rank in each year. Commander-in-Chief is indicated by underline. For example in 1990, Class 5 produced the Commander-in-Chief and they formed the largest group of four in both the ranks of General and Lieutenant-General, while five officers from Class 11 formed the largest group of the rank of Major-General.

as the Defense Minister and party politicians. When Surayut and Samphao became the leading candidates for Commander-in-Chief in the 1998 reshuffle, some within the Army complained that their tenures would be too long. As mentioned, it is extremely difficult to strengthen one's support base during a short tenure. The persistence of this view was, in itself, a significant factor in obstructing the emergence of a strong commander-in-chief. It is virtually impossible to reestablish the predominance of one or two major factions if the Commander-in-Chief has only narrowly won a contest that had no clear favorite. An Army internally divided is not capable of executing a successful coup, and is therefore an Army with little effective political power.

The final blow to the military's declining political power was the new electoral system introduced in the 1997 Constitution. The new rule provided that an elected MP would lose his seat if appointed to a cabinet post, which discouraged local district-based MPs to seek the post. Instead, MPs elected in the newly introduced proportional representation system (party list), which is nationwide, were expected to join the cabinet (see Chapter Three for details). The first general election under the new constitution was held in 2001. The proportional representation list of candidates contained the names of many recently-retired military leaders,[55] who were the most likely candidates for the Defense Ministry. Most of the Defense Ministers (and Deputy Defense Ministers) in the 1990s had also been retired military officers, but some of them had not belonged to the dominant factions in the military hierarchy in the 1990s. In contrast, those likely candidates for the Defense Minister among the party list MPs were all well-known generals who had belonged to the mainstream factions until their retirement. Their appointment would mean that Chawalit would no longer be the only MP with a significant military support base. When appointed as Defense Minister, they would be able to influence military personnel changes just as Chawalit had done.

Formed after the 2001 election, Thaksin's government in February 2001 appointed Chawalit as Minister of Defense and former Defense Permanent Secretary Yutthasak as Deputy Minister of Defense. There was a significant difference between the two appointees. On one hand, as the leader of his own party, Chawalit could pursue his personal interests through military personnel transfers without paying too much attention to other party politicians. At the risk of oversimplification, if Chawalit can be regarded as at one with the military, it can be argued that personnel changes during this period were decided autonomously by the military itself. On the other hand, as a party list MP, Yutthasak was indebted to his party (or more correctly, Thaksin, the party leader) for his position. Thammarak Isarangkun Na Ayutthaya, who became the Defense Minister in October 2002, was also a party list MP. These party list MPs-turned Ministers are almost invariably susceptible to interference in their personnel decisions by highly partisan politicians from their own parties.

Signs of such interference were already evident in the Thaksin administration, clear in the appointment of Thaksin's relatives to important positions. For example, his cousin, Chaiyasit Chinnawat (Class 16), was promoted to the rank of lieutenant-general in April 2001, immediately after Thaksin assumed office, then to the rank of general only one year later. After another six months he was transferred from the Supreme Command of the Armed Forces (in the nominal post of Special Advisor) back to the Army and promoted to Assistant Commander-in-Chief—a post which, as discussed previously, is on the direct path to the top job.[56] Another relative, Uthai Chinnawat of Class 13, was promoted from Deputy Director of Policy and Planning (lieutenant-general) in the Office of Defense Permanent Secretary to Director (general) in October 2001, then to Deputy Permanent Secretary of Defense in October 2002. Thaksin's interference was also seen in the promotion of his classmates from the Army cadet school (Preparatory Class 10). While Thaksin went to the police academy, many of his classmates had gone to the military academy (Class 21). Class 21 officers were promoted to be Divisional Commanders of the First Division and the Second Infantry Division in October 2002. With these two divisions that are closest to the capital, the center of power, in the hands of his classmates, Prime Minister Thaksin intended to posses the capability to deter a coup d'état.

In order to make these personnel changes possible, Thaksin carried out an unprecedented reshuffle of the Supreme Commander of the Armed Forces and the Commanders-in-Chief of the three forces in August 2002, prior to the regular periodic reshuffle in October. He explained that the special reshuffle would enable the new appointees to consult with their predecessors before deciding on the transfers of other officers, so that they could work with staff of their own choosing and thus could operate their commands efficiently from the first day of their appointments. His real intention was, however, to remove Surayut, who would not be submissive to the Prime Minister because he had strong support from Prem, and would thus make it easier to intervene in the Army's personnel matters. If Surayut had retained the authority to select officers for the October reshuffle, Thaksin would not be able to have his way in the restructure. Chief of Staff Somthat Attanan was appointed as next Commander-in-Chief, contrary to Surayut's wishes.[57] During the interim period, Somthat tried to make personnel changes that were contrary to the incumbent's wishes. This created sharp conflicts concerning appointments to the remaining Tiger posts, which resulted in an unusually long negotiation process. Hence, the official announcement of the October reshuffle was not made until 28 September. Despite staunch opposition, the Prime Minister prevailed to achieve the outcomes presented above (see Table 2.4). Furthermore, in a cabinet reshuffle that same October, Chawalit was replaced as the Defense Minister by another retired military officer, Thammarak, who would be more manageable for Thaksin.[58] This appointment created even more opportunity for political intervention in military personnel assignments.

The military's autonomy regarding personnel assignments steadily declined after the May 1992 incident. The decline was particularly marked following the 2001 general election, in which the effects of the 1997 Constitution were felt for the first time. This has entailed a diminution in the power of the Army Commander-in-Chief, and thus a decrease in the military's political power overall. However, as party politicians have increased their influence over military personnel matters, military officers may increasingly align themselves with various party politicians in order to enhance their prospects of promotion. In the mid-1970s, heavy-handed political interference in military personnel matters prompted the military's resentment and a coup d'état.[59] There appears to be a growing possibility of power struggles among party politicians becoming intertwined with the military's internal politics of personnel matters, which may have the unfortunate consequence of dragging the military back into politics.

Moreover, neither the expectation of nor concern about the mounting of another coup has disappeared. Once in a while, influential people have tried to invite the military into politics. Particularly, expectations of a coup d'état intensified for several months from July 1997, when the currency crisis coincided with the final drafting stage of the 1997 Constitution. This was undoubtedly an important factor in political scientist Chaianan Samutthawanit's proposal via the mass media that the people should petition the King to suspend the Parliament for three years and entrust the government to nonpartisan experts (*Nation Sutsapda*, 15 August 1997). In the proposal, the suggested means to suspend parliamentary democracy was a military coup d'état. With the widespread distrust of politicians at the time, many people hoped for the creation of a technocratic government untainted by the electioneering process, like the Anan administration, and expected the military to play the role of a cleaner who could sweep the unpopular politicians from the Parliament (Surachat 1998a: 165–166; 167–173, 174–181; *Athit*, 8 August 1997; 22 August 1997; Chatcharin 1998: 298–304). At the same time, however, it was clear that the military would be held responsible if the 'supposedly competent' administration created by a military coup did not quickly resolve the country's economic problems. Under the circumstances, the military had little to gain and much to lose, and therefore had no reason to accept such a risky role.[60] A few years later, in the lead-up to the January 2001 general election, amidst rising concern that the Election Commission might disqualify numerous candidates for election violations, the leader of the Chat Phatthana Party warned that too many disqualifications and the resultant confusion might lead to a coup d'état (*Bangkok Post*, 15 December 2000). This was an audacious attempt to use the threat of military intervention to influence the Electoral Commission. In March 2002, the deputy leader of the opposition Democratic Party criticized the then Thaksin administration for its repeated mismanagement during its first year in office, suggesting that its continuation could cause a military coup. These remarks by politicians indicated that the idea of a military coup did not become a thing of the past.

To sum up, the shrinking political power of the military is mainly due to the changes in military personnel reshuffling. The military can be powerful in politics as far as there is the possibility of a successful coup. A strong military leader is indispensable for a successful coup. Taking seriously the lesson learned from the political crisis in May 1992, much attention has been paid to prevent such a strong leader from interfering in military personnel changes post-1992. In addition to the concern of the political elite, democratization also affected the military. After September 1992, a prime minister no longer had to depend on the support of the military for the survival of an administration. His power and legitimacy now depend mainly on electoral victory and parliamentary majority. He may interfere with military personnel changes partly because he needs to render Army leaders unable to stage a successful coup.

Part II
Calls for Political Reform and a New Constitution

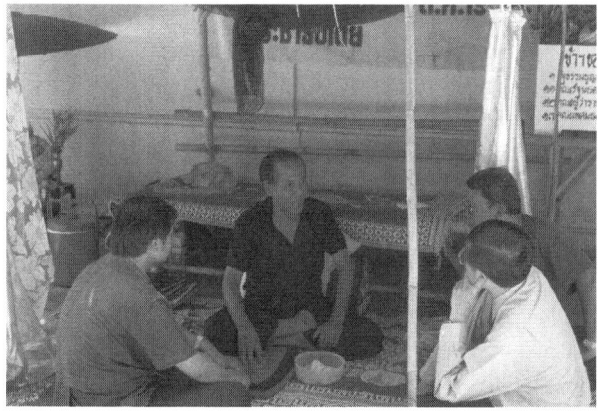

Chalat on hunger strike in May 1994 demanding political reform.

As the military retreated from politics and political parties resumed control in the mid-1990s, the people began to call for political reform. Widespread dissatisfaction with the problems of party politics—corruption, inefficiencies and instability—was expressed through a campaign to demand reform. In 1996, the government decided to conduct a comprehensive revision of the constitution to affect political reform, with the new constitution scheduled to be promulgated and enforced in 1997. The effectiveness of the new constitution was expected to be verified by a Senate election in 2000 and a House of Representatives election in 2001.

The 1997 Constitution for Thailand is the sixteenth since 1932. It was prepared by the Constitution Drafting Assembly (CDA) which was created separately from the Parliament. The members of the CDA were chosen in an election and held numerous public hearings during the drafting process. This broad-based participation was unprecedented in the drafting process; every previous constitution had been drafted by a group of people who had seized power by coup d'état or other non-democratic means. In addition to more democratic procedures, its contents were also more democratic in that it expanded the rights and freedoms of the people. Hence, it was approvingly referred to as the 'people's constitution' (*ratthathammanun chabap prachachon*) and is generally regarded as having contributed to further consolidating democracy in Thailand. In other words, the 1997 Constitution was considered to have remedied the shortcomings of the form of party politics that had come to dominate Thai politics following the May 1992 incident and has thus played an important role in the democratization of Thai politics.

Nevertheless, many aspects of arguments for political reform and the 1997 Constitution warrant closer examination. We might begin by asking why party politics—which had been eagerly anticipated throughout the 1980s—was so harshly criticized as soon as it came into real power. Who were its critics and what were the grounds for their criticisms? Answers to these questions shed light on the provisions of the new constitution, helping to illuminate their intent. Following this we can ask how politics has changed after two elections as a result of the new directions of the constitution.

In seeking answers to these questions, in Chapter Three I examine the course of events beginning from the formulation of arguments for political reform until the enactment of the 1997 Constitution. My intent is to shed some light on questions such as why the campaign for political reform emerged, what it sought to do, who supported it, why the constitution was comprehensively revised, what and how these revisions aimed to reform, why MPs agreed to a draft constitution that restricted their powers, and what the campaign for political reform and the new constitution meant to democratization.

I discuss the effects of the 1997 Constitution in Chapters Four and Five. Chapter Four is an analysis of the Senate election in 2000; the first national election under the new constitution. I consider why many of the successful candidates in this election were former public officials and look into the significance of this fact. Chapter Five is an analysis of the House of Representatives election in 2001 and the cabinet that formed as a result. I consider some of the consequences of the new electoral system and the significance of excluding single-seat-electorate MPs from cabinet. Finally, I discuss the possible political instability that might be generated by the stability of government that the new constitution enables.

3
The 1997 Constitution and its Political Significance

Introduction

The constitution of Thailand was comprehensively revised in 1997, producing the sixteenth constitution since 1932. The intent of the new constitution was political reform. Calls for political reform had begun to increase in 1994. A comprehensive revision was decided upon in 1996 and completed in 1997. The political reform campaign and the 1997 Constitution are often portrayed as the culmination of a democratization movement led by the middle class, whose political influence has grown since 1992.

In the September 1992 general election, four parties (the Democrat, New Aspiration, Phalang Tham and Ekkaphap parties), which were all in opposition during the May incident, won a bare majority, securing 185 of 360 seats. The Social Action Party, which had been a member of the former ruling coalition, joined them with twenty-two seats. The Chuan government was thus formed, with the Democrat Party as the leading party. With almost all of the cabinet members being elected MPs, the government was perfectly democratic *in form*. However not everyone was satisfied. Why was there already notable dissatisfaction with party politics? According to the bureaucratic polity model, which had been dominant until the 1980s, the military and bureaucracy were major obstacles to democratization. After the military had begun to withdraw from politics, the centralized administrative structure was considered to be the biggest problem. In the September 1992 general election, many political parties began to call for decentralization. Because the Interior Ministry and other agencies were strongly opposed to this idea, however, and many party politicians were unenthusiastic about it as well, efforts to effect decentralization stalled at a halfway point in 1994.[1] With the scalpel of reform applied to the centralized administration, albeit half-heartedly, political discontent had lost its focus. It seems as if this was when party politics became the new target. As the military and the bureaucracy, which had long taken the brunt of criticisms, began to fade into the background, political discontent was directed towards the political parties and politicians that had assumed center stage in the political arena. Of course, those who were at risk of losing their vested interests through the rise of party politics were also harsh critics. Regardless of their motives, though, all argued that the political system was not democratic enough and needed further democratization. These were the voices calling for political reform.

In response to these calls for political reform, the government created the Committee on Developing Democracy (CDD) in June 1994. In April 1995 the CDD recommended political reform via a comprehensive revision of the constitution. The Chat Thai Party pledged to implement this recommendation and became the leading party after the July 1995 general election. Immediately after forming the new government, the party established the Political Reform Committee to research the best approach. By September 1996, the procedures for fully revising the constitution had been agreed upon. It was decided that a Constitution Drafting Assembly (CDA) would be established outside of the Parliament (Table 3.1). The CDA began its work in December 1996 and completed drafting a new constitution in August 1997. The draft was passed by Parliament in September and the new constitution was promulgated and put into effect in October 1997. Thus realized the 1997 Constitution was designed to facilitate political reform and is often called the 'people's constitution' (*ratthathammanun chabap prachachon*).

In 1994, political reform was initially only advocated by a very small circle of intellectuals and activists, but it gradually gathered support as dissatisfaction with party politics grew among the people. What was sought by the advocates of political reform? Why was a comprehensive revision of the constitution chosen as the preferred approach to political reform? What did the 1997 Constitution mean to the democratization of Thailand? What did it contribute to democratization? This chapter examines these questions by focusing on the middle class, which, as discussed in previous chapters, is widely regarded as the driver of democratization in Thai politics in the 1990s.

A constitution provides basic rules of politics and stipulates the power relations of the cabinet and the state, hence its revision will effect changes in power relations, which will invariably benefit some and disadvantage others. As the main supporter behind the argument for political reform, what aspects of party politics were the middle class dissatisfied with, and what aspects of the 1997 Constitution served the middle class's interests? In other words, how much consideration did the advocates of political reform and the drafters of the constitution give to the interests of the middle class?

Establishing the Constitution Drafting Assembly

The Committee on Developing Democracy
Political activist Chalat Worachat began a hunger strike in front of Parliament House on 25 May 1994, calling for a new constitution as well as the popular

election of cabinet ministers and local government chiefs.[2] His actions did not attract immediate attention, occurring barely two months after the government's Constitutional Amendment Bill had been voted down by opposition parties in the House on 31 March and the Senate on 1 April, and his demands were considered too bold and unachievable. On 2 June, however, a group of academics and activists gathered at the Law Faculty of Thammasat University for discussions, and formulated a proposal to establish a special constitution drafting committee (*Matichon Sutsapda*, 10 June 1994). On the same day, Prawet Wasi, a prominent intellectual,[3] released a statement entitled 'The death of Chalat Worachat and political reform in Thailand,' (1997b) in which he argued that what Chalat demanded was the democratization of politics. According to Prawet, Thai politics suffers from structural problems and cannot be improved by a change of government unless these structural problems are rectified. Elections are won by contraband traders, illegal loggers, gamblers and ignorant people, and the poor state of politics continues. Therefore, the political structure must be improved by the enactment of a new constitution (Prawet 1997b: 51–6). Prawet's 'political reform' argument was inspired by a series of articles on 'constitutionalism' in the daily newspaper *Phuchatkan*, written by former senior official Amon Chantharasombun (Connors 2003: 155–7), and instantly drew a strong positive response (Prawet 1997b: 52). As support for Chalat grew, Aphirak Chakri, a right-wing organization that had been hostile to Chalat since the May 1992 incident, intensified its attacks on him, and the government began to organize pro-government rallies through the Interior Ministry (*Matichon Sutsapda*, 17 June 1994). The tension soon escalated and demanded a stronger response to the situation. On 8 June, MPs of the Phalang Tham Party, a member of the ruling coalition, requested the government to respond positively. On the same day, about 5000 Chalat supporters gathered in front of Parliament House and criticized the government for its indifference to their demands. To resolve the situation, Democrat MP and Speaker of the House of Representatives Marut Bunnak announced the establishment of the Committee on Developing Democracy (*khanakammakan phatthana prachathipatai* or CDD for short) on 9 June.[4] The CDD was chaired by Prawet and comprised of fifty-eight members. Its terms of reference consisted of drafting a new constitution, drafting new laws concerning elections and political parties, and making recommendations for the short- and long-term development and reform of the national government (CDD 1995: 5).

On 28 April 1995, the CDD submitted its proposal to the Speaker of the House of Representatives, after less than a year of deliberation. The proposal had two major points. First, a committee for political development should be created, modeled after those in the fields of economics and education. Second, they should 'start with political reform in order to solve various problems' (CDD 1995: 6–7). As well as preparing this submission to the Speaker, the CDD was conducting

Table 3.1 The path to establishing the Constitution Drafting Assembly

Date	Event
25 May 1994	Chalat begins a hunger strike demanding: (1) constitutional revision by the house of representatives; (2) popular election of cabinet members; (3) popular election of provincial governors; and (4) popular election of city councilor.
30 May 1994	A democracy group proposes a full constitutional revision by amendment of article 211 of the constitution. Prawet proposes 'political reform,' which is rejected by Prime Minister Chuan.
9 June 1994	Speaker of the House of Representatives Marut sets up the Committee on Developing Democracy to break a deadlock
31 July 1994	Chalat stops a hunger strike.
13–15 December 1994	The fifth constitutional amendment bill is passed by the parliament
10 February 1995	The fifth amended constitution is enforced
15 April 1995	Chuan dissolves the parliament
2 July 1995	A general election is held
8 August 1995	The political reform committee is set up
6 February 1996	The political reform committee proposes six principles for political reform to the government
17 May 1996	The government introduces the article 211 amendment bill to the parliament and sets up a 45-member special committee
22 May 1996	Chaianan is elected to chair the special committee
29 August 1996	The parliament finishes the second reading of the amendment bill. The establishment of a ninety-nine-member Constitution Drafting Assembly (CDA) is the main point.
14 September 1996	The article 211 amendment bill is passed by the parliament
22 October 1996	The amended article 211 is enforced
9–13 December 1996	Applications for CDA candidacy are filed
15 December 1996	Ten candidates are internally elected for each province
26 December 1996	Ninety-nine CDA members are elected by the parliament

Source: *Nation Sutsapda*, 27 December 1996

academic research on political reform financed by a public research grant. This research was led by Bowonsak Uwanno of the Law Faculty of Chulalongkorn University, who played an important role within the CDD (Prawet 1997b: 60). Its findings were published in September 1995 in fifteen volumes collectively titled 'Research reports submitted to the Committee on Developing Democracy for the preparation of a proposal for political reform.'[5]

The CDD's proposal to the Speaker of the House of Representatives was published and turned out to be influential regarding the subsequent political reform. It is therefore worth discussing its contents in some detail. The proposal consisted of three parts: Part 1, 'Problems with the political system of Thailand and the need for political reform,' Part 2, 'Recommendations on the conceptual framework for the reform of Thai politics,' and Part 3, 'Procedures for drafting the constitution.'

Why political reform?

> Political reform will impact on the reform of various other problems in society. While we are plagued by the problem that decisions made ... in politics are neither conscientious nor efficient, we cannot solve other issues such as environmental problems, police reform, bureaucratic reform and educational reform. Political reform is the reform which leads to genuine reforms. (CDD 1995: 15)

In other words, the CDD proposal claimed that politics is the root of all evil and various other problems are unlikely to be resolved until changes are made to politics.[6]

To reform politics, the proposal continues, one must first understand the strengths and weaknesses of the political, economic and social systems before one considers solutions. Eighteen weaknesses are listed, including corruption among politicians and bureaucrats, violation of election rules, political parties controlled by a small number of funding providers, the rural poor dependent on politics for infrastructure development, urban residents who look down on rural areas and politicians and distrust politics, the centralized government administration, weak enforcement of the rule of law, a decline of Buddhism, lack of academic research, and the media in pursuit of commercial interests (CDD 1995: 19–21). The proposal also claims that the Parliament is inefficient and that the Prime Minister is lacking in leadership (CDD 1995: 21–2).

This assessment of the political situation leads to the following conclusions: first, political reform is essential; second, political reform is about making politics honest and efficient; third, political reform is realized by a comprehensive revision of the constitution; and fourth, the democratic political system should be maintained with the King as the head of state (CDD 1995: 25). There is obviously a logical leap here; some of the weaknesses the report identifies are not necessarily political problems, and even those that do result from politics cannot be resolved by honesty and efficiency alone. Hence it seems more likely that from the outset facilitating political reform through constitutional revision was the aim, and that these convenient reasons were merely presented to justify it.

How to reform?
The recommended reform had two main pillars. One was a more strenuous inspection of government administration; the other an attempt to increase the efficiency, honesty and stability of the parliament and cabinet.

Inspecting politics: The Constitution Court, the Administrative Court, the Ombudsman, and the Supreme Court of Justice's Criminal Division for Persons Holding Political Positions were to be established for the more stringent inspection of politicians and bureaucrats. The impeachment system was to be strengthened, and those questioned with improper conduct were to be thoroughly investigated and charged by the Constitution Court or the Supreme Court of Justice's Criminal Division for Persons Holding Political Positions. These organs and the Office of the Auditor-General were to be given significantly greater independence from politics.

Parliamentary cabinet system: The parliamentary cabinet system of Thailand is, the CDD proposal observed, so outdated precluding efficiency and inspection that it must be updated to a contemporary and practical system with reference to examples from other countries (CDD 1995: 50). The proposal discussed changes to the mechanisms of the parliament, political parties and elections, and the promotion of efficiency in the parliament and the government as follows.

A. Parliament
How should one go about maintaining honesty and efficiency while preserving the patron-client relationship with MPs, which is indispensable for rural residents? (CDD 1995: 50–2) The CDD proposal tried to find a solution by restructuring parliament and recommends either two or three houses as desirable. Its preferred option was a parliament consisting of three houses—the House of Representatives, the House of Wisdom (*phruetsapha*) and the House of Advisers. The House of Representatives consists of about 300 MPs elected from single-representative constituencies. A member of the House of Wisdom must be a learned person who is over the age of thirty-five, has a university degree or higher education (or is a middle-level bureaucrat or higher[7]), and does not belong to any political party. He or she cannot become a cabinet member and has a term of six years. Their seats are maximum 100 and they are to be elected from the nation-wide constituency. This is expected to reduce vote buying and create the possibility for people with enthusiasm and abilities to

be elected, even if they lack financial resources (CDD 1995: 54–5). Finally, the House of Advisers consists of two types of members. The first type includes all former Prime Ministers, former Speakers of the Parliament, the highest serving officials of the military and the administration, the President of the Federation of Industry and the President of the Chamber of Commerce. The second type includes vocational representatives selected by the House of Representatives and the House of Wisdom (CDD 1995: 55). Since these Advisers are not subject to the scrutiny of an election, their role is limited to giving advice and exercising a veto. Under the two-house system on the other hand, the House of Wisdom and the House of Advisers are combined to form the Senate (CDD 1995: 57).

The proposal argued that a three-house system is preferable because it allows every sector of society to participate in the political process as well as providing checks and balances (CDD 1995: 57–8). MPs of the House of Representatives represent rural and urban districts and deal with issues to meet the requirements of the people of the districts. Members of the House of Wisdom represent all of the people, not particular constituencies, and concentrate solely on lawmaking as they cannot join the cabinet. They are also expected to set a good example for MPs of the House of Representatives. The House of Advisers represents the bureaucracy as well as vocational organizations and is established in consideration of their vested interests. Having all members of the three houses 'respect each other's role and cooperate with each other amounts to allowing the people belonging to each group (the majority of rural residents, the urban middle class,[8] and vocational organizations) a level of participation in politics appropriate to each group' (CDD 1995: 56).

Importantly, the proposal explains that the three-house system is a mechanism to allow representatives of 'the rural residents, the urban middle class, the bureaucracy and the vocational organizations' to participate. However where does it give consideration to the urban middle class? The House of Representatives, based on the single-seat electoral district system, would naturally favor the majority, the rural populace. The House of Advisers, comprising representatives of organizations for professionals such as doctors, lawyers and accountants, would represent the interests of *some* parts of the urban middle class, but certainly not all. Rather, it is the House of Wisdom that was intended to more directly represent the urban middle class. Members of the House of Wisdom are to be elected from the nationwide constituency and are limited to those who have a university or higher education. There can be little doubt that the authors of the proposal understood that the bachelor clause would favor the urban middle class, as there were hardly any university graduates among the rural populace, particularly among farmers. It is necessary to note here that academic qualification is widely regarded as the criterion that determines the social status of the middle class in Thailand. As rightly pointed out by Funatsu and Kagoya,

> Widespread acceptance of diplomaism, combined with the perception of "more equal opportunities," created an environment in which the urban middle class who achieved success through education could justify its privileged status more easily, and generated social values that support a society in which the low class also accepted authority of the middle class and real class disparity was not easily converted into hostile feelings. (2002: 223)

This bachelor clause was eventually incorporated in the 1997 Constitution.

B. Political parties

According to the proposal, political parties have to be democratized as many of them are controlled by a small number of party executives. There are three means to achieve this. First, they need to be organized properly. Second, they must be provided with public funding so they can remain independent from donors. Third, rules concerning the minimum number of candidates to run in an election from each party are to be abolished[9] while the rule prohibiting independent MPs in the House of Representatives is to remain (CDD 1995: 58–61).

C. Elections

The proposal explains electoral problems as follows.

> The urban middle-class people shun vote buying in elections because they are economically and socially independent and have no need to rely on others. Their circumstances are different from those of rural residents who are deprived of economic infrastructure (roads, electricity, water, etc.). Rural residents are poor and must "rely" on patronage and assistance in order to solve basic problems. This is why a majority of rural residents has been giving their votes to their patrons (*phu uppatham*) as tokens of their "gratitude" in elections. City residents and rural residents interpret "democratic politics" differently and the difference is directly affecting the advancement of democratic politics. *City residents have a "large voice" but a "small number of votes" whereas rural residents have a "small voice" but a "large number of votes".* City residents do not rate the House of Representatives very highly. It is because a majority of MPs are elected by rural residents and a majority of rural MPs are more concerned with the lack of physical social infrastructure (such as roads and bridges) rather than "policies" and "measures" for running the country and fail to deal seriously with issues such as resource management. If the country continues to be run in the way it has been in the past, it is expected to face the recurrence of similar problems in the future. On the other hand, MPs are interested in the Provincial Development Budget (*ngop phatthana changwat*)[10] to compensate for the lack of social infrastructure in their constituencies. (CDD 1995: 61, *emphasis* added)

In view of these differences between the city and rural areas, the proposal argues that there are various means available to alleviate problems while maintaining the benefits of the patron-client relationships between MPs and rural residents. One is to make it more difficult to buy votes. Another is to reduce the importance of the MPs elected on the basis of patron-client relationships. The proposal recommends four specific measures. First, the constituency system must be reorganized, replacing the existing medium-sized, multiple-seat electoral districts with a combination of a nation-wide proportional representation district providing 100 seats and about 300 single-seat districts. Vote buying in proportional representation elections is difficult because the constituency is nationwide. Second, the number of voters should be increased by lowering the minimum voting age from twenty to eighteen, giving overseas nationals the right to vote in elections, and making voting compulsory. The more voters there are the more difficult vote buying becomes. Third, the election campaign period should be shortened to forty-five days and vote counting should be carried out at the district or province level instead of at each polling station. Fourth, a highly independent election commission should be established (CDD 1995: 61–6). In short, the main purpose of the recommendations was to make vote buying difficult, primarily through the introduction of party-list MPs who are not affected by vote buying or patron-client relationships with voters. The only consideration given to rural residents here is to preserve the local district-based MPs, who should continue to look after their voters.

D. Promoting efficiency in Parliament
The proposal cites a study which compares the average numbers of bills passed by the different forms of the legislative branch of the government that existed between 1957 and 1992 in order to highlight the inefficiency of the current parliament. There were three forms of legislature during this period—a revolutionary council with no parliament, a government appointed parliament, and a popularly elected parliament. The average number of bills passed per month was 21.7 for the revolutionary council, 6.4 for the government appointed parliament, and 2.1 for the popularly elected parliament. The proposal argues that a parliamentary session should be solely devoted to lawmaking because of the evident inefficiency of the popularly elected parliament (CDD 1995: 69–71).

The proposal does not mention *why* fewer bills are passed by popularly elected parliaments, although the difference is clearly inherent in the system. The revolutionary council existed immediately after a coup when there was no popularly elected or officially appointed parliament. No deliberation or approval was required, and hence the number of passed bills depended solely on the speed at which government officials could draft them. Naturally many laws were enacted during that period. It was also quite natural that many bills were passed during the period of the government appointed parliament, since most members were pro-government and the bills were not genuinely debated. In contrast, in popularly elected parliaments where the ruling and opposition MPs try to outmaneuver each other, debates about proposed bills invariably take a long time. The emphasis on the differences in the numbers of passed bills without any explanation of why perhaps indicates that the authors of the proposal saw little value in the processes of deliberation by popularly elected MPs.[11]

E. Government stability and efficiency
The proposal makes five recommendations for improving the stability and efficiency of the cabinet. First, the prime minister should be appointed according to a majority vote in the House of Representatives rather than through backstage negotiations. The possibility of becoming prime minister should be open to non-members of the House of Representatives as well as leaders of the minority parties in the Parliament (CDD 1995: 75–7). Second, the prime minister's leadership should be strengthened. Traditionally, governments have been hesitant to introduce far-reaching reform bills for fear of rejection.[12] Measures for addressing a 'state of legislative emergency' should be adopted based on the German model[13] where, if a bill introduced by the government is rejected by the lower house and the prime minister considers the rejected bill to be important (including a budget bill), the prime minister may declare a state of legislative emergency with respect to the bill. The bill is then introduced to the upper house, which must be popularly elected, and becomes law if passed (CDD 1995: 77–8). Third, no more than one motion for a vote of no-confidence should be permitted in the two sessions (or one motion each year). While a motion for a vote of no-confidence in a cabinet member can be carried with the support of a mere 20% of the members of the House of Representatives, a motion for a vote of no-confidence in the prime minister requires at least 50% support, and it must be accompanied by a nomination for the next prime minister, again, as per the German model[14] (CDD 1995: 78–9).[15]

The main purpose of these changes was to strengthen the prime minister's leadership. Yet they include a very interesting proposal in light of the history of democratization in Thailand—the possibility of becoming prime minister without being an elected MP. The reason given for this unique proviso was that, by adopting a 'highly transparent and democratic' selection method—a majority vote in the lower house rather than the traditional method by which the Speaker of the House of Representatives nominated the candidate—'there will be no need to stipulate in the constitution that the prime minister must be an elected MP' (CDD 1995: 76). Perhaps with a feeling of diffidence, the proposal is open to a secret ballot if the candidate is an elected MP while requiring an open ballot if the candidate is not an elected MP. It also recommends that a member of the upper house should be eligible to be elected as prime minister. Recall that a major point of contention in the May 1992 incident was whether or not the prime minister had to be an elected MP. Only three years later, the CDD recommended that the prime minister should not have to be an elected MP. This shows a lack of trust in the members of the House of Representatives.

Towards the new constitution

Recognizing that revising the constitution in order to reform politics would be 'difficult in the current parliament which is comprised of those who have direct interests in it' (CDD 1995: 83), the CDD proposal recommends that the existing constitution (the 1991 Constitution) be amended so that a special committee for drafting a constitution can be established. The proposal sets five principles for the special committee. First, it should be a small scale committee consisting of fifteen to twenty former prime ministers and expert members. Second, members of the House of Representatives would be entitled to offer comments and suggestions but would not have any authority to make a decision with respect to the draft constitution. Third, the draft constitution, explanatory notes, and comments from the members of the House of Representatives should be published and disclosed to ensure transparency. Fourth, a national referendum should be held on two issues—whether the people wish to retain the existing constitution (with possible amendments) and whether they are in favor of the new draft constitution. Fifth, the special committee must finalize the draft constitution within sixteen months of its establishment. A general election should be held within ninety days after the promulgation and enforcement of the new constitution (CDD 1995: 83–5). Note in particular that members of the lower house have been excluded from the drafting process.

The CDD proposal created a significant response; the publication of the first 1000 copies in April 1995 was rapidly followed by a reprint in June.[16] The proposal generated interest in political reform and brought together 'an unlikely alliance between reforming state technocrats and civil servants, public intellectuals, the press, progressive politicians and the developmental NGOs and democracy activists' (Connors 1999: 211).

Although not all of the CDD recommendations were incorporated in the new constitution, it is no exaggeration to say that the proposal set out a clear course that did in fact lead to political reform. First, it declared that political reform was necessary because politics was the root of all social evil. Second, it confirmed that political reform was intended to bring honesty, efficiency and stability to politics. Third, it established that a comprehensive revision of the constitution was the agreed means to achieve political reform and confirmed that the lower house MPs' involvement in the revision process should be kept to a minimum. Fourth, the core members of the CDD played key leadership roles in the political reform that followed. Chairman Prawet became an opinion leader on the subject of political reform and committee member Bowonsak Uwanno and his fellow jurists had central roles in drafting the new constitution.

Prawet published a small book entitled *Political Reform* immediately following the conclusion of the CDD. It is his own summary of Amon's *Constitutionalism* and the CDD proposal. After praising Amon and Bowonsak as the two great public law scholars on the subject of political reform at the start of the book, he explains the need for political reform and the best methodology to facilitate this process. Political reform is needed because of problems such as money politics, the monopoly of politics by a minority, barriers stopping good people from entering politics, corruption, the 'dictatorship of the parliament' (*phadetkan thang ratthasapha*),[17] power struggles and instability, inefficiencies, and poor leadership (Prawet 1995: 3–11). To solve these problems, the whole political system must be reformed by a comprehensive revision of the constitution. The aim of political reform is to achieve honesty, stability and efficiency in politics (Prawet 1995: 12–13). Specific measures include electoral reform, reinforcing inspection and impeachment mechanisms, democratizing political parties, publicly funding political parties, revising relationships between Parliament and government, strengthening the prime minister's status, and changing the operation of Parliament (Prawet 1995: 14–17). Note that his summary completely omits the CDD proposal's consideration for rural areas and the socially disadvantaged, emphasizing instead the conservative perspective of those such as Amon. This suggests that for Prawet, who was actively advocating political reform as an acknowledged opinion leader, the primary objective of political reform was perhaps not to expand personal freedoms and rights among the populace, but merely to restrict the power of party politicians to some extent.[18]

The Political Reform Committee
In the July 1995 general election, the Chat Thai Party campaigned on a platform of political reform[19] and became the leading party.[20] Its leader, Banhan, thus became prime minister. The new government's policy statement declared its intention to develop the political system and set up a political development plan. This plan contained two specific points. First, the government would carry out political reform so that the people could participate in governing the nation and inspecting politics. Second, the government would support the amendment of Article 211 of the 1991 Constitution with reference to the proposal of the CDD[21] (*Nation Sutsapda*, 28 July 1995). In other words, it would amend

the 1991 Constitution to pave the way for a full constitutional revision in an effort to reform politics as recommended by the CDD. In accordance with this policy, Banhan established the Political Reform Committee (*Khanakammakan patirup kanmueang*) on 8 August 1995 and appointed thirty-five members. In the beginning, it seemed that both the ruling and opposition parties were at best half-hearted about the constitutional amendment, doing little more than trying to keep pace with each other (*Matichon Sutsapda*, 15 August 1995). However, Banhan's ascent to the premiership actually led to more calls for political reform. Banhan was generally mocked as a 'walking ATM' and was widely considered to be among the first politicians who should be weeded out in the course of reforms. Hence, the unpopularity of Banhan's administration and the pressure for political reform were proportionate.

The Banhan administration was under pressure from its beginning. Suan Dusit Teachers College polled 8397 people in Bangkok about political reform from 8 to 16 August 1995. The survey showed that 84.9% of them were in favor of political reform, and that 72.1% felt that neither the ruling nor opposition parties were serious about political reform (*Matichon Sutsapda*, 22 August 1995). On 23 August 1995, the military, which had stayed out of politics since May 1992, stated via a radio program that 'we the Thai people are still hoping to find someone who is a strong social administrator (*phuborihan sangkhom*) and courageous social operator (*phuchatkan sangkhom*) and determined to build a fair society in the not-so-distant future' (*Matichon Sutsapda*, 29 August 1995). This statement, with its implied hint of a possible coup d'état, stirred up quite a controversy.

The administration became increasingly unpopular as the prime minister's relationship with the media was severely strained through a series of incidents. On 17 November 1995, the Deputy Secretary-General to the Prime Minister banned a reporter who had been assigned to cover the Prime Minister's Office from accompanying the Prime Minister and his entourage to Tokyo, where they were attending an APEC meeting, because the reporter was a supporter of the opposition Democrat Party. On 20 November, he requested a TV station to reassign a reporter from the Prime Minister's Office to elsewhere because the reporter was asking the Prime Minister blunt questions. On 21 November, he suggested that a program of politics on an FM radio station should be cancelled claiming that it provided its listeners with a chance to criticize the government. On 11 February 1996, a TV station was pressured and 'voluntarily' cancelled a popular program called 'diverse opinions (*mong tang mum*).' On 23 May, the security police sent written warnings to five daily newspapers and one weekly magazine, accusing them of publishing inappropriate and disorderly reports about the Prime Minister's efforts to avoid the deliberation of a no-confidence motion against him in the Parliament (*Matichon Sutsapda*, 20 August 1996). In short, having been subject to harsh criticisms from the very beginning of his administration, Banhan added fuel to the fire by trying to censor the media.

Banhan clearly expressed his irritation in August 1996.

> I am making an effort every day to resolve the problem of trust in the government leaders. To be honest, however, it is difficult. You should ask the residents of more than sixty provinces, not just the residents of Bangkok, whether they trust us. Bangkok is not Thailand. I have visited more than sixty provinces and provided the residents with much of what they want. You should also ask rural residents whether they trust us. I do not want to talk about how people's trust in me has been eroded in Bangkok. Certain matters have been reported contrary to the facts. For example, how is it possible to write [critically] about [the fund-raising by] my wife Chaemsai Sinlapaacha? It is a charitable activity. However, they are eagerly waiting for a chance to damage my reputation and make a mountain out of a molehill in their reports. If this situation is going to continue, to be honest, I cannot remain as prime minister... Media reports are different from the facts... Reporters are making up the stories. The development of our country is stunted because the media does not play fair and it is busy attacking me every day instead of reporting good news... Frankly speaking, I guarantee that even (former Prime Minister) Anan could not continue as prime minister if this situation should continue. Errors are unavoidable in [the government's] work. However, when things are reported in this manner, [when] things contrary to the facts are written, it is natural that trust in the government is eroded... The government does a lot of good things. They are not on the news. If all that is reported is a dispute or a conflict, trust will be lost and democracy will not become reality. (*Matichon Sutsapda*, 20 August 1996)[22]

It was obvious that the media contributed significantly to the administration's unpopularity, and this substantially increased the pressure for political reform.

The slow progress on amending Article 211 of the 1991 Constitution attracted strong criticism, which added to the pressure for political reform. On 11 November 1995, Weng Tochirakan of the Confederation for Democracy announced that it was withdrawing its members from the Political Reform Committee, explaining that the Confederation had doubts about the enthusiasm and real intention of the government and the Committee. The Committee eventually proposed six principles for political reform to the government on 6 February 1996, but the government was slow to act. On 2 May 1996, five members of the Committee tendered their resignations as of 30 April. One of their stated reasons was, again, the prime minister's lack of enthusiasm for political reform. Their resignations stirred up further criticism.

Amid the growing criticism, the government finally introduced a bill to amend Article 211 to the Parliament on 17 May 1996. It contained four major points. First, a constitutional drafting committee consisting of experts and scholars should be set up. Second, political stability and efficiency should be promoted. Third, a national referendum should be held for approval of the draft constitution. Fourth, a democratic political regime with the King as the head of state should be maintained (Decho 1998: 89–90). Once the government bill was presented, a special committee to consider amendments and additions to Article 211 was created within the Parliament. It was chaired by Chaianan Samutthawanit (Chai-anan Samudavanija), a prominent political scientist and government appointed Senator who, together with Amon, advocated political reform based on 'constitutionalism.' The special committee decided on 20 June to proceed with the Constitution Drafting Assembly with ninety-nine members. The fierce debate that ensued over the matter of how to select the members of the Constitution Drafting Assembly coincided with a series of events that shook the government.

On 8 August 1996, Justice Minister Chaloem Yubamrung dropped a bombshell by revealing that hefty bribes had been offered by banks seeking approval for new banking licenses. On 14 August, when the budget bill was put to a vote, the Phalang Tham Party left the ruling coalition. All of this was in the background when the Parliament deliberated the special committee's Article 211 amendment bill on 22 August (the second reading) and reached the following decisions (*Matichon Sutsapda*, 27 August 1996).[23] The drafting body was to take the form of an assembly and its members were not to include MPs. Members were to be elected by the Parliament. The draft constitution was to require parliamentary approval (on the condition that a national referendum should be held if it was rejected by the Parliament). The ninety-nine members of the Drafting Assembly were to be comprised of seventy-six representatives from provinces and twenty-three scholars who were over the age of thirty-five and had a university or higher level of education.

Decision making was relatively easy up to this point but opinions were divided over the method for selecting provincial representatives. Chaianan proposed a general meeting method. An unlimited number of eligible candidates could stand for election to the assembly, come from all over the country to gather in one place and elect 228 candidates from among themselves. Then the Parliament would select seventy-six members out of the 228. The important point was that no distinction would be made according to their provinces at the time of the short-listing of the 228 candidates. All of them could be residents of Bangkok. Bangkok overwhelmed all other provinces in terms of the number of eligible people, the number of candidates, the name recognition of candidates and the abilities of candidates.[24]

The government counter-proposed that candidates should nominate themselves within the province where they are registered as residents. Following this all of the candidates and one representative from every local government body in each province (the provincial administrative organization, municipalities, sanitary districts, *tambon* administrative organizations and *tambon* councils[25]) should meet and elect three candidates. The Parliament would then select one of the three candidates from each province. Many opposition MPs opposed this government proposal. They argued that since there were around 100 local self-government organizations in each province, their representatives might well outnumber the candidates. They were also concerned that these local government representatives would not be able to remain neutral since they were obedient to the Interior Ministry, all the more serious because Prime Minister Banhan was also Interior Minister. Due to these disagreements, it was decided that the special parliamentary committee would reconvene on 29 August.

The committee completed the deliberation (the second reading) on 29 August. The twenty-three expert members of the assembly were to consist of eight public law scholars, eight public administration scholars and seven people with practical experience in the field of public administration and legal affairs. For the selection of provincial members, the committee decided that all the candidates in each province would meet and elect ten candidates from among themselves (each candidate had only three votes) and the Parliament would select one of the ten candidates for each province (*Matichon Sutsapda*, 3 September 1996). Some were dissatisfied that Parliament would be involved in the selection process. They were concerned that only candidates who were favorable to the government would be selected. As one weekly magazine put it:

> Now the possibility to realize such things as the separation of legislative and executive powers and the establishment of "iron rules" to regulate the activities of politicians in order to achieve what everyone sincerely hopes for, for example, to resolve the situation in which MPs are engrossed in becoming cabinet ministers in pursuit of self-interest, has become remote. (*Matichon Sutsapda*, 3 September 1996)

The 'separation of legislative and executive power' here simply means prohibiting elected MPs from becoming cabinet members. Distaste for the elected MPs was perhaps strong enough to lead to a rejection of the parliamentary cabinet system itself.

The opposition had already submitted one no-confidence motion against Prime Minister Banhan by then. Debate on the motion was scheduled to begin on 18 September. With the turbulent period only a few days away, the Bill for the Amendment of the 1991 Constitution was put to a vote on 14 September. It was passed by an overwhelming majority of the 604 members, all except for a handful of absentees and two abstainers[26] (*Nation Sutsapda*, 20 September 1996).

The debate about the no-confidence motion continued from 18 September until the night of 20 September. Sano Thiangthong (Snoh Thienthong), the leader of the largest faction in the ruling Chat Thai Party, and Chawalit, the leader of the ruling coalition's second largest party, the New Aspiration Party, urged Banhan to resign in exchange for a rejection of the motion. Banhan accepted their deal and announced at 11 a.m. on 21 September that he would resign within one week. The no-confidence motion was immediately brought forward and defeated, but the Prime Minister did not keep his word and dissolved the Parliament on 27 September, the deadline date for his resignation. On the same day as this unpopular government was swept from office, the Bill for the Amendment of the 1991 Constitution came into effect, paving the way for the drafting of a new constitution.

In the ensuing general election, in November 1996, the Sano faction abandoned the Chat Thai Party to join the New Aspiration Party which thereby became the leading party. Chawalit, its leader, was appointed prime minister. On 15 December 1996, under Chawalit's administration, a national election was held to select ten candidates for each of the seventy-six provinces. A total of 760 people were elected from 19,329 candidates. A breakdown by occupation indicates that lawyers formed the largest group, followed by businesspeople and bureaucrats.[27] On 26 December, Parliament elected members of the Constitution Drafting Assembly[28] (Figure 3.1).

Drafting the Constitution

Procedures for enacting a new constitution

The Constitution Drafting Assembly met for the first time on 7 January 1997 to elect its chairman. Former Speaker of the House of Representatives Uthai Phimchaichon won forty-four votes in the first round of voting and sixty-five votes in the runoff to defeat former Prime Minister Anan, who received twenty-seven votes and thirty votes in the respective ballots. Five committees were created within the CDA—the Constitution Drafting Committee, the Public Relations Committee, the Policy Research Committee for Science, Information and Constitution-related Legislation, the Assembly Record Committee, and the Public Comment and Hearing Committee. The Constitution Drafting Committee was the most important of all. Once the draft was completed, the Draft Constitution Amendment Committee was created.[29]

The CDA installed the Public Comment and Hearing Special Committee in each province based on the principle provided in Article 211 of the 1991 Constitution that the people's opinions should be incorporated in the constitution enactment process. At the same time, the Constitution Drafting Committee began to prepare a concept plan, which consisted of three pillars; rights and duties, the use of state power, and the political system. As each of the concepts was approved in turn by the CDA on 4 February, 18 February and 4 March 1996 (Montri et al. 1999: 32–3), it was released to the public and comments were invited.[30]

The subcommittee in charge of drawing the part of the plan concerning the political system had five members. Three, including Bowonsak Uwanno, were public law experts who had contributed to the fifteen volume research report at the Committee on Developing Democracy. The other two were academically-oriented with backgrounds in party politics. It is highly likely that the three full-time scholars and the CDD shared many ideological beliefs. According to the subcommittee's concept plan, the House of Representatives was to be comprised of 400 members representing local electoral districts and 100 members elected by a proportional representation system. Members of the Senate were to be elected by direct popular election rather than appointment or indirect election. Senators would have to have a university or higher education. Members of the House of Representatives would not be allowed to concurrently hold cabinet posts (*Nation Sutsapda*, 18 April 1997). The provisions in the final product, the 1997 Constitution, were very close to these draft proposals.

On 24 March, three subcommittees were established to draft a constitution based on the subcommittee's concept plan and the public's comments. Each subcommittee completed its own part of the draft during the period 1–10 April and the Office of the Council of State responsible for drafting law for the government integrated the three parts from 13 to 16 April. A working group comprising representatives from the Constitution Drafting Committee, three subcommittees and the Public Comment and Hearing Committee prepared a working draft of the new constitution in a Bangkok hotel from 17 to 20 April. The Constitution Drafting Committee worked to finalize the draft in a Phatthaya hotel from 21 to 27 April. CDA members who were not on the Drafting Committee were allowed to attend but were prohibited from speaking to save time (Montri et al. 1999: 35–7). The finalized first draft consisting of 339 articles was submitted to the CDA on 7 May. On 8 May, it was passed by an overwhelming majority: ninety-one in favor, one abstention and seven absent. The Draft Amendment Committee was then established within the CDA. The CDA members were given thirty days from 8 May to 7 June to submit their motions for amendment. Fifty-five motions were submitted for amendments to as many as 224 articles (Montri et al. 1999: 39–40).

The Public Comment and Hearing Committee printed and distributed 800,000 copies of a two-part booklet. Part 1 was the draft constitution. Part 2 was an

The 1997 Constitution and its Political Significance 133

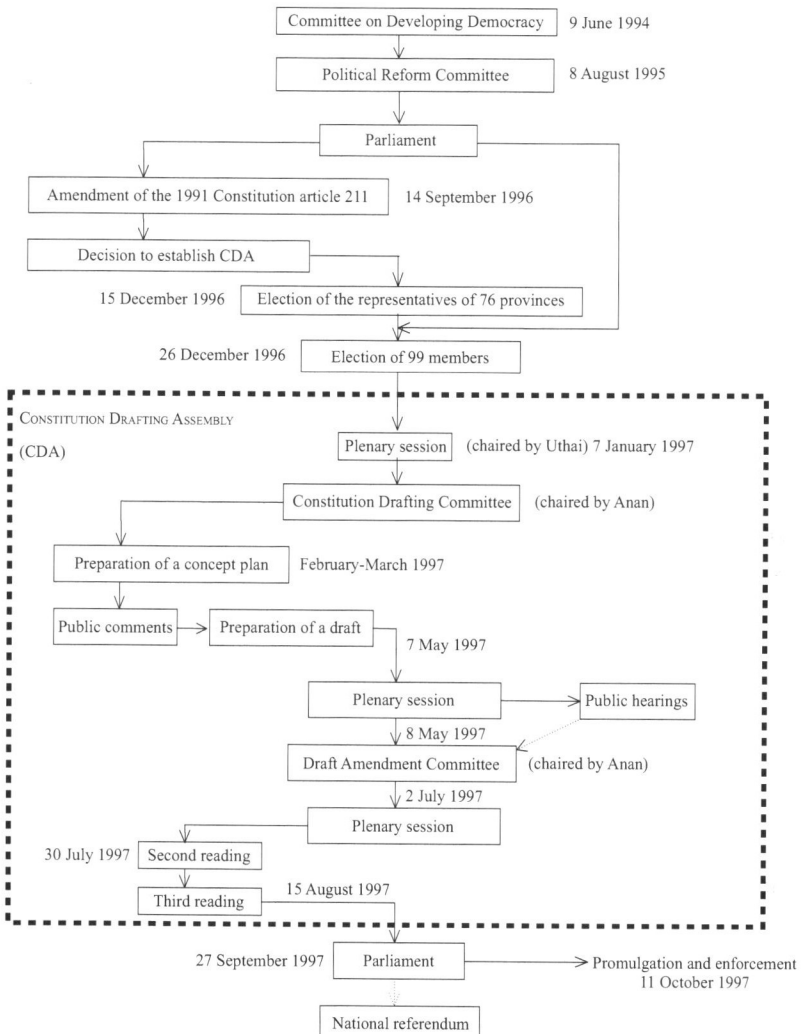

Figure 3.1 The 1997 Constitution drafting process

Source: Prepared by author.

explanatory note entitled 'What will the new constitution bring to the people?' written by Bowonsak, a jurist and secretary-general of the CDA. The booklet was widely publicized by the media and various public and private organizations. Members of the Provincial Public Comment and Hearing Special Committees around the country gathered in Bangkok from 9 to 11 May to prepare for public hearings based on the booklet. Public hearings were held in each province from 15 to 30 May. There were also five regional hearings (east, northeast, central, south and north) held from 16 to 25 May and one national public hearing in Parliament House on 10 June (Montri et al. 1999: 38–9).[31]

The Constitution Draft Amendment Committee considered the amendment motions with reference to the public's comments, finalized the second draft on 27 June and submitted it to the CDA on 2 July. The CDA began deliberating the draft on 3 July and spent nearly one month before completing the final draft with 336 articles on 30 July. The final draft was put to a vote in the CDA fifteen days later on 15 August and adopted by an overwhelming majority: ninety-two in favor, four abstained and three absent. It was presented to the Parliament on the same day (Table 3.2).

Rights and freedom

The 1997 Constitution was dubbed the 'people's constitution' by its creators. The concept plan prepared by the CDA members for hearing before March 1997 had been titled the 'Concept plan for drafting the people's constitution (*krop bueangton ratthathammanun chabap prachachon*)' (Decho 1998: 96), which appears to be the origin of the rhetorical expression. The praise refers to the fact that the opportunity to participate in the drafting process was made available to more people than ever before (Wanmuhamatno 1998: 19; Khanin 1998: 272), and it was made possible because Article 211(3) of the 1991 Constitution stipulated that the opinions of the people should be respected when drafting any new constitution. To meet this requirement, representatives of the provinces were included in the CDA; public meetings and hearings on the concept plan and the draft were conducted around the country; the Special Committee for Public Comments and Hearings met in each province; and other public hearings were conducted for business organizations, professional associations, the media, educational institutions and political parties. In the light of this unprecedented public consultation process, it was regarded as a 'genuine people's constitution' (Decho 1998: 107).[32] Moreover, there were provisions made for a national referendum if the draft was rejected by Parliament. Thus, there is no doubt that this constitution was far more participatory in the drafting process than any previous constitution in Thailand's history.

Table 3.2 The CDA work schedule

7 January 1997	The first session. Election of the speaker.
14 January 1997	Decision to set up five committees – drafting, public hearing, public relations, science and records.
20 January 1997	The first session of the drafting committee (twenty-nine members including chairman Anan). Work continues to 30 April.
8 May 1997	The CDA approves the committee's draft following deliberation on 7 and 8 May and sets up the draft amendment committee (thirty-three members including chairman Anan). Amendment work continues from 13 May to 2 July.
30 July 1997	The CDA finishes the second reading of the amended draft (examination of each article). Nation-wide public relations activity for fifteen days before a vote.
15 August 1997	The draft is passed (approved) by the CDA folowing the third reading. Ninety-two votes in favor, four abstention, one walkout and two absent.
4 September 1997	The parliament deliberates the draft from 4 to 10 September.
27 September 1997	The draft is passed by the parliament. Five-hundred and seventy-four votes in favor, sixteen against and seventeen abstention.
11 October 1997	Promulgation and enforcement of the new constitution.

Source: Prepared by author.

However, a constitution written *by the people* is not necessarily a constitution *for the people*. Its contents should be carefully examined to judge whether it will bring benefits to the people at large or not. The then Speaker of the Parliament expressed his pleasure that 'the people's rights and freedom were substantially expanded' (Wanmuhamatno 1998: 18). Bowonsak, one of the drafters, claimed that it 'expanded civil rights and freedom more than ever before,' observing that the new Constitution had fifty-three articles concerning rights, freedom and equality whereas the 1991 Constitution only had thirty (Bowonsak 1998: 52–3).[33] The new Constitution does include new provisions for social rights such as education, health services and assistance for the aged and the disabled. The concept of community rights proposed by the CDD was also incorporated, although its precise meaning remains somewhat ambiguous. These rights and freedoms were the selling points of the new Constitution, each of which was explained in detail in the pamphlet distributed by the CDD in August 1997. However, these provisions for social rights perhaps stand out primarily because they had been rather poorly dealt with in the past. At the same time, an increase in obligations tends to go unnoticed. Although the total number of articles concerning obligations was halved from ten to five, giving a surface impression that the number of obligations had actually been reduced, this was an illusion created by cramming seven articles of the 1991 Constitution into a single article in the new Constitution. The new Constitution added two new obligations—the obligation to vote and the obligation of public servants—while retaining the existing ten obligations (Bunloet 1998: 210–16.)

Among the rights and freedoms, provisions were made to increase the general public's participation in politics. Bowonsak highlights four such points: the right to petition for legislation by 50,000 signatures, to petition for the dismissal of ministers and MPs by 50,000 signatures, national referenda, and the popular election of senators (rather than government appointment) (Bowonsak 1998: 60–2). However, these come with conditions. For example, in a petition for legislation, petitioners must provide a draft bill as well as the requisite signatures. Further, this procedure is only applicable to legislation concerning rights, freedoms or fundamental state policies provided in the constitution.[34] On the provision for a referendum, there was heated debate about whether it should be included and whether its results should be binding. The 1974 Constitution was the only previous Thai constitution to have provisions for a national referendum, and it was limited to enacting or amending the constitution. Furthermore, no such referendum had ever been held. Hence, while drafting the 1997 Constitution, some people insisted that there not be any provision for a national referendum. They argued that the King should not be bothered with questions of which issues could be decided by referendum and were concerned that the King might be compelled to ratify the results of a referendum with no room for his discretion. After much discussion, it was finally decided that the provision should be included in the constitution on the condition that the referendum result should be taken as advice to the cabinet and not binding (Khanin 1998: 269–70).

The final decision was made in the CDA on 22 July 1997. Let us examine the minutes of the debates to see how the assembly reached the conclusion that the referendum would not have binding force. In response to the Constitution Drafting Committee's original proposal, which denied the referendum any binding force, Assemblyman Bunloet Khachayutthadet argued that it was wrong to treat referendum results as mere advice and that they should be binding on the government of the country (RPSR 24, 179 (88/1)). Assemblyman Suni Chaiyarot argued that they might as well abandon the provision because the complex implementation procedure raised doubts about its feasibility and that without binding force it would be a sham even if it was implemented (RPSR 24, 180–2 (88/2–89/20)). Assemblyman Sawat Khamprakop, a veteran politician, criticized the proposal sarcastically:

> If what the government wants is just advice, it does not need to hold a national referendum. It can ask *kamnan*, village chiefs, provincial governors, district officers or even the media. A national referendum is a very expensive exercise. The last general election cost 550 million baht. The government should cut expenditure in the current situation. As there are MPs and Senators it should be sufficient for the cabinet to consult them. Even if the government consults the people, they would not know the answer. Questions that the government wants to consult are always difficult ones. How can you expect the people to know the answers that the cabinet and the Parliament do not know? (RPSR 24, 183–6 (90/1–91/2))

In response to these criticisms, political scientist Suchit Bunbongkan of the Draft Amendment Committee explained that there are two types of referendum. According to Suchit, one is used when Parliament is unable to make a decision and asks the people instead. In this case, the result is binding and equivalent to law. Examples include the issues of divorce and abortion in Catholic countries. The other type of referendum is used by the government as a source of guidance and does not necessarily result in legislation.

> We need to recognize the fact that national referendum is fraught with problems in Thailand. Because national referendum is a new device and preparations have not been made, there is a risk that certain types of law may come into existence unless some restrictions are put in place. Some people may exert pressure to have a national referendum held in an attempt to create a particular law. It may threaten our national security or have an adverse effect[35] on our country.

For this reason, Suchit continues, it seems appropriate at this stage to treat a referendum result as advice to the cabinet with no legislative effect, and it should not go beyond seeking the opinions of the people on controversial bills that have divided the Parliament. Besides, Thailand has a House of Representatives and an elected government, which plays a major role in the country's decision making on behalf of the people. He concludes that there is no need to hold a national referendum on every issue,

Because the people are not necessarily capable of understanding the issue clearly and making a decision carefully. (RPSR 24, 182–3 (89/2–90/1), emphasis added)

The combination of consideration for the King and the view that the people are ignorant seems to have won the day. The original proposal was put to a vote where it was decided that referendum results would not be binding, with twenty-seven votes in favor and fifteen against. Hence, while the constitution drafters congratulated themselves on creating the 'people's constitution' which they claimed was open to increased participation by the people, they actually considered the people to be too ignorant to govern themselves wisely and feared their numbers.

This is just one of the more striking illustrations of why careful examination of the provisions of the 1997 Constitution are needed without simply accepting that it genuinely is the people's constitution. It should be kept in mind that the greatest point of contention in drafting the fifteen previous constitutions (and their amendments) since 1932 has always been the provisions concerning power relations. These are the provisions about the governing structure, especially the Parliament and the cabinet: Who is eligible to become prime minister and cabinet ministers? Can serving military officers and bureaucrats be cabinet ministers? Can popularly elected MPs join the cabinet? How much control does the Parliament have over the cabinet? Should the Parliament use a single-house or a two-house system? Should MPs be popularly elected or government appointed? If Parliament has both types of MPs, in what proportions should they be represented? What respective powers should the two types of MPs have? What electoral system should be used? The interests of the drafters have always been strongly reflected in these fundamental issues underlying the parliamentary system of government. Let us now look at how these particular issues were dealt with in the 1997 Constitution.

Honest politics: Changes to power relations
In drafting the new constitution, changes were made to the electoral system and the relationship between the Parliament and the cabinet, and the system for inspecting politicians was strengthened, with the aim of reducing corruption and cleaning up politics. This section examines three major areas of change that were meant to ensure honest politics, namely, reforms in the electoral system, addition of bachelor clause to MP's eligibility, and the establishment of several independent bodies to inspect politicians' activities. A repeatedly and widely acknowledged problem with the electoral system was that MPs who were elected owing to vote buying became cabinet ministers according to factional dynamics (which are defined by the number of MPs in each faction) and then worked to

recover their 'invested' funds using improper means. Several new measures were incorporated into the 1997 Constitution with the aim of resolving this problem.

Electoral system: The selection method for senators changed from government appointment to popular election.[36] It marked the creation of a Senate that had the potential to dilute the legitimacy conferred on the House of Representatives by its status as the only popularly elected house and to confront it squarely. 'The most important functions of the Senate are inspection and dismissal. In other words, it is the house of review' (Bowonsak 1998: 77).[37] The powers unique to the Senate include the power to select Election Commissioners, the Ombudsman, members of the National Human Rights Commission, judges of the Constitution and the Administrative Courts, and members of the National Counter Corruption Commission, as well as the power to dismiss members of the cabinet and the House of Representatives. It was explained that the power of dismissal was conferred to the senators because their constituencies were larger than those of lower house MPs and because they were not allowed to become cabinet members (Bowonsak 1998: 77). The total number of senators is 200. Each province forms an electoral district and is allotted a certain number of senators in proportion to its population. Election campaigning and re-election are banned. It was considered that, if electioneering similar to that of lower house MPs was allowed, senatorial candidates might as well engage in vote buying, then once they are elected turn to corruption in an effort to recover funds. Because the Senate is expected to perform different functions from those carried out by the House of Representatives, the eligibility criteria for appointment are also different. Senators are not allowed to become cabinet members during their term of office and for one year after the end of their term. They are not allowed to belong to any political party. Former members of the House of Representatives must wait for at least one year before standing for Senate election. These stipulations are designed to sever ties with cabinet members and political parties, who are the subject of senatorial inspection, and to make the inspection work easier. Senators must have a university or higher education and must be at least forty years old. This age limit is higher than the minimum of twenty-five for lower house MPs because senators are expected to have appropriate knowledge and experience.

The composition of the House of Representatives was changed to 100 seats for proportional representation plus 400 seats for single-seat districts. This was a significant change from the previous system with the maximum of three seats per electoral district.[38] Voting for the proportional representation seats is based on a fixed-list system in which political parties prepare a list of ranked candidates and voters choose a preferred political party. Seats are allocated to parties on the basis of their share of the vote, then to candidates of each party according to their rank on the list. According to Bowonsak, the closed list system was adopted for several reasons. First, vote buying is difficult because it is a nation-wide constituency. Second, wasted votes are minimized. Third, it will strengthen political parties. Fourth, it opens the door to the political world to those who are competent but not good at election campaigning. Fifth, people with a national perspective will be added to the House of Representatives. Sixth, parties are expected to rank their ministerial candidates higher in the list, which means that voters are indirectly selecting cabinet members (Bowonsak 1998: 64). Bowonsak points out that some improvements were also made to the single-seat electorate system. First, equality in voting has been achieved in that one person casts one vote regardless of which electoral district one lives in.[39] Second, it creates closer relationships between MPs and their constituencies. Third, the practice of vote buying is curtailed, so competent candidates with no financial resources can now enter Parliament (Bowonsak 1998: 66).

It is unlikely that anyone was convinced that the introduction of the single-seat district system would directly curtail vote buying. Most were expecting other effects, one of which was a closer relationship between each MP (or potential candidate) and his or her electorate in a smaller electoral district, as Bowonsak points out. Some candidates may win because they look after their electorate well, rather than simply because they are financially resourceful (Khanin 1998: 234).

More importantly, the CDA chairman Uthai Phimchaichon, a lower house MP for many years, pointed out that the main purpose of the new system was to 'fight off the kingpin (*luk phi*).' According to Uthai, electoral districts under the previous system were too large for candidates to achieve any significant name recognition among their voters, hence they had to rely on local influential figures (kingpins) and resort to vote buying. Uthai explained by telling a hypothetical story citing the name of the president of the Songkhla provincial Chamber of Commerce Chan Itsara, who is also known in Bangkok: Chan is a well-known businessperson in his local town of Hat Yai, but three kilometers out of town, no one has heard of him. If he wants to run for election, he must rely on an influential figure to cover the large electoral district. Operators of illegal lotteries (*huai taidin*) are perfect for the job. An operator has many lottery ticket sellers under him who each deal with many more customers. In the lead-up to an election, lottery ticket sellers distribute 500 baht to each of their customers in exchange for casting their vote to a particular candidate. Customers are free to put the money in their pocket or to purchase more lottery tickets. Either way, they are obliged to vote for a particular candidate. There is a relationship of trust between the lottery ticket seller and his customers (otherwise transactions could not be effected). It becomes possible to estimate the number of votes based on the number of people who accepted the sellers' distributions. The illegal lottery operator can thus decide who will win the seat. If politicians do not comply with the wishes of these influential figures, they will not receive their support in the next election, and hence, they will not be re-elected. This is solely because of the difficulty involved for candidates to gather votes on their own in a large electoral district under the previous system.[40] In smaller district, there is less need for candidates to turn to a local kingpin or to buy votes (Uthai 1998: 25–6).

The image of a 'kingpin' who controls MPs refers to the boss of a political faction rather than to an influential local figure who remains behind the scenes. Under the previous electoral system, voters could cast one vote for each of the seats in their electoral district. Some districts had one or two seats but most had three. It was not difficult, or uncommon, for a powerful MP to form a team with two unknown candidates and make a clean sweep of the three seats. This MP has already become the boss of a minor faction at that stage. MPs such as this have helped many of their factional colleagues to win seats in other districts of the same province or neighboring provinces. Under the 1991 Constitution, there were nearly 400 lower house seats and a maximum of forty-six cabinet posts. If there were, for example, 230 MPs in the ruling coalition, this equated to one cabinet post for every five MPs. Hence, any MP who headed a faction of five MPs, including three from his own electorate plus two from elsewhere, was almost guaranteed a cabinet position regardless of his administrative ability or aptitude. In contrast, in single-seat electorates, each candidate would have to achieve at least a minimal level of popularity or profile on his or her own. The assumption was that this would make winning difficult for candidates whose only real credentials were to be someone's underling, and also make it hard for kingpins to secure cabinet posts. It should also be noted that the 1997 Constitution increased the number of MPs in the House of Representatives while cutting the number of cabinet posts by ten to thirty-six.

The real significance of the new electoral system becomes clearer when considered in conjunction with the new rule that lower house MPs must resign their seats if they take cabinet posts—i.e., they cannot concurrently hold a lower house seat and a cabinet post. This was not unprecedented—the 1968 Constitution under a military government prohibited lower house MPs from becoming prime minister or cabinet members. In comparison, the 1997 Constitution provides that the prime minister must be a lower house MP and allows lower house MPs to become cabinet members.[41] However, once they become cabinet members, they lose their seats in the House of Representatives.[42] When a lower house MP takes a cabinet post, a by-election will be held if he is a single-seat district MP, or the candidate ranked next on the list of the same party will be elected as a substitute if he is a party-list MP. This may have the effect of restraining the desire of single-seat district MPs to enter cabinet.[43] If an MP joins the cabinet and his rival wins the by-election, the next general election will inevitably be a fierce battle between de facto incumbents. Moreover, if an MP is appointed to a cabinet post but later dismissed for corruption or incompetence, he cannot return to the House of Representatives until the next election. This constitution thus discourages single-seat district MPs, who tend to strongly represent the interests of their local constituencies, from taking cabinet posts and thus, by default, encourages party-list MPs to enter the cabinet. According to Bowonsak, the party-list MPs supposedly have a more 'national' perspective and the proportional representation system is intended to curtail vote buying.

The new constitution has also taken a number of other 'measures to reduce and eliminate vote buying' (Bowonsak 1998: 63). Specifically, voting has been made compulsory and voting by overseas nationals is allowed, as well as absentee voting and blank voting (voting for no one)—all aimed at increasing the number of voters and making vote buying more difficult. The new constitution also stipulates that the approval of the Election Commission is required for any personnel change in government following dissolution of the Parliament in order to prevent improper interference by the cabinet. Third, the government will provide a certain level of financial support for election campaigning in order to ensure fairness. Fourth, the Election Commission has been established. Fifth, ballot boxes are to be gathered and counted all together at one place in each electoral district rather than at each polling station. Of the measures highlighted by Bowonsak, the most important is the establishment of the Election Commission, followed by the changes in vote counting methods. Responsibility for the conduct of elections has been handed over to the newly established Election Commission from the Interior Ministry. The Commission is independent from Parliament and the cabinet and has large powers.

Uthai points out that the new vote counting method will help prevent moneyed elections. A decade ago, 'voters… were criticized for being preoccupied with power poles (in hopes of electrification)' (Uthai 1998: 29). According to Uthai, this was because ballot boxes were opened and votes were counted at each polling station. Pledges made by candidates to vote-gathering brokers, including the erection of a temple, the construction of an irrigation pond, or the purchase of a pickup truck, were honored if they won the number of votes promised by the brokers. This was why voters cast their votes diligently. Even school teachers cast their votes in order to have a library or a kitchen at their schools. Under the new constitution, ballot boxes will be opened all together in each district to prevent this situation. Candidates and voters will not be able to have a breakdown of votes of each polling station, thus candidates will not have to honor their promises to the brokers (Uthai 1998: 29–30).[44] Furthermore, it was not unheard of for candidates to bribe or threaten election officials when the ballot boxes

Table 3.3 Proportion of university graduates in the total population (%)

Year	No education	Primary	Secondary	University
1960	38.1	58.4	3.0	0.5
1970	26.4	68.0	4.9	0.7
1980	16.0	72.4	9.4	2.2
1990	10.7	70.7	13.6	5.0

Source: Based on data published on the website of the national statistical office of the prime minister's department (http://www.nso.go.th/thai/stat/pop-hou/tab6.htm)

were opened at individual polling stations. This conduct should be more readily preventable with vote counting carried out all together.

The new constitution also aimed to block bribery from another angle. In Thailand, election-related bribery has been rife at four levels: businesspeople buying off political parties, political parties buying off candidates, candidates buying off vote brokers, and vote brokers buying off voters.[45] The last two were considered to be the most problematic by the advocates of political reform. It was expected that the newly created Election Commission would be able to impose some controls on these practices, aided by the introduction of a proportional representation system, and the prohibition on concurrently holding a lower house seat and a cabinet post. Furthermore, donations to parties and politicians would be regulated to some extent by the auditing of politicians for improper moneymaking, improved transparency of political donations, and public funding for political parties. To address the problem of political parties buying serving MPs before elections, the new constitution provided that lower house MPs should be members of political parties and should remain members of one party for at least ninety days prior to the registration of their candidacy. It also provided that an election should be held within forty-five days from the full term of the Parliament or sixty days from the dissolution of the Parliament, making it impossible for serving MPs to switch parties immediately before a general election.[46]

These and other changes to the election system were expected to help reduce vote buying and thus curtail MPs' pursuit of self-interest. In addition, an inspection mechanism for MPs and cabinet members was developed. Before we discuss the inspection mechanism, though, we must consider another important change to the election system: the provision that cabinet members, Senators, Members of the House of Representative, and the members (and judges) of some independent inspection authorities must have a bachelor's degree or higher education qualifications.

Why bachelor clause?: The new constitution has a novel rule that Members of Parliament and the cabinet must have a bachelor's degree or higher education qualifications. According to an estimate by Pasuk and Baker, 90% of the adult population, 95% of the adult rural population and 99% of farmers are disqualified by this rule (2000: 188).[47] Considering that only 5% of the total population had a bachelor's degree or higher qualification as of 1990, it is an extremely uncommon and severely limited 'democracy' that only grants eligibility for election to such a small section of society (Table 3.3).

As is generally known, election systems around the world have evolved from limited suffrage for wealthy men based on the amount of tax paid to universal and equal suffrage following the abolition of restrictive rules concerning property and sex. The principle of equality, which is the foundation of democracy, has been taken into consideration. Thailand had been conducting universal and equal elections since 1933 when the representative parliamentary system was introduced after the coup d'état in the previous year against absolute monarchy. Although there were times when a popularly elected parliament was abolished, suffrage had never been limited on the grounds of wealth or sex. It is somewhat ironic, then, that the 1997 Constitution introduced a limited electoral system to Thailand for the first time—a stark contrast to the much lauded notion of the 'people's constitution.' This contradiction, in turn, is a clear indication of the fundamental nature of this constitution.

Why is a bachelor's degree required to be eligible to stand for election? There is no persuasive argument for this stipulation in any of the numerously published commentaries on the 1997 Constitution.[48] Bowonsak touches on this bachelor clause for parliamentarians and cabinet members as an example of expanded freedom of education and research (Bowonsak 1998: 53). He argues that this provision will promote the spread of higher education. He is virtually saying that those who want to become politicians should go to university, an admonishment that makes little sense to those who are already past school age. This point-of-view ignores the fact that financial and time constraints make it very difficult for many primary and secondary school students to pursue higher education, should they want to.

What exactly was the reasoning for introducing the bachelor clause? The CDD's initial proposal had included this qualification for the Senate because it was expected to perform the special function of inspecting the House of Representatives and the cabinet. The rule came to be extended to members of the cabinet and the House of Representatives about halfway through the drafting process. According to the CDA minutes, the bachelor clause for lower house MPs was added at a plenary session of the CDA on 15 July 1997 and for cabinet members, at a plenary session on 22 July. Let us review the discussions at these sessions through the minutes, beginning with the session on 15 July.

1. Bachelor clause for lower house MPs

Kamon Sukkhasombat (member for Sing Buri province) was the first to propose the addition of the bachelor clause at the 15 July session. According to interviews and various opinion polls in his province, he says, 'most people prefer lower house MPs who are university graduates because they want them to have a certain level of knowledge and ability... [and] Article 211 of the [1991] constitution provides that the opinions of the people must be respected in drafting a constitution.' Furthermore, he argued, politics has nothing to lose and much to gain from the inclusion of this clause, because it helps to screen candidates for the House of Representatives. 'A bachelor's degree is useful in determining a person's knowledge and abilities.' His argument followed like this: the objective of the draft constitution is political reform; the educational qualification is essential because political reform means making improvements to politics so that it is more adaptable to current and future changes; particularly in the present global environment, the country needs virtuous and knowledgeable people. The third point of his argument addressed the powers of lower house MPs. He pointed out that the bachelor's clause was included for senators whose power is limited to review bills and for the Election Commission members whose sole duty is to conduct free and fair elections. Similarly, he noted that the clause was being proposed to be included for provincial council members in a bill then under discussion in the Parliament. Therefore, he concluded, the bachelor clause should be included for members of the House of Representatives as well, because those who are given broad and important powers should possess virtue, knowledge, ability and a broad perspective (RPSR, 19, 81/1–81/2, 82/1).

Thawon Chansom (member for Buri Ram province) proposed a similar amendment, stating:

> Educational qualifications show facts. By receiving university or higher education, people can acquire knowledge in philosophy and various other areas and understand various social and human issues. People with just four years of primary education or secondary education do not learn that much and do not have the capacity to understand issues deeply enough to be involved in the governance of the country... In the old days, it was not appropriate to include such a clause since there were very few university graduates. These days, the number of university graduates has increased, and compulsory education is extended to twelve years (in the draft constitution). People will have higher educational qualifications from

now on, which is the prime reason for my proposal... There are people who have excellent knowledge and ability without a university education. I do not deny that. However, there is no doubt that their knowledge and ability are not as good as those of university graduates. (RPSR, 19, 84/1–84/2, 85/1)

Panya Singsakda (member for Nakhon Ratchasima province) also proposed an amendment which included the education qualification clause on the grounds that it would ensure that competent people would enter the Parliament (RPSR, 19, 87/1–87/2).

Political scientist Amon Raksasat (expert member) threw cold water on these arguments. He observed that in countries such as France, Japan, Italy, Germany, Switzerland, Australia, Cambodia and Netherlands age requirement is the only difference in the eligibilities for voting and holding office. Having more conditions for eligibility, he argued, would 'narrow the range of choices for voters and keep candidates remote from the people' (RPSR, 19, 88/1–88/2).

Lueam Phanloek (member for Surin province), after a long, meandering statement during which he was cautioned by the chairman several times, said, 'Those of us who are sitting here now are university graduates according to Article 211 of the Constitution. We are all university graduates. It is a really wonderful idea.' When he was asked by the chairman to clarify the point, he said, 'I would like to express my support for assembling university graduates at the CDA. I am in favor' (RPSR, 19, 89/1–89/2, 90/1–90/2).

Sanan Inthraprasoet (member for Nakhon Nayok province) agreed that the requirement for a bachelor's or higher degree should be added.

> The draft proposed by the committee has no educational qualification requirement at all. Not even things like a certificate of completion of the four-year primary education or a level of literacy. I think it is very dangerous, because to become a Member of Parliament—representative of the people—does require a certain level of knowledge. I once conducted a survey to ask people with various educational backgrounds such as four years of primary education, three years of secondary education and six years of secondary education about their own educational qualifications and their expectations for educational qualifications of parliamentarians. Most of the people with primary and secondary education qualifications wanted their MPs to have a bachelor's degree. University graduates wanted MPs with a master's degree and those with a master's degree wanted MPs with a doctorate... It is necessary to stipulate an education qualification requirement clearly. In fact, it does not matter whether it is six years of secondary education, a bachelor's degree or a master's degree as long as the education qualification requirement is stipulated. It is assuring to know that our MPs have

satisfied a certain education qualification requirement. Surprisingly, however, no such clause is found in the draft. It is conceivable that someone from the Meo hill tribe, for example, makes fortune in opium trades, buys votes and wins an election despite having no education at all. What will happen to this country then? I would like to ask my fellow esteemed members of the assembly. Please include a clause that honorable members of the House of Representatives must at least have a bachelor's degree. This is for the country, the people, all of us, not for a particular individual. (RPSR, 19, 94/1–94/5 (193–4))

Jurist Phongthep Thepkanchana (member for Samut Sakhon province) acknowledged, 'We received a lot of feedback from people at public hearings that they wanted a certain education qualification requirement. They believe that the higher the education qualification, the higher the standard of lower house MPs.' Yet he pointed out that the committee deliberated this issue carefully and decided not to include an education qualification rule for three reasons.

The majority of the people have not completed university education. If we stipulate that candidates for the House of Representatives must be university graduates, we would exclude a majority of the people and deprive them of the opportunity to become Members of Parliament. Second, although education means more knowledge, higher standards and greater work efficiencies, education is not confined to classrooms nor limited to the acquisition of a bachelor's degree or certificates. It is possible to develop human resources through education outside of classrooms, that is, learning through experiences and day-to-day work. Third, another important point is that I believe we should let voters exercise their right to decide what kind of people they want to choose as their MPs. We are introducing compulsory voting. However, voters are supposed to have the right to decide who to elect. Are we justified in depriving voters of this opportunity?

He also observed the gradual rise in the educational qualifications of lower house MPs, that is, an initially small but now larger number of university graduates, and even some master's and doctoral degree holders are in the lower house. He upheld the decision of the draft amendment committee not to add the education qualification requirement in order to give the people the right to a wide range of choices (RPSR, 19, 95/1–95/2 (195–6)).

After the discussions, the issue of a bachelor clause was put to a vote by a show of hands. Thirty-three members were in favor and twenty-six were against. Thongchat Rattanawicha requested another vote as the voting result had a narrow margin. Others seconded and another vote was taken. This time, thirty-five voted in favor and twenty-seven voted against (RPSR, 19, 98/1–98/2

(201–2)). Consequently, it was decided that the bachelor clause for lower house MPs would be included in the constitution.

2. Bachelor clause for cabinet members
As mentioned, there was no bachelor clause for cabinet members in the original draft. It was first proposed at the draft amendment committee on 21 June but was voted down. However, a week after the bachelor clause for members of lower house MPs was adopted, a plenary session of the CDA on 22 July decided that the same requirement should be adopted for cabinet members.

a) Discussions at the draft amendment committee on 21 June
It was the former Education Ministry official Decho Sawananon (member for Surat Thani province), who proposed that the bachelor clause should apply to cabinet members. He argues:

> While the CDA is targeting lower house MPs, cabinet members who are in charge of governing the country carry a greater responsibility about misgovernment than lower house MPs, who are only responsible for legislation. Strangely, the draft has a more stringent rule for senators than for cabinet members by requiring senators to have a bachelor's or higher degree.
>
> The people at public hearings and meetings mentioned two things as desirable qualities in cabinet members. One quality related to knowledge and ability (*khunnawutthi*). They indicated their strong preference for someone with comprehensive knowledge and multilingual skills, i.e., an expert or a specialist. The other quality related to morality, integrity and honesty. These two qualities mean, in short, being a university graduate. The education policy of our country has consistently placed equal emphasis on academic ability and morality. It has aimed to produce university graduates who have both the knowledge of a philosopher and the morality of a good observer of the Buddhist precepts. Therefore, a bachelor's or higher education is a desirable qualification requirement. Equivalent qualifications are not permissible. One must have graduated from university. Graduates of socially unacceptable universities are not permissible either. (RPKP, 21 Mithunayon 2540, 2/4–2/6)

Thongchat (member for Nakhon Si Thammarat province) supported this proposal, arguing:

> We are trying to carry out political reform and would like to entrust the running of the country to the hands of people who have widely recognized abilities and knowledge. Therefore, cabinet members must be persons who are at least endorsed by the education system of this country as being capable of making proper

judgments. This means having a bachelor's degree. Second, the new constitution aims to have cabinet members selected from party-list MPs. Candidates on the party-lists will be those who have a nation-wide profile. Having a nation-wide profile means that the person is highly educated and trusted by most people. It is thus appropriate to have a bachelor's degree as the criterion for such a person. Finally, the people at public hearings and meetings all said that cabinet ministers should have a bachelor's or higher degree. (RPKP, 21 Mithunayon 2540, 2/6)

Samat Kaeomichai (member for Chiang Rai province) proposed an amendment to include qualifications equivalent to a bachelor's degree while expressing his support of the rule in principle:

Despite the desire of some of the people to require a university or higher qualification for lower house MPs, the draft does not have such a requirement for lower house MPs. This is because lower house MPs are the representatives of the people and reflect the real situation with the people. They may not be university graduates but may have sufficient knowledge and ability to understand their problems. This is why the bachelor clause for lower house MPs has not been included. However, cabinet positions require a certain level of academic qualification and work experience. I have two reports from public hearings. One is a report on the results of public hearings conducted by the CDA in each province. According to the report, many people expressed the view that cabinet members should at least have a bachelor's degree. Moreover, many people wanted their prime minister to have at least a master's degree and the ability to speak at least one foreign language. The other report, which is a public opinion poll conducted by a college, shows a similar result. A bachelor's degree for cabinet members and a master's degree for prime minister. Accordingly, it is appropriate to use a bachelor's degree as the education qualification requirement for cabinet members. (RPKP, 21 Mithunayon 2540, 2/7)

Scholar Kasem Sirisamphan (expert member) countered that the bachelor's clause would

Disqualify those with excellent abilities and ethics who have missed the opportunity to receive a university education. There are people who did not have the opportunity for education but are well equipped with experience, abilities and ethics, and these people would not be able to become cabinet members. For example, people such as Prime Minister John Major and former Prime Minister Winston Churchill of the United Kingdom could not become prime minister in Thailand. These outstanding people would not be given a chance.

He also pointed out that the leaders of farmers' and workers' groups, no matter how competent and virtuous they are, would be disqualified because they are not university graduates. Since he was not a CDA member elected from a province, he states

> I cannot say what the people want. I need to listen respectfully to what provincial representatives say. If provincial representatives tell me that that is what the people of their provinces want, I must respect their wishes. Still, I ... would like to state that having such a clause would deprive some outstanding people who missed out on an education of the chance to assume important political posts. (RPKP, 21 Mithunayon 2540, 2/8)

Phongthep Thepkanchana followed, arguing against the requirement. He said he could understand how the people feel when he reflects on politics in the past. There were cabinet members who had no university education. They did not perform well at work. However, many of the cabinet members who had a bachelor's, master's or doctor's degree equally performed poorly.

> Education is not about studying at university for four years. Some people are still empty-headed after four years at university. By learning for ten, twenty years... other than at university, people can gain far greater practical experience than those who study at university... There are many examples in Thailand. Thai businesspeople are conducting business extensively, even overseas, but many of them only have had a primary education... I feel that we might take away opportunities from capable people and narrow down our choices of suitable candidates for the prime ministership. (RPKP, 21 Mithunayon 2540, 2/8–3/1)

Phinthip Lilaphon (member for Songkhla province) added an astute observation:

> Bachelor clause is being proposed in search of virtuous and competent people, but virtuous and competent people are not found only among university graduates. People are seeking cabinet members with virtue, integrity and ethics. Therefore, the rule should stipulate that a cabinet member should be a person of ethics, knowledge and integrity instead of one with educational qualifications. (RPKP, 21 Mithunayon 2540, 3/1)

The vote was a 12–12 tie (four abstained). The draft amendment committee chairman cast the deciding vote for the original proposal according to precedent.

As a result, it was decided by only one vote that the bachelor clause should not be included (RPKP, 21 Mithunayon 2540, 3/2–3/3).

b) Discussions at the plenary session on 22 July
Despite the decision by the draft amendment committee, Thongchat started the argument again in favor of inserting the bachelor clause.

> Because we have received a lot of feedback from the people saying that cabinet members should be equipped with appropriate scholarship and knowledge and sufficient ability to run the government and should possess at least a bachelor's degree-level of knowledge. This is the view expressed by my fellow countrymen at the hearings.

Since the bachelor clause for lower house members was added, he argued, 'cabinet members also should have a university or higher education to ensure consistency' (RPSR, 24, 71/2 (145)).

Former member of the House of Representatives, Prathuang Khamprakop (member for Nakhon Sawan province), requested the inclusion of an extra requirement that a cabinet member should be 'a person with an excellent background in his work, ethics, morality, conduct, knowledge and ability' worthy of a cabinet minister, in addition to the bachelor clause (RPSR, 24, 71/2 (145)).

Phinthip requested the addition of a requirement for 'proven knowledge, morality and integrity,' arguing:

> A minister is required to be a person who has abilities, who has no trouble with morality, and who is at least honest; a person who is capable of carrying out his duties efficiently. I believe that these points should be included in the provision. Some may say it is unrealistic. However we want a minister to be equipped with such qualities. (RPSR, 24, 72/1 (146))

Decho declared that the required qualifications for ministers should be stricter than those for lower house MPs and suggested that the wording should be changed to 'not lower than a bachelor's degree' by omitting 'or its equivalent' (RPSR, 24, 72/1 (146)). Samat countered that the word 'its equivalent' should be included just like the adopted requirement for lower house MPs because they were also allowed to become cabinet members (RPSR, 24, 72/1–72/2 (146–7)). Amnuai Thaiyanon (member for Prachuap Khiri Khan province) proposed the wording, 'not lower than a bachelor's degree recognized by the Civil Service Commission' (RPSR, 24, 72/2 (147)).

After this exchange of arguments, the amendment to add 'not lower than a bachelor's degree or its equivalent' was put to a vote. A majority voted in favor of the amendment and the education qualification requirement for cabinet members was adopted (RPSR, 24, 72/2 (147–8)).

3. Reasons for the inclusion of the bachelor clause

As we have seen, the CDA members who proposed the addition of the bachelor clause cited three main reasons. First, and most frequently, they claimed that it was proposed by many of the people at the public hearings and meetings. Second, they argued ethical and competent individuals are essential to realizing honest and efficient politics and only university graduates could meet this requirement. Third, they suggested that senators have to be university graduates, and therefore lower house MPs should be university graduates, and therefore cabinet ministers should be too. All of these reasons are superficial and unconvincing.

Although the 'wish of the people' was cited as the strongest reason, it should be noted that the CDA did not always have great respect for the people's opinions. For example, despite very strong demands for the prime minister to be directly elected by popular vote, the CDA was determined to dissuade the public from pursuing this idea (Uthai 1998: 32–5; Connors 1999: 217).[49] It is also important to note that the people who actively attended public hearings were typically highly educated, i.e., university graduates. Very few members of the general populace attended the hearings and they did not seem to voice their opinions. Furthermore, when presented with multiple hypothetical candidates of the same age, background, appearance and other conditions and asked to choose solely on the basis of educational qualifications, there is no reason not to choose the one with the higher educational qualification. Some people may say that a lower educational qualification is acceptable, but it is inconceivable that they would find it preferable. Since it is likely that the survey questions about desirable educational qualifications were asked in this manner, we must be wary of their findings. Finally, the CDA members were themselves university graduates. Even allowing that Uthai, Chairman of the CDA, was correct when he wrote: 'This is based on the majority opinion of the people. Drafters did not include the bachelor clause because they themselves were bachelor's degree holders. Mr. Anan is a university graduate but he argued that they did not have to be university graduates' (Uthai 1998: 12–13). We must nevertheless consider that the drafters, or at least the majority, were unlikely to be sensitive to the suffering caused by this rule since they were themselves university graduates. Moreover, because there are only a small number of university graduates in Thailand, this rule puts them in a considerably advantageous position in elections. From the perspective of the personal interests of the CDA members, then, there was no

Table 3.4 Educational qualification of lower house candidates and winners in recent years

	March 1992		July 1995		November 1996	
	Candidates	Winners	Candidates	Winners	Candidates	Winners
Below bachelor's degree	55.28%	30.97%	42.12%	27.37%	50.56%	26.46%
Bachelor's degree	35.32%	48.86%	44.85%	47.06%	38.05%	44.78%
Master's degree	5.89%	15.34%	8.43%	17.39%	8.14%	21.12%
Doctorate	2.74%	4.83%	3.63%	6.14%	2.81%	7.12%
Other	1.72%	2.27%	0.97%	2.05%	0.43%	0.51%
	100.00%	100.00%	100.00%	100.00%	100.00%	100.00%

Source: Based on data from Kromkanpokhrong (1992; 1995; 1996)

reason to actively oppose the inclusion of this rule. Hence, very few of them gave serious consideration to Amon's and Phongthep's warnings that the rule would deprive the majority of the people of the right to stand for office.

The second assertion—that ethical politicians are needed to reduce corruption and clean up politics and only university graduates are equipped with such ethics—is simply a groundless presumption. As is evident in some of the arguments cited above, many of the CDA members' intelligence and wisdom was highly questionable although they were all university graduates. Another, more important, substantiation is the proportion of university graduates in the House of Representatives, rising from 52.5% in 1983, to 60.8% in 1986 and 63.0% in 1988 (Manut 1986: 382–4, 493–5; SLR 1989: 228). This figure increased further to over 70% in the 1990s, as indicated in Table 3.4. The increasing proportion of university-educated MPs directly corresponds to an increasing proportion of university-educated cabinet members. Yet it is widely accepted that political corruption became quite blatant following the beginning of the Chatchai administration in 1988. In other words, corruption seems to have worsened as the number of university-educated lower house MPs and cabinet members increased. This suggests that a high educational qualification does not guarantee honesty or cleanliness and, worse still, might even suggest that highly-educated people thrive on corrupt activities. Hence, the assertion that a higher educational qualification would lead to more ethical politics was merely empty speculation. Another important fact revealed in Table 3.4 is that while 70% of successful candidates had a bachelor's or higher degree, one-half of the total candidates had an education level lower than university.

The third reason is simply and completely illogical. The requirement for senators to have a bachelor's or higher degree was introduced because senators were expected to perform the important function of inspecting lower house MPs and cabinet members, who were deemed to be 'neither competent nor ethical.' In short, the qualification requirement was intended to distinguish senators from lower house MPs and cabinet members. Clearly, this original intention was forgotten as function came to be confused with power. Soon it was argued that since lower house MPs had more power than senators, and cabinet members had more powers than lower house MPs, the minimum educational qualification for lower house MPs and cabinet members should not be any less than for senators, contrary to the original objective. That a number of CDA members cited this as a reason suggests either poor reasoning abilities or poor memories, or both.

After we dismiss these superficial and illogical 'reasons' we can perhaps attribute the inclusion of the bachelor clause to the generalized distrust of or distaste for the populace that is expressed throughout the minutes of the constitution drafters' discussions about the merits of a referendum. Biased by distrust or arrogance, they disregarded the fact that the majority of lower house MPs were already university graduates when they claimed that university graduates would run politics more ethically and efficiently. In a real sense, then, their condemnation of political practices was directed at the uneducated voters rather than the standing lower house MPs. They appear to believe that not only are the candidates to blame for corrupt money politics, but also the uneducated, poor and vulgar populace who take their money; and, hence, the governance of the country should not be left in their hands. The drafters' contempt for the populace was shared by both the intellectuals and the mass media advocating political reform, as well as by many urban residents. For example, Prawet argued at the commencement of the drafting process in December 1996 that there was no need to hold a national referendum to enact a new constitution. He claimed that a sufficient level of participation would be achieved by the public hearings, and therefore Parliament should approve the draft bill without delay. 'A national referendum at the final stage of the enactment process is unnecessary. The people have already participated in it.' Another reason was that 'the holding of a national referendum may cause some problems because of the immaturity of Thai society' (Prawet 1997a: 125–6). Although Prawet did not specify, the 'problem' referred to here means 'rejection of the proposal.' He feared that the draft constitution might be rejected if the final decision was left to the masses. From the outset Prawet hoped for the participation of the 'public (*satharana*)' comprising 'academics, the media, development NGOs, community leaders... the business community (*phak thurakit*)' (Prawet 1997a: 81).[50] He excluded the populace, including farmers and laborers. Prawet also points to 'a major conflict' in Thai politics that 'lies between the city and rural areas. Poor rural areas, bound by the patron-client relationship, elect people like the current MPs for the House of Representatives. Although politicians claim the legitimacy of their elections, the media and city residents are not impressed' (Prawet 1997a: 95). While he recognizes this conflict, though, he considers the drafting of a constitution to be a matter of concern only to city residents and does not expect rural residents to participate. We can assume similar views were widespread in certain influential circles, since the bachelor clause received hardly any criticism from intellectuals and the media who supported political reform, not to mention the drafters themselves.[51]

Inspection: The new constitution provides for the establishment of several agencies to inspect politicians.[52] The Election Commission mentioned above is one of them. This Commission not only organizes elections but also validates and invalidates winning candidates and identifies election irregularities. The most anticipated tasks of the Commission are prevention and prosecution of vote buying offences. The Commission has five members who are required to be at least forty years old and have at least a university degree or equivalent qualification. They are not allowed to hold any other job, and their term of office is seven years with no reappointment. A selection panel of ten members, including the President of the Constitution Court, the President of the Supreme Administrative Court, four people mutually elected among the Rectors of all state higher education institutions and four representatives of political parties, nominates five candidates, while the Supreme Court of Justice also nominates its own five. Among the ten nominees, five will be elected by the Senate through a secret ballot and appointed by the King.

The second such agency is the National Counter Corruption Commission. It verifies the personal assets declared by politicians and examines their financial records for signs of improper accumulation of assets. If a declaration is found to be false, the case is referred to the Constitution Court for its decision for a five year-suspension of the offender's civil rights. A case of suspected improper accumulation of assets is referred to the Supreme Court of Justice's Criminal Division for Persons Holding Political Positions for further investigation. If a complaint alleging corruption or improper accumulation of assets by a prime minister or parliamentarian[53] is signed by more than three-quarters of lower house MPs or more than 50,000 voters and submitted to the President of the Senate, the Commission investigates the allegation and refers any suspicious case to the Senate for dismissal proceedings and to the Attorney General for trial. The Attorney General sends the case for indictment to the Supreme Court of Justice's Criminal Division for Persons Holding Political Positions if the accused is a politician or to a regular court if the accused is not a politician. This Commission is a powerful watchdog against corrupt activities of politicians.

The Commission is comprised of nine members. Candidates are nominated by the selection panel, selected by the Senate and appointed by the King. The selection panel has fifteen members consisting of the President of the Supreme Court of Justice, the President of the Constitution Court, the President of the Supreme Administrative Court, seven people mutually elected from among the Rectors of all state higher education institutions, and five people mutually elected from among representatives of all political parties that have any seat in the Parliament. The National Counter Corruption Commissioners must be at least forty-five years old. The term of office is nine years. They are not allowed to hold any other job and are required to retire by the age of seventy. Under these conditions, bureaucrats and university professors around their retirement age of sixty are naturally the most likely candidates.

The third is the Supreme Court of Justice's Criminal Division for Persons Holding Political Positions. In the past, all civilians were tried at regular courts under the three-instance court system.[54] Under this system, it took a very long time to conclude a trial, especially in the case of a parliamentarian, because the hearing had to be adjourned when Parliament was in session unless otherwise approved by Parliament. Therefore, the Criminal Division for Persons Holding Political Positions was created within the Supreme Court to deal exclusively with offences committed by politicians under the 1997 Constitution. It considers cases such as misuse of authority and corruption. Nine Supreme Court judges serve as judges of this division. Concluding a trial is expected to take only one or two months in this division, since it does not accept appeals and its decision is final (Phongthep 1998: 317–18). As mentioned earlier, cases involving politicians suspected of improper accumulation of assets by the National Counter Corruption Commission are tried at this division.

The fourth is the Constitution Court. A similar institution was provided by seven of the past constitutions: 1946, 1949, 1952, 1968, 1974, 1978 and 1991. However, none of them adequately ensured its independence from politics—for example, its judges were selected by Parliament. The previous Constitution Court made only thirteen judgments between 1946 and 1991. The 1997 Constitution aims to guarantee the Court's independence. The Constitution Court has fifteen judges, including five Supreme Court judges, two Supreme Administrative Court judges, five legal experts and three political science experts. For the last two categories, the President of the Supreme Court, four deans each from law and political science faculties and four political party representatives form a panel and select candidates in their respective fields. Experts also include those who have experience as cabinet members, members of independent inspection bodies, Deputy Attorney General or higher, bureaucrats at the level of Director-General or its equivalent, and university professors, and must be forty-five years of age or over. For expert members, a list containing twice as many candidates as the quota is prepared, then narrowed down to the quota by the Senate. The term of office is nine years with no reappointment. The retirement age is set at seventy, the same as for Counter Corruption Commissioners, which makes it suitable for bureaucrats who are due to retire at sixty.[55]

Stability and efficiency: Seeking a strong prime minister

Based on the understanding that politics must be stable as well as honest (Bowonsak 1998: 73), several measures have been taken to strengthen the prime minister's leadership. First, it has been made more difficult to submit a no-confidence motion against the prime minister. A no-confidence motion can be submitted against a cabinet member with support from one-fifth of lower house MPs, but in the case of the prime minister, support from not less than two-fifths is needed. Furthermore, a motion against the prime minister must be accompanied by the nomination of a prime ministerial candidate (Khanin 1998:

256–7). In the lower house that has 500 MPs, if the number of MPs from the ruling coalition reaches 300, it would be very difficult to submit a no-confidence motion against the prime minister.

Second, the prime minister was previously elected behind closed doors but is now selected by open vote in Parliament. Parliamentarians are free to cast their vote as they wish, without being bound by party decisions. This selection format was expected to increase the legitimacy and leadership of the prime minister (Likhit 1998: 293–8).

Third, members of the House of Representatives who become cabinet members are disqualified from holding their seats in the house. The House of Representatives members and the cabinet members are clearly separated so that it becomes easier for the former to supervise the latter (Bowonsak 1998: 74).[56] More importantly, cabinet members who have lost their cabinet posts are not entitled to return to the House of Representatives. This rule was made for the purpose of imposing stricter discipline on cabinet members. It was also 'expected to reduce pressure on the prime minister within the cabinet' if those who lose their cabinet posts in a cabinet reshuffle have no place in the cabinet or the House of Representatives (Likhit 1998: 306). This rule would thus strengthen the prime minister's authority over cabinet members and lead to a stable administration.

Fourth, under the combined proportional representation and single-seat electoral system, it was expected that political parties would run their prospective cabinet members in the proportional representation constituency. It was hoped that this would eradicate the bad practice that larger factions could secure cabinet posts for their members regardless of ability or aptitude. If political parties register their prospective cabinet members on the party-list, voters can in effect indirectly elect cabinet members. The order of the candidates on the party-list would effectively be determined by the leader of each party who would become the candidate for prime minister. In this sense, the prime minister (and the leaders of the ruling coalition parties) would have more freedom in choosing cabinet members. Moreover, the vote-gathering ability of political parties in the single-seat electorates was also expected to increase due to the synergetic effect of their party-lists. It would stabilize political parties, strengthen their authority over their members and contribute positively toward stabilizing an administration.

The fifth measure was intended to prevent lower house MPs from bargaining with the prime minister in exchange for the passage of a bill. This measure was expected to alleviate the problem that the parliament's rejection of a government bill could directly result in the resignation of a prime minister or the dissolution of the parliament. If the bill is related to the government policy speech or the constitution and also if the number of negative votes does not exceed one-half of the lower house members, the government is entitled to resubmit the bill to a joint session of both houses (Khanin 1998: 247–8; Bowonsak 1998).

These rules would provide more stability to the prime minister's status than before. Other rules were implemented to prevent the prime minister from becoming too stable and behaving despotically. First, the prime minister cannot dissolve the Parliament while it is debating a no-confidence motion against the prime minister. That is, the prime minister cannot dissolve the Parliament in order to avoid the debate or passage of a no-confidence motion. Second, it is possible to petition for the impeachment of the prime minister or to pursue criminal prosecution with the support of at least 50,000 voters or one-fourth of lower house MPs. Third, parties that secede from the ruling coalition are allowed to join forces with opposition parties in submitting no-confidence motions and to nominate either their leader or the opposition leader as the next prime ministerial candidate (Bowonsak 1998: 73–6).

Passage of the constitution

Distrust of politicians permeated the draft constitution. It stipulated that some of the relevant laws (*kotmai prakop ratthathammanun*, organic laws)—the constitution's operational regulations—should be promulgated and enforced within specified time periods. The organic laws on election, on the political parties and on the Election Commission had to be enacted within 240 days of the enforcement of the constitution and the organic laws on Ombudsmen, on counter corruption, on criminal procedure for persons holding political positions, on State audit and on referendum within two years. The first three organic laws were given a short 240-day deadline because they were considered especially important, being directly related to the supervision of politicians, which was the primary objective of political reform. These laws had to be implemented prior to a general election which, in turn, was essential for the constitution to produce the intended effects. These deadlines were an expression of a strong determination to prevent Parliament from delaying the reform process by failing to enact the organic laws.[57] In comparison, no specific deadlines were set for laws to establish the National Human Rights Commission and the National Economic and Social Advisory Council called for by the constitution. Similarly, the constitution ensures civil liberties and social rights 'as provided by law' but no specific deadlines were set for such laws. This indicates that the eight organic laws that had stipulated deadlines had particular importance. In addition to setting deadlines, the constitution drafters meticulously detailed the organic laws. For example, they specified the eligibility details for candidates for the Parliament, including age and educational requirements, in the constitution rather than leaving them to the organic law on election. In this regard, the constitution drafters were concerned that the legislation process in Parliament would reflect the interests of the Members of Parliament. Also, while they specified the eligibility requirements and the selection methods in detail for members of the Election Commission, the Constitution Court and the National Counter Corruption Commission—regarded as essential for inspecting politicians—they only provided broad rules for bodies not directly involved in political reform, such as the National Human Rights Commission.[58] The difference here indicates that the constitution drafters took precautionary measures to protect the political inspection bodies, whose job was to police politicians' pursuit of self-interest, from interference by those politicians.

A draft constitution was completed on 30 July 1997 and presented to Parliament on 15 August. This draft contained a threat not only to lower house MPs, but also to the vested interests of senators, changing their selection method from government appointment to popular election. A strong backlash was expected in Parliament.[59] However, it just so happened that a currency crisis broke out in July.

On 2 July the Ministry of Finance and the Bank of Thailand announced that the country was adopting a managed float system of exchange rate for baht. This was the beginning of a currency and economic crisis.[60] Among the various factors that have been mentioned as likely causes of this crisis, the most commonly accepted version of events is that the government had embarked on an ill-prepared economic liberalization program while keeping the baht pegged to the dollar, resulting in a huge influx of foreign capital and producing an economic bubble (Takahashi, Kwan and Sano 1998). There is no doubt that the slow response of the Chawalit administration, formed in November 1997, amplified the crisis. The Anan administration in 1991, however, had taken the first, and arguably the largest, steps toward economic liberalization. The Democrat Party inherited their policies while in government from September 1992 to May 1995. During this period, it was the private sector that borrowed heavily from foreign lenders and amassed huge debts, not the government. Signs of a forthcoming economic slump were already becoming apparent in 1996. Nevertheless, the Chawalit administration met the most severe criticism.

Amongst those who borrow a lot of money to get rich quickly, it seems only natural that one takes credit for one's success and blames others for one's failures. Hence it is no surprise that those who were hurt by the economic crisis blamed the government and politicians for their woes.

> Entrepreneurs were hit directly by the crisis. Employees also suffered misfortunes. One would expect that the most resentful would be sacked lower-class workers... but it was not the lower-class workers but the so-called "white-collar workers" in

English ... people of the "middle class"[61] in everyday Thai language who were most resentful. (Surachat 1998a: 156–7)

Numerous reformers took advantage of the frustration of those suffering during the crisis, fueling it to convince them to pass the draft constitution in order to realize the necessary political reform to break out of the crisis. For instance, former Prime Minister Anan pointed out during an address to a group of businesspeople on 6 August 1997 that the Thai people welcomed the the IMF's intervention and relief program because they trusted the IMF's financial management abilities more than their own government's, and then argued that they should enact the new constitution in order to achieve efficient and honest politics. The next day, he participated in a panel discussion at the law faculty of Chulalongkorn University where he argued that inefficient government was one of the main causes of the economic crisis (*Matichon Sutsapda*, 12 August 1997). Although 'the intervention by the IMF was not welcomed by other Asian countries hit by the currency crisis, most Thais received it with open arms' (Surachat 1998a: 164) because they had no confidence in the economic management skills of their party politicians and desperately wanted to grab hold of a helping hand. One available hand was the IMF; another was the new constitution. Many people hoped that 'once the new constitution is enacted and politics is reformed and strengthened, the economy will be strengthened too.' 'For those who were on the verge of desperation due to the economic crisis, the draft constitution was the last resort' (*Matichon Sutsapda*, 9 September 1997). The details of the draft were thus not so important; it is highly doubtful that many people have read all 336 articles of the most voluminous constitution in Thai history. What was important was that the new constitution represented a magic wand that could save their economy and politics from the crisis. Once the new constitution's passage came to be seen as a certain remedy for the economic crisis, the constitutional issue became an economic issue. There was growing concern that if this constitutional revision failed, the economic crisis would deepen.[62]

Members of Parliament might have been dissatisfied with all or part of the draft constitution, but they were not permitted to propose any amendments. They had only a simple choice—reject the entire draft on whatever grounds or pass it in its present form. The situation might be likened to a ready-made suit versus a custom-made suit, where you can complain about a less-than-exact fit, but no alterations are allowed. Your only choice is either to buy it or not. There was a very high possibility that, without the economic crisis, the draft constitution would have been rejected by Parliament and put to a national referendum. However the 'divine wind' called the economic crisis was blowing. The CDA helped to use this wind to further its own cause. Anan led a campaign for the draft constitution's passage, adopting green as the symbolic color for his campaign, and distributed a large number of free copies of the draft constitution.[63] As Michai Ruchuphan, the then President of the Senate, recalls:

> When the draft constitution was presented to Parliament, the CDA stepped up its pressure. It organized demonstration marches. It asked the people to carry green flags, to wear a green headband and to put a sticker on. It was trying to show off the strength of support and urge Parliament to pass the bill. It threatened explicitly and implicitly that rejection by Parliament would lead to violent incidents. I must admit that the CDA was immensely successful in rallying support for the draft constitution. (Michai 2001: 23)

The media also lobbied hard for the passage of the draft. Any MPs who criticized the draft or its advocates in public or in interviews were sharply attacked by the media. This discouraged MPs from voicing their concerns about or opposition to the draft. As the devastating economic crisis worsened day-by-day and the new constitution increasingly came to be seen as essential for the country to overcome the economic crisis, the draft constitution bill became a litmus test of how strongly each member of the ruling party and Parliament was motivated to resolve the economic crisis. There was no longer any option of rejecting the draft.[64] By 2 September, Prime Minister Chawalit had begun to voice his support for the draft constitution.

Still, a wave of criticism against the draft constitution arose during deliberations in Parliament from 4 to 10 September. For example, Representative Charoen Karun condemned the draft on 5 September: 'This is a draft constitution of university graduates, by university graduates, for university graduates. It divides the people into two classes. One of them is the ruling class consisting of people with a university or higher education.' He pointed out that it provides that members of the House of Representatives, Senators and cabinet members have to have at least a university education, yet, the subordinate class is 'obligated to vote. They are told to go to vote and choose someone to be their ruler. Such a constitution is absurd' (RPRS, khrang thi 3: 85). Representative Kawi Supphathira also criticized the bachelor clause: 'It is a matter of human dignity... farmers can't go to university and can't obtain a degree. Aren't they allowed to have human dignity? Why are they discriminated against in this way?' He reminded that no other country in the world had a constitution with such a clause, and none of the past fifteen constitutions of Thailand had such a clause, either (RPRS, khrang thi 3: 115–16). He went to the length of saying, 'Support for the draft will be a betrayal of our countrymen. There are only two million university graduates in the total population of sixty million people. For the remaining fifty eight million people, it is as if they are being deprived of their rights and executed' (RPRS, khrang thi 3: 119). Representative Seksan Saenphum stated on 8 September that the CDA was 'wrong from the beginning' because its membership was limited to university graduates. He pointed out that those who create a law usually do it for their own class, attributed farmers' low educational attainment not to their stupidity but to their circumstances, and called the constitution a 'class version' because 'it forsakes farmers.' He further noted that it was capitalists who supported political parties in conventional Thai politics: 'When capitalists supported political parties, various laws, regulations and benefits were made not for the people... but for capitalists. These capitalists... all of them have higher educational qualifications and only these people with higher educational qualifications have enjoyed these benefits' (RPRS, khrang thi 4: 51–3).

Yet the draft constitution was destined to be approved when the resolution of the economic crisis was tied to its passage. The MPs cited above were merely venting their frustration. The more they criticized, the more the pressure to pass the draft increased. Under these circumstances, the draft was put to a vote on 27 September, with each member of both houses in attendance asked one-by-one whether they agreed or not. The draft constitution passed by an overwhelming majority: 578 in favor, sixteen against and seventeen abstained (RPRS, khrang thi 7: 91). Once it was approved by Parliament, a national referendum was no longer required, and the new constitution was scheduled to be promulgated and enforced on 11 October. As discussed, the new constitution provided that the organic laws on election, on political parties and on the Election Commission had to be enforced within 240 days of the enforcement of the new constitution so that a general election could be held according to the new constitution as early as possible. On this basis, many people expected an early dissolution of the Parliament. For instance, Chaianan and Parichart predicted that 'once the organic laws are prepared, the first general election under the new constitution will be held, perhaps in the first half of 1998' (Chaianan and Parichart 1998: 167).

However, Prime Minister Chawalit resigned on 6 November following a large rally on 20 October 1997 to demand his resignation attended by 5000 people on Silom Street, the nation's foremost business district where all leading Thai and international companies were situated, and a continual decline in the value of the baht coinciding with growing discord within the ruling coalition.[65] When Chuan, the leader of the opposition Democrat Party, succeeded in his aggressive maneuver to win a majority of votes and became the next premier,[66] the pressure for an early dissolution of parliament weakened. To put it bluntly, political reform took priority over economic policies during the Chawalit administration. Excitement over the constitutional revision created such a big fuss that the people almost forgot about the economic crisis. However, once a new government came to office, the excitement subsided and the resolution of the economic crisis was given the highest priority. Perhaps, for many people, the pressure for constitutional revision meant much the same thing as pressure for the cabinet to resign.

New constitution and democratization

Chaianan once said,

> It [a constitution] has been used as a major tool in maintaining the power of the group that created it. What Thailand has experienced is not constitutionalism and constitutional government, but rather different kinds of regimes that adjusted and readjusted institutional relationships between the executive and the legislative branches according to their power position vis-a-vis their opponents. (Chaianan 1989: 320)

Despite this view, however, Chaianan has high praise for the new constitution:

> The 1997 Constitution is the first constitution, of which rules were not determined by power groups competing for the state power. It was achieved by the complete change in the method and process of constitutional revision to allow broad participation of the people and a new consensus to generate. (Chaianan 2000: 58)

The 1997 Constitution is purported to be completely different from the previous fifteen constitutions. The PR booklet by the CDA containing the final draft proudly declared, 'This is the first time in the history of Thailand that a constitution is drafted by a group of people who have no vested political interests which is the Constitution Drafting Assembly consisting of provincial representatives and experts' (SR 1998: 117).

Chai Uengphakon (Ji Ungpakorn) (2000), however, squarely challenges this view. For Chai, examination of the provisions of the 1997 Constitution reveals that they were drafted by capitalists by stealth. Poor people, workers and farmers were not involved in the election of the drafters, much less the actual drafting. University graduates elected the drafters from among themselves. Granted, a series of 'public hearings' was held in the drafting process, but the CDA, made up of prominent capitalists and politicians, did not incorporate any of the important suggestions put forward by workers and farmers in the draft. Chai observes that the fundamental goals of the constitution drafters were to ensure stability of the government and to defend a free market economy; provisions concerning the election system are typically more advantageous to larger political parties and they aim to stabilize the government and avoid the confusion inherent in coalition governments. Chai counters the argument that the constitution also reflects the interests of the people by expanding freedom and rights and allowing more participation in politics by pointing out the following: that if it is to be called the people's constitution, it should more extensively reflect the interests of workers and farmers who account for 80% of the population; that the new constitution does not provide anything that benefits the people; that regrettably, many people, including NGOs and labor unions, were misled by the 'ostentatious concept' of rights and freedom and supported the constitution on that basis; that under this constitution, the lower classes are deprived of their right to be elected to Parliament while being obliged to vote, because the right to be elected to Parliament is granted to university graduates only (Chai et al. 2000: 64–6). For Chai, then, it is not a constitution by the people nor for the people.

Even if the drafters have no vested interest in the constitution, it is inevitable that its provisions will benefit some people and disadvantage others. As Chaianan points out, Thailand has revised its constitution so frequently because those who have seized power by unconstitutional means such as a coup d'état have remodeled it to suit their convenience.[67] Drastic changes to the election system and the relationship between the House of Representatives and the cabinet were incorporated in the 1997 Constitution. The 1997 Constitution is no different from its predecessors in terms of determining power relations. Changes to power relations create advantages and disadvantages. Of course, any group who expects to benefit from the new constitution will support it. So, who supported it?

The full revision of the constitution was triggered by calls for political reform. Political reform was called for because of dissatisfaction with the state of politics at the time. Pasuk and Baker divide pro-reform forces into two camps based on the location of dissatisfaction. One was the conservative camp which was dissatisfied with party politics. They were led by Amon, who wrote a series of essays titled 'constitutionalism' in the daily *Phuchatkan* and published them in book form in 1994. He was a leading conservative who had served as the Secretary-General of the Office of the Council of State from 1979 to 1990. He argued that there were problems with parliament being too powerful and parliamentary politics being inefficient and unstable, and his solution was to enact a constitution that was capable of controlling the parliament by separating the three powers. This camp aimed to curtail the power of party politicians and restore it to the bureaucracy. The other camp consisted of NGOs and some intellectuals who were dissatisfied with any politics that ignored social equity and citizens' participation.[68] Chalat, who went on hunger strike in 1992 and

1994, belonged to this camp. Party politics was far more desirable than military or bureaucratic politics in their eyes but it still failed to properly consider the weak (Pasuk and Baker 2000: 111–12).

These two camps were instigators, but for the political reform movement to achieve a new constitution, it needed powerful supporters. It found them among urban residents. Bowonsak, who played a significant role in the drafting process, was keenly aware of this. His explanation immediately after the new constitution was passed tells all: patron-client relationships are rampant in Thailand, most notably between rural residents and lower house MPs; urban residents dislike these patron-type MPs who occupy 75% of the seats in the House of Representatives, but a few of them are also engaged in patron-client relationships and rely on politicians in order to obtain government contracts, honorable positions and decorations; a majority of urban residents do not have patron politicians, not because they are free from the patron-client culture, but because they have no contact with politicians, and if they find such a point of contact, they are not different from rural residents; the new constitution cannot destroy this patron-client culture, and is thus designed to stop the spreading of the patron-client relationship by setting up independent inspection bodies; it offers inspection opportunities to the people who cannot find any contact with politicians (Bowonsak 1997).[69]

Bowonsak divided the people into those who were clients of politicians and those who were not—in other words, the beneficiaries and non-beneficiaries of party politics—and gave consideration to the non-beneficiaries in the drafting process. White-collar workers, professionals, shop owners and intellectuals belonged to the non-beneficiary group. These people largely correspond with the usual definition of the urban middle class. Bowonsak (1997) claims that the drafting process gave primary consideration to the interests of this class and therefore assumes that the supporters of political reform are to be found among the people of this class.

According to Bowonsak, political reform is intended to achieve three objectives: 'The first objective is to take politics out of the hands of politicians' and turn it into *citizens' politics* by expanding citizens' rights and freedoms and transforming a representative democracy into a citizens' participatory democracy. The second aim is to ensure that powers are exercised *honestly and justly* in the political and administrative systems by strengthening citizens' rights to efficiently supervise the exercise of political power. The third objective of political reform is to *stabilize* the government, strengthen the prime minister's leadership and make the parliament more *efficient* so that it can properly resolve various problems' (1998: 52, emphasis original).

Bowonsak claims that 'the new constitution treated citizens as the leading actor in politics and tried to bring politics closer to citizens' (Bowonsak 1998: 52). From his perspective, the citizenry is not identical to the people, as can be seen in his statement: 'The question of whether the new constitution can achieve its intended results depends on whether the people who supported it will wake up to civic awareness and consider that the affairs of a city are as important as their personal affairs' (Bowonsak 1998: 79). The citizenry is not the mass or a mob but the people who have developed a civic awareness. It should be identified and nurtured among those urban residents who have little access to the benefits of party politics. Expanding these citizens' rights and freedoms to limit the power of lower house MPs elected from rural districts was one of the principal objectives of political reform. Specific measures included the introduction of a proportional representation system and the creation of inspection bodies.[70] Conflicting interests between urban areas and rural areas were unmistakably reflected here.[71]

Anek Laothammathat vividly illustrated the conflict between the city and rural areas. Anek had spearheaded Thai political research at home and abroad in the 1990s. As calls for political reform were gathering force, he pointed out that the urban residents' view of politics was totally different from the rural residents' view and attempted to analyze the differences (Anek 1996; 1995). According to Anek, 'What lies at the root of problems surrounding democracy since the mid-1980s is the conflict between farmers in rural areas and the urban middle class' (Anek 1995: 11). He observed that the urban middle class consists of two groups, one comprised of corporate people and professionals and the other consisting of social reformers. The former group includes corporate managers, executives, technicians, doctors, nurses, lawyers, architects, engineers and other professionals. The latter includes students, teachers, progressive academics, activists from development NGOs, etc. The former group demands efficient government and free economic activity while the latter demands the expansion of rights and freedoms and economic fairness (Anek 1995: 10). Both groups look for policies, ideals, ethics and competence in politics and maintain their independence without being bound by obligations or connections in elections (Anek 1995: 7). This is in clear contrast to rural residents who vote for the people who they think looked after them best or paid for their votes. As the political system became more democratic, election results were increasingly decided by rural residents who far outnumbered the urban middle class. Hence, political power ended up in the hands of those politicians who were preferred by rural residents (Anek 1995: 9). The urban middle class was dissatisfied with these MPs, complaining that their politics was rife with vote buying and corruption (Anek 1995: 8, 9).

This discontent and criticism has a historical background. Since administrative centralization was achieved in the late nineteenth and early twentieth centuries, the capital and other urban districts had continued to rule over rural areas. Urban residents felt that they had a higher status than rural residents. Rural residents were thus regarded as 'second-class citizens.'[72] The conflict between the city and rural areas came to a head after the Communist Party of Thailand start to wage guerrilla warfare in rural areas in the mid-1960s. The Party pursued a strategy of 'countryside surrounds cities' and tried to extend its influence among rural residents. When the struggle for the people ended in victory for the military in the early 1980s, urban areas no longer needed the military to provide a barrier for rural areas against communist infiltration. Party politicians then increasingly ingratiated themselves among rural residents.

In a democracy elections are important, and elections are numbers games. The population of Bangkok accounts for only 10% of the total population and the total urban population accounts for a mere 30%; thus 70% of voters live in rural areas. The majority of lower house MPs are elected from rural districts and therefore they dominated the cabinet. Although almost all of the rural-constituency MPs lived in regional cities themselves, they had won the majority of their votes in rural districts and hence had to return the favor by implementing public works projects in their constituencies. The rural MPs' domination of the national government became apparent from the start of the Chatchai administration in 1988. Since the country had never had rural representatives at the helm of the government during the periods of monarchial and military rule, metropolitan residents came to feel as if the master-servant relationship had been reversed, or to stretch the point slightly, as if a suzerain state was being ruled by its colonials. Metropolitan residents were highly dissatisfied with the party politics that had brought about this reversal, and their dissatisfaction was expressed in calls for political reform.

When the Banhan administration came to office in 1995, it added momentum to the process of political reform. First, it incorporated political reform into its policy platform, and then into its political agenda. Second, the country's unprecedented economic boom, which had begun in the late 1980s, began to show signs of weakening during Banhan's administration and the business community and urban residents began to call for government action (*Matichon Sutsapda*, 20 August 1996). As their frustration with the government's inability to take effective action grew, they increasingly felt the need for political reform (Pasuk and Baker 2000: 112–15). In response to this growing sentiment, the major political parties all pledged in the 1996 general election to entrust economic management to a 'dream team' of experts (*nak borihan mue achip*, economic bureaucrats and managers of major corporations) rather than party politicians.

In order to cater to the demands of businesspeople and urban residents, they had to restrain their lower house MPs' strong desires to be cabinet members.

Third, the tone of criticism hardened, moving beyond the inability of politicians to govern and extending to the party politicians themselves. As discussed above, from the 1980s, the power center of party politicians began to shift towards rural MPs. Cabinet positions and the major political party offices were assumed by rural-constituency politicians rather than capital-based ones.[73] The majority of cabinet members in both the Chatchai administration in 1988 and the Chuan administration in 1992 were MPs elected from rural districts. The Banhan administration followed the same trend. All three of these prime ministers were elected from constituencies outside of Bangkok, but Banhan was by far the most notorious for dispensing favors in his constituency in Suphan Buri province. It was well known throughout the country that Suphan Buri province had an incongruously magnificent national highway network. Banhan was regarded as the epitome of a rural-constituency MP, thus his accession to the premiership removed any lingering doubts about the fact that national government was now run by rural MPs. Metropolitan residents considered these 'old provincial boss politicians ... as the threat to Thailand's democracy and economic success' (Pasuk and Baker 2000: 138) and there was a gathering groundswell of opinion that national government should not be left in the hands of such politicians.

In the 1980s, a new term came into use to denigrate party politicians: *chao pho*. The term refers to influential people whose influence is obviously acquired through illegitimate activities. They ran illegal businesses such as contraband trading, gambling and unlicensed logging and typically had no hesitation in killing their enemies.[74] Only a small percentage of local bosses and MPs were *chao pho*.[75] In the 1990s, however, there was a growing tendency for the mass media to brand many rural-constituency politicians, especially the more influential ones, as *chao pho*. As soon as an MP is called a *chao pho*, his illegality is assumed and he becomes a villain who must be vanquished (Pasuk and Baker 2000: 135–6, 231). The expression was used not because there were more MPs who were involved in illegal businesses but because condemning the politicians was a convenient way to criticize the political system.[76] While lower house MPs insist that they are legitimately elected in democratic elections, critics can claim that they are elected by rural votes that are bought with funds raised through suspicious businesses or corrupt activities and that people so elected are devoted to recovering their funds through further corrupt behavior once they are elected.[77] These criticisms proved highly effective in encouraging metropolitan residents to strongly support political reform, primarily in the form of curtailing the MPs' power.[78]

City residents used a powerful weapon to attack the rural MPs and their supporters—public opinion. The readership of newspapers and magazines, particularly the quality print media, was almost exclusively urban residents.[79] And while the consumers of the broadcast media (radio and television) included many rural residents, the program producers were exclusively urban residents, as in the print media. In other words, the urban middle-class 'were the main consumers and producers of public opinion' (Anek 1995: 11).[80] Consequently, the mass media came to represent the views of urban residents as 'public opinion,' and the sources of information for both the print and broadcast media were concentrated in the capital. Hence, for example, the regional newspapers were insignificant while the national newspapers had hardly any local editions.[81] Accordingly, the opinions of city residents became almost synonymous with the opinions of metropolitan residents—to the extent that when a headline in any of the English-language newspapers says 'city,' it means Bangkok. This became quite obvious in the debate about political reform.

There were also other reasons behind the city residents' opinions coming to be treated as public opinion. One cause was that so-called opinion polls came into wide use in the 1990s. Social surveys had been monopolized by the National Statistical Office until the end of the 1980s. Niyom Purakham in particular, its director from 1984 to 1989, was the reigning figure in the field of social and public-opinion surveying during this period. However, the media and educational institutions began to frequently poll public opinion in the 1990s.[82] It was common practice, particularly until the mid-1990s, to limit the survey area either to Bangkok or to the metropolitan area plus a few regional cities. Surveying in rural areas was costly and there was no reliable resident record for sampling, so nation-wide random sampling surveys were rarely conducted. Some surveys were conducted on the Internet, which had a very limited user base. The results of these surveys (*phon*, derived from the English word 'poll') were therefore considerably biased in favor of urban residents' opinions, but they were nevertheless reported as if they were the opinions of the general public.

Still, there was another, more important reason underlying this shift. As discussed in previous chapters, the interpretation of the May 1992 incident as a democratization action driven by the urban middle class became widely accepted. There was no doubt that the May 1992 incident had contributed to the military's withdrawal from politics and the consolidation of party politics. Hence, supporters of the incident were hailed as the heroes of democratization. It was further widely accepted that these 'heroes' were urban middle-class people. Consequently, the urban middle class was officially labeled democratic and respectable, and hence their opinions were deemed worthy of special attention. Although theirs were minority views in comparison to the size of the rural population, they gained currency as 'just' opinion or the consensus opinion of the general public. Hence, the CDD's claim that 'city residents have a "large voice" but a "small number of votes" whereas rural residents have a "small voice" but a "large number of votes"' (CDD 1995: 61) accurately describes the situation in which urban residents' views are treated as genuine public opinion.

An apt anecdote for this situation is Interior Minister Sano Thiangthong's critical comment in August 1997 about the CDA waving the flag of 'the people,' and the response from a regular commentator in the weekly *Matichon*. The commentator presumed what Sano 'really means' as follows:

> Although members of the CDA have held many public hearings and meetings, they have only targeted intellectuals and the middle class. The people in rural areas have never expressed their opinions. To put it bluntly, they don't understand anything about the constitution. Therefore members of the CDA should stop referring to the majority of the people.

According to this commentator,

> No matter how true (Sano's) remark is, what we need to understand first is that members of the House of Representatives or the Senate have no right to decide whether they accept the draft constitution or not. It is public opinion expressed via the media and other means that decides whether the draft constitution should be accepted or not. It is a big mistake to jump to a hasty conclusion that the people support lower house MPs and therefore the people do not approve unless lower house MPs approve. The people might sell their votes in elections but it does not mean that they sell their patriotism or souls.

He then insists that:

> As far as the middle class who have expressed their views (at public hearings and consultations or audience-participation television programs) are concerned, they cannot stand the present state of politics any longer and desperately want political reform. This minority group is more fearsome than the majority people in rural areas. If you cannot believe it, trace back in your memory. (Yuenyat 1997)

The 'memory' referred to here is the May 1992 incident. The commentator asserts almost overconfidently that the middle class is the pillar of democratization and that the opinion of city residents, whose core is the middle class, *is* public opinion even though they are a minority. He warns that the middle class will rise up again if their 'public opinion' is ignored.

In fact, this was the first instance in Thailand in which the political process was substantially influenced by public opinion.[83] Politicians became increasingly annoyed by the way that urban middle class opinions were reported by the media as if they were sound arguments. One example is Prime Minister Banhan's criticism that the media should seek opinions across the country, not just in the capital city. On 17 September 1997, shortly before a vote on the draft constitution bill, Prime Minister Chawalit told a delegation of northeastern region residents who had visited Government House to express their support, that 'The majority of the people have the right, power and duty to care about their country. You are the only owners of this country. Others merely reside in this country. When they (*man*) suffer a loss, they complain loudly that they can't get what they want.' The word 'they' obviously referred to 'opposition parties, city residents, the middle class and the media.' Pressed by the angry media the following day to explain who 'they' were, Chawalit replied jokingly, 'potatoes,' drawing even more criticism (*Matichon Sutsapda*, 23 September 1997).[84] Yet the media reacted hysterically when critics of the draft constitution gathered in the capital or rural residents visited to express support for the government from August until September 1997, branding it 'a strategy to surround cities by countryside' (*Matichon Sutsapda*, 16 September 1997; *Matichon Sutsapda*, 23 September 1997), perhaps because it knew that the city residents whose opinions it voiced were in fact the minority group.

Sane Chamarik, a political scientist, scathingly observed that, in the debate over political reform which intensified in the wake of this conflict, the middle class, the media and intellectuals exhibited 'narrow-mindedness for "being preoccupied with their own interests" and "giving no regard to the feelings and lives of rural residents"' (Sane 1998: 4). The urban middle class became dissatisfied with party politics as it began to take root, because it shifted the center of power from the capital to rural areas. According to Anek, their ideal government was the Anan administration (Anek 1995: 9),[85] an undemocratic administration with no popularly elected parliament. The urban middle class pursued stability and efficiency so eagerly that they appeared to be willing to abandon democracy. For example, a proposal for separating the legislative and executive branches, i.e., prohibiting elected MPs from serving as cabinet ministers, was central to the type of political reform being advocated. If the parliamentary cabinet system is undermined in this way (at least partially), the cabinet would be dominated by (active or retired) bureaucrats and prominent corporate executives. The former accounted for a majority of cabinet members until the 1980s, while the latter gradually increased their numbers in the cabinet in the 1990s. These were the people who had been successful either in the government or the business sector. In Thailand, anyone who aims to succeed in one of these sectors must be in Bangkok.

Although this proposal was rejected, the 1997 Constitution contained numerous measures with similar repercussions, such as the introduction of a proportional representation system, bachelor's degree requirements for MPs and cabinet members, the creation of inspection bodies to supervise politicians, and a prohibition on concurrently holding a seat in parliament and a cabinet post. The bachelor's degree requirement is clearly advantageous to city residents since one in three university graduates lives in Bangkok and 70% of them live in urban areas. The introduction of the proportional representation system and the ban on concurrently holding a parliamentary seat and a cabinet post virtually divide lower house MPs into first- and second-class MPs. The party-list MPs who risk less by joining the cabinet are first-class MPs while single-seat MPs who risk everything by joining the cabinet are second-class MPs. The party-list MPs, who are expected to represent the interests of the nation rather than a particular constituency, are typically more well-known across the country.[86] Most of these well-known people live in Bangkok. The only people living in provinces who frequently appear in the media are (usually notorious) influential politicians or *chao pho*. Consequently, a large proportion of the 100 party-list MPs are essentially elected from the Bangkok electoral district, which effectively means that the capital produces a disproportionate number of lower house MPs. Further, because these party-list MPs are the most likely candidates for cabinet posts, the cabinet naturally includes a large number of Bangkok representatives. Furthermore, most of the members of the various inspection bodies are bureaucrats or academics living in Bangkok. In these ways, According to Pasuk and Baker, the political reforms implemented in the 1997 Constitution helped the urban areas, particularly the capital city, recapture the leading role in national government from rural areas (Pasuk and Baker 2000: 238, 250). As the warm welcome given to the new constitution indicates, it alleviated urban middle-class discontent at the expense of party politicians and rural residents. The significance of the 1997 Constitution was that it helped to ensure the survival of the parliamentary system, which had been subject to harsh criticisms and widespread discontent, and helped to consolidate democratic politics.

No less important is the fact that these political reforms did not alienate another powerful group—the businesspeople who played a major role in party politics as MPs, supporters of MPs, and donors to political parties (Tamada 1988). In Thailand, party politics has been supported from below by provincial businesspeople and from above by large-scale Bangkok businesspeople since the 1970s. Money politics was regarded as a major problem for the political reform advocates. Members of the drafting committee must have been aware of the importance of and methods for regulating political funding, having studied the constitutions and political systems of various countries. However, the 1997 Constitution and the 1998 Organic Law on Political Parties did not go beyond newly establishing public subsidies for political parties and requiring the disclosure of political donations. Public subsidy reduces the financial burden on businesspeople, and only the political parties, not the donors, can be punished for breaching the disclosure requirements. These provisions cannot regulate off-the-book contributions, and only the politicians who accept bribes are subjected to political corruption inspection; the bribe-givers are not called to account at all.[87] The 1997 Constitution provides for community rights and fair distribution of income to cater for the demands of those who seek the expansion of freedom and rights, but that is not without dispelling the uneasiness of the wealthy class, including businesspeople, by including provisions for the right to ownership and inheritance of personal property (Article 48) and upholding a 'free economy based on the market mechanism' (Article 87) to protect against excessive pressure for wealth redistribution. In this sense also, the new constitution contributed to the consolidation of democratic politics.

At the same time, in the short term, it is extremely important to note that the constitutional revisions prevented the turmoil caused by the economic crisis from destabilizing the political regime by diverting people's attention to the drafting of the new constitution. When the currency crisis broke out, a number of proposals were put forward to suspend the Parliament and create a special administration. If the constitutional revision had not become the central issue, there is a good chance that a coup d'état-style undemocratic government might have been established. Because the constitution happened to be the central issue at the time, however, such chaos was avoided. It was clearly a stroke of good fortune that the economic crisis coincided with the drafting of the new constitution.

4
The 2000 Senate Election: Return of the House of Public Officials

Significance of the Senate election

The Senate election under the new 1997 Constitution was held in March 2000.[1] It was held in 2000 because the four-year term of the senators who were appointed under the 1991 Constitution on 22 March 1996 was due to end on 21 March 2000 and there would be no senators unless an election was held. Since the first House of Representatives election under the 1997 Constitution was delayed until January 2001, this Senate election became the first national election to be held under the 1997 Constitution. It can therefore be considered to be the first test of the 1997 Constitution's political reforms.

The 2000 election was the first popular election of the Senate in the history of Thailand. Until then, the word 'senator' was virtually synonymous with 'appointed parliamentarian.' The Thai Parliament was restructured every time a new constitution was enacted, sometimes with one house, sometimes with two. During the times of a single house, between one-half and all of the Members of Parliament were appointed. During two-house periods, the senators were appointed, with one exception: those senators who were elected by the popularly elected lower house MPs on 26 May 1946 (this Senate was dissolved by a coup on 8 November 1947).

Most of the time, it was the cabinet who did the selection of senators and naturally, the cabinet would prefer those who would be beneficial for the administration's survival. Looking at the occupations of senators in the past (see Figure 4.1), it is clear that more than half of the senators in all periods were formerly public officials (*kharatchakan*: national government employees, both civil and military). In fact, it was common for more than 90% of the senators to be former public officials when there were no popularly elected MPs (lower house MPs). Even when increasing numbers of popularly elected MPs were entering the cabinet during the 1980s, 80% of senators were public officials (both active and retired). Once the cabinet came to be comprised almost solely of elected MPs, i.e. during the party cabinet era, the proportion of public officials decreased slightly.[2] Among the 260 senators appointed in March 1996, when party politics

Figure 4.1 A breakdown of appointed legislators by occupation, 1932-1996

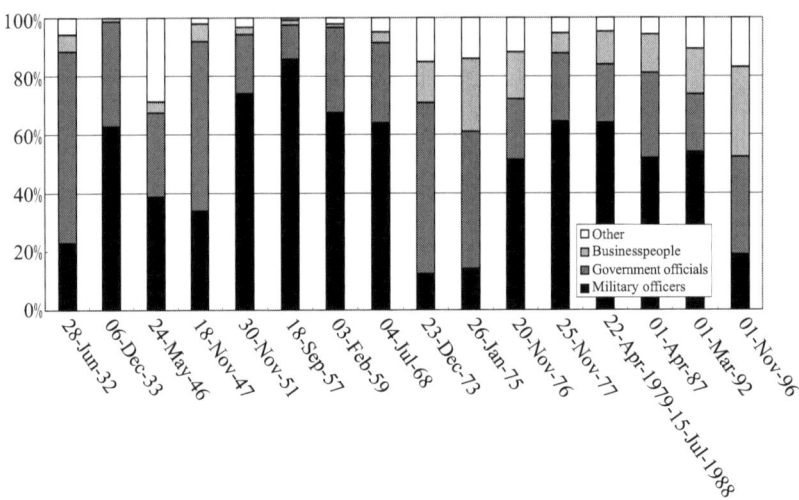

Source: Data prior to 1988 are based on information compiled by Rangsan (Rangsan 1989: 174-178), data for 1987 are based on information compiled by Pathan (Pathan n. d.: 381), data for March 1992 are compiled by author based on the list of senators (Kromkanpokkhrong 1992: 25-92) prepared by the Department of Local Administration, Ministry of Interior, and data for 1996 are taken from the Senate secretariat's statistics (SLW 1996: 154).

Note: Rangsan's data prior to 1977 show the numbers at the time of appointment while the data from 1979 to 1988 show a breakdown of all 500 members by occupation. Pathan's data shows a breakdown of 260 sitting members as of 22 April 1987.

was considered well-established, only 53.1% were public officials (SLW 1996: 154).[3] This gap was filled mainly by businesspeople, who accounted for 30.4% of senators in 1996.[4] The proportion of businesspeople increased during the party cabinet era because they were political parties' primary support base, especially financially. Clearly then, whether a party government or a military junta, the government always gave preference to its supporters in appointing Members of Parliament.[5]

Despite these fluctuations, the proportion of public officials had never fallen below 50%. The appointed Senate was thus effectively always a 'house of public officials.' This arrangement was harshly criticized by the bureaucratic polity model,[6] the most widely accepted view in studies on Thai politics until the 1980s. Public officials, who dominated the cabinet lineup from the prime minister down, appointed high ranking military and administrative officials to the Senate in order to ensure as many government supporters in the legislative branch as possible. In most cases, they were military generals in key posts ranging from the Five Tigers to divisional commanders (sometimes including regimental commanders) and high-ranking administrative officials at the level of department chief or higher. These high officials were, in a way, representatives of their departments or ministries who endeavored to build a solid footing in the Senate in order to protect the interests of their organizations. When they were unable to protect or further the interests of their organizations, they were at least able to supplement their incomes by adding their senators' allowances to their public office salaries. It was unlikely that these senators would oppose the government that appointed them. Of course, it would be somewhat naive to expect that these government-appointed senators, particularly active military and administrative officials, would act as watchdogs over the government. Thus any bills that were passed by the elected lower house against the wishes of the cabinet were likely to be voted down by these government-appointed senators. Chaianan calls the military and bureaucrat dominated Senate the 'informal political party' or the 'legislative arms' of the bureaucracy (Chaianan 1989: 333–4). In other words, the government-appointed Senate has played an important role in protecting and promoting the interests of the bureaucracy.

The appointed Senate had been criticized as one of the main impediments to democratization, which is why the 1997 Constitution introduced the popular election of senators despite strong opposition from certain quarters. It should be noted, however, that the change was not made on the grounds that changing from appointment to popular election would in itself contribute positively to democratization. Since the principal aim of political reform was to strengthen the supervision of lower house MPs, the Senate was expected to play a central role in controlling the House of Representatives. In order to control the House of Representatives, the Senate had to have popularly elected members so that it could claim the same democratic legitimacy as the popularly elected House of Representatives. Recall, as discussed in Chapter Three, that the constitution provided different election rules for senate and lower house candidates, including eligibility for election, in the hope that those who were elected to the Senate would have the right qualities to inspect and oversee the lower house MPs.

So what were these Senate election rules in the 1997 Constitution and what outcomes did they produce? Did it create a Senate that was different from the house of bureaucrats? This chapter aims to highlight one aspect of the political reform by examining how it changed the Senate.

Senate election procedures and features

Number of seats
The 1997 Constitution provides that the House of Representatives has a total of 500 members, including 100 elected on a party-list proportional representation basis and 400 elected on a single-seat electoral district basis, and that there

are 200 senators. Since the 1991 Constitution provided that there should be two-thirds as many senators as lower house MPs, the relative size of the Senate was considerably reduced by the new constitution.[7] Each province forms a Senate electoral district, with seats distributed to each district in proportion to its population at the end of the year prior to the election. Based on the total population of 60 million, each Senate seat is allocated to a constituency of about 300,000 people. The most populated city, Bangkok, gets eighteen seats. Any province with a population less than 300,000 gets one seat. This method of allocating seats follows that of the lower house.

Eligibility for election

Section 125 of the Constitution stipulates that to be eligible for election to the Senate, one must be:
1. A Thai national by birth (which excludes naturalized Thai citizens);
2. Of not less than forty years of age on the election day;
3. A university graduate (with not lower than a Bachelor's degree or its equivalent).

These are the same requirements as for the lower house except for the age requirement.

Section 125 also provides that a candidate may stand in a province (electoral district) if he or she satisfies any of the following conditions:
1. Being a registered resident of the province for a consecutive period of not less than one year;
2. Having previously been an elected Member of Parliament, a councilor or executive of local self-government organizations of the province;
3. Born in the province;
4. Having studied in an education institution in the province for a consecutive period of not less than two academic years;
5. Having served in the official service before or having been a registered resident in the province for a consecutive period of not less than two years.

This provision is the same as for lower house candidates.

Section 126 stipulates, however, that certain people who may meet the above requirements are nevertheless ineligible, including political party members and serving public officials. The members and executives of political parties are ineligible, and former lower house MPs are ineligible for one year after leaving the lower house. This is in contrast to lower house MPs who have to be members of political parties—an attempt to block political party influence in the Senate.[8] Serving senators are also ineligible; i.e., senators cannot be re-elected. Public officials, however, may stand as candidates as soon as they leave their jobs.

Election procedure

The foremost feature of Senate election is a ban on political campaigning. The involvement of political parties is prohibited, as is wining and dining and, of course, bribery. The only activity candidates and their supporters are allowed to participate in is 'introducing' the candidates. To ensure fairness, the Election Commission prepares the following for the introduction of candidates: designated billboards for posters, printing and distribution of candidate profile booklets, designated locations for candidate introductions, and campaign broadcasts on television and radio.

What candidates can include in the introduction materials (flyers and posters) is limited to: a personal profile (which may include a photograph of the candidate either with or without spouse and/or children), education history, work history, and the candidate's registration number.[9] Importantly, no election promises or policies may be included. Accordingly, candidates must rely solely on name recognition to attract votes, unless they resort to vote buying.

Winning-out style election

The Senate election was held on 4 March 2000. There were 1522 candidates competing for 200 seats. Voter turnout was 72.08%, which was relatively low considering that voting had been made compulsory,[10] but it was higher than in any previous national election.[11]

The Election Commission announced winners in each electoral district from 8 to 20 March and confirmed the election of 122 senators (Kho. Ko. Tho. 2000a). The number was seventy-eight short of the full 200 because, in many provinces, some candidates who came within the winning range were issued a red card (*bai daeng*) or a yellow card (*bai lueang*) and could not be declared winners. A candidate who polled within the winning range is someone who is, for example, among the top three candidates in a three-seat province. The two types of 'penalty card' originate from soccer, as their names suggest. A candidate who is found to have committed a clear-cut election violation is issued a red card and ordered out of the election immediately. A candidate who is suspected of an election violation but without any clear evidence is issued a yellow card and allowed to participate in a second ballot.

The remaining seventy-eight seats were put to another ballot. As in the first round, those who polled within the winning range without any election violations were declared winners. The polling was repeated until there were no more vacancies. There were two notable features of this process. First, no new candidates were allowed to enter after the first round of polling. Only the original

Table 4.1 Senate elections, 2000–2002

Voting date	Number of voters	Electoral districts (provinces)	Number of seats	Declared winners	Candidates	Voter turnout (%)	Invalid & blank votes (%)
4 March 2000	42,557,583	76	200	122	1,532	72	6.3
29 April 2000	26,877,074	35	78	66	1,054	54	7.2
4 June 2000	8,001,267	9	12	8	255	41	7.2
24 June 2000 / 9 July 2000	3,479,800	4	4	3	124	31	6.9
22 July 2000	1,177,323	1	1	1	54	31	4.4
21 April 2001	5,537,209	8	11	10	78	41	5.2
26 May 2001	994,482	1	1	1	12	46	3.5
24 February 2002	711,564	1	1	1	13	32	3.0
4 August 2002	1,037,713	1	1	1	17	53	3.1

Source: Compiled by author based on the Election Commission website
(http://www.ect.go.th/english/national/senate/nat1.html and
http://www.ect.go.th/thai/senate/result/0400845/result.htm).
Note: Elections from 2001 onwards were by-elections.

candidates were permitted to stand for these subsequent ballots, and they were not allowed to withdraw their candidacy.[12] Second, those who received either one red card or two yellow cards were eliminated from the list of candidates. In short, it was a winning-out series.

The second ballot for seventy-eight seats was held on 29 April in thirty-five provinces. Sixty-six candidates were elected in this round. Voter turnout was 53.85%, almost 20% less than the first round. Seven candidates were red-carded and ordered out. The third round of voting for the remaining twelve seats in nine provinces was held on 4 June. Eight winners were declared and four were eliminated. Voter turnout decreased by 10% to 41.23%.

Although a fourth round for four seats in four provinces was scheduled to be held on 18 June, the Constitution Court ruled on 15 June that the yellow card system was unconstitutional.[13] Hence, four candidates who had been eliminated after receiving a second yellow card in the second and third rounds were allowed to stand again in the fourth round. Following this decision, voting for one seat in Ubon Ratchathani province was held on 24 June. Then, the ballot for the remaining three seats in three provinces was held on 9 July. Ubon Ratchathani province was the only district that could not find a winner in this round. A fifth round of voting was held in Ubon Ratchathani province on 22 July and, finally, all 200 seats were filled. More than four months had passed between the first round of Senate elections and its conclusion (Table 4.1).

This winning-out style not only took a long time to confirm all of the winners, but also violated the principle of one person one vote, as some of the candidates complained. Let us look at the case of Ubon Ratchathani province where votes were cast five times. The province had six seats. In the first round, the top five candidates were issued a yellow card and only the sixth-ranked candidate was proclaimed winner (Table 4.2).

In the second round of voting, the top three candidates received a yellow card and the fourth and fifth candidates were declared winners. Although Wichai Khrongyut came first in the first round, he only attracted half the number of votes in the second round. Still, he managed to come fifth and secured a seat. Maliwan Ngoenmuen, who came second in the first round, also got only half the number of votes and failed to reach the winning range. In contrast, Amon Ninprem came seventh in the first round, then first in the second round. Wilawan Tanwatthanaphong was tenth in the first round and third in the second round. However, they were both yellow carded in the second round. Adisak Phokkhakuniakanon who polled third in the first round and second in the second round was red-carded and disqualified. Wirasak Chinarat received almost as many votes in the second round as the first and managed to win.[14] In the third round of voting, Maitri Naiyakun came first with more than double the number of his second round votes but received a yellow card. Maliwan, who ranked second in the first round and sixth in the second round, came third and won. Amon, who ranked seventh in the first round and first in the second round, came second and also won. Wilawan, who came third in the second round, polled so poorly this time that he was nowhere near the winning range. In the fourth round of voting for the remaining seat, Maitri secured almost the same number of votes

Table 4.2 Higher ranked candidates in five rounds of voting in Ubon Ratchathani

	Name	1st	2nd	3rd	4th	5th
1	Wichai Khrongyut	81,034	○ 38,152			
2	Maliwan Ngoenmuen	77,866	36,928	○ 50,527		
3	Adisak Phokkhakunlakanon	60,066	54,534			
4	Wirasak Chinarat	48,393	○ 42,551			
5	Sanit Chanthrawong	42,303	29,844	44,523	50,532	48,162
6	Niran Phithaknawatchara	○ 41,926				
7	Amon Ninprem	39,523	59,890	○ 52,607		
8	Maitri Naiyakun	39,443	25,943	66,914	69,382	39,578
9	Nitisak Ratchanit	39,015	28,371	-		
10	Wilawan Tanwatthanaphong	33,634	48,964	27,917	105,077	○ 102,167

Source: Compiled by author based on the results of each round of voting released by the Election Commission.

Note: The names of declared winners and the numbers of votes within the winning range are in bold letters.

A diagonal line across the number of votes indicates a yellow card, a cross indicates a red card, and a circle next to the number of votes indicates a declared winner in that round of voting.

as he did in the third round but lost to Wilawan, who managed to poll more than 100,000 votes. However, Wilawan was issued a yellow card and failed to win. In the fifth round, Wilawan again secured more than 100,000 votes and finally won a seat in the Senate.

There is some possibility that votes in the first round were secured by vote buying or other irregular means. It is not surprising that each candidate polled less in the second round since fewer voters turned out. However, some candidates won more votes. Besides possible irregularities,[15] this was because those who had voted for winning candidates in previous rounds now drifted towards other candidates. Amon was a typical example. There is little doubt that he increased his votes in the second round and almost maintained the same level in the third round because he managed to attract the votes that in earlier rounds had gone to the winners. This was also the primary factor in the substantial increase in former provincial Governor Maitri's votes in the third round.

One of the effects of this winning-out style election was that any voter who diligently participated in each round of voting effectively cast four votes (five, if the fourth round, which produced no winner, is included). Hence, some voters must have contributed to the victories of as many as four candidates, for example, Niran Phithakhawatchara in the first round, Wirasak in the second, Amon in the third and Wilawan in the fifth. In many provinces there were some candidates, who would otherwise have lost, who won seats in later rounds on the basis of the early winners' votes drifting to them. In Bangkok, for instance, a second round was held for two of its eighteen seats. Chotchoi Sophonphanit came thirty-fifth in the first round with a mere 10,351 votes, less than half as many as the lowest ranked winner with 22,925 votes, but increased her votes nearly eight-fold to 82,579 in the second round and won a seat. The other candidate who won in the second round, with 92,515 votes, had come seventh in the first round with 50,322 votes but received a yellow card. In effect, in the second round Chotchoi jumped over seventeen candidates who had polled better than her in the first round. Obviously, many of the early winners' votes drifted to her. In Nakhon Ratchasima province, three of its eight seats were decided in the first round. In the second round, winners were decided by similarly fluctuating results in which a candidate who came tenth with 31,000 votes in the first round led the second round with 53,000 votes, the eighth-ranked candidate came second, the second-ranked candidate came third, and the ninth-ranked candidate came fourth.

This is clearly against the principle of equality in election. For example, if a group with a particular leaning (say, people who are interested in conservation) preferred a particular type of candidate (e.g., environmental activists), the group could keep voting for the particular type of candidates in all rounds to ensure their victory. Besides, a candidate who was not within the winning range in the first round and thus supposed to be a loser could turn to be a winner due to the repeated rounds of voting.

Who were the winners?

Who stood as candidates in this Senate election and who won? Were they different from those who had previously been appointed by the government? Fortunately, the Election Commission published detailed information about candidates and winners on its website for this Senate election.[16] An example cited here is that of Pramot Maiklat of Bangkok district, who received the highest number of votes in the country (Figures 4.2 and 4.3). In both figures, the left side is a reproduction of the original Thai text and the right side is a translation. (Certain information such as house numbers and telephone numbers are deleted to protect privacy.)

Candidates: Predominance of former public officials

Initially there were 1532 people who filed for candidacy. This number was later reduced to 1522, as ten people were found to be ineligible. One of the 1522 candidates died before polling was complete. According to the *Bangkok Post*'s reports of the official data released by the Election Commission (*Bangkok Post*,

Figure 4.2. Example of the introduction of an election candidate (Pramot Maiklat)

เอกสารแนะนำตัวผู้สมัคร
จังหวัด กรุงเทพมหานคร
หมายเลขผู้สมัคร เบอร์ 151
คำนำหน้าชื่อ / ยศ นาย
ชื่อ ปราโมทย์ นามสกุล ไม้กลัด
อายุ 59 บ้านเกิดจังหวัด กรุงเทพมหานคร
ระดับการศึกษา ปริญญาโท
ปริญญาตรีจากสถาบัน
วิศวกรรมชลประทาน เกษตรศาสตร์ 2506
ปริญญาโทจากสถาบัน
วิศวกรรมศาสตร์(วิศวกรรมชลประทาน)
ม.แคลิฟอร์เนีย,สหรัฐอเมริกา
ปริญญาเอกจากสถาบัน
อาชีพ / ความเชี่ยวชาญ
การจัดการทรัพยากรน้ำและทรัพยากรเกษตร
ประสบการณ์
อธิบดีกรมชลประธาน
รองปลัดกระทรวงเกษตรและสหกรณ์
	Personal Information of Candidate
	Province: Bangkok
	Candidate No. 151
	
	Title: Mr.
	First name: Pramot
	Family name: Maiklat
	Age: 59
	Place of birth: Bangkok
	Education: Master's degree
	  B.A. (Irrigation Engineering), Kasetsart University 1963
	  M.A. (Irrigation Engineering) University of California
	Occupation/Specialty:
	  Management of water and agricultural resources
	Career:
	  Director-General, Irrigation Department
	  Deputy Permanent-Secretary, Ministry of Agriculture and Cooperatives

Table 4.3 A breakdown of the 2000 Senatorial election candidates by occupation

Occupation	Number of candidates	ratio (%)
Public official	600	39.4
Politician	21	1.4
Farmer	56	3.7
Legal professional	259	17.0
Businessperson	318	20.9
Laborer	61	4.0
Other	207	13.6
Total	1,522	100.0

Source: *Bangkok Post*, 2 March 2000.

2 March 2000), of 1522 candidates, 600, or almost 40%, were public officials (retired military officers or civil servants), followed by 318 businesspeople (20.1%) and 259 legal professionals (17.0%) (Table 4.3).

This breakdown appears to be based on information provided by the candidates themselves, but it does not seem to properly reflect the reality for several reasons. The candidates' personal information published on the Commission's website had one item labeled 'occupation/specialty' and another labeled 'career.' The description given in these sections, particularly in the former, varies greatly between individuals (and provinces). For example, in Pramot's case (Figure 4.2), the occupation/specialty is listed simply as 'management of water and agricultural resources,' which appears to be his 'specialty,' not his occupation. It is the career section that indicates Pramot was a 'Director-General of the Irrigation Department,' that is, a civil service official. Yet the career section does not include dates, so it is not immediately known if the candidate was, say, a provincial governor immediately prior to the election or more than ten years earlier. Because of this ambiguity, there was even some variation in the numbers reported by the Election Commission. For example, one of the Commission's reports published after the Senate election stated that 601 of 1532 candidates (39.2%) were public officials (Kho. Ko. Tho. 2001a: n.p.) while another stated that 571 of 1521 candidates (37.5%) were public officials (Kho. Ko. Tho. 2000d: 12). Either way, though, public officials undoubtedly formed the largest group. Since serving public officials were not allowed to run for the Senate under the 1997 Constitution, almost all of these 'public officials' (about 570) were pensioners (*kharatchakan bamnan*), that is, they were 'retired' in terms of occupation. However, they were classified as 'former public officials' distinct from, say, private sector retirees, because of the significance and high value attached to jobs in the national public service in Thai society.

Furthermore, in many cases a declared occupation is hard to accept at face value. For example, the occupation of retired general Han Linanon, who was

Figure 4.3   Example of the introduction of an election winner (Pramot Maiklat)

ประวัติสมาชิกวุฒิสภา จังหวัดกรุงเทพมหานคร	Personal Information of Senator Bangkok

คำนำหน้าชื่อ / ยศ นาย ชื่อ ปราโมทย์ นามสกุล ไม้กลัด
เพศ ชาย เลขที่บัตรประชาชน x-xxxx-xxxxx-xx-x
จังหวัดที่เกิด กรุงเทพมหานคร วันเกิด 12/12/1929
สัญชาติ ไทย
ชื่อ บิดา กฤษณา สัญชาติ บิดาไทย
ชื่อ มารดา ปิ่น สัญชาติ มารดาไทย
จังหวัดที่เกิด กรุงเทพมหานคร
ภูมิลำเนาเดิม
xx หมู่ที่ x แขวงบางประกอก เขตราษฎร์บูรณะ กรุงเทพมหานคร 10140
ที่อยู่ปัจจุบัน
xxx ซอยประชาชื่น xx ถนนประชาชื่น แขวงบางซื่อ เขตบางซื่อ กรุงเทพมหานคร 10800
ที่อยู่ที่ติดต่อ
xx ซ.ประชาชื่น xx ถ.ประชาชื่น บางซื่อ กทม. 10800
โทรศัพท์ xxxxxxx FAX xxxxxxx
อาชีพ/ความเชี่ยวชาญ
ข้าราชการบำนาญ
ระดับการศึกษา
ปริญญาโท
ปริญญาตรีจากสถาบัน
วิศวกรรมชลประทาน เกษตรศาสตร์ 2506
ปริญญาโทจากสถาบัน
วิศวกรรมศาสตร์(วิศวกรรมชลประทาน)
ม.แคลิฟอร์เนีย,สหรัฐอเมริกา
ปริญญาเอกจากสถาบัน
 	
ประสบการณ์ทำงาน
อธิบดีกรมชลประทาน
รองปลัดกระทรวงเกษตรและสหกรณ์
 	
คะแนนเสียงที่ได้จากการเลือกตั้ง
421,515 คะแนน
	Title: First name: Pramot
	Family name: Maiklat
	Sex: Male
	Citizen's ID: x-xxxx-xxxxx-xx-x
	Place of birth: Bangkok
	Date of birth: 12 December 1929
	Nationality: Thailand
	Father: Kritsana Nationality: Thailand
	Mother: Pin Nationality: Thailand
	Place of birth: Bangkok
	Registered domicile: No.XX, Mu X, Bangprakok, Khet Ratburana, Bangkok 10140
	Current address: xx Soi Prachachun XX, Prachachun Road, Bangsu, Bangkok 10800
	Contact address: xx Soi Prachachun XX, Prachachun Road, Bangsu, Bangkok 10800
	Telephone: xxxxxxx Fax: xxxxxxx
	Occupation/Specialty: Retired public official
	Education: Master's degree
	    Bachelor's degree: School of agricultural & irrigation engineering 1963
	    Master's degree: University of California (water engineering)
	Occupation/Specialty:
	    Management of water and agricultural resources.
	Career:
	    Irrigation bureau director.
	    Deputy undersecretary of the agriculture and cooperative ministry
	Votes polled: 421,515

elected in the southern province of Satun, was listed as 'self-employed.' Perhaps he was running some kind of business, but his electoral success had nothing to do with his being a business owner and everything to do with having been the Commander of the Fourth Army Region in the south, where his successes in anti-Communist operations and restoring civil order were so spectacular that the Army Chief was green with envy. After retirement from the Army, Han was elected to the House of Representatives and became a cabinet member on the strength of his military achievements. His success in the political world was solely due to his reputation as a military man. Another example was Sunthon Chindain, elected in Kamphaeng Phet province, who listed his occupation as 'legal professional.' While this is technically correct, many 'legal professionals' are lawyers; Sunthon is a retired judge who served in both provincial and high courts in the province. It is certain that he was elected on the strength of his career as a judge.

It is likely that many of the candidates who were former public officials were listed in other categories. It is also highly probable that not a few of them were elected on the basis of their career in the public service, as with Han and Sunthon above. Hence, it is important to re-classify their occupations with greater emphasis on their work history. It should be noted, however, that while this re-classification is expected to be much closer to the reality than the Commission's original data, complete accuracy is unachievable because a number of candidates changed their jobs frequently or else had more than one job at a time. The result shows that 874 of 1522 candidates (57.4%) had worked as a public official at some point in their life, 414 (27.2%) had never worked in the public service and it is unclear whether the remaining 234 (15.4%) had worked in the public service or not. Hence, the proportion of public officials is substantially higher than that reported by the Election Commission. A breakdown of the public officials shows that primary and secondary school teachers form the largest group (328; 21.6%), followed by Interior Ministry officials (98), police officers[17] (65), university teachers (54), Public Health Ministry officials (46) and Agriculture and Cooperatives Ministry officials (22). As well as these administrative officials, there were eighty-six military officials among the candidates. Sixty-one were from the Army, sixteen from the Navy and nine from the Air Force. The largest group outside of the public service was businesspeople (170), followed by lawyers (164) (Table 4.4).

Winners: Predominance of former public officials

The breakdown of the election winners by occupation, according to the Election Commission report, indicates seventy-three of 200 successful candidates were former public officials (36.5%), forty-nine were self-employed (24.5%) and

Table 4.4 A breakdown of the 2000 Senate election candidates and winners by occupation

Occupation	Candidates		1st round		2nd round		3rd round		4th round		Total winners		Success rate
Public officials (a)	874	57.42%	71	58.20%	32	48.48%	4	50.00%	4	100.00%	111	55.50%	12.70%
Interior Ministry	98	6.44%	16	13.11%	6	9.09%	2	25.00%			24	12.00%	24.49%
Police	65	4.27%	8	6.56%	6	9.09%					14	7.00%	21.54%
University (b)	54	3.55%	8	6.56%	3	4.55%			2	50.00%	13	6.50%	24.07%
Primary & secondary school	328	21.55%	6	4.92%	6	9.09%	1	12.50%			13	6.50%	3.96%
Public Health Ministry	46	3.02%	6	4.92%			1	12.50%			7	3.50%	15.22%
Agriculture Ministry	22	1.45%	3	2.46%	1	1.52%					4	2.00%	18.18%
Justice Ministry	5	0.33%	2	1.64%							2	1.00%	40.00%
Prime Minister's Office	8	0.53%	2	1.64%							2	1.00%	25.00%
Finance Ministry	8	0.53%			2	3.03%					2	1.00%	25.00%
Transport & Communication Ministry	8	0.53%			1	1.52%					1	0.50%	12.50%
Army	61	4.01%	12	9.84%	3	4.55%			1	25.00%	16	8.00%	26.23%
Air Force	9	0.59%	1	0.82%							1	0.50%	11.11%
Navy	16	1.05%	1	0.82%							1	0.50%	6.25%
State-run company	34	2.23%	3	2.46%	1	1.52%					4	2.00%	11.76%
Unknown/other	112	7.36%	3	2.46%	3	4.55%	1	25.00%			7	3.50%	6.25%
Other than public officials	648	42.58%	51	41.80%	34	51.52%	4	50.00%	0	0.00%	89	44.50%	13.73%
Subtotal	414	27.20%	30	24.59%	19	28.79%	2	25.00%	0	0.00%	51	25.50%	12.32%
Businessperson	170	11.17%	11	9.02%	13	19.70%	2	25.00%			26	13.00%	15.29%
Lawyer	164	10.78%	10	8.20%	4	5.06%					14	7.00%	8.54%
Farmer	5	0.33%	1	0.82%							1	0.50%	20.00%
Journalist	16	1.05%	1	0.82%							1	0.50%	6.25%
NGO	16	1.05%	6	4.92%	1	1.52%					7	3.50%	43.75%
Religion-related	8	0.53%	1	0.82%							1	0.50%	12.50%
Doctor (c)	5	0.33%			1	.52%					1	0.50%	20.00%
Other	30	1.97%									0	0.00%	0.00%
Unknown	234	15.37%	21	17.21%	15	22.73%	2	25.00%	0	0.00%	38	19.00%	16.24%
Total	1522	100.00%	122	100.00%	66	100.00%	8	100.00%	4	100.00%	200	100.00%	13.14%

Source: Compiled by author based on the personal information of candidates published by the Election Commission (Kho. Ko. Tho. 2000b; Kho. Ko. Tho. 2000c).

Note: Winners in the 5th round are not included in the winners of the 4th round.

(a) Refers to retired public officials and includes those who are in business or practice law after retirement. Successful candidates include 14 provincial governors, 10 provincial police chiefs, 7 department heads, 11 generals, 5 state-run hospital directors.

(b) Includes teachers of not only the institutions under the jurisdiction of the Ministry of University Affairs but also the higher education institutions under the jurisdiction of the Ministry of Education such as teachers' colleges and technical colleges.

(c) Includes only those who are not confirmed as having worked for Ministry of Public Health. Doctors employed by the Ministry of Public Health are classified as officials of the ministry. Graduates of medical schools of state universities are required to work for government agencies for a certain period.

twenty-five were legal professionals (12.5%) (Table 4.5). Other occupations included ten farmers, ten unemployed, eight salaried workers, six politicians and five medical professionals[18] (Kho. Ko. Tho. 2001a: n.p.). Considering that public officials accounted for nearly 40% of the total candidates according to the Commission report, their success rate was lower than those of other occupations.

The re-classified data, however, indicates that there were 111 former public officials (55.5%, including four former state-run company employees), fifty-one in other occupations (26.0%) and thirty-eight unknown (19.4%).[19] The public officials included twenty-four Interior Ministry officials, sixteen Army officers, fourteen police officers, thirteen primary, secondary and university teachers, and seven Public Health Ministry officials.

So, what is the significance of the proportion (55.5%) of former public officials? To answer this question, comparison with the past appointed Senate is deemed useful. The very high proportion of public officials in the appointed Senate has been frequently noted, as they had accounted for more than 90% of appointed legislators for much of the period prior to 1973. During those relatively rare periods of party politics, however, they accounted for just over 60% in 1946 and about 60% in 1975. In these periods, the ratio of administrative officials to military officials tended to increase markedly. The proportion of public officials gradually but steadily declined from the late 1970s, during which time the proportion of businesspeople has steadily increased. In 1996, when the government last appointed senators, 52.3% of them were public officials (18.9% military and 33.5% administrative). At the same time, the proportion of businesspeople reached 30.1%. Even though the Senate was still a house of public officials with more than one-half of its members being employed in the public sector, this characteristic was steadily becoming less pronounced.

The proportion of public officials to the total number of winners in the first Senate election in 2000 (55.5%) compares favorably to the 1996 figure in terms of preserving the Senate's public official character. It would, of course, be inappropriate to directly compare the two. After all, many of the appointed senators were serving public officials rather than retired ones. For example, 194 of 267 senators as of June 1995 were public officials, of which 110 were active and eighty-four were retired. In March 1996, 138 of 260 senators were public officials, of which eighty-five were active and fifty-three were retired (SLW 1996: 154). In both cases, there were more serving public officials than retired ones, at a ratio of about six to four. Under the 1997 Constitution, however, serving public officials were not eligible to run for the Senate, and therefore all of the public officials who stood for office in the 2000 election were retired. Perhaps more importantly, the 55.5% included public officials in a broader

Table 4.5 A breakdown of the 2000 Senate election winners by occupation

Occupation	Election Commission Data		Tamada Data	
	Number	%	Number	%
Public official	73	36.5	111	55.5
Political official	1	0.5	-	-
Agriculture	10	5.0	1	0.5
Law	25	12.5	14	7.0
Medical	5	2.5	-	-
Professional	4	2.0	-	-
Self-employed	35	17.5	26	13.0
Commerce	14	7.0		
Salaried worker	8	4.0	-	-
Politician	6	3.0	-	-
Unemployed	10	5.0	-	-
Other	9	4.5	48	24.0
Total	200	100.0	200	100.0

Source: Data published by the Election Commission (Kho. Ko. Tho. 2001a) and data compiled by author based on the personal data published on the Election Commission website.

sense—counting those who had worked in the public service in the past but who were not necessarily living solely on a public service pension after retirement. If this same, broader definition had been used for appointed senators, their proportions would have been even higher.[20]

Despite these important reservations, though, it is undeniable that former public officials continued to command a majority in the Senate even after this inaugural popular election. Another important consideration is that many of the former public officials owed their electoral success to their public service career. That is, they were elected because they were former public officials. In this sense, the Senate did not entirely change its character under the new popular election system. It continued to be very much a house of public officials thanks to an election system that was favorable to certain types of former public officials.

High success rates among certain public officials

Two-hundred winners of 1522 candidates equates to an overall success rate of 13.1%. The success rate for former public officials was 12.7%; 111 of 874 candidates were successful. Although this is slightly lower than the overall success rate, it should be noted that the success rate fluctuates greatly from one government ministry to another. For example, primary and secondary school teachers accounted for 21.6% of the total candidates and 37.5% of public official candidates but only thirteen or 6.5% of the total winners were successfully elected, making for a success rate of less than 4%. Once these are removed, the remaining public officials account for 35.9% (546) of the total candidates and 49.0% (ninety-eight) of the total winners, making the success rate 17.9%. This is substantially higher than the 13.7% success rate for those who fall into non-public official and unknown categories.

A breakdown of winners by ministry shows that twenty-four were former Interior Ministry officials, followed by eighteen from the Defense Ministry, fourteen from the police, thirteen each from the Education Ministry and the University Bureau, seven from the Public Health Ministry and four from the Agriculture and Cooperatives Ministry. In terms of success rates, the Justice Ministry was 40.0%, Office of the Prime Minister and the Finance Ministry 25.0% each, the Army 26.2%, the Interior Ministry 24.5%, universities 24.1% and the police 21.5%.

A closer look at those ministries that produced relatively high numbers of winners reveals interesting relations between candidates' careers and their electoral districts (provinces) of choice. Of the ninety-eight former Interior Ministry officials who stood as candidates, thirty-three were former provincial governors. Fourteen of them were elected, which meant a success rate of 42.4%. Of these former provincial governors, at least nine filed candidacy in the province in which they had served as governor. Five of them were elected, which boosted their success rate to 55.6%. Another occupation with a high success rate in provinces where the candidates had worked as high officials was director of the state-run hospital. Among the seven candidates in this category, five were successful (a success rate of 71.4%). The situation was similar for former provincial police chiefs: there were seventeen candidates and ten were successful (58.8%). More particularly, of the eleven candidates who ran in the province in which they had previously worked as police chief, eight were successful (72.7%).[21] In the case of the Army, thirty of sixty-one candidates were generals. Ten were elected, a success rate of 33.3%. There were also five Navy admirals but none of them were successful, while only one of six air chief marshals was successful. Similar results were observed for lieutenant-generals. There were thirteen lieutenant-generals from the Army, three vice admirals from the Navy and two air marshals from the Air Force. Only three Army lieutenant-generals were elected.

Former military officials in Bangkok and the provinces had markedly different fortunes. As mentioned above, a total of thirty Army generals ran throughout the country and ten succeeded. In Bangkok, however, seven former Army generals ran and none was successful. In fact, they suffered a crushing defeat, not even attracting 10,000 votes each. Two air chief marshals and two Navy admirals also ran in Bangkok and failed. This means that twenty-three Army generals ran in the provinces and ten—nearly one-half of them—succeeded (a success rate of 43.5%). In short, Army generals were popular in the provinces and quite unpopular in Bangkok, and in this case, the successful candidates did not necessarily run in the provinces where they had worked. In fact, those who did were a minority. Five ran in the provinces where they were born. For example, Phanom Chinawicharana, a Class 11 Army Academy graduate who was the Second Infantry Division Commander at the time of the May 1992 incident, ran in his home province of Sukhothai. High officials of the military are often regarded as local heroes in their home provinces.

Why so many public officials?

Former national government employees accounted for 57.4% of the candidates and 55.5% of the winners. Why were there so many public officials in the election? The 1997 Constitution and Thailand's social structure offer reasons for this.

First, under the 1997 Constitution, eligibility for election is limited to those who have a university or higher education, as discussed in Chapter three. According to the preliminary results of the 2000 Population and Housing Census conducted by the National Statistical Office,[22] the population six years of age and over in 2000 was 55,250,000 and only 3,114,000 or 5.6% of them had a university or higher education qualification (bachelor's, master's or doctorate degree).[23]

These university graduates were not distributed evenly throughout the country, either. Of 3,114,000, 2,196,000 (70.5%) lived in an urban area (*nai khet thetsaban*) and only 919,000 (29.5%) lived in rural areas (*nok khet thetsaban*). Of the university-educated urban residents, 1,050,000 lived in Bangkok while only 1,146,000 lived in cities other than Bangkok. In short, the population with a higher education qualification was divided into three almost equal parts: 33.7% in Bangkok, 36.8% in other cities and 29.5% in rural communities. This, however, is inconsistent with the general population distribution. Of 55,250,000 people who were six years of age and over, 37,820,000 (68.5%) lived in rural communities, 11,520,000 (20.8%) lived in cities other than Bangkok and only 5,910,000 (10.7%) lived in Bangkok.[24] Accordingly, there was considerable disparity in the proportion of people with a higher education to the population six years of age and over for the three regions: 17.8% in Bangkok, 9.9% in other cities and 2.4% in rural areas (Table 4.6). According to the 1997 Population Migration Survey by the National Statistical Office,[25] we can estimate that 37% of the people with a higher education qualification were born in Bangkok. These figures show that over one-third of those who were eligible for parliamentary election were either born or living in Bangkok. Reflecting the distribution of university graduates,

264 candidates ran for the Senate in Bangkok, accounting for 17.3% of a total of 1522 candidates. This high number of candidates was not just because Bangkok was the largest electoral district (eighteen seats). In fact, Nakhon Ratchasima province, the second largest electoral district with eight seats, had only fifty-four candidates, Ubon Ratchathani province with six seats had sixty-one candidates, Chiang Mai province, Nakhon Si Thammarat province and Udon Thani with five seats each had fifty-one, forty-eight and thirty-four candidates respectively. Since Bangkok had a much higher number of eligible people, the competition was also proportionately tougher.[26]

It is not immediately known exactly how these precious few university graduates were employed. There is no doubt, however, that a significant proportion of them were public officials. According to data released by the Civil Service Commission,[27] the total (actual) number of national government employees (regular full-time personnel) in 1999 was 1,209,000,[28] and 764,000, or 63.2%, of them had a university or higher education. There were also 91,000 local government employees, of which 53,000 or 57.7% had a university or higher education. Hence, the total number of serving public officials with a university or higher education was 817,000, which accounted for almost one-quarter of the total number of university graduates (Table 4.7). There were about 300,000 non-regular full-time employees as well,[29] including a considerable number of university graduates. The military service also had many officers who were graduates of military academies—the equivalent of university graduates. We can assume that there was also a sizeable number of civil and military service retirees.

Looking at the places of work for the 1,210,000 or so national government employees, we find that almost 80% of them were working in the provinces. In particular, 96.1% of 528,000 primary and secondary education personnel, the largest group, were based in the provinces. Of the education personnel, 88.9% had a university or higher education.[30] It was perhaps only natural, then, that nearly 330 of the Senate election candidates were former teachers. Moreover, it is important to note that, besides education personnel, more national government employees worked in the provinces than in Bangkok. For example, 72.5% of general administrative agency employees worked in the provinces. When local government employees were added, almost 1,000,000 public officials were working outside of Bangkok. About 60% or 600,000 of them had a university or higher education. Since the total number of university graduates living outside of Bangkok was about 2,000,000, public officials accounted for about one-third of them. These individuals had the option of running for office in the provinces where competition was not as keen as it was in Bangkok. In other words, when age requirement is disregarded, one-in-three

Table 4.6 Distribution of people with a higher education (university or higher) in 2000

	Total	By area			By region				
		Urban		Rural	Metropolitan	Central	North	Northeast	South
		Metropolitan	Non-metropolitan						
Population 6 years of age and older (000)	55,253.2	5,913.7	11,517.6	37,821.9	5,913.7	12,968.8	10,415.8	18,711.1	7,243.9
Population with a higher education (000)	3,114.5	1,049.8	1,145.7	918.9	1,049.8	774.6	393.1	616.4	280.5
Bachelor's degree	2,880.4	918.3	1,071.5	890.5	918.3	727.4	368.5	595.2	271.0
Master's degree	217.8	122.7	68.6	26.6	122.7	43.2	23.3	19.2	9.5
Doctorate degree	16.3	8.8	5.6	1.9	8.8	4.0	1.4	2.1	0.1
Area or regional population / Total population (%)	100.0%	10.7%	20.8%	68.5%	10.7%	23.5%	18.9%	33.9%	13.1%
% of population with a higher education by area or region	100.0%	33.7%	36.8%	29.5%	33.7%	24.9%	12.6%	19.8%	9.0%
% of population with a higher education in each area or region	5.6%	17.8%	9.9%	2.4%	17.8%	6.0%	3.8%	3.3%	3.9%

Source: Compiled by author based on the data released by the National Statistical Office (www.nso.go.th/pop2000/table/tadv_tab6.xls).

Table 4.7 Numbers, education and places of work of national public officials in 1999

Categories	Number	% of university graduates	Place of work		
			Central	Regional	Regional (%)
National government officials	1,208,623	63.2%	236,388	972,235	80.4%
General	394,814	51.4%	108,770	286,044	72.5%
Teaching	527,682	88.9%	20,543	507,139	96.1%
University (a)	51,083	79.8%	51,083	-	0.0%
Parliament	1,397	52.3%	1,397	-	0.0%
Judges	2,455	100.0%	850	1,605	65.4%
Prosecutors	1,677	100.0%	761	916	54.6%
Police	229,515	20.3%	52,984	176,531	76.9%

Source: Compiled by author based on data published by the Civil Service Commission. (http://www.ocsc.go.th/PersPoli/manpower/manth/slide8.htm)

Note: Additionally, about 60,000 local government personnel (91,117 total minus 29,643 Bangkok Metropolitan Administration personnel) are regionally-based.

(a) There are regional universities but they are directly under Ministry of University Affairs. It seems that their employees are not considered to be assigned in region.

of the people eligible for the 182 Senate seats in the regions outside of Bangkok were serving public officials.

Furthermore, a candidate for Senate election must be at least forty years of age under the 1997 Constitution. Most of the university graduates who were forty years of age or older at the time of the 2000 Senate election would have graduated from university before 1980.[31] The number of university graduates in 1980 was far smaller than in 2000: only 2.2% of the total population.[32] These precious few university graduates prior to 1980 were almost exclusively employed by various government agencies. It is thus highly probable, under the condition that an eligible candidate must be forty years old or more with a university or higher education, that former public officials accounted for well over one-half of the total eligible population.[33]

As mentioned previously, the constitution banned campaigning in Senate elections beyond the uniform campaign activity that was permitted. For businesspeople who traditionally produced many candidates and winners in lower house elections, such constraints made it difficult to take advantage of their financial resources.[34] In contrast, former public officials would not be disadvantaged by their relative financial weakness. The ban on electioneering meant that one's election outcome was more dependent on name recognition than financial resources. Former public officials who had held important posts in the provincial outlets of central government agencies, including provincial governor, provincial police chief, state-run hospital director, etc., often enjoyed excellent name recognition among the voters. One notable characteristic of Bangkok in this regard was that those candidates who appeared frequently in the media attracted far more votes than others.[35] Although Bangkok had a high concentration of former ministry executives such as permanent secretaries and department chiefs, they could not compete with the darlings of television and newspapers in terms of public profile. But very few media celebrities lived in the provinces. Hence, in terms of public profile, provincial agency chiefs ranked very highly in the provinces.

Another important issue was the constitutional ban on the appointment of senators to cabinet posts. Traditionally, businesspeople formed the largest group among popularly elected MPs in the House of Representatives. For the MPs after 1983, the occupational category of 'politician' refers to the incumbent MPs, most of whom in fact are businesspeople. In the 1990s, they accounted for more than one-half of all MPs. The main personal goal for most MPs was to land a cabinet post, as former Prime Minister Anan commented on 6 August 1997: 'The problem with Thai politics is to win power by unfair election and try to recover funds... They invest money (in election) to get a cabinet post, not to become a member of the House of Representatives' (*Matichon Sutsapda*, 12 August 1997). The proportion of businesspeople in the House of Representatives had increased since the 1970s because they could recover the funds invested in their election campaigns by becoming cabinet members (Rangsan 1993: 61–76). However, the Senate was not as attractive as the House of Representatives for such people once the possibility of entering the cabinet was eliminated. Presumably, then, many businesspeople would not have stood for this Senate election even if they did have a chance of winning. This, of course, would have worked in favor of eligible candidates other than businesspeople, such as former public officials.

The constitution had another, albeit minor, provision that was favorable to former public officials. As discussed, it stipulated conditions for eligibility to stand in particular provinces (electoral districts). Usually, a candidate could run in the province in which he or she was born, or was a registered resident. One exception to this requirement was that one could stand in a province in which he or she had served as a Member of Parliament, a local government head or a member of local council. This was typically the province in which the candidate resided. But there were two further exceptions: eligibility in a province in which the candidate had studied for at least two years or had worked as a public official for at least two years. In this case, he or she did not have to be a registered resident of this province. The latter provision was clearly a special benefit for former public officials. Many public officials are transferred every two to four years, often from province to province, all over the country. If they decide to run for the Senate, they have the privilege to choose from many available options the most winnable province. Obviously, a province in which the candidate had served as the head of a provincial agency would be an attractive option. In this respect, it should be recalled that former provincial governors, provincial police chiefs and hospital directors recorded higher success rates when they ran in the provinces in which they had formerly held these posts. Bangkok was no exception. They had former directors-general (three out of seven candidates were successful) instead of former chiefs of provincial offices and a former metropolitan police chief (one candidate ran and won) instead of former provincial police commanders.

What the election meant for political reform

The effect of the bachelor clause

Had a bachelor clause not been set as the eligibility requirements for Senate candidacy, a far wider range of candidates could have been nominated, especially since political party affiliation was not required and the cost of candidacy was relatively low. As indicated in Table 3.4 in the previous chapter, the proportion of House of Representatives candidates with an education below university level was 55.3% in March 1992, 42.1% in 1995 and 50.6% in 1996. These candidates had to be members of political parties. Without the requirement for political party membership, any person could have run for Senate election and the number of candidates with a lower education qualification would have increased. Further, because financial strength was not a deciding factor, they could have achieved a higher success rate than they did in lower house elections. However, the bachelor clause was included in the supposedly democracy-oriented 1997 Constitution and deprived less-educated people of the opportunity to run in any election.[36] As the appointed Senate served some, albeit nominal, function of vocational representation, some appointed senators did represent laborers and farmers. Thus, this bachelor clause was clearly not conducive to democratization.

Recall that the CDA claimed that the bachelor clause was adopted because voters at public hearings and meetings wanted MPs with a higher education. Did the Senate election outcome reflect this preference of voters? In fact, 59.3% of the candidates had a bachelor's degree, 32.7% had a master's degree and 8.0% had a PhD. If voters really preferred people with a higher education, candidates with a master's degree and a PhD would have achieved higher success rates. However, 57.5% of the winners had a bachelor's degree, 35% had a master's degree and 7.5% had a PhD (Table 4.8). There was no significant difference between the proportions of candidates and winners. Looking at the success rate for each group, the success rate for the total of 1522 candidates was 13.1%; it was only 12.7% for bachelor's degree holders, 14.1% for master's degree holders and 12.4% for PhD holders. Master's degree holders achieved a slightly higher than average success rate, but PhD holders were less successful than bachelor's degree holders, whose success rate was already below average. Contrary to the CDA's claim, then, voters did not necessarily prefer candidates with higher education.[37] The figures speak for themselves, showing that although the so-called majority who demanded higher education qualifications at the CDA hearings and meetings might have been the majority of certain vocal groups, it was clearly not the majority of the voters as a whole.

The house of public officials

The 2000 Senate election was the first time in the history of Thailand that senators had been popularly elected and was thus a completely new experience for both the voters and candidates. More than a few candidates would have nominated themselves without really knowing what to expect. The constitution drafters had great expectations that intellectuals would be the most eligible Senate candidates. As it turned out, though, intellectuals were not equally successful throughout the country. For example, it was in Bangkok where four of seven successful NGO candidates and four of thirteen successful university teachers were elected. As we have seen, former public officials were much more successful than intellectuals in the provinces.

It is important to note that the former public officials' high success rate stemmed directly from the provisions of the constitution. The education qualification and the minimum age requirements, alongside the ban on cabinet appointment and election campaigning—both disincentives for wealthy businesspeople—gave former public officials an advantage against party politicians. The drafters probably could have anticipated this outcome, at least to some extent. The criticisms of bureaucratic governance which had recurred until the end of the 1980s had completely disappeared by then. The predominance of (former) public officials in the Senate was no longer a topic of major concern. When the Chatchai administration was created in 1988, the accession of a party politician to the premiership, instead of a military man, was widely and warmly welcomed as an important step towards democratization. Bowonsak, the central figure in drafting the 1997 Constitution, was an advisor to Prime Minister Chatchai. Yet, those who led the drive for political reform in the 1990s considered party politicians, not the military or administrative bureaucrats, to be the enemy of democracy. Further, once the party politicians had taken over the role of villain, their opponents—public officials—were re-located in the good guy camp.

Similarly, it should be noted that former public officials were also expected to join some of the inspection bodies stipulated by the 1997 Constitution, judging, again, from the eligibility requirements. In fact, the first thirteen judges of the Constitution Court consisted of five Supreme Court judges, two ambassadors,

Table 4.8 A breakdown of the 2000 Senate election winners by education

Degree	Candidates		1st round winners		2nd round winners		3rd round winners		4th round winners		Winners subtotal		Success rate
	Number	%	Number	%	Number	%	Number	%	Number	%	Number	%	
Bachelor's	903	59.3%	71	58.2%	36	54.6%	6	75.0%	2	50.0%	115	57.5%	12.7%
Master's	498	32.7%	41	33.6%	26	39.4%	2	25.0%	1	25.0%	70	35.0%	14.1%
Doctorate	121	8.0%	10	8.2%	4	6.1%	0	0.0%	1	25.0%	15	7.5%	12.4%
Total	1522	100.0%	122	100.0%	66	100.0%	8	100.0%	4	100.0%	200	100.0%	13.1%

Source: Compiled by author based on the personal data of all candidates published on the Election Commission website (http://201.183.254.190/report).

two university teachers, two officials from the Office of the Prime Minister (the Council of State and the Bureau of Budget), one public prosecutor and one military judge. The five members of the Election Commission consisted of three Supreme Court judges, one university teacher and one director-general of the Interior Ministry. The fifteen judges of the Supreme Administrative Court consisted of six high officials of administrative agencies (a department head of Finance Ministry, a deputy permanent secretary of the Interior Ministry, a deputy permanent secretary of the Labor and Social Welfare Ministry, a department head of the Agriculture and Cooperatives Ministry, a deputy secretary-general of the Civil Service Commission, and a deputy director of the Bureau of Budget), four Supreme Court judges (one of them was the secretary-general of the Supreme Court), two university teachers, one public prosecutor, one military judge and one deputy governor of the Central Bank (a former judge). All were retired public officials. Once party politicians were identified as the problem, public officials came to be seen as the most suitable inspectors. As discussed, the Senate was also expected to inspect party politicians.

The tendency for former public officials to predominate in the Senate was confirmed again by the by-election for eleven seats in eight provinces held on 21 April 2001. Amid mounting pressure for a senator from Surat Thani province to resign after his sexual misconduct came to light, the Election Commission decided on 13 March 2001 to disqualify ten senators, including the Senate president, for vote buying and other irregularities in the previous year's election. The senator who was accused of sexual misconduct also resigned the following day.[38] Consequently, an election was scheduled for eleven seats in eight provinces all together.[39] All of the previously disqualified senators sought re-election except for the one who resigned over the scandal.[40]

A breakdown of seventy-eight candidates in eight provinces shows that there were forty-four former public officials (56%), followed by sixteen businesspeople and eight politicians (Table 4.9). The average voter turnout for eight provinces was only about 41.37%. Eleven winners included six former public officials, three businesspeople, one politician and one lawyer. Former public officials accounted for 55% of the winners.[41] The proportion of former public officials to candidates (56%) and to winners (55%) was almost the same as for the 2000 Senate election. The Senate continued to be dominated by public officials. It is no exaggeration to say that the job of senator is ideally suited to many former public officials. Public officials have presumably learned from the two Senate elections that they have an advantage in Senate elections. They now know what to expect. Unlike the House of Representatives, the Senate is never dissolved, so the timing of election is predetermined. Would-be candidates can thoroughly prepare for the next election. Thus it is highly likely that there will soon be more

Table 4.9 Number of former public officials in the April 2001 Senate by-election

Province	Seats	Candidates	Number of public officials Candidates	Winners
Khon Kaen	1	9	5	0
Ubon Ratchathani	2	9	2	2
Si Sa Ket	2	13	6	1
Lop Buri	2	12	8	1
Ayutthaya	1	9	4	0
Phayao	1	8	7	1
Ranong	1	8	5	0
Surat Thani	1	10	7	1
Subtotal	11	78	44	6

Source: Compiled by author based on data published by the Election Commission.

public officials near retirement age who will aim for the Senate as a place for postretirement employment.[42]

Another point to note is that it took nearly one year from the original election for the Commission to investigate complaints from voters and determine what election violations occurred. Many of those elected probably expected that their election violations would go unquestioned once their election victories were declared. However, those who were found guilty of violations were retrospectively disqualified and ordered to repay their Senate allowances. This was a strong warning against future election violations. Considering that most of these cases involved vote buying, these financially strong candidates will have to be more cautious in future elections.[43] This will create even more favorable conditions for former public officials.

5
The 2001 General Election: Did It Change Politics?

The aim of the political reformers and the 1997 Constitution was to achieve clean and efficient politics. It was not until a House of Representatives election was held under the 1997 Constitution and a new cabinet was formed that the effects of various constitution's provisions became apparent. Members of Parliament and the cabinet under the Democrat Party government, which was formed in November 1997, shortly after the new Constitution came into force, were selected according to the previous system. The government finally dissolved Parliament on 9 November 2000, immediately before the end of its full term. Despite the intentions of constitution drafters, more than three years had passed since the new Constitution was effected. The first general election under the new Constitution was held in January 2001, followed by the formation of the first cabinet under the new system.

This chapter examines the extent to which the desired objectives of the political reformers were achieved in terms of elections, political parties and the cabinet's composition. Since some provisions were not applied to this first general election in accordance with the interim measures provided by the Constitution for the transitional period, the Constitution's full effects were still not realized. Several more elections must be held before one will be able to fully evaluate the extent to which the reformers' aims have been achieved. Still, general tendencies or directions may be estimated. The main objectives of the political reformers included eradicating vote buying, emphasizing political parties rather than candidates in elections, realizing a two-party system, appointing cabinet members from MPs elected on a party-list basis, strengthening the leadership of the prime minister in cabinet and stabilizing the government.

This chapter concludes that, to a large extent, the aims of the new constitution have been achieved. While vote buying has not been wholly eradicated, political parties with clear policy promises have emerged and won a majority of the seats in Parliament. No single-seat constituency MP was included in the cabinet. The prime minister's position became strong and the administration became stable. However, the increased administrative stability also contained seeds of instability for the political system.

The 2001 general election

Implementing the election

The 1997 Constitution changed the election format for the House of Representatives from a multiple-seat electoral constituency system to a combination of 400 seats in a single-seat electoral constituency system and 100 seats in a party-list proportional representation system. The single-seat constituencies are allocated to each province in proportion to population. In the party-list system, voters cast votes for the party of their choice based on a list of ranked candidates for each party. Seats are allocated to each party in proportion to the number of votes it polls nationally.[1] Any party that fails to poll at least 5% of the total votes fails to win a seat.[2] Each voter casts one vote for the single-seat constituency and one vote for the party-list system. Unlike senators, House of Representatives MPs are required to belong to a political party.

The applications for candidacy were filed from mid to late November 2000 for the general election scheduled to be held on 6 January 2001. Thirty-seven parties nominated candidates on the party-list basis and thirty-nine parties in the single-seat constituencies. The New Aspiration, Democrat, Chat Thai, Chat Phatthana and Thai Rak Thai parties each nominated the maximum 100 candidates for the party-list system (Kho. Ko. Tho. 2001b: 22). In the single-seat constituencies, only the Thai Rak Thai Party nominated 400 candidates. The Democrats nominated 398, Chat Phatthana 320, New Aspiration 311 and Chat Thai nominated 257. Only eight parties, including those just mentioned, nominated more than 200 candidates, or more than one-half of all the single-seat constituencies (Kho. Ko. Tho. 2001b: 151).

The Election Commission assessed the candidates' eligibility in November and disqualified those found to be ineligible. Thirty-seven candidates in twenty-two provinces were ruled ineligible among the initial 2782 single-seat constituency candidates. Twenty-seven of them were disqualified because they did not vote in the previous year's Senate election and six were disqualified due to their lack of educational qualifications (*Bangkok Post*, 3 December 2000).[3] During the campaign period, four candidates were disqualified for electoral violations.

Meanwhile, registered voters who were planning to abstain from voting had to report their reasons to the Election Commission by 29 December. Thai nationals living overseas cast votes in sixty-five countries during December.[4] Domestic absentee voting was conducted on 29 and 30 December. The general election was finally held on 6 January 2001.

The election recorded high voter turnouts: 69.94% in the single-seat constituencies and 69.95% in the proportional representation. Although these figures were slightly lower than those of the previous year's Senate election, they were the highest for any House of Representatives election in Thailand's history.[5] At the same time, the rate of invalid votes (except among absentee voters) was a very high 10.01% in the single-seat constituencies but only 2.49% for the party-list system (Kho. Ko. Tho. 2001b: 22).[6] This was markedly higher than the 2.89% of invalid votes in the 1995 general election and 2.63% in the 1996 general election.[7]

The Election Commission gradually announced the polling results, red-carding eight candidates and yellow-carding fifty-four candidates in the single-seat constituencies on 23 January (*Bangkok Post*, 24 January 2001). The red-carded candidates (each was the leading candidate in their respective constituencies) included five from the Thai Rak Thai Party, two from the New Aspiration Party and one from the Chat Thai Party. Consequently, a revote was scheduled to be held on 29 January in the electoral constituencies of these sixty-two candidates. The revote was limited to the single-seat constituencies and the results of the voting on the party-list basis on 6 January were validated as they were. Only seven of fifty-four yellow-carded candidates failed in the revote; the remaining forty-seven candidates were elected again with the highest number of votes in each constituency (Table 5.1).

Election results

All the winners were confirmed following the revote on 29 January.[8] In the 400 single-seat electoral constituencies, the Thai Rak Thai Party won 200 seats, exactly one-half of the total number, followed by the Democrats (ninety-seven seats), Chat Thai (thirty-five), New Aspiration (twenty-eight), Chat Phatthana (twenty-two), Seritham (fourteen), Ratsadon (two), Thin Thai (one) and the Social Action (one) parties (Table 5.2).

Table 5.1 Red and yellow-carded candidates and by-election winners by party

Party	Invalidated candidates in the original election			By-election winners	Difference
	Red	Yellow	Subtotal		
Thai Rak Thai	5	27	32	24	-8
New Aspiration	2	6	8	9	1
Chat Phattana	0	8	8	10	2
Democrat	0	7	7	7	0
Seritham	0	3	3	4	1
Chat Thai	1	2	3	5	2
Ratsadon	0	1	1	2	1
Thin Thai	0	0	0	1	1

Source: Compiled from Election Commission data
(http://202.183.203.226/sorsor/report-6jan44/newvote.html).

Table 5.2 Single-seat district winners by party and region

Party	Central	North	Northeast	South	Metropolitan	Total
Thai Rak Thai	47	54	69	1	29	200
Democrat	19	16	6	48	8	97
Chat Thai	21	3	11	0	0	35
New Aspiration	3	1	19	5	0	28
Chat Phatthana	4	2	16	0	0	22
Seritham	0	0	14	0	0	14
Ratsadon	1	0	1	0	0	2
Thin Thai	0	0	1	0	0	1
Social Action	0	0	1	0	0	1
Total electoral districts	95	76	138	54	37	400

Source: Data as of 2 February 2001 on the Election Commission website
(http://202.183.203.226/sorsor/numbermp.html).

The leading Thai Rak Thai Party acquired seats evenly throughout the country except in the south. While it managed to win only one seat in the southern region, it won approximately half of the seats in the central and northeast regions, 70% in the northern region and almost 80% in the metropolitan region. The Democrat Party won nearly 90% of the seats in the southern region, which has been a solid constituency for the second leading party since the 1980s. The forty-eight seats it won in the south accounted for almost half of the ninety-seven seats it won nationally. While it managed to gain about 20% of the seats in the central, northern and metropolitan regions, it only won about 4% of the seats in the northeastern region, which was the largest constituency with 138 seats. Besides the two major parties, the Chat Thai Party won a relatively large number of seats in the central region, as did the New Aspiration, Chat Phatthana and Seritham parties in the northeastern region. Like the Democrats, to some extent these parties retained their traditional constituencies.[9]

Let us compare the numbers of seats won by each party in this election with the four previous general elections (Table 5.3). Among the established parties, the Democrat Party won forty-four seats in March 1992, seventy-nine in September 1992, eighty-six in 1995, and 123 in 1996. In 2001 it won slightly fewer seats at ninety-seven, but this was far from an election loss. The New Aspiration Party won seventy-two seats in March 1992, fifty-one in September 1992, fifty-seven in 1995 and 125 in 1996. In 2001 it suffered dismally, winning only twenty-eight seats. The Chat Thai Party won seventy-seven in September 1992, ninety-two in 1995, thirty-nine in 1996 and thirty-five in 2001, which was a negligible reduction. The Chat Phatthana Party won sixty in September 1992, fifty-three in 1995 and fifty-two in 1996. Its number of seats was reduced by more than half to a mere twenty-two in the 2001 election. The Seritham Party lured some powerful MPs from the Chat Phatthana Party and the new look helped the party

Table 5.3 District-based seats won in the 2001 election and those in the previous four elections

	2001	1996	1995	Sept 1992	Mar 1992
Total number of seats	400	393	391	360	360
Thai Rak Thai	200	-	-	-	-
Democrat	97	123	86	79	44
New Aspiration	28	125	57	51	72
Chat Thai	35	39	92	77	74
Chat Phatthana	22	52	53	60	-
Seritham	14	4	11	8	-
Thin Thai	1	-	-	-	-
Ratsadon	2	-	-	1	4
Social Action	1	20	22	22	31
Prachakon Thai	0	18	18	3	7
Phalang Tham	0	1	23	47	41
Sammakkhitham	-	-	-	-	79
Other	0	11	29	12	8

Source: Compiled by author.

increase its seats. The Social Action Party had maintained about twenty seats since September 1992 but lost a lot of ground in 2001, winning just one seat. The Phalang Tham Party, which had won many of the available seats in the metropolitan area in the early 1990s, failed to win any in 2001.[10]

At the same time, there were only five parties that won more than 5% of the total votes cast on the party-list basis. The 100 seats were distributed to these five parties in proportion to the number of votes won by each of them.[11] Forty-eight seats were awarded to the Thai Rak Thai Party, thirty-one to the Democrat Party, eight to the New Aspiration Party, seven to the Chat Phatthana Party and six to the Chat Thai Party (Table 5.4).[12] The fifth-ranked Chat Thai Party won its seats by a mere hair's breadth after polling 1,523,807 votes or just 5.32%.[13]

The Thai Rak Thai Party won 200 seats in the single-seat constituencies and forty-eight seats on the party-list basis. Its total of 248 seats was marginally short of an absolute majority but very close to it. The only time a single party has won a clear majority of seats in a general election in Thailand was the February 1957 election won by the Seri Manangkasila Party. This party had been formed by Prime Minister Plaek Phibunsongkhram and did everything in its power to ensure an election victory. It secured a narrow majority by winning eighty-three of 160 seats (52%) (Murashima et al. 1991: 131). Its victory was largely due to wide-spread election fraud and was an underlying cause of the coup in September 1957. The Sahapracha Thai Party was also formed by the incumbent Prime Minister of the time, Thanom Kittikhachon, in the lead up to the general election in 1969. It only won seventy-five of 219 seats (34%), however; far from a majority.[14] Other than these 'government parties' (Fujiwara 1994), 114 of 279

Table 5.4 Seats won by party in the 2001 election

Party	Party-list	Single-seat districts	Total
Thai Rak Thai	48	200	248
Democrat	31	97	128
Chat Thai	6	35	41
New Aspiration	8	28	36
Chat Phatthana	7	22	29
Seritham	0	14	14
Ratsadon	0	2	2
Thin Thai	0	1	1
Social Action	0	1	1
Total	100	400	500

Source: Election Commission data
(http://202.183.203.226/sorsor/numbermp.html).

seats (41%) won by the Democrat Party in the 1976 general election was the highest previous record (Murashima et al. 1991: 131). Hence the 2001 result was clearly an overwhelming victory for the Thai Rak Thai Party. The reasons for this victory will be discussed in this chapter.

Did the 2001 general election change political parties?

One of the objectives of the drafters of the 1997 Constitution was to develop the political party system. This involved popularizing political parties by encouraging general voters to become party members, democratizing party operations, imposing stricter discipline on MPs and so on. To what extent had these aims been achieved by the time of the first general election to be held under the new constitution?

Expanding party membership and branches
The Election Commission publishes official data about the number of branches and members of each political party at the time of election. As of June 1999, the Democrat party had 130 branches, but the other major parties had less than ten each.[15] As of December 2000 when campaigning had already started, the Democrat Party increased its number of branches to 163, while the New Aspiration Party substantially increased its number of branches to 207. The Chat Phatthana Party grew more moderately—from six to thirty-three—and the Chat Thai Party added only one new branch—from five to six. The newly formed Thai Rak Thai Party, which eventually won nearly half of the seats, only had four branches (Table 5.5). As there were seventy-six provinces in the country, only the New Aspiration and Democrat parties had more branches than

the number of provinces. It is obvious that the parties were slow in developing their organizations.

In terms of membership, while the New Aspiration Party had two million members and the Thai Rak Thai Party over one million, the Democrats had 740,000 members, Chat Phatthana had 150,000 and the Chat Thai Party had only 40,000 as of 20 December 2000, a few weeks before the polling date. However, membership numbers jumped sharply in a rather short period of time: 6.25 million for the Thai Rak Thai Party, 3.73 million for the Democrats, 3.58 million for Chat Phatthana, 3.08 million for New Aspiration and 1.59 million for the Chat Thai Party as of 1 February 2001, immediately after the election. The total party membership as of 1 February 2000 was 19.86 million, which was an impressive number. It looked as if the political parties had transformed from mere parliamentary factions into popular political parties in a very short time. However, considering that there were 42.88 million eligible voters and only 29.93 million of them actually voted, the total party membership of almost 20 million people seems to be excessive. This extraordinary increase in the number of party members can probably be attributed to a phenomenon reported by the media in which voters were paid cash to join the parties during the election campaign rather than, as is the norm, having to pay a fee to join a party (*Bangkok Post*, 1 December 2000 and 16 January 2001). This method of recruiting new party members was a *de facto* means of buying voters. As mentioned below, though, it is quite likely that the membership drive was actually aimed at maximizing the government subsidy for each party, since the number of party members was one of the factors used to determine how public money was allocated to the parties. This abnormal condition shortly before the general election becomes obvious when these membership numbers are compared with those of June 2002. Although the Thai Rak Thai and New Aspiration parties increased their memberships by absorbing the Seritham Party, and Chat Thai also substantially increased its membership and number of branches, the numbers for the Democrat and Chat Phatthana parties did not change much after February 2001. This pre-election activity and post-election inactivity should be interpreted as evidence of a weak party following combined with too few branches, i.e., all show and no substance, rather than a new-found stable support for the parties.[16] This will be verified shortly by examining the relative insignificance of membership fees in the parties' finances.

Subsidies for political parties

The Organic Act on Political Parties of 1998 established a system of state subsidy for political parties and required the disclosure of all donations, which had previously been given in secrecy. Under the new system, part of the national budget is allocated to the newly-established Fund for Development of Political

Table 5.5 Number of branches and members of major parties

Party	June 1999 Branches	June 1999 Members	20 Dec 2000 Branches	20 Dec 2000 Members	1 Feb 2001 Branches	1 Feb 2001 Members	1 June 2001 Branches	1 June 2001 Members	15 June 2002 Branches	15 June 2002 Members
Thai Rak Thai	-	na	4	1,031,088	4	6,249,777	4	6,249,777	8	13,826,203
Democrat	130	na	163	740,516	164	3,729,633	166	3,729,633	191	3,762,436
Chat Thai	5	na	6	42,383	6	1,590,606	6	1,590,606	17	2,045,977
New Aspiration	5	na	207	2,112,140	207	3,081,449	192	3,081,449	-	-
Chat Phatthana	6	na	33	152,908	33	3,581,142	34	3,581,142	35	3,688,423
Seritham	7	na	na	na	13	604,936	13	604,936	-	-

Source: Compiled from Election Commission data (http://www.ect.go.th/doc/num-party.xls; http://202.183.203.226/neo/new/party/newparty/; http://202.183.203.226/neo/new/party/mainparty/html; http://www.ect.go.th/newthai/eection/party/newparty/; http://www.ect.go.th/newthai/party/newparty/).

Note: The New Aspiration Party was dissolved in 2002 but the party name was taken over by a new party. Since this party is totally different from the previous one, blank spaces are left under the heading of June 2002 in the above table.

Table 5.6 State subsidy for major parties, 1999 and 2000 (in Baht)

Party	1999 (26 parties)		2000 (29 parties)	
	Subsidy	Ranking by amount	Subsidy	Ranking by amount
New Aspiration	33,403,400	2	63,727,200	1
Democrat	34,075,400	1	58,822,900	2
Chat Phatthana	6,719,700	3	13,916,200	3
Chat Thai	4,480,000	5	8,866,000	4
Social Action	5,072,900	4	8,311,300	6
Prachakon Thai	3,362,400	6	5,905,400	8
Thai Rak Thai	649,400	19	4,389,500	9
Kaona	1,336,500	13	3,700,300	10
Phalang Tham	1,627,600	8	2,990,500	12
Ratsadon	1,525,400	11	2,815,100	13
Ekkaphap	1,538,800	10	2,805,700	14
Seritham	1,425,740	12	2,565,000	16
Other	12,770,175	-	37,184,900	-
Total	107,987,415		216,000,000	

Source: Compiled from Election Commission data
(http://202.183.203.226/neo/new/party/p2-5.html and
http://202.183.203.226/neo/new/party/p2-3.html).
Note. Parties that received large amounts but had no seat in the house were
included in 'other,' e.g. the 5th, 7th, 11th and 15th parties in 2000.

Parties (*kongthun phuea kanphatthana phakkanmueang*), from which subsidies were distributed to political parties. The amount allocated to each party is calculated based on the number of MPs, the number of votes polled on the party-list basis, the number of party members and the number of branches. The total subsidy was 108 million baht in 1999 and about 200 million baht in 2000.[17] The amount allocated to each party in 2000 was 63.72 million baht to the New Aspiration Party, 58.83 million baht to the Democrats and 13.91 million baht to Chat Phatthana (Table 5.6). Although the major parties with more MPs were ranked higher, the subsidy rankings did not directly correspond to the number of MPs because other factors, such as the numbers of party members and branches, were also taken into account.

Following the 2001 general election, which for the first time allowed parties to receive votes on the party-list basis, it was decided that the fund allocation should be calculated according to the ratio of 35% for the number of MPs, 30% for the number of party-list votes, 20% for the party membership and 15% for the number of branches. Eight of the nine parties that won seats[18] and thirty-five parties with no seats were eligible to receive the subsidy. Among the major parties, the Thai Rak Thai Party received 89.46 million baht, the Democrats 57.92 million baht, New Aspiration 27.32 million baht, Chat Phatthana 19.45

Table 5.7 Breakdown of income of major parties, 1998 and 1999

	Democrat		New Aspiration		Chat Thai		Thai Rak Thai	
	1998	1999	1998	1999	1998	1999	1998	1999
Membership fee	6,258,100	7,451,920	0	0	7,022,723	2,433,420	0	0
Donation	5,846,690	13,679,592	6,400,000	22,647,802	0	5,461,600	32,264,498	12,318,395
Subsidy	0	34,075,400	0	33,016,868	0	4,480,000	0	649,000
Other	5,206,573	1,198,587	59,620	0	8,333	0	46,061	3,017,829
Total	17,311,363	56,405,499	6,459,620	55,664,670	7,031,057	12,375,020	32,310,559	15,985,224

Source: Compiled from the annual report on political party activity published by the Election Commission (Kho. Ko. Tho. 1999: 97, 116, 190, 252; 2000e: 154, 193, 265, 342).

Table 5.8 Donations to major parties, 1998–2000 (in Baht)

Party	1998	1999	2000	Total
Thai Rak Thai	31,111,630	12,273,995	304,409,954	347,795,579
Democrat	1,074,300	12,195,758	148,942,702	162,212,760
Chat Thai	0	5,461,600	151,472,000	156,933,600
New Aspiration	0	22,647,802	32,210,000	54,857,802
Chat Phatthana	1,500,000	6,000,000	54,100,000	61,600,000
Seritham	0	1,160,340	37,858,500	39,018,840
Ratsadon	0	0	22,130,000	22,130,000

Source: Compiled from Election Commission data
(http:// 202.183.203.226/neo/new/party/p2-7.html;
http://202.183.203.226/neo/new/party/month/dec43.html;
http://ect.go.th/party/give/41-44.htm).

million baht, Chat Thai 12.49 million baht, Seritham 6.59 million baht, Ratsadon 3.04 million baht and the Social Action Party received 1.71 million baht. Six of the parties with no seats received more than one million baht in subsidies. Two of them received more than the Seritham Party, which had fourteen MPs.[19]

How important was the subsidy for party finances? Judging by the financial statements for 1998 and 1999 lodged by each party, prior to the introduction of state subsidy, the income sources for each party included donations, membership fees and other sources (for example, interest) (Table 5.7). In 1998, the leading party, the Democrats, received 17.31 million baht in income, consisting of 6.26 million baht in membership fees, 5.85 million baht in donations and 5.21 baht in other income. The leading opposition party, New Aspiration, received 6.46 million baht, of which 6.40 million baht was in donations. They had no membership fee income at all. In 1999, the first year following the introduction of a state subsidy system, the subsidy of 34.08 million baht allocated to the Democrats was almost twice its total income for the previous year. New Aspiration's subsidy was five times its income for the previous year. Chat Thai's subsidy was almost two-thirds of its income for the previous year (Kho. Ko. Tho. 1999: 97, 116, 190, 252; 2000e: 154, 193, 265, 342). While it is unclear whether the membership fees were actually paid by party members or contributed by party executives, the New Aspiration Party, with 1.69 million members as of 1 January 1998 and 1.71 million members as of 1 January 1999, recorded no membership fee income for the two years. Chat Thai, which maintained a stable membership of 33,000 people over this period, recorded a drastically reduced membership fee income in 1999 (Kho. Ko. Tho. 1999: 114, 185). The financial statements of other parties over the same period also show little income from membership fees. When parties cannot rely on their members for income, they have little choice but to turn to political donations for their funding. The introduction of a state subsidy was thus very fortuitous for many parties.

Political donations

Any political party that receives a donation is required to report the name of the donor, as well as the date and amount of the donation under the 1998 Political Parties Act. Political donations, which had traditionally been given in secret, are now disclosed to the public through the Election Commission. This was a major change.

The records of donations to major parties from 1998 to 2000 indicate that many of the donations in 2000, shortly before the general election, were in excess of one digit larger than those of the previous year. The Thai Rak Thai Party, for example, which received the largest amount of donations, decreased from 31.11 million baht in 1998 to 12.27 million baht in 1999, but then jumped more than twenty times to 299.41 million baht in 2000. The three-year total of 342.80 million baht was almost twice the 181.93 million baht donated to the second-ranked Chat Thai Party (Table 5.8).

Disclosed donors included various individuals and corporations. Among them, there were many party executives, their relatives, and MPs. In 2000, the largest donation to the Thai Rak Thai Party, the top donation recipient, was Photchaman Chinnawat (Pojaman Shinawatra), the wife of party leader Thaksin Chinnawat, who contributed a total of 75 million baht. In other words, almost one-quarter of the party's donations came from Mrs. Chinnawat alone. In the case of the New Aspiration Party, 23 million baht of the total 32.21 million baht was contributed by deputy party leader Sukkhawit Rangsitphon. Party secretary-general Suwat Lippataphanlop and his family members donated 9.45 million baht of 93.3 million baht to the Chat Phatthana Party. Similarly, the biggest donor to the Seritham Party was party leader Prachuap Chaiyasan, who contributed 10 million baht of the total 34.86 million baht donated to the party. In 2001, Thai Rak Thai received a total of 140.07 million baht in donations, 120 million baht or 86% of which was contributed by Photchaman.[20]

However, party executives and MPs were not the only donors. Uthai, the CDA speaker, once commented that 'The parties that wish to be in government would include in their party-lists the candidates who may not be good at electioneering but have suitable abilities to enter the House of Representatives. For example, someone like Chotchoi' (Uthai 1998: 23). Chotchoi was a member of the Sophonphanit clan, which owned a Bangkok Bank conglomerate.[21] What Uthai meant was that a wealthy person such as Chotchoi was accustomed to a comfortable life and would not be able to bear campaigning in a single-seat electoral constituency where she would have to sweat under the sun and ask the lower classes of people for votes. Voters would endlessly try to solicit monies and gifts from her. Therefore it would be more appropriate for her to stand in the party-list system.

From the point of view of political parties, individuals with high levels of name recognition or popularity that could attract many votes or who are suitably qualified to be cabinet members with excellent political and administrative skills would be very welcome. But of course, the parties would want something in return if they were to include someone on their list. Political donation is one way to reconcile the interests of the wealthy who want to enter the House of Representatives without effort and the interests of the parties in need of funds. Therefore, it was expected that the party-lists would include major contributors.

Indeed, comparing the party-lists of proportional representation candidates with their lists of major donors reveals significant correspondence between the two. Putting this more directly, one finds that the names of major donors frequently appear on the candidate lists. Among relatively small-scale donors to the Democrat Party, Phothiphong Lamsam of the Lamsam family, which owned the Thai Farmers Bank group, made a large donation of 25.06 million baht and won a seat on the party-list basis as the party's twenty-seventh ranked candidate.[22] Phonwut Sarasin, a son of the head of the Sarasin family, Phong, whose extensive business interests include the Thai subsidiary of Coca Cola, donated one million baht and took the thirtieth place on the candidate list.[23] From the Sophonphanit family, which donated 2.75 million baht, Kanlaya, a well-known social activist (philanthropist), was listed as the nineteenth candidate.[24] Phonsek Kanchanachari of Siew-National, a Thai joint venture company with Matsushita Electric Industrial Co., Ltd., donated 3.6 million baht and became the twenty-sixth candidate on the list. In the Chat Thai Party, Det Bunlong, a longtime fund contributor and former MP, made fifteen donations totaling 25.48 million baht and became the third-ranked candidate on its party-list. Kao Pinyo Company, which donated 25 million baht, was effectively owned by Sawat Horungrueang. Sawat also owned the NTS steel company, which was burdened with enormous levels of bad debt during the economic crisis. His four other companies also donated a total of 640,000 baht (*Matichon Sutsapda*, 18 December 2000).[25] Sawat was ranked ninth on the party-list of the Chat Thai Party.[26] Although the rankings on the party-list do not necessarily correspond exactly to the size of donations, it is clear that there is a strong relationship between donations and inclusion on candidate lists.

There is no doubt, either, that despite the new laws, many of the donations to political parties or politicians remain undisclosed.[27] For example, Banhan, the leader of the Chat Thai Party, complained that he had given four to five million baht each to some of his MPs before the general election to entice them to stay with the party but they defected anyway (*The Nation*, 18 November 2000). The Chat Thai Party had thirty-nine MPs elected in 1996. If, for example, five million baht was given to twenty of them, the total expenditure would be 100 million baht, which would be more than one-half of the value of donations received by the party in 2000. It was common for most of the parties to try to retain their existing MPs while trying to poach MPs from other parties. In an election, the parties must pay costs for printing posters and other promotional materials and for advertising on television and radio as well as the cost of buying MPs.[28] For instance, the Chat Phatthana Party reportedly spent 120 million baht on campaigning in seven electoral constituencies of Phetchabun province. The campaign fund was given in a lump sum to the party executive and candidate in the first constituency, Pancha Kesonthong, who was supposed to distribute 15 million baht to each candidate (*Bangkok Post*, 31 December 2000).[29] It is obvious that such an enormous expense could not be fully covered by disclosed donations. In the Thaksin cabinet, there were some prominent capitalists such as Pracha Malinon and Adisai Photharamik as well as some capable people (e.g. Finance Minister Somkhit Chatusiphithak) and faction leaders with many underling MPs (e.g. Minister for the Office of the Prime Minister Somsak Thepsuthin). These capitalist cabinet members did not have factional followers or any special skills as cabinet members. Although their names did not appear on the list of donors to the Thai Rak Thai Party, it would be reasonable to assume that their appointments to the cabinet were directly related to their financial contributions to the party, which suggests that not all of the financial contributions to political parties were disclosed.

Did the 1997 Constitution change elections?

The 1997 Constitution aimed to make it easier for competent and honest candidates to win an election while bringing an end to money-driven elections. To what extent have these aims been achieved? This section examines the impact of the 1997 Constitution on local bosses and on vote buying, then analyzes how it helped to develop the conditions for Thai Rak Thai Party's landslide victory.

Did it destroy local bosses?
The new election system had little effect on the level of competition; aside from 100 seats on the party-list basis, there were 400 seats on the constituency basis, not much different from the 393 seats in the 1996 election. But candidates had to adjust to the drastic changes in their constituencies from a multiple-seat

constituency to a single-seat constituency. As discussed in previous chapters, under the previous system, electoral constituencies typically had three seats and voters could choose up to three candidates. They could choose three candidates from one party or from two or three different parties. Candidates did not have to poll the highest number of votes to win. Those with the second and third highest numbers of votes also won. Under the new single-seat system, only the one candidate who polled the most votes would win.

There were also other factors that made traditional vote-gathering activities more difficult. First, vote-gathering brokers, who were indispensable for campaigning, now had to deal exclusively with one particular candidate. In the three-seat constituencies, each broker could support candidates from different parties simultaneously, since more than one could be elected. All he or she had to do was to encourage voters to cast their votes to individual candidates for whom he or she had promised to gather votes. In the new single-seat constituency, a broker could no longer work for multiple candidates. Further, since there were only a limited number of shrewd brokers, candidates now had to face fierce competition to secure an exclusive contract with a competent broker. Another major change was that vote counting was now to be carried out at a single, centralized location in each district rather than at individual polling stations. When the votes were counted at individual polling stations, brokers and candidates could closely monitor their votes in each polling precinct, and it was typically not very difficult to bribe the ballot-counting officials. However, with all ballot boxes to be opened in one place, it was more difficult to check whether the residents of particular villages had voted as promised. In short, it became difficult for candidates to secure vote-gathering brokers and for brokers to gather votes. One more important factor was that the Election Commission was supposed to police vote buying and other election fraud more rigorously.

Under the previous multiple-seat system, there were some cases in which all three seats in a constituency were won by candidates from a particular clan, or where the candidates and winners in several neighboring constituencies were effectively decided by one local boss. Such bosses also wielded strong influence in local government councils. In some places, influence of these local bosses in the general election was effectively eliminated under the new constitution. Samut Prakan province, Bangkok's neighbor to the south, is one example. The Atsawahem clan led by Watthana had held many seats in this province. In the 1996 general election, Watthana's group won all six seats in the province. Three of them were won by members of the Atsawahem family. Watthana's elder brother was the chairman of the Samut Prakan provincial council and one of his sons was the mayor of Samut Prakan city. In the 2001 general election, they ran for the Ratsadon Party and four of them, including two family members, were

Table 5.9 Example of the impact of electoral changes

Candidate	1996		2001	
	District	Votes	District	Votes
Tun Chintawet	Old 2nd	106,938	New 11th	27,501
Panya Chintawet	Old 2nd	88,339	New 9th	8,927
Chatri Phiriyakitphaibun	Old 2nd	77,139	New 11th	30,738

Source: Compiled by author.

nominated as candidates in the party-list. In the six single-seat constituencies of the province, two of Watthana's sons and the wife of one of his sons ran as candidates (*Bangkok Post*, 8 January 2001). However, the party failed to win a seat on the party-list basis, having attracted less than the required 5% of the total votes, and only won a seat on the constituency basis. As a result, the Atsawahem family no longer had anyone in the House of Representatives. In Chiang Mai province in the north, Thawatwong Na Chiang Mai, his wife (both incumbent MPs) and their daughter all ran as candidates, and all suffered defeat. In Pathum Thani province, adjacent to Bangkok, members of the Hansawat clan won all three seats in the 1995 general election. Two won again in 1996. In 2001, all three ran again, this time as candidates of the Thai Rak Thai Party. One was nominated on the party-list basis and the other two on the constituency basis. All three failed this time, with the party-list candidate ranked ninety-fifth on the list. Thus the clan no longer had any members in the House of Representatives.[30]

Besides the clans, winning also became more difficult for politicians who had no real vote-gathering abilities of their own and had previously won their seats as members of three-candidate teams who were totally dependent on the team leader. In single-seat constituencies they had to rely on their own efforts. The second constituency of Ubon Ratchathani province in the 1996 general election provides an example. The winners here were the Chintawet brothers, Tun and Panya (New Aspiration), who came first and second, and Chatri Phiriyakitphaibun (Chat Thai), who came third. In the 2001 election, the brothers (Chat Thai) ran in the newly-established ninth and eleventh constituencies and Chatri (Thai Rak Thai) ran in the eleventh constituency. In the 1996 election, Tun was the leading candidate, polling almost 30,000 more votes than Chatri. But in 2001 Tun polled about 3000 less than Chatri, coming second in the eleventh constituency. Panya received less than 9000 votes in the ninth constituency, a dismal failure that clearly stemmed from the electoral changes that removed the opportunity for him to benefit from his brother's vote-gathering power (Table 5.9).[31] These examples might be interpreted as suggesting that the new election system did indeed bring about major changes.

However, for those candidates who enjoyed strong popularity throughout an old multiple-seat constituency or had a firm electoral base in a particular area which happened to largely coincide with a new single-seat constituency, the implications of the changes were not as serious. In fact, it often provided more favorable conditions for the latter type of candidates. Furthermore, the changes benefited many of the provincial council members in running for the House of Representative election, because each of those relatively large districts—with populations of around 100,000 people—came to form a single-seat constituency under the new system, thus coinciding with the district-based election for provincial council. In many of these districts, the center where the district office is located is demarcated as the city (*thetsaban*) and each city has a city council. Until 2000 the mayor was internally elected from among the city councilors, but today he or she is directly elected by city residents. Mayors therefore surfaced as significant candidates in the single-seat electoral system. In some provinces, the provincial and city councilors mobilized personal connections in their electorates during campaigns. For example, the Thai Rak Thai Party backed city mayors and their relatives as candidates in Ratchaburi's first constituency, Songkhla's second and third constituencies and Phetchabun's fourth constituency.

Furthermore, quite a few clans retained a firm grip on their traditional seats in the House of Representatives—some even acquired more seats. Take for example, the family of Anan Chaisaeng, an MP from Chachoengsao province in the east since 1969. His eldest son, Chaturon, had won every lower house election since 1986 except in September 1992. His second son, Konlayut, was elected to the Chachoengsao City Council in 1985 and became mayor in 1995 (Chaturong et al. 1996). His third son, Wutthiphong, ran for the 1996 general election with his brother but came second by a narrow margin. He was then elected to the CDA at the end of the year. In this general election, Anan and Wutthiphong were elected in two of the four electoral constituencies in the province and Chaturon was elected as the fifteenth proportional representation candidate of the Thai Rak Thai Party. Thus, one family produced three House of Representatives MPs. It was widely known that a *chao pho*, Somchai Khunplum (nicknamed Kamnan Po), had controlled the results of the elections in the eastern province of Chon Buri. In the 1996 general election, seven candidates led by his son, Sonthaya, were successful. This time, six candidates backed by Kamnan Po were elected. They lost in the seventh constituency (Satahip district) where a naval base was located and there were many Navy people among its residents as a result of the change to the single-seat constituency system. However, Kamnan Po's eldest son was elected as a proportional representation candidate of the Chat Thai Party and two other sons were elected in single-seat constituencies. This increased the number of MPs in the clan from two to three. Another example was the Limpaphan clan in Sukhothai province. The family's patriarch, Pheng, had been elected to the House of Representatives in 1946 and was the former mayor of Sawankhalok city. His second son, Praphat, had been elected to the House of Representatives for many terms except in 1996. His third son, Somchat, was the incumbent mayor of Sawankhalok city. In this general election, the clan belonged to the Chat Phatthana Party and Praphat was elected in the proportional representation system. In the single-seat constituencies, Somchat's son Somchet, the provincial council member from Sawankhalok district, ran in the third constituency and Praphat's son Piyawat ran in the fourth constituency. Somchet was successful while Piyawat was not.

Similarly, there are numerous cases in which family members ran for seats vacated by incumbent MPs who were shifting for the party-list candidacy. Former House of Representatives MP Akon Huntrakun, who was planning to run for the Senate when he passed away in March 2000, complained during the drafting of the constitution that if MPs were banned from concurrently holding cabinet posts, the 'party heavyweights (would be given the privilege of) making their wife or child or financial backer into a House of Representatives MP as proxy for themselves who would be taking cabinet posts' (Akon 2000: 140). This was precisely what happened. One example is the Adireksan clan in Sara Buri province. Praman Adireksan was the inaugural leader of the Chat Thai Party and had been an MP for the province since 1952, holding many cabinet posts along the way. He and his eldest son, Pongphon, were elected together in March 1992 and again in 1995. Praman retired before the 1996 election but his two sons ran and won. Pongphon was the secretary-general of the Chat Thai Party but he fell out with party leader Banhan. In the 2001 election, he defected to the Thai Rak Thai Party and ran as a candidate on the party-list. The seat he vacated was won by another of his younger brothers. The family produced one party-list MP and two constituency-based MPs in this election, an increase of one. In the eastern province of Sa Kaeo, Sano Thiangthong's clan won all three seats in the 1996 general election. This time, Sano switched to the party-list candidacy but the clan kept a firm hold on the three single-seat electoral constituencies. The number of MPs in the family increased from three to four. Also in the southern region, Democrat Party executives Surin Phitsuwan and Suthep Thueaksuban, while they themselves became party-list candidates, put family members up as proxy candidates and made them successful constituency-based MPs.

Did it eliminate vote buying?
Under the 1997 Constitution, the Election Commission replaced the Interior Ministry as the body responsible for administering elections and kept a closer watch on the provision of material benefits to voters. Its new, tough stance was demonstrated during the Senate election. For example, the *Bangkok Post* reported that 'In the past, people [in Bang Khen district in the north of

Bangkok] wanted an election as often as possible. It was a time filled with the joy of receiving but things are different now' (31 December 2000). They could no longer expect such rewards because of more rigorous policing. If this can be taken at face value, candidates would have to win votes on account of policies and personal merit rather than financial resources.

The ruling party MPs, particularly cabinet members, fought their campaigns by emphasizing their track records in efforts for the development of their electoral constituencies. The Chat Thai Party leader Banhan, for instance, spoke to about 3000 people at a campaign rally in front of Chainat City Hall and encouraged them to vote for the candidates of his party if they wanted roads, telephones, water and electricity because Chainat should be developed, just like the neighboring Suphan Buri province had been (*Bangkok Post*, 22 December 2000). Banhan's constituency was in Suphan Buri province, which had somewhat excessively developed infrastructure that was the envy of residents in nearby provinces.

However, the practice of vote buying never disappeared. Rival candidates all over the country accused each other of paying voters anywhere from 200 to 500 baht each. Various commodities were provided in lieu of direct cash payments, too. Rice, seasoning products, clothes and wrist watches were distributed in most provinces, while offers of free holidays or meals were not uncommon either (*Thai Post*, 26 November 2000). A Democrat Party candidate in the second constituency of Phrae province accused his rival of paying local fabric producers 300 to 500 baht for products which usually only cost 100 baht (*Bangkok Post*, 7 December 2000). In the first constituency of Chiang Rai province, the Mayor of Chiang Rai city—the husband of a Chat Phatthana Party candidate—was issued a warning by the Election Commission for distributing gifts to residents in the name of social welfare (*Bangkok Post*, 22 December 2000). Stimulant drugs were reportedly distributed in Chiang Rai and Mae Hon Song (*Thai Post*, 26 November 2000). The traditional illegal lottery method was also used.

Purchasing insurance policies was another method that was reportedly used in many electoral constituencies. Candidates paid premiums of 400 to 500 baht per voter for a group life insurance policy and handed the policies to the voters. In the hotly contested electoral constituencies of Nakhon Ratchasima, Phichit and Buri Ram provinces, life insurance was purchased for campaign workers. According to one insurance company, the Thai Rak Thai and Chat Phatthana parties bought group insurance for voters in Nakhon Ratchasima province.

> It is our company policy not to sell insurance cover to political parties. However, political parties usually organize voters into clubs (*samoson*) or vocational groups and take out group policies with their family members as beneficiaries, not the

parties. In some cases, the company is not sure whether or not the premiums are paid by politicians. The Provincial Insurance Bureau (the provincial office of the Insurance Department of the Commerce Ministry) has issued an order not to accept insurance applications from politicians during the election period. (*Krungthep Thurakit*, 11 December 2000)

In this province, the parties organized groups of more than 100 voters in occupational groups and took out insurance at lower premiums. In Buri Ram province, the Chat Thai Party and the Thai Rak Thai Party took out insurance on their vote-gathering brokers for the duration of the election period.[32] Deputy Minister of Commerce Phaithun, a former MP from Phichit province, commented:

> I have tried to buy insurance against accidental death and severe disability for 1000 to 2000 supporters of the Democrat Party in my province. However, I had to give up on this group insurance idea because of strict rules set down by the Election Commission. These days, insurance companies invite politicians to buy insurance. The important points are how much discount they will give us and whether it is difficult to receive insurance payouts. Once the election is over, I will buy insurance for the party's campaign workers. The premium is not a lot of money and they can receive insurance money if they have accidents or die. (*Krungthep Thurakit*, 11 December 2000)[33]

It appears that insurance was purchased to reward campaign workers as well as to buy voters.

In the first constituency of Khon Kaen province, a building collapsed after five tons of fertilizer was housed in it. A candidate had organized the delivery of 1530 bags of fertilizer for distribution to voters. The candidate was not held responsible for the incident, however, as one of the provincial council members came forward as the owner of this fertilizer and offered to pay the cost of rebuilding (*Bangkok Post*, 25 December 2000). Gifts of fertilizer and free or discounted rice harvesters were reported in more than one province. In the northeastern provinces of Surin and Buri Ram, women and young people were encouraged to form cooperatives of about fifty members, open bank accounts and prepare development plans. When a development plan was submitted, 45,000 baht was paid to the cooperative from the state-run Bank of Agriculture and Agricultural Cooperatives. Through similar processes, a total of 4.5 million baht was deposited in the accounts of 100 cooperatives in the bank's Sangkha branch in Surin province (*Bangkok Post*, 18 December 2000 and 4 January 2001). This is but one example of Agriculture and Cooperatives Ministry subsidies being used to buy votes.

Similar examples, particularly of bankrolled elections, are too numerous to detail. Hence Chai concluded that 'clearly the new Constitution has failed to stop vote buying' (2002: 197). One campaign worker in Khon Kaen province commented that the candidate who invested the most money would win and, therefore, his candidate would inject funds while spying on the rival candidates' movements (*Bangkok Post*, 3 January 2001). Democrat Party leader Chuan complained that his party did not have sufficient campaign funds. His fellow party executive Athit Urairat attributed his party's loss to the huge amount of funds injected by the Thai Rak Thai Party to buy votes (*Bangkok Post*, 17 January 2001). The executives of the New Aspiration Party, who had even fewer financial resources than the Democrats, expressed a hope that the Election Commission would more readily issue red cards. They clearly believed that their candidates would have better prospects if their Thai Rak Thai and Chat Phatthana party rivals were disqualified. The fact that the election results were so clearly influenced by the amount of gifts doled-out to voters indicates that the election was fought in virtually the same manner as previous elections.

Thai Rak Thai's success

The people who drafted the 1997 Constitution claimed to be pursuing an ideal of stable politics under a two-party system. The Thai Rak Thai Party suddenly emerged as one of the two parties. This section attempts to explain the party's landslide victory through the analysis of its appealing points and its ability to invest in strong candidates. What were the characteristics that distinguished it from the other parties?

Appealing party: Several factors appear to have contributed to the new party's landslide win:

1. A long lead-up time prior to the election;
2. Voter weariness with the existing parties;
3. The appeal of a prime minister from the northern region;
4. The popularity and high profile of party leader Thaksin;
5. Sympathy for asset concealment charges;
6. Appealing policies;
7. Skillful responses to the new election system;
8. Abundant financial resources;
9. Wooing strong candidates through a variety of legitimate and illegal incentives.

Since the importance of the last factor depends upon the voter appeal of the individual candidates in question, this section will focus instead on the first eight factors—those that can be attributed to the party itself.

First, the Thai Rak Thai Party was well prepared for the first general election under the 1997 Constitution, although it was a new party formed in July 1998.

The size of its financial resources and its membership list as of December 2000, as discussed, is indicative of the party's readiness for the election.

Second, from the outset, the ruling Democrat Party was expected to struggle in this election. Recovering from the economic crisis was the administration's most important and urgent task, but the pace of recovery had been slow since 1999. They had retained power by putting off the election until 2001, but even then they had no real achievements to boast about. Meanwhile, the people were clearly growing more and more tired of the longtime government every day. At the same time, like the Democrats, the leading opposition New Aspiration Party had so many MPs defecting to other parties already in 2000 that they no longer looked very attractive either. With the remaining parties looking even less attractive than these two, the Thai Rak Thai Party emerged as a new choice for voters.

Third, the party's campaign in the north emphasized that its leader, Thaksin, was a northerner and, if elected, would be the first northerner in Thailand's history to become prime minister. This parochialism had great appeal to the northern voters, as is evident in the fact that the party won over 70% of the seats in the north. Particularly in seven provinces in the narrower northern region,[34] including Thaksin's home province Chiang Mai, the party overwhelmed its opponents, winning twenty-eight of thirty-three seats.

Fourth, Thaksin's popularity was not limited to the northern region. He was a self-made entrepreneur who had amassed a fortune on his own in Bangkok, not Chiang Mai, and was widely recognized for his business acumen. Many people believed that someone who had achieved remarkable success in the business world was necessary to competently steer the country, particularly the economy. No less important were the twin facts that he was the captain of the telecommunications industry and that he used his brilliant advertising skills to promote his party.

Fifth, once the election campaign had officially begun, the National Counter-Corruption Commission concluded that Thaksin had failed to declare his assets properly when he joined the Chawalit cabinet in 1997 and asked the Constitution Court to disenfranchise him.[35] Thaksin insisted that the omission was a minor oversight caused by an innocent mistake and lodged an appeal with the Constitution Court. If the Court ruled that Thaksin had tried to conceal his assets, he would lose the right to be elected. However, the Counter-Corruption Commission had found no wrongdoing in the earlier cases brought against Prime Minister Chuan and Interior Minister Banyat Banthatthan for failure to declare assets. Hence, the Commission's decision, more than three years after the alleged offence and in the middle of the official election campaign period, was treated with suspicion by the public, and all the more so because it directly contradicted the earlier findings in favor of the ruling party ministers. A considerable proportion of the population suspected that there were political considerations involved in the Commission's decision and timing; and in many cases this suspicion translated into sympathy for Thaksin. An image formed of Thaksin being harassed by the ruling Democrat Party, who had seemingly become politically ineffective.[36]

Sixth, the Thai Rak Thai Party offered appealing policies. Thailand's political parties had traditionally been lukewarm about using public pledges to increase votes. All parties to date had been conservative parties that went along with the established norms of adopting empty and ambiguous policies. As one former finance minister and economist put it: 'When I am asked what I think of the economic and monetary policies of our major parties, I cannot answer the question. To be frank, they have no policies. Even if they do, their policies do not interest anyone, including myself' (Wiraphong 2001: 137–8). In this general election, however, the Thai Rak Thai Party adopted policies with concrete benefits that were easy for the residents of large rural constituencies to understand. They included giving farmers a three year moratorium on debt repayment and establishing a one-million-baht development fund for each of over 70,000 village communities throughout the country. Everyone understood that the repayment of his or her debt would be postponed for three years and his or her village would receive development funds. These policies were extremely appealing. The party also proposed that healthcare fees would be fixed at thirty baht per visit, which was similarly appealing. There is no doubt that these policy measures contributed to the party's overwhelming victory in a significant way. Moreover, the party also proposed positive financial policy measures for the business community, including the establishment of an asset management organization to write off bad loans (Wiraphong 2001: 148–9).

Seventh, Thaksin used a clever tactic in the new party-list system. Major parties, except Chat Thai, included party executives, incumbent MPs, and academics, bureaucrats and military officers who were prospective cabinet members in their party-lists. Thai Rak Thai followed suit, but they differed in listing prominent candidates not only in the higher ranks but also in the lower ranks of the list. It was common practice to rank incumbent MPs higher so that they had a better chance of winning. However, Thai Rak Thai listed as many as five incumbent MPs in the ranks below the fifty-first position, where they had significantly smaller chances of winning a seat.[37] Furthermore, six recently retired military and police generals were listed below the eightieth position. Among the candidates from the business world, Phanloet Baiyok, the famous owner of the tallest building in Thailand, was ranked ninety-second. In other words, the party's proportional representation candidate list could be compared to the finest quality pancake packed full of bean paste from one end to the other—it looked far more delicious than the other parties' lists.

The eighth factor was the party's abundant financial resources. As mentioned earlier, Thaksin's wife had donated large sums of money to the party and there can be little doubt that Thaksin himself did too. The party's relationship with the business community was also important. Many businesspeople were dissatisfied with the Democrats' ineffective economic policies. Many of them came to place their hopes on Thai Rak Thai as a viable alternative to the Democrats. When Thai Rak Thai began to show strong signs of becoming the leading party, more businesspeople joined the bandwagon, boosting the party's financial strength even further.

In earlier elections, large-scale businesspeople supported particular parties behind the scenes—they rarely did so publicly. The situation was quite different in this election. For example, Thanin Chiarawanon (Dhanin Chearavanont), head of Thailand's leading corporation, Charoen Phokkhaphan (CP), commented on 27 October 2000 that Thailand was in the middle of an economic war and needed a prime minister who was well versed in economic matters; although Thaksin was not perfect, he understood the economy better than the other prime ministerial candidates (*Bangkok Post*, 28 October 2000). Further, Thanin met Thaksin over dinner during the election period and arranged for two of his relatives, including a nephew, to join the Thai Rak Thai Party as proportional representation candidates (*Matichon Sutsapda*, 26 February 2001). Nor was Thanin the only businessman to publicly support a Thaksin administration. Chairman Chatri Sophonphanit of the Bangkok Bank, the largest commercial bank in Thailand, invited Thaksin and other Thai Rak Thai executives to a meeting on 27 November where he praised Thaksin for his ability to deal with economic issues (*The Nation*, 28 November 2000; *Matichon Sutsapda*, 11 December 2000).

Many other businesspeople also expressed their support, or at least goodwill, for Thaksin. For example, Bunyasit Chokphatthana of Saha Phatthana Group and Bunchai Bencharongkhakun of TAC, Thaksin's main competitor in the telecommunications industry, made sympathetic noises about Thaksin's alleged assets concealment.[38] Those who stood as candidates on the party-list basis for the party were even more explicit in their support for Thaksin. These included Adisai Photharamik of the telecommunications company Jasmin and Pracha Malinon, who operated a television station (Channel 3). Thailand's foremost businesspeople supported Thaksin because they saw him as the best hope for an economic recovery, having given up on the Democrats' economic policy. Thanin commented:

It is obvious if you think about it. How much assets he (Thaksin) owns in Thailand. Twenty to thirty billion baht in the stock market alone. If economic conditions improve and the share price index goes up from 300 to 400, Thaksin's fortune will increase by more than ten million baht. He must put forth his best efforts (to restore the economy). (*Matichon Sutsapda*, 26 February 2001)

These businesspeople would certainly have put their money where their mouths were.

Recruiting strong candidates: The new single-seat constituency system was a disadvantage to small- to medium-sized parties that held only a few seats each. It should have been even less favorable for new parties. Yet, the election resulted in a landslide victory for the new Thai Rak Thai Party. Did the party overcome this disadvantage solely on the strength of the factors discussed above? Who were the candidates fielded by Thai Rak Thai? Let us look at the movements of incumbent MPs, i.e., the winners of the 1996 election, to find out. Among the 393 candidates who succeeded in the 1996 House of Representatives election, 358 ran again in this general election.

Thai Rak Thai fielded eighty-six incumbent MPs among its 400 single-seat constituency candidates and thirty among its 100 proportional representation candidates. The total of 116 was almost one-third of the 358 incumbent MPs running for re-election. New Aspiration, which had been the leading party with 125 MPs immediately after the 1996 election, now had only forty-four incumbent MPs. The second largest party, the Democrats, had 100 of 123 incumbent MPs running for re-election this time. Chat Phatthana had thirty-seven of fifty-two, Chat Thai had thirty-six of thirty-nine, Social Action had one of twenty, and the Prachakon Thai Party had one of eighteen (Table 5.10). Thus Thai Rak Thai was already the largest party in the lower house before the election.

New Aspiration's crushing defeat can be attributed to the same causal factors as Chat Thai's crushing defeat in the 1996 general election: their MPs defected in droves. The same group of MPs was involved in both cases. Chat Thai became the leading party in the 1995 general election and assumed office. Sano Thiangthong's faction fell out with Prime Minister Banhan, mainly because Sano was not given the Interior Ministry post, and defected to New Aspiration before the 1996 general election. This became the impetus that pushed New Aspiration to the top in 1996. The Sano faction then switched to Thai Rak Thai in the 2001 general election.[39]

Sano's faction members were not the only MPs who made this move. Virtually every party lost MPs to Thai Rak Thai. History reveals that incumbent MPs are far more likely to be re-elected than candidates who are trying to get elected

Table 5.10 Number of incumbent MPs and former candidates among candidates of major parties, 2001

Party	Incumbent MPs			Former 1st runner-up candidates			Former 2nd runner-up candidates		
	Single-seat candidate	Party-list candidate	Subtotal	Single-seat candidate	Party-list candidate	Subtotal	Single-seat candidate	Party-list candidate	Subtotal
Thai Rak Thai	86	30	116	34	5	39	13	5	18
Democrat	75	25	100	17	1	18	16	2	18
Chat Thai	33	3	36	12	1	13	3	0	3
Chat Phatthana	32	5	37	12	1	13	9	0	9
New Aspiration	33	11	44	7	4	11	16	0	16
Seritham	11	5	16	5	0	5	4	0	4
Ratsadon	2	4	6	3	0	3	0	0	0
Social Action	1	0	1	0	0	0	0	0	0
Prachakon Thai	1	0	1	0	0	0	0	1	1
Kaset Mahachon	0	1	1	0	0	0	0	0	0
Phalang Tham	0	0	0	1	0	1	0	0	0
Thin Thai	0	0	0	1	0	1	0	0	0
Thai Maharat	0	0	0	0	1	1	0	0	0
Retired, etc.	-	-	35	-	-	-	-	-	-
Subtotal	274	84	393	92	13	105	61	8	69

Source: Compiled from the list of successful candidates for the 1996 and 2001 general elections.
Note: Includes all 393 successful candidates in 156 districts in the 1996 general election but only 153 first runners-up and 114 second runners-up due to limited availability of data.

for the first time. Hence, it was highly likely that Thai Rak Thai would become the leading party once it could count more incumbent MPs as candidates than any other party.

The number of candidates who are incumbent MPs of the major parties and the number of successful candidates of each party in this election are as follows: Thai Rak Thai significantly increased from eighty-six to 200 in the single-seat constituencies and thirty to forty-eight in the proportional representation; the Democrats also grew from seventy-five to ninety-seven and twenty-five to thirty-five. The other parties did not see a significant change in number: from thirty-three to thirty-five and three to six for Chat Thai Party, from thirty-three to twenty-eight and eleven to eight for the New Aspiration Party, and thirty-two to twenty-two and five to seven for the Chat Phatthana Party. Thai Rak Thai did not only have their incumbent MPs re-elected: it gained MPs dramatically. Why did this occur?[40]

While incumbent candidates enjoyed a high probability of re-election, those candidates who lost by narrow margins would be next in line for election. Among the 156 electoral constituencies in the country in the 1996 general election, 153 runners-up and 114 second runners-up were traced. The Thai Rak Thai Party had thirty-nine runners-up among its candidates; the Democrat Party was a distant second with eighteen (Table 5.10). When a party cannot poach incumbent MPs from other parties, it looks to the runners-up as the second best candidates. If it still cannot find strong candidates, it looks to the next runners-up. At this level, the Thai Rak Thai Party, the Democrat Party and the New Aspiration Party fielded similar numbers of candidates. Another type of strong candidate is a former MP who had won at least one of the three general elections in the 1990s (March 1992, September 1992 and 1995) but either failed or did not run in 1996. The Thai Rak Thai Party had forty-one of them in the single-seat constituencies and twelve in the proportional representation. Furthermore, the party had six runners-up in the Senate election in 2000 among its candidates. These numbers suggest that the party fielded a number of most promising candidates.

And that was not all. In addition to these former MPs, Thai Rak Thai also secured the support of local politicians such as provincial and city councilors, and many people who had extensive experience as vote brokers in national elections. For example, in Khon Kaen province in the northeastern region, Charoen Phatdamrongchit (known as Sia Leng), had been the most important vote broker in every general election since the 1980s. In the 2001 general election, his son, Chakrin, stood as a candidate in the first constituency of Khon Kaen and won by a huge margin. In addition to having nominated four incumbent MPs as candidates, Sia Leng's support is generally considered to have been an important factor in the party's victories in eight of the eleven constituencies in the province.⁴¹

There is evidences that the Thai Rak Thai Party was not hesitant to brazenly secure promising candidates. For example, in the second constituency of Chiang Mai province, party leader Thaksin's home province, the party nominated his younger sister Yaowapha Wongsawat as its candidate. In the first constituency, Pakon Buranupakon in his second term as the city mayor of Chiang Mai had been preparing to run for the House of Representatives for Chat Phatthana Party. Pakon's younger brother had come third in the five-seat Chiang Mai province in the Senate election a year earlier.⁴² Thaksin drew Pakon into his party shortly before the election (*Bangkok Post*, 2 December 2000). Further, the party persuaded Somphong Amonwiwat, a powerful Chiang Mai MP and acting secretary-general of Chat Thai, not to run for this election.⁴³ In a similar case in Pathum Thani province, a provincial councilor who was planning to run in the first constituency for Thai Rak Thai was forced out of the party when it decided to endorse a candidate from the Hansawat family, which had held many seats in the House of Representatives for many years (this candidate moved to Chat Phatthana).⁴⁴

The Thai Rak Thai Party did not wait until immediately before the general election to begin headhunting strong candidates. The activity had already peaked by the end of June 2000, when over ninety MPs resigned en masse from the leading opposition New Aspiration Party (*Nation Sutsapda*, 24 July 2000).⁴⁵ With the ruling party camp losing MPs one after another, in July 2000, a serving cabinet member from Chat Thai complained that Thai Rak Thai was aggressively using its financial strength to buy MPs by the '2–3–5–15–15+10' method. Under this scheme, the party would pay two million baht if an MP agreed to transfer to the party, three million baht followed by five million baht if the transfer was confirmed prior to the dissolution of the parliament, fifteen million baht if the MP actually ran for the party, a further fifteen million baht if the candidate had a good chance of winning, and an additional ten million baht in campaign assistance if it was a close contest one week before the polling date (*Nation Sutsapda*, 17 July 2000).⁴⁶ That was a total of fifty million baht, with at least one-half of it guaranteed for an incumbent MP who changed parties.⁴⁷ One candidate in Chiang Rai province who moved from the Democrats to Thai Rak Thai, for instance, strenuously denied rumors that he had sold himself for fifty million baht (*Bangkok Post*, 2 January 2001).⁴⁸ For most candidates, however, an offer of forty to fifty million baht was too good to refuse, and well worth the cost of being accused of selling out.

Thai Rak Thai had already recruited about 100 incumbent MPs by July 2000, thanks to a large-scale injection of funds, thus significantly increasing its chances of becoming the leading party. This in turn made the party even more attractive to politicians who were eager to secure government posts, thus further increasing the number of defectors to the party.[49] It also became a safe haven for candidates who were unsure of their chances and wanted the help of a large and powerful party organization. As one regional politician observed: the Sasomsap family, which had secured three of five seats in Nakhon Pathom province in the 1996 general election,

> would be wiped out under the new electoral system unless they joined the Thai Rak Thai Party. Because the Election Commission is clamping down on election irregularities under the new system, they cannot bombard voters with cash and it is difficult to manipulate voting and vote counting. This is why those who have no track record must rely on their party's popularity. They also must avoid a showdown with their main rivals, therefore they must move to their rivals' party and try to win. For these reasons, the three Sasomsap brothers had to find a way to join the Thai Rak Thai Party, to which (their strong rivals) Chanchai, Rawang and Phonsak belonged, for the general election on 6 January 2001, although their candidacy from the Democrat Party had been almost confirmed. (*Nation Suisupda*, 17 September 2001)[50]

The 1997 Constitution effectively prohibits political parties from 'buying' incumbent MPs immediately before a general election. While Section 107(4) retains the earlier prohibition of independent MPs, it also stipulates that a candidate is required to be 'a member of any and only one political party, for a consecutive period of not less than ninety days, up to the date of applying for candidacy in an election.' At the same time, Sections 115 and 116 provide that a general election must be held within forty-five days from the end of the term of the Parliament or sixty days from the dissolution of Parliament. Hence, under the provisions of the new constitution, a mass defection of MPs could not occur after the election was called. However, looking at the articles (Section 314 onwards) that provide temporary exemptions from the application of the 1997 Constitution as a transitional measure, Section 325 stipulates that 'the period of time under section 107(4) shall not apply to the first general election of members of the House of Representatives after the promulgation of this Constitution.' Accordingly, the ban on independent candidates was applicable but the ninety day rule for party membership was not, and candidates were thus able to switch parties until the moment that they filed their candidacy. Many incumbent MPs took advantage of this loophole and moved *en mass* to Thai Rak Thai, including some of the cabinet members of the coalition party led by Democrats.

Thai Rak Thai used its ample funds to recruit many candidates with a high chance of winning election. If we were to compare candidates to gems and stones, these strong candidates would be gems. The most probable winners would then be superior quality gems. Those who are expected to poll very few votes are stones. Thai Rak Thai had formed more than two years before this election, and it had not wasted this time trying to polish stones. Instead, it concentrated on collecting gems, such as incumbent and former MPs, their relatives, Senate candidates and local politicians. It supplied sufficient campaign funds to its gems and superior gems for them to acquire more luster. As Democrat leader Chuan complained at a seminar in June 2002, Thai Rak Thai injected the largest-ever sum of money into the first general election under the new constitution to recruit MPs from other parties (*The Nation*, 29 June 2002). This was the principal factor behind the party's overwhelming victory in the 2001 election. Hence, in terms of preventing political parties from buying candidates, the 1997 Constitution did not have the intended effect at this general election.

However, the 1997 Constitution was effective in another area. Ironically, Thai Rak Thai was able to boldly and generously invest in this recruitment campaign due to provisions found in the new constitution itself. The transitory provisions will not apply at the next general election. This will produce a powerful enclosure effect, preventing incumbent MPs from leaving their party unless their party dissolves or they retire or resign.[51] This provision also means that MPs cannot run for the next election if they fail to leave their party (resign from Parliament) before the ninety-day deadline since they could not then receive party endorsement. The constitution thus gives political parties the effective power to decide the fate of lower house MPs.

Until these rules came into effect, MPs could only be bought for the upcoming election. Under the new constitution, they have been bought for life. It is thus understandable that the price skyrocketed. The real effect of these provisions intended to stop the buying of MPs will be felt in the next general election, which Thai Rak Thai will fight with a large number of incumbent MPs who are captives of the party.

Administrative stability and political instability

Thai Rak Thai's landslide victory and the formation of the Thaksin administration met the expectations of the constitution drafters to a large extent. In terms of the election, a large party emerged paving the way for a prospective two-party system and defined a policy to gather votes. In forming a cabinet, it excluded single-seat MPs and selected cabinet members mainly from among the party-list MPs, as discussed. In terms of government administration, the Prime Minister exercised strong leadership and tried to fulfill his election promises. It seemed like a model administration that conformed to the intent of the constitution drafters.

So, what are the weaknesses or problems of the Thaksin administration? Many commentators argued that the fate of this administration depended on the success or failure of its populist pork-barrel policies and its economic recovery measures. There is some doubt as to whether its generous election promises, which earned the administration the nick-name the 'Santa Clause administration' (*Dokbia*, February 2001), can be delivered without breaking the back of an economy already severely stressed by the economic crisis.[52] These doubts are reasonable enough, but I see some other, even more serious, destabilizing factors. They are serious because the risk of falling into these pits increases for any administration, not just Thaksin's, which conforms closely to the model envisaged by the 1997 Constitution. Let me note two of these factors. One is the exclusion of single-seat constituency MPs from cabinet. They accounted for around 80% of the ruling coalition MPs, and many of them are eager to join the cabinet. It is probably not going to be acceptable in this democracy based on the principle of majority rule to continue to categorically exclude the majority of MPs from the cabinet. The other is that Thaksin's leadership is very strong and the administration is too stable. In Thailand, administrative instability and prime ministerial weakness were in fact important factors contributing to political stability. It appears, though, that the political reformers failed to recognize that. They identified administrative instability as a problem and set out to fix it. In the next sections these two factors will be discussed in more detail. First, the problems with excluding the single-seat constituency MPs from cabinet will be discussed, then the reasons why the traditional stabilizing mechanism of Thai politics is incompatible with a model administration under the 1997 Constitution will be elaborated.

Cabinet members and constituency MPs

On the back of his party's landslide win, Thaksin formed a coalition with the New Aspiration Party, the Chat Thai Party and the Seritham Party and became Prime Minister on 9 February. The ruling coalition parties held in excess of 300 seats. It was a safe majority from the point of view of the Constitution's requirement that more than 200 MPs were required to endorse any no confidence motion against the prime minister.

Section 201 of the 1997 Constitution provides that a cabinet should comprise a prime minister plus a maximum of thirty-five members. As mentioned, the drafters expected that cabinet members would be selected from among the party-list MPs. Although the Constitution does not ban the constituency MPs from entering the cabinet, they are discouraged from doing so by the stipulation

Table 5.11 Members of the House of Representatives in the Thaksin Cabinet, February 2001

Category	Number	Subtotal
2001 election candidates		34
Party-list		
Successful	27	
Unsuccessful	7	
Single-seat district		
Successful	0	
Unsuccessful	0	
Non-candidates	2	2
Total		36

Source: Compiled from *Nation Sutsapda*, 26 February 2001.

that their acceptance of cabinet posts will result in a loss of their parliamentary seats and will therefore lead to by-elections in their constituencies. Moreover, the Election Act was amended in 2000 to add a new provision: 'In the case where a member of the House of Representatives elected on a constituency basis is appointed as the Prime Minister or a minister, such member and the political party to which he or she is affiliated shall be jointly liable for the re-election expenditures in the vacant constituency in accordance with the rules and procedures as prescribed by the Election Commission' (Section 113/1).[53]

Thus, even though they are all members of the same House of Representatives, the distinction between the first-grade party-list MPs and the second-grade constituency MPs grew even sharper.

Thaksin's cabinet consisted of thirty-six members, the maximum allowed. Thai Rak Thai secured twenty-seven posts, New Aspiration and Chat Thai were given five each and Seritham was given one. There were thirty-six members for thirty-eight posts because Deputy Prime Ministers from the New Aspiration and Chat Thai parties concurrently held the posts of Defense Minister and Labor Minister respectively. All twenty-seven members from Thai Rak Thai, all four from New Aspiration, and three of the four from Chat Thai were party-list candidates. One from Chat Thai and one from Seritham were non-candidates (*Nation Sutsapda*, 26 February 2001). No winners or candidates from the single-seat constituencies were included. This overwhelming majority of thirty-four party-list candidates out of thirty-six cabinet members included both successful and unsuccessful candidates. Thai Rak Thai had forty-eight of its party-list candidates elected. Five of its cabinet members were ranked below forty-ninth on the proportional representation candidate list. They were ranked sixty-eighth, ninety-third, ninety-fifth, ninety-ninth and hundredth. Both New Aspiration and Chat Thai had one unsuccessful candidate each among their four cabinet members. In other words, the thirty-six cabinet members included nine non-MPs: seven unsuccessful party-list candidates and two non-candidates (Table 5.11).

Thus, elected MPs accounted for only 75% of the cabinet members. While there were calls to include constituency MPs in the cabinet, these ultimately went un-answered. Only seventeen of thirty-four party-list MPs in the cabinet were former House of Representatives MPs. Hence, the cabinet's makeup corresponded, in this respect at least, with the intentions of the constitution drafters who had envisaged a cabinet of party-list MPs. But the constituency MPs accounted for around 80% of the ruling coalition party MPs. If the door to the cabinet remained closed to them, a general sense of dissatisfaction was likely to develop in the lower house. If constituency MPs were as indebted to the party for their victories as the party-list MPs were, this dissatisfaction might remain below the surface. Yet if they were relatively more independent of their respective parties, this dissatisfaction was more likely to come to the surface. On this point, then, the relationship between parties and their MPs in the new election system needs to be examined.[54]

Party or individual?: Did MPs owe their electoral success to their parties or to their own efforts? This is a question of how voters behaved. In the old system, voters, particularly rural voters, tended to vote for candidates rather than political parties. This tendency is evidenced by the many MPs who were elected for many successive terms despite having switched parties at almost every election. So, next question is: Was there a new tendency among the voters to attach more importance to political parties?

If support for parties and support for constituency candidates perfectly coincided, synergy would be evident and the numbers of votes for the party-list

Table 5.12 Comparison of votes polled by major parties in party-list and single-seat districts in the 2001 election

Party	Party-list		Single-seat districts		
	Votes	Share	Votes	Share	Districts with candidate
Thai Rak Thai	11,634,495	40.6%	9,617,665	37.2%	400
Democrat	7,610,789	26.6%	6,729,638	26.0%	393
New Aspiration	2,008,948	7.0%	2,437,552	9.4%	309
Chat Phatthana	1,755,476	6.1%	2,313,810	8.9%	318
Chat Thai	1,523,807	5.3%	2,216,010	8.6%	256
Seritham	807,902	2.8%	1,026,889	4.0%	195
Thin Thai	604,029	2.1%	278,864	1.1%	200
Ratsadon	356,831	1.3%	852,400	3.3%	183
Other	2,326,925	8.1%	412,974	1.6%	-
Total	28,629,202	100.0%	25,885,802	100.0%	-

Source: Compiled from Election Commission data.

and the constituencies should match. However, the total number of valid votes for the constituencies was about 10% lower than for the party-list. It is thus appropriate to compare the proportions rather than the numbers of votes (Table 5.12).[55] The share of votes was higher in the party-list than in the constituencies for Thai Rak Thai and the Democrats among major parties. For Thai Rak Thai, the share of votes in the constituencies was 0.91 of their share of votes in the party-list. It was 0.98 for the Democrats. Thai Rak Thai's share of votes in the party-list was 3.5 points higher than in the constituencies. It can be surmised that the party's vote gathering power had some impact here. The shares of votes for the party-list and the constituencies were almost the same for the Democrats. Even though these parties polled better in the party-list, it is difficult to say that the party's vote-gathering power significantly exceeded that of their constituency candidates.[56]

The other five parties polled substantially better in the single-seat constituencies. New Aspiration's share of votes in the single-seat constituencies was 1.34 times higher than in the party-list. The figure was 1.41 times for Chat Phatthana, 1.46 times for Chat Thai and 2.63 times for the Ratsadon Party. Although there were variations between constituencies, given that these parties did not field any candidate in many constituencies, there is little doubt that, over all, the vote-gathering power of their single-seat constituency candidates substantially exceeded that of these parties.

One way to determine the relative importance of the vote-gathering powers of a party and a candidate would be to compare the party-list votes a party received from a particular single-seat constituency with votes the party's candidate received in that constituency. Thai Rak Thai was the top gatherer of party-list votes in more then 270 electoral constituencies, almost 70% of all electoral constituencies. If support for the party directly translated into support for its single-seat constituency candidates, the party would have had over 270 winners in single-seat constituencies and achieved a substantial majority. Moreover, differences in the parties' power tend to be amplified in elections by single-seat constituencies in comparison to the party-list, which usually works in favor of the larger parties. However, Thai Rak Thai produced only 200 winners in the single-seat constituencies. This suggests that the party's vote-gathering power was not as strong in this arena; party endorsement did not guarantee victory.

This is a question of whether voters cast their votes for the same party in both their single-seat constituency and the party-list. If voters prioritized parties over candidates in the single-seat constituencies, the candidate from the highest polling party on the party-list basis should win in that constituency. Reversals offer some insight into this relationship. Reversals refer to the constituencies in which the single-seat constituency winner belongs to a different party than the one that polls highest for that constituency on the party-list basis. Reversals occurred in sixty-nine constituencies across thirty-four provinces, almost one-half of Thailand's seventy-six provinces. Reversals are not uncommon in close contests between multiple parties. But did they only occur in closely contested seats?

Let us look at some examples, using the numbers of votes in the first round of polling on 6 January. Reversals occurred in all three constituencies in Chanthaburi province in the east (Table 5.13). Thai Rak Thai received the highest number of party-list votes from the first electoral constituency: 26,331. The Democrats received second highest number with 22,395 votes. However, a candidate from Chat Phatthana Party received 37,731 votes and won the single-seat constituency by a large margin, although the party itself attracted only 15,999 votes in the party-list ballot. In the second constituency, Thai Rak Thai won 42,716 votes in the party-list ballot but its constituency candidate only attracted 32,137 votes. Instead, a Democrat candidate won the seat with 41,258 votes, over 10,000 votes more than his party attracted in the party-list ballot. In the third constituency, the Democrats attracted 31,679 votes in the party-list ballot, over 3000 votes more than Thai Rak Thai, but a Thai Rak Thai candidate defeated the Democrat candidate by a margin of 15,000 votes in the constituency. By way of contrast, Chat Phatthana produced a winner in the first constituency but did not nominate a candidate in the second constituency and its candidate in the third constituency only managed to attract 7400 votes. In this case, the 1600 votes Chat Phatthana polled in the second constituency without any candidate could be regarded as votes for the party, i.e. the baseline votes for the party. The polls in the second and third constituencies suggest that in these cases, the vote-gathering power of the Democrat and Thai Rak Thai parties was less than that of their respective single-seat constituency candidates.[57]

In Nakhon Sawan province in the central region, Thai Rak Thai received the highest number of votes for the party-list in all seven electoral constituencies (Table 5.14). However, only three of its candidates won the respective single-seat constituencies. The Chat Thai Party produced three winners and the Democrats produced one. The successful candidates from these two parties attracted far more votes than their parties did in the party-list election, clearly suggesting that they owed their victory to their own efforts rather than their parties'.

In Khon Kaen province in the northeast, Thai Rak Thai on the party-list basis received the highest number of votes in all eleven constituencies, garnering a total of 426,120 votes in the province. However, the party lost in three single-seat constituencies; Social Action won the third constituency, Seritham won the eighth constituency and New Aspiration won the eleventh constituency. The Social Action Party attracted a provincial total of only 5086 votes in the

Table 5.13 Votes polled by major parties in Chanthaburi province in the 2001 election

Party	1st district		2nd district		3rd district		Total	
	Party-list	Single-seat	Party-list	Single-seat	Party-list	Single-seat	Party-list	Single-seat
Thai Rak Thai	26,331	16,985	42,716	32,137	28,486	33,593	97,533	82,715
Democrat	22,395	10,659	30,823	41,258	31,679	17,909	84,897	69,826
Chat Phatthana	15,999	37,731	1,603	-	5,461	7,369	23,063	45,100

Source: Compiled from Election Commission data
(http://203.185.151.5/mpresult/6jan/sh_kate_city.asp?CID = 7&KATE = 1 to http://203.185.151.5/mpresult/6jan/sh_kate_city.asp?CID = 7&KATE = 3, and http://203.185.151.5/mpresult/6jan/page3.asp?page = 1&CID = 7).

Table 5.14 Votes polled by major parties in Nakhon Sawan province in the 2001 election

Party	1st district		2nd district		3rd district		4th district	
	Party-list	Single-seat	Party-list	Single-seat	Party-list	Single-seat	Party-list	Single-seat
Thai Rak Thai	27,460	21,700	37,992	30,189	29,091	23,117	33,959	31,117
Democrat	21,687	11,323	25,220	34,184	15,634	7,510	13,126	9,081
Chat Phatthana	15,572	32,012	1,714	960	17,568	29,619	16,698	23,612

(Continued)

Party	5th district		6th district		7th district		Total	
	Party-list	Single-seat	Party-list	Single-seat	Party-list	Single-seat	Party-list	Single-seat
Thai Rak Thai	39,172	35,230	27,461	24,252	20,194	10,900	215,329	176,505
Democrat	8,021	16,602	22,022	20,257	12,855	8,396	118,565	107,353
Chat Phatthana	11,721	4,130	7,683	12,106	14,615	22,073	85,571	124,512

Source: Compiled from Election Commission data
(http://203.185.151.5/mpresult/6jan/sh_kate_city.asp?CID = 23&KATE = 1 to http://203.185.151.5/mpresult/6jan/sh_kate_city.asp?CID = 23&KATE = 7, and http://203.185.151.5/mpresult/6jan/page3.asp?page = 1&CID = 23).

Table 5.15 Votes polled by major parties in Khon Kaen province in the 2001 election

Party	1st district		2nd district		3rd district		4th district		5th district		6th district	
	Party-list	Single-seat	Party-list	Single-seat	Party-list	Single-seat	Party-list	Single-seat	Party-list	Single-seat	Party-list	Single-seat
Thai Rak Thai	40,228	30,742	42,229	29,721	37,349	10,983	41,910	33,584	42,499	29,548	43,317	40,349
New Aspiration	3,018	3,956	3,602	5,196	11,799	14,039	6,863	6,353	4,066	6,852	1,972	1,029
Chat Phatthana	6,374	8,121	15,643	23,576	5,465	11,712	6,699	10,967	4,337	7,860	14,511	21,589
Seritham	5,179	9,789	7,001	7,467	3,140	3,735	7,154	10,315	9,098	13,832	1,231	923
Democrat	12,280	15,509	9,054	7,506	4,378	3,851	4,521	3,480	4,130	3,383	3,505	2,001
Ratsadon	209	307	1,701	4,648	1,163	2,501	2,201	4,118	1,831	4,204	144	-
Thin Thai	4,546	-	2,627	1,351	845	488	909	-	774	451	821	-
Thai Chuai Thai	256	-	618	-	827	-	639	-	748	-	541	-
Chat Thai	485	-	620	758	200	-	228	-	378	692	214	-
Chat Phatthana	38	-	93	-	4,074	19,966	221	-	76	-	89	-

(Continued)

Party	7th district		8th district		9th district		10th district		11th district		Total	
	Party-list	Single-seat	Party-list	Single-seat	Party-list	Single-seat	Party-list	Single-seat	Party-list	Single-seat	Party-list	Single-seat
Thai Rak Thai	33,573	17,799	33,295	21,663	37,596	24,948	37,605	30,619	36,519	23,293	426,120	293,249
New Aspiration	4,588	3,190	2,114	2,034	15,335	20,637	12,093	9,625	18,708	31,575	84,158	104,486
Chat Phatthana	5,875	12,844	1,953	2,779	5,364	8,770	15,502	25,253	949	259	82,672	133,730
Seritham	7,124	10,416	22,128	26,334	5,438	7,030	698	543	1,832	1,950	70,023	92,334
Democrat	2,802	1,276	3,403	2,408	2,458	1,817	1,216	727	7,383	8,702	55,130	50,660
Ratsadon	2,252	6,051	9,493	16,893	229	395	91	-	128	129	19,442	39,246
Thin Thai	570	-	552	216	609	290	676	-	1,302	935	14,231	3,731
Thai Chuai Thai	886	-	582	-	467	-	362	-	400	-	6,326	-
Chat Thai	928	2,492	160	-	1,864	3,781	259	-	265	-	5,601	7,723
Chat Phatthana	125	-	96	-	117	-	64	-	93	-	5,086	19,966

Source: Compiled from Election Commission data (http://203.185.151.5/mpresult/6jan/sh_kate_city.asp?CID = 6&KATE = 1 to http://203.185.151.5/mpresult/6jan/sh_kate_city.asp?CID = 6&KATE = 11, and http://203.185.151.5/mpresult/6jan/page3.asp?page = 1&CID = 6 and http://203.185.151.5/mpresult/6jan/page3.asp?CID = 6&page = 2).

proportional representation system, 4074 of which were garnered in the third constituency. The party virtually had no vote-gathering power. Its candidate in the third constituency was a former MP who won on his personal merits. This is a typical example of voters choosing a candidate, not a party.

These examples of reversals may be considered to be unique cases—exceptions to the rule, so to speak. Yet they reveal something important about the behavior of voters that was otherwise occluded by Thai Rak Thai's overwhelming victory in both the party-list ballot and the single-seat constituencies. Similar cases can be found in other provinces such as Roi Et, Phetchabun, Buri Ram, Sakon Nakhon and Si Sa Ket. These examples all suggest that many voters attached greater importance to the candidates than to the parties in the single-seat constituencies. This is not, of course, to deny that Thai Rak Thai enjoyed very strong support and that its victorious single-seat candidates received many votes from party supporters. At the same time, though, the party's performance on the party-list basis was helped by the popularity of many of its single-seat candidates. There is no reason to believe that the voters had a significantly different attitude towards Thai Rak Thai than all others, or that they would have voted for simply any candidate that the party had endorsed for their constituency. As mentioned, the party fielded many incumbent MPs—who had previously been elected without this party's support—and its lineup was not significantly different from that of the other parties.[58]

Grievances of constituency MPs: Under the parliamentary cabinet system, the party with a majority of seats forms government. This is why political parties have been trying to win as many seats as possible. There are two ways to increase one's seats. One is to strengthen the party's ability to attract votes and get more candidates elected. The other is to recruit more candidates likely to be elected to secure more seats. Thailand's political parties have long relied almost exclusively on the latter method. They have tried to recruit as many strong candidates as possible prior to a general election. Incumbent MPs have a high probability of winning. In the general elections in September 1992 and 1995, the success rate for incumbent MP candidates was 60%. The figure was close to 80% if former MP candidates were included (Horikoshi 1997: 51).[59] Therefore their primary strategy has been to retain their own MPs while poaching incumbent MPs from other parties. This strategy was the key to survival for new parties on the scene, such as the New Aspiration Party, which formed in 1990, the Sammakkhitham Party formed in 1991 and the Chat Phatthana Party formed in 1992. Despite being new parties, they each won fifty to eighty seats in the first general elections after their formations. However, the existing parties were just as active as the new ones in buying MPs before general elections. This practice often evoked strong criticism that MPs were selling out; and, as mentioned, the new Constitution was designed to stop this practice. But Thai Rak Thai employed this traditional practice to great effect in the 2001 general election.

Since most parties have relied on this method to secure MPs, each party has fragmented into various factions. What is important here is that many MPs have won elections through their own efforts and never felt indebted to their parties. Their relative independence gave them power to exert some degree of influence on their parties. Thus any faction larger than a certain size (the number of ruling party MPs divided by the number of cabinet posts) could demand a cabinet post, which was a universal aspiration of House of Representatives MPs. But of course many MPs' aspirations would never be fulfilled due to the limited number of cabinet posts. Hence factions pressured their prime minister or party leader for cabinet posts, thereby threatening the stability of the administration. In this sense, the buying of incumbent MPs has been the central cause of administrative instability.

Can the Thai Rak Thai Party overcome this problem? As mentioned earlier, the Thaksin administration consisted of thirty-six cabinet members, including twenty-seven party-list MPs and nine non-MPs. The Thaksin administration was created by the shear strength of numbers. Around 80% of the ruling coalition parties' MPs were from single-seat constituencies. This arrangement ensures that no matter how many votes a party attracts with its lineup of prospective cabinet ministers in the proportional representation system, it cannot secure a parliamentary majority unless it wins in the single-seat constituencies. Power in the parliament is determined by the number of seats a party holds, not the caliber of its party-list candidates.[60] In the most extreme case, it is doubtful that a party could be the leading party if it did not win any single-seat constituencies, even if it won all 100 of the proportional representation seats with an array of appealing policies and brilliant candidates.

As we saw earlier, party endorsement did not mean very much to the single-seat MPs of the ruling coalition parties. In comparison, there is no doubt that Thai Rak Thai's single-seat constituency candidates received a boost from the party's policies and popularity but won largely through their own efforts. If anything, financial assistance was the party's most important contribution to its single-seat constituency candidates. This was also true of the Sammakkhitham and New Aspiration parties in the 1990s. The end of money was the end of attachment for these two parties. Many of the constituency MPs of the Thai Rak Thai Party had been headhunted by the party for their ability to win seats. These people therefore did not feel deeply indebted to the party. Thus, filling the cabinet solely with party-list MPs as per the constitution drafters' intent is inconsistent with the party's internal balance of power, as constituency MPs would continue to demand cabinet posts. If this disgruntled majority gets together and rises in revolt, the administration will be quickly pushed to the brink of collapse.[61]

The party needs to employ some compensatory measures if it continues to deny these MPs cabinet posts. One way is to give them alternative posts such as secretaries or advisors to cabinet ministers or parliamentary committee chairs. If secretaries and advisors to ministers and various parliamentary committees begin to enjoy more involvement in policy-making (which means more room to hunt for personal benefits) on the back of more rigorous supervision of politicians and cabinet members, these posts may make better career choices than cabinet posts for MPs.[62] It goes without saying that this situation runs counter to the efforts to eradicate corruption. Another way is to continue the practice of party or faction leaders (most of them ran under the party-list and either they or their close aides got cabinet posts) paying allowances to single-seat constituency MPs. For example, the Thai Rak Thai Party MPs received a monthly allowance of 50,000 baht on average from their faction leaders as well as their parliamentary salary of 70,000 baht per month (*Matichon Sutsapda*, 8 July 2002). This was not a large sum of money,[63] and rival factions of party MPs repeatedly made allegations of corruption against cabinet members from other factions[64] because their grievances with the distribution of perks and benefits were building up (*Matichon Sutsapda*, 8 July 2002).[65] This problem was expected to get worse in each subsequent election. Many former MPs switched to the party-list in the first general election under the new electoral system. They were able to do so because they were faction leaders with many MPs under their command. Once they became party-list MPs, however, their ability to bargain with the party leader is diminished; and if their ability to assist with election campaigns and election funds for their faction's single-seat MPs is reduced, their control over other MPs would be weakened. The single-seat constituency MPs will become increasingly bold in their demands if there are no leaders to control them. The party will have to top up allowances in order to silence these unhappy MPs. To that end, the party will have to tolerate the faction leaders in cabinet pursuing their own interests as they try to find the money necessary to control their MPs, unless the party leader can provide the funds himself. The former means deepening political corruption. The latter may be an option for the mega-wealthy like Thaksin, but not for anyone else.

The third possible measure is to give MPs more say in preparing the budget, that is, to revive the House of Representatives Members' Development Budget (*ngop so. so.*). This system allows MPs to decide how to use a certain amount of government money. This budget allocation was introduced in 1979 (the 1980 budget) and abolished in 1997. The Kriangsak government that introduced it was indifferent toward the House of Representatives. Prem, who took over the government in 1980, included some MPs in his cabinet but the prime minister himself was not an elected MP. For these ex-military prime ministers, *ngop so. so.* was an effective measure for securing Parliament's support quickly and efficiently. The budget was retained after Prem stepped down in 1988, and as various party leaders came to occupy the prime minister's office. The funds from this budget came in handy for lower house MPs preparing for re-election.

This budget was evenly distributed to all MPs. It began at 1.5 million baht per year in the 1980 budget, was gradually increased to 2.5 million baht during the Prem administration, 3 million baht in 1989, 4 million baht in 1990 and 5 million baht in 1991 under successive party governments. The distribution of an additional 15 million baht from a separate fund began in 1994. The reason for establishing the separate fund lies in the budget preparation process. The (1978, 1991 and 1997) Constitution(s) provided that any bill that required budget expenditure should have the Prime Minister's consent prior to its introduction to Parliament and prohibited the House of Representatives from revising a government budget bill upward. They could only make downward revisions. Under these circumstances, government agency budgets were cut as much as possible in budget committee deliberations, and the surpluses created by the cuts were redistributed in the way MPs wanted. For example, 13.5 billion baht was cut from the 1993 budget and 8.8 billion baht was cut in 1994. MPs eagerly trimmed the budget in order to increase their share. This naturally created great difficulties for government agencies. From the 1994 budget onwards, the MPs' budget was fixed at five million baht from the development budget plus fifteen million baht from the separate fund. The total amount allocated to all MPs was seven to eight billion baht: around 1% of the annual government expenditure. This was not an excessive amount for government agencies to sacrifice in order to secure their desired budgets, and it suited both the cabinet and House of Representatives MPs (Tamada 2001: 4–6). Nevertheless, after increasingly strident criticism that the development budget was a hotbed of corruption among MPs it was removed from the 1998 budget—prepared in the aftermath of the economic crisis—and subsequent budgets. But, as mentioned, there was talk of reviving this development budget (or something similar) under the Thaksin administration, because it is an effective means of alleviating discontent in the House of Representatives.[66]

The appointment of serving MPs to cabinet posts was once prohibited in Thailand under the 1968 Constitution enacted by Thanom's military government. This arrangement caused the Thanom administration to have some difficulties with the Parliament after the general election in 1969. Support in the House of Representatives is essential for the passage of government bills, and MPs were demanding a share of perks and benefits, particularly in the distribution of at least some budget funds, in exchange for passing bills. In the end, Thanom resorted to a coup d'état in November 1971 to abolish the Parliament and silence the House of Representatives. The 1997 Constitution contains contradictions that are similar to those in the 1968 Constitution. Today's MPs have experienced the benefits of being in the cabinet and receiving funds from the development budget in and after the 1980s. The revival of the House of Representatives development budget alone may not be enough to compensate for the ban on cabinet appointments. Continuing support from constituency MPs is critical for the survival of the administration. The administration must provide generous compensation to constituency MPs if it is to continue to deny them cabinet posts. This will not be an easy task. No matter who becomes prime minister, failure to appease their discontent will lead to destabilization of the administration.

Administrative and political stability

Stabilizing factors for politics: Politics in Thailand has become quite stable since the 1980s. Lack of interest in the results of general elections can be seen as indicative of its stability. This is not because general elections were not being held, nor because elections were mere confidence tricks, nor because election results were predetermined. In fact, the situation in Thailand is quite the opposite. General elections were held three times in the 1970s, three times in the 1980s and four times in the 1990s. In 1983, Social Action was the last party to win the most seats in two consecutive elections. Since then, the leading party has changed in every election. In the 1990s, increasing democratization meant that election results directly reflected the makeup of the administration and there was a change of government at every general election. These were extremely competitive elections. Frequent changes of government mean that administrations are unstable. However, few people take much notice of a change of government in Thailand. Party executives are probably the only people who are genuinely concerned by the ruling party's defeat. Although voters and the business community may expect a change of government, they do not have any real concern. In their experience, a change of government does not change politics. Unstable administrations and political stability have been the major characteristics of Thai politics.

According to the arguments for political reform and the drafting committee for the 1997 Constitution, administrative instability was one of the major problems of Thai politics, and strengthening the political parties and the prime minister's office were necessary correctives. These objectives have been achieved to some extent and the administration has become more stable. However, such administrative stability can undermine the mechanisms that have maintained Thailand's political stability. To make this point, let us briefly look at the reasons for this political stability.

The first was the conservative political parties' growing dominance. One reason for the coup in October 1976 that brought a temporary end to party politics after only one and a half years was the emergence of left-wing forces. Containing left-wing political parties was widely seen to be crucial for the resumption of party politics. This need was addressed by the 1978 Constitution and the 1981 Political Party Law. Both were designed to promote the emergence of large conservative parties with abundant financial resources. They made it more difficult for minor parties to survive, and left-wing MPs in the 1970s were typically faced with a choice between retiring from politics or switching to a conservative party. The old socialist parties managed to produce a few MPs during the 1980s but none in the 1990s. By then, politics in Thailand was ruled by conservative parties.[67]

The second reason was the lack of policies in elections. Political parties concentrated on recruiting MPs from other parties and neglected efforts to attract votes directly from voters. The Social Action Party is a good example. The party increased its number of seats in Parliament in the 1970s by implementing attractive policies, including the legendary capital-back-to-rural project (*khrongkan phan ngoen su chonnabot*).[68] However, the party stopped proposing specific policy measures that appealed directly to voters. The absence of policies shielded political parties and administrations from direct voter pressure. Since they made no specific policy promises they were not bound by any policies. The political parties were also lacking in organizational infrastructure, especially for lay members and local branches. Thus in order to increase the number of sitting MPs, their best option was to recruit MPs with proven vote-gathering power. They began buying highly electable politicians in the lead-up to elections. The only thing that mattered to these parties was money. Once a party ran out of money, it became defunct; but its demise never threatened the stability of politics itself, because there was no shortage of similar parties to take its place.

The third reason was the rise of the MP's re-election rate during and after the 1980s thanks to the widespread use of vote-gathering brokers and the prevalence of vote buying. Vote brokers converted swinging votes, who might otherwise vote for left-wing parties, into organized votes by looking after voters. This transformed election campaigning completely. The number of swinging votes influenced by the oratorical skills of candidates decreased substantially and most votes were controlled by brokers. Thus conservative party candidates vied with each other to secure effective vote-gathering brokers in the 1980s.

In this type of party politics, parties need not listen to voters. MPs barely need to acknowledge the requests and complaints of individual voters. Under the circumstances it was the vote brokers who looked after voters rather than MPs or parties. If we take fishing as an analogy, candidates (and their vote brokers) catch the fish called voters; political parties merely buy a catch.[69] Political parties rarely dropped a line into the water, and when they did, they did not use any bait. Their reliance on the practice of buying MPs and their failure to develop policies and organizations can be seen, in a sense, as collusion between the political parties to neglect voters. Yet this neglect has greatly bolstered the stability of party politics. The voters' voices do not reach MPs. The MPs' opinions go unheard by their parties. The conservative parties' dominance, the policy-vacuum and the use of vote-gathering brokers have all contributed to the relatively long-term stability of Thai politics.

Another thing that helped stabilize politics was regular general elections. An election carries symbolic meaning as a festival of democracy and bestows legitimacy on the winners (Compton 2000: 175). In Thailand, each party's share of parliamentary seats fluctuated considerably at every election due to intense competition. Particularly when a groundswell of political discontent arises among voters, the parties that become identified with the seeds of discontent lose the election. This does not mean, however, that the voices of voters are necessarily reflected in the election result: there has almost always been a buffer in between the two, which is businesspeople's financial support. They usually abandon their support of unpopular parties and begin to channel their funds to others. The new favorites develop bigger coffers, buy more MPs and come to power. Since 1988, when it became customary for the leader of the party with the most lower house seats to assume the premiership, every leading government party has lost the subsequent election: the Chat Thai Party in March 1992, Sammakkhitham in September 1992, the Democrats in July 1995, Chat Thai in March 1996 and the Democrats again in January 2001.[70] Individual MPs blame the ruling party executives for misgovernment and continue to be elected under the new party affiliations, nonchalantly making a living as professional politicians. The number of seats held by each party may fluctuate but the faces of the winners of those seats do not change very much. Hence, changes of government may produce outward appearances of change even though the politicians and their mode of operating—the 'substance' of politics—barely changes. There is no doubt that these superficial changes reduce the pressure that develops from the voters' frustration. While elections were dogged by corruption such as vote buying, even the ruling parties did not use government institutions arbitrarily—or rather, they did not blatantly use their incumbency to retain political power. Hence elections, although rife with fraud, were always fought competitively. In this way, the instability of successive administrations has stabilized the political regime. As Yamakage (2001: 5) pointed out: 'Democracy has an interesting characteristic.

It pursues a stable regime by incorporating the instability of the administration into the system.'

There was another important stabilizing factor beyond party politics: the plurality in the power structure. This plurality was built into the system as a system of checks and balances among political actors, to put it nicely. A less generous perspective, though, might refer to it as a system of ensuring mutual sabotage and thereby minimizing the excessive abuse of power by the government. Checks and balances extended well beyond the political parties to include the military, administrative agencies, the monarchy, the media and various other groups. The effectiveness of these checks and balances explains why, in Thailand's long list of military prime ministers, Sarit was the only one to achieve the kind of strong leadership that characterized the Soeharto regime in Indonesia or Ne Win in Myanmar (Burma). During the frequent periods of military rule in Thailand, the military leaders' power has been limited by government agencies, the monarchy and competing factions within the military.

During the periods of elected government, no party has ever held an absolute majority in Parliament. Hence a multi-party coalition has always been necessary to form government, and such coalitions ensure continuing competition between coalition partners as well as between the factions within each party. It is curious, then, that none of the parties ever seriously tried to win an absolute majority of the seats, even though by the 1990s it was almost guaranteed that the majority party in the House of Representatives could appoint the prime minister. A party could secure the post of prime minister if it was the largest party of the ruling coalition, in other words, if it won about a quarter of the House of Representatives seats. The Chat Thai Party only won 24.4% in 1988, Sammakkhitham 21.9% in March 1992, the Democrats 21.9% in September 1992, Chat Thai 23.5% in 1995 and New Aspiration 31.8% in 1996. Because these leading parties controlled far less than a majority of seats, they had to make considerable compromises to form and sustain ruling coalitions. Fierce rivalry between the ruling coalition and the opposition parties as well as between the coalition parties contributed to political stability by creating a pluralistic power-base that could put the brakes on excesses and abuses. The military, administrative agencies and the monarchy all helped to restrain party politicians. As a result, individual parties and politicians were prevented from exercising excessive power and leadership, thus avoiding drastic policy changes. The effectiveness of this pluralist system has been confirmed by comparative studies on corruption. Due to a high degree of fragmentation and hostility among the political elites, rent-seeking activities remain open to new entrants and thus remain competitive (Doner and Ramsay 2000: 153–5; Khan 2000: 103). There is no doubt that the entrenched plurality of the political power structure has minimized oscillations and kept Thai politics on a relatively even keel.

Destabilizing factors for politics: The Thai Rak Thai Party's phenomenal rise at the beginning of the twenty-first century seems to be capable of upsetting this stabilizing mechanism. There are three destabilizing factors associated with this rise to power: making specific policy commitments in elections, decreasing plurality in the power structure and the advent of a sole proprietor-type political party.

As mentioned, Thai Rak Thai Party departed from precedent and proposed specific and attractive policies during the election campaign. These were not vague and general policies such as national development, law and order or anti-drugs. They were offered with specific details so that the general public could later assess the extent to which they had been implemented. Having appealed directly to the voters, though, the party would now be bound by its election pledges. Unlike earlier administrations, the party has left itself little leeway to neglect voters. This of course is not simply a problem for Thai Rak Thai. If it successfully delivers on its election promises, it will set a precedent that forces other parties to propose even more attractive policies at the next election. Successful implementation will also decrease the distance between the government and voters. When policies and politicians reflect the voters' wishes, it certainly is a case of increasing democratization. At the same time, however, it increases the likelihood that the government will be swayed by public pressure, thus destabilizing the political system. Conversely, if the government does not deliver on its campaign promises, it will lose voter support. In past elections, voters have held particular administrations to account for their shortcomings and thrown the ruling parties out. But if making and breaking unrealistic election promises becomes common to all parties, the public is likely to lose trust in the political system itself, not just particular administrations or parties. Election promises raise voters' hopes and weaken the shock absorbing mechanisms that insulate governments/political parties from the voters, possibly destabilizing the political regime.

The second factor is Prime Minister Thaksin's unprecedented grip on power. The strength of his leadership has stabilized the administration and improved government efficiency. Bases for his leadership are found both in Parliament and the cabinet. In Parliament, as we have seen, Thai Rak Thai won almost half of the seats in its landslide victory, swallowing minor parties like a corporate raider since assuming power. After absorbing the Seritham and New Aspiration parties in 2002, it had more than 290 seats in the House of Representatives. It has also set its sights on absorbing its coalition partners—the Chat Phatthana and Chat Thai parties. Since the coalition government holds a firm majority of over 300 seats, there is no chance of government bills being voted down in the lower house. There is likewise little chance of a no confidence motion being made against the prime minister, since the 1997 Constitution provides that such a motion requires the support of at least 200 MPs in the House of Representatives—in contrast to the 100 required for a no confidence motion against other ministers.[71] Furthermore, Thai Rak Thai's influence is spreading to Senators, who are constitutionally required to remain nonaffiliated. It is also important to note once again that most cabinet members were appointed from the party-list MPs. As discussed previously, unlike their constituency counterparts, party-list MPs owe their seats to their party and are therefore easily controlled by the party. Recall, also, that they lose their seats in the House of Representatives when they accept cabinet posts, so any rebellion against the prime minister might result in their immediate dismissal from cabinet and hence unemployment. There is thus very little chance of the prime minister meeting serious opposition within his cabinet.

This, too, is laden with risks. First, the administrative instability which had long served effectively to maintain political stability has been lost. Thaksin made this clear in April 2003 when he declared that Thai Rak Thai would hold the reins of government for twenty years (*Matichon Sutsapda*, May 2, 2003). The 1997 Constitution's provisions to stop incumbent MPs from switching parties means that Thai Rak Thai will go into the next general election with nearly 300 incumbent MPs. No previous party administration has managed to serve a full term, because invariably driven into corners and out of options, ruling parties resorted to dissolution of Parliament. But Thaksin's majority allows him to choose the most opportune moment to dissolve Parliament and hold a general election. Even if he should fail to fully deliver on his election promises or should his popularity slip, it will be very difficult for either the ruling or opposition parties to remove him from office against his will. The history of every ruling party being defeated at election has to date contributed to the stability of the political regime. However, resentment against an administration that cannot be removed from power may well lead to resentment against the parliamentary cabinet system as a whole and thus destabilize the political system itself.

His stable and secure support base has enabled Thaksin to exercise CEO-type power to such an extent that he is increasingly being criticized for being arrogant and tyrannical. The restraints of pluralism within the ruling coalition camp no longer exist, replaced by the dominance of the Thai Rak Thai. Within the party, Thaksin has a faction of party-list MPs under his direct control and his younger sister Yaowapha leads a large faction of constituency MPs on his behalf. Some factions try to keep their distance from the leader, but he continually chips away at the resistance by pressuring faction leaders and converting their MPs. Unlike the ruling parties of the past, there is no force within the party that is strong enough to effectively restrain or check Thaksin.

Thaksin has secured a considerably stronger position than any of his predecessors against the other significant forces that constitute the Thai political world: government agencies, the military and the monarchy. For example, he extensively reorganized central government agencies in October 2002. It is hard to imagine that high levels of autonomy will be evident among many of the newly appointed permanent secretaries and department heads. They have effectively become employees of CEO Thaksin, just like his cabinet members and ruling party MPs, rather than counterforces that might contain the prime minister. He has also intervened in the military hierarchy, promoting his cousin Chaiyasit, who had been languishing in an insignificant post in the military, to lieutenant-general in April 2001, to general only one year later, and then to an Assistant Commander-in-Chief of the Army six months later. This strategic positioning gives him even more room to intervene in military personnel matters, creating a risk that the military could become the prime minister's 'private soldiers' rather than a counterforce to the party government. Similarly, while complete obedience to the monarchy has been demanded of all prime ministers since the 1980s, Thaksin has been asserting some degree of autonomy, evidenced by reports of discord. Even the Constitution Court, which the constitution drafters had expected to remain independent from politics, decided in favor of the Prime Minister on allegations of false asset declarations in August 2001. Meanwhile, he retaliated against media organizations that were critical of his administration, launching investigations into their affairs on the basis of alleged suspicions of illegal money laundering.[72]

These high-handed tactics have raised concerns about the concentration of power. While Thaksin was the head of the executive branch of the government, Somchai Wongsawat, the husband of Thaksin's younger sister Yaowapha, was a serving permanent secretary in the Justice Ministry. Thaksin's cousin, mentioned above, was the leading candidate for the most powerful post in the military, the Army Commander-in-Chief. Phriophan Damaphong, the brother of Thaksin's wife Photchaman, was an assistant commander of the Royal Thai Police and had the potential to become the commander (*Nation Sutsapda*, 19 August 2002). If all of these positions come under Thaksin's effective control, there will be no one left to stop any abuse of power. As one columnist observed, while the tiger (Thaksin) with success in the business world claimed to be a 'vegetarian tiger' in the political world, the people should keep a close watch to see if it is true (*Phuchatkan*, 29 August 2002). This is a warning that he may show his true carnivorous nature and embark on a wild hunt for personal benefits.

The third factor is the sole proprietorship-like character of Thai Rak Thai. This is an unprecedentedly large party, which allows Thaksin tremendous power. Yet the substance of the party is no different from any other party. The 1997 Constitution aimed to transform political parties from the personal property of party executives into democratically operated organizations. To this end, it requires political parties to report all donations and provides public funds in proportion to membership and branch numbers. Certainly, political donations are (increasingly, if not entirely) disclosed and the numbers of party members and branches have increased. However, political parties continue to be overly-dependent on their leaders, whose actions determine the fate of their parties. Kasem Sirisamphan, a former university academic who joined the Social Action Party in the 1970s and held the secretary-general's post, deplores this situation. From his well-informed perspective he pointed out that the Thai Rak Thai Party was formed to install Thaksin in the prime minister's office and this purpose had already been achieved. He observed that this gigantic party is still a one-man party just like the Chat Thai Party, the New Aspiration Party and the Chat Phatthana Party, considering the fact that the party's major fund contributor is Thaksin's wife and there is no other financial backer who can replace her. According to Kasem (2002), survival of the party is inconceivable without the party leader and his wife.

In terms of dependency on the party leader, Thai Rak Thai far surpasses Chat Thai, New Aspiration and Chat Phatthana. These three parties typically have a secretary-general or deputy leader who is very much a co-proprietor. In contrast, Thai Rak Thai is controlled by Thaksin alone in CEO style because its massive war-chest has been provided almost solely by Thaksin and his wife.[73] Although it is a much larger party than others, its organizational structure remains undeveloped and it retains strong characteristics of sole proprietorship. With Thai politics revolving around this party—which is not viable without Thaksin—the entire political system could immediately plunge into chaos if he withdraws from politics for any reason. It is common knowledge that a political regime with power excessively concentrated in one individual contains the seeds of serious instability over the medium to long term.

6
Epilogue: Democratization of Thai Politics

This book has considered the democratization process in Thailand from a perspective that places greater emphasis on the appeasement of and compromise with opponents to democratization than on appreciation of proponents for it. Having discussed many of the specific issues involved in this process in the preceding chapters, I would now like to review the democratization process as a whole in an attempt to highlight its context more clearly. Then, I feel I have a duty to provide a brief explanation of a coup that happened on September 19, 2006.

Looking back on democratization in the 1990s

Connection with the pre-1990s era

The most commonly accepted theory in the field of Thai political research prior to the 1990s was the bureaucratic polity model. With the exception of the illegal Communist Party, the first counterforce to arise was the student movement, which played the leading role in the 14 October 1973 uprising. Farmers' and workers' movements became more active in the wake of this uprising. Once the parliamentary system was established, metropolitan and regional businesspeople began to participate in the national government through party politics. Businesspeople formed political parties, ran for Parliament, joined the cabinet, provided funds to and lobbied political parties and MPs. These businesspeople became the majority group in the popularly-elected House of Representatives in the 1970s and increased their presence in cabinet in the 1980s. The business community also increasingly pursued their interests through business and industry organizations. These groups lobbied government agencies and the government at government-and-private-sector joint committees. The prominence of these groups generated the popular perception that Thai politics moved from bureaucratic domination to bourgeois domination or corporatism in the 1980s (Anek 1992). On this view, businesspeople were seen to be the central pillar of democratization, as they made in-roads against the military and bureaucratic monopoly of power.[1]

The political system in Thailand in the 1980s was referred to as 'half democracy,' as the military retained significant political powers and the parliament and parties were not always the central players in political matters. Under these circumstances, in which the military continued to be influential, the military's most obvious rival for power—the party politicians—came to be admired as a pillar of democratization. Hence the people came to be more tolerant of corrupt party politicians than corrupt military or administrative officials. However, in a complete about-face, in the 1990s the party politicians came to be seen as the principal obstacle to democratization. This change was brought about by three main factors. First was the Anan administration, formed in March 1991. Second was the May 1992 incident, which was interpreted as a democratization movement led by the urban middle class against the military. Third was the military's withdrawal from politics following this incident.

The 1991 coup and the Anan administration
There was a growing belief in the late 1980s that there would be no more military coups in Thailand. This proved to be merely wishful thinking when a successful coup d'état was executed in February 1991. Yet there was very little negative reaction to this coup, as its pretext of cleaning up politics was warmly welcomed.[2] The military entrusted the government to Anan, who was appointed head of government twice, from March 1991 to March 1992 and from June to September 1992. Anan's cabinets were filled with high-level bureaucrats. This was precisely the type of bureaucratic government that academics had criticized until the end of the 1980s. It soon came to be seen, however, as an object of praise rather than criticism. It was credited with being far more stable and efficient, and less corrupt, than its immediate predecessor or any of the administrations that came to power after September 1992.[3] Few seemed to notice that the administration's effectiveness was largely due to the absence of an elected parliament, with the interference and compromise that would have entailed.

Nevertheless, a significant development in the democratization process occurred during the first Anan administration. The Interior Minister launched a major campaign against vote buying in the lead up to the general election in March 1992. This brought discussion about the wide-spread practice of vote buying into the public domain, where its illegality was strongly emphasized (Arghiros 2001: 170–2). Further, an election monitoring team—called the 'neutral organization' (*ongkon klang*)—was organized with Prime Minister Anan's support to supervise the March 1992 general election and monitor vote buying activity (Callahan 2000). This increased the amount of criticism of vote buying practices. Competitive elections that reward the winners with power invariably increases the amount of campaign funding required. When political parties have no internal vote-gathering power, as is the case in Thailand, the injection of large sums of money in electioneering is essential. The growing concerns that MPs won seats by buying votes and engaged in corrupt activities after the election in order to recover their 'investments' tarnished the image, and hence the legitimacy, of elections, thus weakening the foundations of democracy. Furthermore, some of the harshest criticisms regarding vote buying was directed at the voters who sold their votes rather than towards the MPs who bought them, since a majority of the vote sellers were rural residents and urban lower-class people (while, of course, the critics were intellectuals and the educated upper-classes). This general disparagement of the 'populace' further undermined the foundations of democracy.

The May 1992 incident

As discussed in earlier chapters, Suchinda reneged on his promise and became prime minister on 7 April 1992. When a protest rally calling for his resignation grew into a massive demonstration in the central metropolitan district of Bangkok in May 1992, troops opened fire on the crowd, killing many and injuring many more. The backlash from this incident forced Suchinda to resign and the military to retreat from politics.

The incident was extremely significant for democratization. First and foremost, the military's withdrawal from the center stage of politics was crucial. The military withdrew because it was held accountable for the shooting, triggered by the massive scale of the rally. Rallies of this scale were rare in Thailand; the previous time a rally attracted a crowd in excess of 100,000 was in October 1973. The unexpected gathering of protesters in early May owed much to Chamlong, highly popular among the metropolitan populace at the time and with a great capacity to draw crowds. He was not merely an ornament, but was a skilled performer who went to great lengths, including a hunger strike, to mobilize as many people as possible. The rally was almost wholly the fruit of his efforts.

During the incident the print media began to report that there were many urban middle-class people among the rally participants. After the incident the print media began making claims that the rally was part of a democratization campaign led by the middle class. In this regard, Chamlong began to be overshadowed by the middle class. At the same time, though, the military and some political parties accused Chamlong of leading the people to their deaths. The print media happily repeated these criticisms. Certainly Chamlong was at least partially responsible for the casualties as he directed the rally and provoked the shootings. However, those who value the outcomes of the rally—such as the resignation of the prime minister and the military's withdrawal from politics— have no right to criticize him. Chamlong moved the rally and continued street protests, although he knew it was risky, in order to force the military leadership into deciding whether to withdraw their support or open fire on the protesters. To say that a peaceful gathering of 100,000 middle-class people could have achieved the same results without Chamlong is a complete fantasy. The rally was not a festival; it was a power struggle. Support for Chamlong would certainly have diminished if the battle had dragged on. He therefore needed a short, decisive battle. It is simply self-contradictory to try to blame Chamlong for the casualties while applauding the successful removal of the prime minister.

The downplaying of Chamlong's role and the overrating of that of the middle class by the print media had two important political consequences. First, Chamlong's tactics for mass mobilization were widely condemned, as the various risks involved were seen, in hindsight, as too great. It is also important to note that Chamlong's challenge was not only directed towards the prime minister and the military, but also to the parliament. Chamlong gave up on the parliament and resorted to extra-parliamentary politics. As Prime Minister Suchinda pointed out, it is difficult to maintain a stable parliamentary system if minority parties take their concerns outside of the parliament and mobilize the masses as a tactic to achieve their demands. Thus, branding Chamlong as a dangerous rogue was a highly effective way of rejecting mass mobilization politics and indirectly contributed to consolidating a parliamentary democracy.[4]

Second, the middle class gained discursive power. Public opinion (*mati mahachon* or *pracha mati*) began to carry political weight. It was quite possible to interpret the May 1992 incident as an action taken by the people (*prachachon*), along the lines of the 1986 'people power' uprising in the Philippines. However, as discussed, rather than reporting it as a 'people's uprising,' the print media defined it as middle class action. The middle class was the print media's principal market as well as the producer of mass media content. Based on occupation classifications, the middle class (professionals, managers, administrators and clerks) grew from a mere 2.6% of the total workforce in 1960 to 12.1% in 1995. In the capital city, it had reached 33.4% of the workforce by 1990. With its strong purchasing power, the middle class was also the main target of advertising for housing, cars and household goods—and this advertising was an important source of revenue for media companies. The media, naturally, tends to reflect the views of their customers, and casting their customers in the role of leaders of democratization undoubtedly boosted sales.

The ability to control public opinion was even more important. By casting their readers in the role of the champions of democratization, the print media effectively transformed the middle class's opinions into the *vox populi* worthy of special attention. The print media subsequently increased the number of serialized columns penned by academics and other intellectuals (who belonged to the middle class themselves). The lively discussions about politics and policies in these columns were understood only by those who had what Michael Mann (1993) calls discursive literacy—the ability to participate in public discussions—a majority of whom were well-educated, middle-class people. It was natural that the tone of argument in these columns would be responsive to the reactions of the middle class, their main readership. Although the middle class was certainly neither monolithic nor united under common values or ideals, they do tend to be relatively homogenous vis-à-vis other classes. The middle class's opinions were thus amplified by these columns and editorials and gained even more currency. By conferring legitimacy on the middle class, the media's own legitimacy was enhanced,[5] and in the process, public opinion began to steer the government of the country. In Thailand, until the end of the 1980s, 'public opinion' was typically understood either as the opinion of the people or the official opinion that the government preached to the masses, and neither rarely had power to steer government.[6] However, the opinion of the middle class, which was elevated to the status of the 'enlightened public' in May 1992, gathered authority once it found a strong partner in the media. Despite rare involvement in political activities after the May incident, the middle class has dominated political discourse since the incident because 'the middle class has always constituted a significant portion both of consumers and producers of the public opinion' (Anek 1995b: 11).

The middle class was a minority, however, accounting for just over 10% of the national population. Hence, the source of this recently elevated 'public opinion' was gradually expanded to encompass all of so-called civil society (or the public, the citizenry, etc.) and includes the intelligentsia, NGOs and the business community. Regardless of how the boundaries of the group were defined, though, at the core was the middle class with the media as their voice. And this form of public opinion soon began to call for political reform with a very loud voice.

Arguments for political reform

After the military retreated from politics in 1992, the political parties assumed the central roles in politics. Various groups soon became critical of party politics, however, each for different reasons. There were three major groups: bureaucrats, the urban middle class, and NGO activists. As party politicians began to intervene in the bureaucracy's personnel matters, they slowly ate into the vested interests of bureaucrats, who became increasingly dissatisfied with this situation. They became basically opposed to party politics and sought to curtail the powers of party politicians. The urban middle class's discontent was quite different. Democracy is based on the principle of majority rule, and House of Representatives seats are allocated in proportion to population. Since only 10% of the population lives in Bangkok and 30% in all urban areas, rural-based MPs came to dominate the parliament, and then the cabinet. Although numerically a minority, urban residents, particularly in Bangkok, believed that they were superior to their rural counterparts and felt aggrieved by the rural MPs' domination of national government. Finally, the activists from NGOs were frustrated by the fact that the benefits of democracy had not yet reached widely enough into society. They had hoped that local people would enjoy increased participation in politics and administration.

Although the interests of these groups did not necessarily coincide, they shared a dissatisfaction with party politics. The Anan administration became their perfect model, and was highly respected in Bangkok and other cities (Table 6.1). Its integrity, efficiency and stability were considered to be its key strengths. People pointed to these positive traits as ideals, pointed out how party politics fell short, and began to call for political reform. The political reform movement attracted strong support. Of course, no one could object to the argument that integrity, efficiency and stability were desirable for politics, and these lofty ideals were far removed from the realities of party politics and extremely difficult to realize. It was very easy to criticize party politics for falling short of this ideal; and a groundswell of criticism would give momentum to political reform. Furthermore, democratization was seen to be the purpose of political reform. Claims that politics had to be reformed for the sake of democratization, rather than in the interests of particular groups or forces, were virtually bullet-proof. Third, public opinion—the voice of the urban middle class—firmly supported political reform.

The assertion that the 1997 Constitution was drafted by people who had no stake in it (SR 1998: 117) was an illusion. True, the party politicians who had

Table 6.1 Most respected prime minister by region, 1994 (%)

Prime minister	Metropolitan	Urban				Rural			
		Central	North	Northeast	South	Central	North	Northeast	South
Sarit Thanarat	12	7	7	6	3	4	0	3	0
Thanom Kittikhachon	1	1	0	1	-	-	0	1	-
Sanya Thammasak	0	1	2	1	0	-	-	0	-
Khuekrit Pramot	3	4	4	1	1	2	1	2	1
Seni Pramot	0	0	0	0	-	0	0	-	-
Thanin Kraiwichian	1	0	0	-	-	0	-	-	-
Kriangsak Chamanan	1	0	0	-	-	1	-	1	-
Prem Tinsulanon	22	24	19	24	45	23	20	27	23
Chatchai Chunhawan	9	8	5	7	3	22	10	9	1
Anan Panyarachun	28	27	23	18	10	17	9	5	4
Suchinda Khraprayun	1	2	-	-	-	2	0	-	-
Chuan Likphai	15	22	28	25	35	26	39	43	69
Other	7	3	10	16	3	2	18	10	1

Source: IDE (1995: 72)

the highest stake in it were largely excluded from the reform process. Their involvement was limited to selecting the members of the Constitution Drafting Assembly and then voting in Parliament on the final draft. Nevertheless, it would be quite mistaken to believe that the drafters and supporters of the constitution had no vested interests in it. The interests of the people who demanded political reform and supported calls for a new constitution to this end were more or less reflected in the draft. The 1997 Constitution thus aimed to accommodate some of the demands of groups who were dissatisfied with party politics and to alleviate their discontent. Such considerations helped to garner support for the political reform movement.

Conciliatory democratization

Appeasing the opponents

Rueschemeyer and others focus on social class structures and argue that formal democracy cannot achieve stability unless the rights and interests of the elite are protected (Rueschemeyer et al. 1992: 267). Reviewing the processes of democratization in Thailand from the 1970s in this light, it does seem to have been these reluctant groups, rather than active proponents, who held the key.

When the military government collapsed in 1973 and businesspeople were harshly criticized for having colluded with the military government, they became active participants in party politics in order to protect their interests. At the time, Thailand's neighbors were turning communist, the Communist Party of Thailand was increasing its influence at home, left-wing MPs were gathering strength in the parliament, and students, farmers and workers were campaigning for various demands outside the parliament. Conservatives and royalists, seriously concerned about the survival of capitalism and the monarchy, supported the military coup to put an end to the democratic regime in 1976.

However, this regression to an authoritarian regime lacked any legitimacy. On the back of mounting frustrations about the massacre at Thammasat University immediately before the 1976 coup and the highly repressive regime, the Communist Party of Thailand's influence grew rapidly. To counter this, the country was steered back toward a resumption of democratic politics. This time, however, democratic politics had to be non-threatening to the conservative elite. According to comparative research, 'The dominant classes accommodated to democracy only as long as the party system effectively protected their interests. Strong clientelistic, non-ideological multi-class parties as well as strong conservative parties could perform this function' (Rueschemeyer et al. 1992: 287). This was precisely the party system that emerged in Thailand.

Many medium to small-scale conservative parties were formed, most of which received funds from businesspeople in Bangkok. A majority of MPs were themselves provincial businesspeople or were supported by them. Ideology and policy were never openly discussed in election campaigns; what was important was the financial strength to secure vote-gathering brokers and buy voters, particularly among rural residents and the urban lower-classes. The party system and electoral politics were very helpful for businesspeople in maintaining and promoting their own interests. Although the number of seats held by each party fluctuated wildly and a different party came to power in every election, it did not worry the business community because all parties were conservative and unlikely to introduce any policies that would threaten their interests. Regular changes of government worked to re-legitimize each administration and thus served to stabilize government by conservative parties.

The middle class found a greater political voice in the aftermath of the May 1992 incident. The middle class's attitude to democratization is influenced by its relationship with other classes (Rueschemeyer *et al.* 1992: 267). The middle class could ally themselves with either the upper or the lower class in their view of democratization. If they were to side with the upper class, they would be indifferent or even adverse to demands from rural residents and the urban lower-class to rectify social and economic disparities. In Thailand, the middle class people exerted their newly acquired discursive power to criticize party politics. Businesspeople buying political parties, political parties buying MPs and MPs buying voters were all equally damaging to the legitimacy of democratic politics, but the main target of the middle class's criticism was the MPs buying of voters. The middle class supported those arguments for political reform that proposed the ideals of clean, efficient and stable politics. The fruit of the political reform, the 1997 Constitution, substantially changed the power relationships between MPs and cabinet members. The rural district MPs' authority was diluted and the new proportional representation MPs were given a higher status. Hence the relative importance of urban residents was increased through party-list MPs as their proxies to compete with rural representatives.[7] While Thailand's middle class appeared at first glance to be reformist, it was in fact as conservative as the middle class in other Asian countries and allied itself with the upper class.

Another important point was that these political reforms did not threaten the vested interests of the businesspeople who had benefited from party politics. The focus of the political reformers was firmly on the shortcomings of party politicians; the practice of businesspeople buying political parties was considered to be insignificant compared to the problem of politicians buying voters. For this reason, no effective regulatory measures were introduced for political funding. Although all political donations must now be reported, the penalties for non-reporting are imposed on the political parties, not the donors. As Kasian Techaphira observed in 1996, the political reform movement was merely an internal squabble between the large-scale businesspeople of Bangkok and the small- to medium-scale businesspeople of the provinces (Sane 1997: 401). While many of the constituency MPs in the new parliament were provincial businesspeople, the party-list MPs were either leaders of party factions, well-known figures, or major donors to political parties. Under the previous system, it was difficult for large political donors to join the cabinet because elected MPs opposed such appointments on the grounds that unelected people were not qualified to become cabinet members. Under the 1997 Constitution, wealthy businesspeople had better chances of becoming party-list MPs and entering the cabinet, by simply contributing large sums of money to a political party. Political power relations in Thailand now more closely reflect economic power relations. The wealthy businesspeople of Bangkok were thus major beneficiaries of these political reforms and could continue to transform their economic power into political power as before.

These political reforms did not do much in terms of reducing social and economic inequalities. The word 'democracy' is often used to mean 'liberal democracy,' which lumps together very incompatible desires for freedom and equality (Katsuda 1970; 1979; 1994). In the party politics which began to take root in Thailand in the 1990s, the slim relationships between political parties and voters has kept the demands of the masses from boiling over. However, party politics has the potential to head toward mass democracy, as was the case with India (Kimura 1996). Because the proponents of political reform did not relish the prospect of giving a greater voice to the masses, they changed the election system to make the masses ineligible for election and restricted the power of the constituency MPs who most directly represented the masses. These moves forestalled the country's shift to mass democracy, effectively turning back the clock. When there is a conflict between equality and freedom, the 'haves' choose freedom. In this sense, the 1997 Constitution is tinged with elitism.

Constituency MPs and rural people were forced to pay the price of political reform. However, there is no doubt that the political reform contributed to entrenching party politics by placating the discontent of the middle class, which had been the most vocal critic of party politics, and almost eliminating dissenting voices. On this point, the clever slogan of 'the people's constitution' coined by constitution drafters was important, even though 'the people' referred to here is virtually synonymous with the political reform supporters. They include the conservative bureaucrats and NGOs, who were dissatisfied with party politics, as well as the middle class. Those who demanded and supported the political reform took this slogan at face value and argued strongly against those MPs who criticized the draft constitution. Their defense of the draft basically amounted to a concession that the constitution was drafted in the way they wanted. It would be contradictory for these people to complain about the 1997 Constitution or the political regime it produced. In other words, the supporters of political reform were burdened with a responsibility to uphold the new political regime under the 1997 Constitution.

Stable conservative democracy

Thai politics since the late 1970s has been characterized by stability. This stability derives mainly from three reasons: the gradual democratization process marked by the appeasement of critical groups, conservative party rule excluding leftist parties, and government instability. Democratization in Thailand is not a direct product of radical movements but a product of attempts to slowly remove the sharp edges from radical demands. This process was required to reassure the opponents of such demands. There are different groups of people who do not always welcome democratization, including the business community, the military, bureaucrats and the urban middle class. They were concerned about the egalitarian or redistributive policies of a democratic government. This is why the conciliating and appeasing process took so long and Thailand had to wait until the 1990s before it could boast of its political democracy to the rest of Southeast Asia. Thailand's democratization can be described as 'democratization from above' or 'managed democratization,' since it proceeded in parallel with the conciliation process.

Party politics from the 1980s onwards has had the following characteristics. First, what was established was an all-conservative party order. Government policy did not change much regardless of which party came to power. Second, political parties did not make any significant efforts to attract voters. They never tried to expand the party membership or to present appealing policies. Hence, there was no party that used religious, regional, class or ethnic differences as a point of contention in elections—electoral politics did not create or amplify social divisions. Third, political parties concentrated on buying powerful candidates before each election in order to increase their number of parliamentary seats. They therefore had to give special consideration to the people who provided the funds for this purpose rather than general voters. Fourth, mechanisms by which parties bought candidates, candidates bought brokers and brokers bought voters were established. These mechanisms kept parties and governments away from voters, allowing party politics to, in a sense, remain aloof from voters. That is, parties could remain unresponsive to the needs of voters.

Another stabilizing factor for the political system was the instability of administrations. In all five general elections from the 1990s to 2001, the leading government party lost and a new government was installed. But government instability did not only surface during elections: no administration managed to stay in power for a full four year term. This was typically because the leading parties only held one-third or so of the seats in the House of Representatives and the system of checks and balances—or mutual sabotage—was at work within the ruling coalition. Furthermore, the stability of each party was constantly under threat internally by MPs who did not yield to party control since they did not owe their electoral success to the party. This pluralistic power situation prevented particular parties or politicians from exerting excessive power, created room for compromise to accommodate various conflicting interests and had the effect of stabilizing the political system. Further, due to the instability and fragility of administrations, which was the prime target of political discontent and the reason they were replaced in an election every few years, political discontent was not easily transformed into criticism of the political system itself.

However, the 2001 general election, held under the 1997 Constitution, produced a stable administration, which was very rare in Thailand. The administration was formed by the Thai Rak Thai Party, which won almost half of the seats in the House of Representatives, led by party leader Thaksin. Prime Minister Thaksin was a very strong leader while his potential rivals within the parliament, the ruling coalition and his own party weakened. He was also effective in getting the military and the bureaucracy under his control. The rapid decline in the plurality of power eroded the system of checks and balances and almost eliminated the administrative destabilizing factors. At the same time, Thaksin made specific election pledges and endeavored to fulfill them since his administration was formed. While a direct reflection of the desires of voters in politics should be welcomed as a democratization move, it does mean that a stabilizing factor for politics, neglect of the voters, was being lost. As of 2003, the political situation and the administration were both very stable. It was obvious that Thai politics had changed.

Postscript: democratization and the 2006 coup

I did not expect another coup to happen in the near future when I wrote this book (in Japanese) in 2003, although I thought it was possible that democracy would be placed in a predicament. Even with the increasing dissatisfaction with the Thaksin administration, a coup was almost unimaginable because the unpopular government could be defeated democratically at general elections and it was evident that developed countries would not recognize a military government. Nevertheless, the military staged a successful coup on September 19, 2006. The

Table 6.2 Votes polled by Thai Rak Thai and other major parties in party-list district in 2001, 2005 and 2006

Party	2001		2005		2006	
Thai Rak Thai	**11,634,495**	**38.9%**	**18,993,073**	**58.7%**	**16,420,755**	**56.5%**
New Aspiration	2,008,948	6.7%	-		-	
Chat Phatthana	1,755,476	5.9%	-		-	
Seritham	807,902	2.7%	-		-	
Subtotal	16,206,821	54.2%	-		-	
Democrat	7,610,789	25.4%	7,210,742	22.3%	-	
Chat Thai	1,523,807	5.1%	2,061,559	6.4%	-	
Other	3,287,785	11.0%	2,782,849	8.6%	1,935,647	6.7%
Votes of all parties (A)	28,629,202		31,048,223		18,356,402	
Blank votes (B)	530,599	1.8%	357,515	1.1%	9,051,706	31.1%
Valid votes (A+B)	29,159,801		31,405,738		27,408,108	
Invalid votes	745,829	2.5%	935,586	2.9%	1,680,101	5.8%
Total votes	29,909,271	100.0%	32,341,330	100.0%	29,088,209	100.0%

Source: Compiled from Electoral Commission Data (Kho. Ko. Tho. 2001b: 22, 282–283; 2005: 24, 253; 2006).

Note: The numbers of valid votes, invalid votes and total votes in 2001 and 2005 do not correspond but they are kept as original.

coup council led by the Commander-in-Chief of the Army called itself 'The Council for Democratic Reform under a Constitutional Monarchy.'

This coup was a crucial step in a series of attempts to topple the Thaksin administration. The attempts seemed to begin in earnest in 2005 after the Thai Rak Thai Party scored a historic victory in general elections in February 2005. The party won 377 seats (310 constituency MPs and sixty-seven party-list MPs), about 75% of the total seats in the Parliament. The party received 19 million votes for the proportional representation system with nation-wide constituency (see Table 6.2). Although it was not the electorates but MPs that chose the Prime Minister, it was apparent that many people cast votes for the Thai Rak Thai party with eager expectation of Thaskin's premiership. The nation-wide constituency had an effect similar to the presidential election (Sombat 2006). The electoral victory attested to Thaksin's great popularity and gave him a firm democratic legitimacy. His strong leadership was a kind of 'presidentialization of politics' which has been observed widely in many Western countries in recent years (Poguntke and Webb 2005: 1). The presidentialization of Thai politics was not abnormal at all but suited well to cope with challenges accompanying globalization.

The royalists could not tolerate such a strong leadership, however. For them, political leaders should not outshine the monarchy, but should try to enhance the monarchy. Problematic for the royalists is the fact that Thaksin enjoyed democratic legitimacy and, unlike non-democratic leaders in the past, did not have to depend upon the monarchy for political legitimacy. Chaianan, a leading advocate of the royalist camp, spoke at a seminar on May 24, 2006.

> There have been few national leaders who gained power owing to electoral victory in Thailand. Field Marshall Sarit Thanarat did not enjoy [democratic] legitimacy deriving from political parties. ...Important is the fact that the Thai Rak Thai party has made efforts to muster support not for the party itself but for the leader. This support should be considered from a broader viewpoint. If we do not stop it, the monarchy will become only a symbolic figure and fulfill only a ceremonial role. ...There is a significant difference between Sarit and Thaksin. Sarit did not have democratic legitimacy because he rejected electoral democracy. Sarit established closer rapport between the monarchy and the people [in order to get legitimacy from the monarchy]. This was why the people supported Sarit. In contrast, it is apparent that various policies of the present government led by Thaksin do not conform to the royal will. (*Matichon*, May 25, 2006)

Anek, a political scientist-cum-politician, provides further revealing information about the misgivings of the royalists, as follows:

> We should apprehend that the populist policies [of the Thaksin administration] may undermine policies under the patronage of the monarchy. If government leaders would pursue populist policies without great care, they might come into conflict with the royal patronage for preeminence. The author has heard a resident in Northeast Thailand say frankly, "His Majesty the King has been on the throne for sixty years and has always helped the poor. Regarding medical treatment, however, the royal assistance cannot match Thaksin's '30-baht-a-visit health care scheme.'" (Anek 2006: 100–101)

A book titled *Royal Power* (*phraratchaamnat*) published in July 2005 was noticeable among early efforts to criticize Thaksin. To my astonishment, the author writes on the first page of the book: "'I read the book. I love it very much. The author writes nicely and rightly,' said His Majesty the King to Mr. Pi Malakun na Ayutthaya' (Pramuan 2005: 6). Anti-Thaksin forces used the monarchy as a symbol of their movement consistently from beginning to end. The monarchy was a powerful and useful symbol for two reasons. In Thailand royalist value is indisputable and the people are loyal to the monarchy. In the power struggle against Thaksin who boasted his democratic legitimacy, the monarchy could countervail Thaksin's legitimacy to some extent. The royalists insisted that the morality, purity and integrity of the monarchial authority were more valuable than dubious electoral victories. For example, on July 15, 2006, the Secretary to the Chief Judge of the Supreme Court spoke at a seminar and tried to dilute Thaksin's legitimacy. Although Thaksin boasted that his party got 16 million votes in the April 2006 election, 'we must ask how he got 16 million votes. If one vote is 1000 baht, 1000 multiplied by 16 million is only 16 billion baht. Sixteen billion baht is not expensive as a cost to control state power' (*Matichon*, July 16, 2006). Moreover, among the people royalist sentiment became by far the stronger in 2006 because of the 60th anniversary celebrations of the King's accession to the throne in June 2006. The people responded to the royalist advocacy and, already in 2005, began to wear yellow shirts to express their love and respect for the monarch.

The anti-Thaksin forces tried to put pressure on Thaksin to step down. First, they organized rallies to criticize Thaksin and demand his resignation. When the scale of the rallies became large in February 2006, Thaksin dissolved the Parliament and scheduled general elections on April 2. While Thaksin was sure of electoral victory, the opposition parties boycotted the election because they had little possibility of winning the election. Second, the court started judicial trials concerning election irregularities after the election. The anti-Thaksin forces longed for the courts to dissolve the Thai Rak Thai party and convict Thaksin. Although the court decided in May that the April 2 election was void and there should be a re-election, it seemed to take much time to convict the Thai Rak Thai party and its politicians of a crime. In September 2006, it became clear that re-election should be held within two or three months. Since the re-election would result in Thaksin's victory, the anti-Thaksin forces had few options. At that juncture, the military staged a coup.

Why could the military stage a successful coup? First, the military officers were encouraged to be loyal to the monarchy rather than the government. On July 14, 2006, General Prem, the President of the Privy Council, said at the Army Academy, 'Why are we the King's soldiers? In horse-racing, horse owners hire jockeys to ride the horses. The jockeys do not own the horses. They just ride them. A government is like a jockey. It supervises soldiers, but the real owners are the country and the King' (*Bangkok Post*, July 15, 2006). Second, immediately after the speech, pro-Thaksin officers were transferred. There are three Army divisions stationed in Bangkok, the First Division, the Second Cavalry Division and the Anti-aircraft Division. As these divisions are critically important for staging and suppressing coup attempts, Thaksin appointed his reliable classmates as the division commanders. However, three commanders could not resist the coup attempt because the Army chief transferred commanders of strategic battalions under them in July 2006 without consulting the division commanders. Battalion commanders loyal to Thaksin were sidelined to positions not responsible for commanding fighting troops (*Bangkok Post*, 21 July 2006). A good example was the Fourth Cavalry Battalion of the Second Cavalry Division. The battalion had played a significant role in many coup attempts in the past. The battalion commander who was the son-in-law of the Second Cavalry Division commander was transferred in July. The new commander led the battalion tanks and troops and moved into Government House and other strategic points in Bangkok on September 19, up to the appointer's (Army Chief's) expectations, and he said after the coup, 'We are ready to do what the King asks. We are soldiers who belong to His Majesty' (*Bangkok Post*, September 24, 2006). The clear and serene loyalty to the monarchy in this manner should be the third reason for the success. Probably due to this loyalty, the coup leaders easily succeeded in gaining royal approval and neutralized the opposing officers. Since there were many military officers who supported the Thaksin administration or disagreed with the coup, royal approval was crucial to its success.[8]

The military was not in isolation. The third announcement of the coup council states:

1. The current constitution, drafted in 1997, is now abrogated.
2. The House of Representatives, the Senate, the cabinet and the Constitution Court are dissolved.
3. The Privy Councilors will remain at their duties.
4. The courts of justice, except the Constitution Court, will retain their full power. (*Bangkok Post*, September 20, 2006)

It is quite natural that an institution will remain intact if it is not abolished or dissolved by means of a coup. Almost all institutions are not affected by the coup, and the coup announcement does not refer to them. Why then did the coup council announce it was retaining the Privy Councilors and the courts? It would be rational for us to think that the Privy Councilors and the courts have special importance for the coup leaders, probably as indispensable allies in their fight against Thaksin. Although the Privy Councilors have hardly been directly involved in politics, subordinates or close aides of the President of the Privy Council occupied important positions in the cabinet, the appointed legislature and the Constitution Drafting Assembly after the coup. On the other hand, the courts have tried cases conducive to the eradication of Thaksin and his supporters and are going to have a larger role in politics under the 2007 Constitution. Among the three branches of government—legislative, administrative and judicial—while the 1997 Constitution attempted to weaken legislative power to strengthen administrative power, the 2007 Constitution aims to strengthen judicial power to weaken administrative and legislative power.

Since Thaksin's political power derived from his personal wealth and the 1997 Constitution, the coup council had to abolish the popular 1997 Constitution and draft a new one which would not engender a strong leader. Understanding this point very well, the Constitution Drafting Committee chairman, Prasong, said in August, 'We have Mr Thaksin to thank for setting a bad example and parading it for people to see. We did not draft the charter to destroy you [Mr Thaksin], but we wrote it to prevent others from acting like you and your men' (*Bangkok Post*, August 18, 2007). What the coup council needed to eradicate was not only Thaksin but a strong and popular leader like Thaksin. It is quite absurd to stage a coup and abolish the constitution in order to oust a prime minister who ascended to power democratically and never refused elections, however corrupt he is. Nevertheless, as far as the opponents or antagonists to democracy are powerful, conciliation is inevitable. This coup attests to the importance of the opponents. The anti-Thaksin forces, especially the royalists, want to return politics to the pre-1997 era. Their ideal is a weak national leader and an unstable coalition government. Yet the possibility that politics will move forward in the direction espoused by them does not seem high. To their dismay, despite heavy criticism and legal action against him, Thaksin remains to be more popular than any other party politicians as of 2007. Democratizing effects of party politics after 1992 and political legacies of the Thaksin administration cannot be cleared away easily by a coup or a new constitution.

Finally, I would like to briefly discuss the middle class. In 2006 the middle class was invited to join the anti-Thaksin forces. Since Thaksin was very popular among the electorate, and apparently the anti-Thaksin forces were a numerical minority, they needed powerful allies. The middle class, praised as a pro-democracy force, could thus be a helpful ally. The anti-Thaksin leaders, then, tried to divide the people into the poor (lower class) and the middle or upper class, and classify the poor as Thaksin's supporters who were willing to sell votes. The leaders tried to put the people into an either-or situation, stating: 'you should choose loyalty to the monarchy, otherwise you are a corrupt Thaksin supporter.' Although a person could be a royalist and a democrat at once, many middle class people took the royalist side and joined anti-Thaksin rallies. Moreover, it was important that the print media was firmly on the anti-Thaksin side since early 2006. As the media needed essays or comments which were critical of Thaksin, critical intellectuals or NGO activists became highly visible. Some of them not only criticized Thaksin, but also tried to criticize the poor and justify the coup. Although not a few intellectuals disagreed with the anti-Thakin movement and opposed the coup, opportunities for expressing opinions were limited. Interestingly, it was not quality papers such as *Matichon*, *Krungthep*

Thurakit, The Nation, or *Bangkok Post* which became increasingly critical of the coup in 2007, but was instead popular papers such as *Thai Rat* or *Daily News*. My impression is that the middle class gave assistance to the royalists and conservative forces in the struggle against Thaksin which ended in the coup. No one could deny that the middle class has lost their authority as a pro-democracy force and the discursive power that it has enjoyed since 1992.

Notes

Introduction

1 On the trend of democratization studies, Tilly points out that we should focus on how democratization starts rather than how it progresses, stating, '[A]nalysts of democratization favor path-tracing. No doubt detecting a path's existence makes a crucial move to toward learning how to walk it. But even an excellent map does not teach plodding urbanites how to climb mountains' (2000: 1). This book is no exception to this criticism. Considering the lack of sufficiently convincing study on democratization in Thailand, however, I believe that path finding is still a worthwhile exercise.

2 Anderson (1977) has published a study that emphasizes the role of the petit bourgeoisie in the politics of the 1970s. However, 1970s' Thai politics can be adequately explained without turning to the middle class. Furthermore, the middle class did not participate in any major political activities during the 1980s. This is why some people have resorted to unsubstantiated claims that the politically active students of the 1970s became the middle class of the 1990s, or to regard the businesspeople (company owners and managers) who assumed major roles in the party politics of the 1980s as members of the middle class, or to categorize certain intellectuals as representatives of the middle class, in order to establish the continuity of the role played by the middle class. All of these arguments are rather farfetched.

3 The main reason for the widespread use of this model despite criticism would be that it has been used mainly for critique, not analysis. A tool for critique does not require careful elaboration.

4 Parichart's (1997) discussion provides a valid criticism of this analysis. First, provincial bureaucrats did not have much power. 'Because of the centralized system of administration, provincial officials do not have much real policy- or decision-making authority, having to follow policy lines set by the ministries in Bangkok. As a result, lobbying for policy change at the provincial level has not been particularly effective. Thus, provincial business people have not been able to do much more than curry favors and seek special treatment at the local level' (Parichart 1997: 252). Second, corporations registered in provinces accounted for only 34%

of all registered corporations. 'In 1995, of 328,498 active businesses, 111,588 (34 percent) were registered in the provinces, with the rest being in Bangkok' (Parichart 1997: 252). 'By and large, small- and medium-scale provincial entrepreneurs have had to be self-reliant, having been relatively neglected by state authorities. However, as they have done reasonably well for themselves, especially when compared with farmers and workers, this neglect by the state has been, if not acceptable to both parties, at least not a major cause of conflict' (Parichart 1997: 256–7).

5 It is important to note that the middle class, which came to be regarded as the nucleus of the democratization forces, originally referred mainly to white-collar workers (new middle class) and small to medium-scale self-employed people (old middle class), but the interpretation was gradually broadened to include businesspeople (*phokha nakthurakit*). Businesspeople who straddle both the old middle class and the upper class (owners and managers of large corporations) thus came to be lumped together in the middle class. This modified interpretation has placed businesspeople on the periphery of the 'good-guy' middle class. Around the same time, the word 'capitalist (*nai thun*)' fell out of favor and was replaced by 'businesspeople,' while the 'state' or 'public sector (*phak rat*)' was countered by the 'private sector (*phak ekkachon*),' rather than the 'capitalist class.' These changes stemmed partly from the rise of neo-liberal ideologies in the field of economics.

6 For instance, the 'public' by Prawet, a leading political reform advocate, refers to 'academics, mass media, NGOs, community leaders, poll-watch organizations and the business community.' (Prawet 1997a: 81).

7 Potter (1993) himself had previously taken the structural approach to explain democratization in Asia.

8 Whether to use the 'bourgeoisie' or the 'middle class,' and the 'strict definition' of each term, 'depends on the individual; there is no unified view.' It has been pointed out that 'the middle class is often used roughly to mean a group of people whose sense of class identification is not as strong as that of the bourgeoisie but who position themselves in the middle stratum of society' (Sonoda 2002: 79). For convenience, the term 'middle class' will be used in this book to refer to people who work as 'skilled professionals, managers or administrators, or clerks' according to a relatively clearly-delineated occupational classification. Since most of these types of people in Thailand reside in cities, the term is almost synonymous in this context with the 'urban middle class.'

9 Regarding the last point, Bunce states that 'one of the problems facing many new democracies today is that they tend to be hybrid regimes, combining authoritarian elements with democratic elements…Many of these regimes

combine the uncertain results of democracy with the uncertain procedures of authoritarianism' (2000: 714–15).
10 Democratization is not necessarily governed by universal laws. However, it does not occur in individual countries totally independently of the international environment either. Some commonalities of the process—both strengths and weaknesses—can be found within each region, due to 'external agency and regional contagion' (O'Loughlin et al. 1998: 568).
11 Predominantly Catholic East Timor had to wait until 2002 for its independence.
12 From the perspective of the transition approach, Takeda (2001) has identified subcategories of authoritarianism and conducted a detailed comparative analysis of the actions taken by establishment and antiestablishment elites in the transition process.
13 Analysts who compared democratization in Latin America and Asia point out that the difference in the attitudes of respective aid-donor countries was one of the reasons why, although both regions were undemocratic from 1960 to 1977, subsequent democratization processes occurred at different velocities in the two regions. While the US encouraged democratization as a condition for aid in Latin America, Japan did not set any similar condition for her aid in Asia (O'Loughlin et al. 1998: 567).
14 Sonoda (1998) is also helpful on this point.
15 'The middle class was originally reluctant about the democratization of the economy and grew more critical and conservative as the labor movement became more active. The "confrontation between the conservatives and the reformists," which was ideologically defined as a struggle between the conservatives who tried to maintain the capitalist economic order and the revolutionaries who tried to destroy the existing order by a violent revolution, led the middle class to lean toward conservatism' (Moriyama 1998: 132).
16 Itō (2002: 114–15) also comments that 'the interests of the middle class in democratization would be defined by their interests in the demands of the authoritarian regime or the lower classes and accordingly, they would demonstrate a wide range of attitudes concerning the merits of democratization.'
17 Anek has 'a liberal and quite democratic view of civil society' (1999: 39).
18 Iwasaki (1998a: 23, 25) observes that the 'Americans believe that the bourgeoisie is the core of civil society' and claims that 'the argument to equate the bourgeoisie with civil society can be considered valid although to a limited extent.'
19 In addition to the proportion of elected MPs in the cabinet, another important indicator is whether the Prime Minister is an elected MP or not.

The past prime ministers who were MPs include Pridi Phanomyong and Thawan Thamrongnawasawat in 1946, Phibun in 1957, Khuekrit in 1975, Seni in 1976, Chatchai in 1988 (see Rangsan 1993: 96–103 for details) and all prime ministers since September 1992.

20 Also, by-elections were held in August 1946 and June 1949 when the number of seats was increased substantially.

21 By way of clarification, Pridi was first elected to the parliament in August 1946 and was not an MP when he became Prime Minister. Also, the parliament was dissolved in November 1947 following a coup d'état and therefore Khuang was not an MP for a period immediately after the coup (Prasoet 1974: 504–5, 583).

22 See Katō (1995) for the political history of this period.

23 Of the seventy-one victims who died in the 14 October uprising, twenty-six were students. Among them, seven were high school students, twelve were vocational college students and only seven were university students. Only five out of the seven died on the spot (SNNT 1974: 454–71).

24 Four members of Sanya's cabinet were appointed as Privy Councilors in 1975, which confirms the notion of a 'King's government.' While the Privy Council was originally dominated by members of the royal family and the pre-1932 royalists, it admitted an increasing number of jurists from the 1970s onward. This seems to reflect the King's concern to increase and institutionalize his power and authority.

25 These political parties could not win a single seat in the capital Bangkok. The Democrat Party had a stronghold in the capital, where they won all of the available seats in 1976. Samak Sunthorawet of the right-wing faction was a key figure in helping the Democrat Party to attract votes. When Samak left the Democrat Party to form a new party, the latter won an overwhelming victory in the 1979 general election, securing twenty-nine out of thirty-two seats. It is worth repeating that voters in the capital have been consistently conservative.

26 Many activists, including the students who escaped the crackdown, ended up joining the guerrilla campaign organized by the Communist Party of Thailand.

27 The military was divided into a number of factions following the 14 October incident. The most influential figure was the Commander-in-Chief of the Army, Krit Siwara. He retired on 30 September 1975 and took the position of Defense Minister on 21 April 1976 but died suddenly two days later. Since the Commander-in-Chief of the Army who succeeded him was not as powerful as him in unifying the Army, the retired Navy commander led the coup d'état.

28 When Sangat had an audience with the King in February 1976, he was told to 'consult Thanin, a jurist, before doing anything' (Matichon 1989: 55). Thanin became a Privy Councilor after his retirement.
29 Chalat was promoted from Head of Strategic Education of the Army to Deputy Chief of Staff on 1 October 1974, then promoted with exceptional speed to Deputy Commander-in-Chief of the Army on 1 October 1975 when Praman (the then leader of the Chat Thai Party) was Defense Minister, but retired from the national high command on 1 May 1976 (*Ratchakitchaanubeksa*, vol. 91, pt. 159, p. special 12, vol. 92, pt. 203, p. special 7, vol. 93, pt. 78, p. 1221). Sanan Khachonprasat, who later became Secretary-General of the Democrat Party, was Chalat's *aide-de-camp*.
30 See Chapter Two for a discussion of the significance of Class in relation to military power structures.
31 The Communist Party expanded its influence in the late 1970s as government troops intensified their attacks on guerillas. Anticipating what could potentially be the greatest threat to the Thai government since the creation of the modern military, the military itself advocated abandoning its hard line approach, one that was solely reliant on suppression by force, and focused more on dissuading the people from supporting the guerrillas instead by improving their relative conditions. Prem, a former regional commander of the northeast region where the guerrillas had their strongest presence, formally adopted this soft approach as soon as he became Prime Minister in 1980, by proclaiming the Prime Minister's Office Order No. 66/2523 discussed in the text.
32 The Prem administration was supported by the military and political parties at the front and by the King from behind. It maintained the appearance of democracy by including many party politicians in the cabinet to secure support from a majority faction in the parliament but still had an unelected former military official as the Prime Minister and was subject to the political influences of the military. This political form has been called 'half democracy' (Prudhisan 1992), 'demi-democracy' (or 'halfway democracy') (Likhit 1992), 'quasi-democracy' (Suchit 1996: 18–19) and 'premocracy' (Sombat and Montri 1991: 160).
33 It has often been presumed that the national security-related posts and economic posts in Prem's cabinet were always occupied by non-MPs. For example, Chaianan and Parichart comment that 'General Prem adamantly refused to allocate key cabinet portfolios to the coalition parties; he reserved these desirable seats for his political appointees. Prem's appointees were professionals and technocrats who steered the country through an economic recession and laid a solid foundation for the

double-digit growth rates of the late 1980s' (1998: 154). This, however, is a rather static view that overlooks the steady changes made during the eight years of his administration and is inaccurate.

34 In Thailand where indiscreet words and conducts in relation to the royal family are punishable as *lese majesty*, it is an extremely bold move to make such an appeal directly to the King and publish it in a weekly magazine. Of the ninety-nine signatories to the petition (see *Su Anakhot*, 8 June 1988), some were intellectuals who were well-known royalists, including the petition's author. It is thus possible that the King's informal consent had been granted for this petition in advance.

35 Surin (1997: 158–61; 1999: 361) points to 'pressure' and 'attacks' from the middle class as factors forcing Prem's retirement, but the author disagrees with this overstatement and extension of the role of the middle class before the May 1992 incident. Similarly, Hewison's view that he retired due to 'enormous pressure from various groups and political parties' (1997: 1) is unwarranted.

36 Among former prime ministers, he was the third person after Sanya and Thanin to be appointed as a Privy Councilor, the fourth person since 1932 after Phibun, Pridi and Sarit to be given the highest decoration, and only the second person after Pridi to receive the title of 'Senior Statesman.' Before Prem, Sarit had been the only person to have been bestowed such an honor by the current King. Prem was conferred both the highest decoration and the title of 'Senior Statesman.' This clearly shows how much the King valued Prem. Prem replaced Sanya as President of the Privy Council on 4 September 1998.

37 The conservatives were seriously alarmed with the rise of the left-wing forces at home and in neighboring countries and relentlessly attacked them, even attempting assassinations in several cases. As a result, the 1976 general election saw a dramatic reduction in the left-wing camp with the Socialist Party reduced to two seats, the Socialist Front Party to one seat and the New Force Party to three seats.

38 The minimum number of nominated candidates was reduced to one third of the total number of parliamentary seats under Article 112 of the 1991 constitution and further down to one fourth in the 1995 amendment. These amendments might have been made partly because their concerns about the left-wing had diminished. As described later, independent MPs were still banned from the lower house but the minimum number of candidates was removed under the 1997 Constitution. However, a 5% minimum share of the vote was required for proportional representation candidates where the left-wing candidates might have a chance to win.

39 The Prem government's inaction in the face of widespread vote buying can be counted as another of its contributions.
40 As rising expectations intensified competition, the killing of rival candidates and their campaign workers was not uncommon (Anderson 1990).

Chapter One

1 The committee was set up with seven members and later expanded to nine members.
2 Certain perspectives highlight the antagonism between Chawalit and Class 5 officers (Hewison 1993: 164–167, 182; Pasuk and Baker 1997: 24–25). Certainly, their relationship began to deteriorate at some point after the 1991 coup. This was because, while Chawalit tried to work his way to the premiership through party politics, the Class 5 group seized political power by way of a coup and tried to preserve that power. The Class 5 group ended up blocking Chawalit's dream of becoming prime minister. The rift between Chawalit and the Class 5 group reached a crucial point not at the time of coup d'état but when the Class 5 group began maneuvering to preserve their power. Accordingly, the views that regard Chawalit and Class 5 as rival factions from the beginning are superficial perspectives that ignore the course of events since the 1980s and are totally incorrect.
3 Commander-in-Chief of the Air Force Kaset Rotchananin commented on 7 May 1991 that he had no plan to form a political party and he personally supported Chawalit (*Matichon Sutsapda*, 19 May 1991). Aside from his real intent, this kind of comment did not sound unnatural before the formation of the Sammakkhitham Party. However, Suchinda later revealed that Kaset disliked Chawalit from the outset, as Kaset insisted at the time of the 1991 coup that he would not participate in the coup if it was staged to make Chawalit prime minister (Watsana 2002b: 280).
4 The Interior Ministry under Itsaraphong Nunphakdi conducted campaigns to promote democracy in rural areas. They were intended to increase political awareness among rural people, encourage them to vote and prevent vote buying. 71,933 teams of operatives were organized, with each team consisting of four members including soldiers and teachers (Mahatthai 1992: 20–23). One interior ministry official, who was assigned in a northern province at the time, told the author that some of these teams were promoting voting for any party other than the New Aspiration Party. There is also an observer's report that suggests they were encouraging

people to vote for pro-military parties in the central region (Arghiros 2001: 171).

5 Surin (1992: 8) aptly points out that this party was formed to counter the New Aspiration Party.

6 Anan enrolled in the faculty of political science at Chulalongkorn University in 1952 but left to join the Air Force academy, where Kaset was his classmate in Class 1. In October 1987 when Anan was the Air Force Assistant Chief of Staff, Kaset was nominated by a retiring Air Force Commander-in-Chief as his successor. The appointment was blocked, however, by the then Prime Minister Prem. A group of Air Force officers who supported Kaset went to see the Prime Minister to demand a reason for this move. Anan was in the front row of the delegation. When Kaset was transferred to the post of Deputy Supreme Commander of the Armed Forces in October 1988, Anan was transferred to the post of Deputy Permanent Secretary of Defense. The both were, in effect, driven out of the Air Force. In October 1989, Kaset was appointed as the Air Force Commander-in-Chief and Anan was appointed as the Air Force Chief of Staff at the same time. Anan was later promoted to the deputy Commander-in-Chief, and then left the Air Force six months prior to his compulsory retirement to become the Interior Minister in the Suchinda cabinet in April 1991. The interior minister is the second important post after Prime Minister in a Thai cabinet. The appointment of a high official of the Air Force rather than the Army to this post meant that Anan was there specifically on behalf of Kaset who remained active in the posts of Supreme Commander of the Armed Forces and Commander-in-Chief of the Air Force concurrently. If the parliament was dissolved and a general election was called, the interior minister could influence the election result to a certain extent. For Kaset, Anan held the key to realizing his ambition to enter politics. Therefore, there was a certain authority to what Anan said.

7 The real power of the Chat Thai Party was in the hands of Secretary-General Banhan. For this reason, Banhan was given the most lucrative post of transport and communication minister in the Suchinda administration. This shows that Banhan was given the best treatment among party politicians.

8 Although Khasem was an Army officer, he was a graduate of the School for Reserve Officers (*nai roi samrong*), not the Army Academy. Suchinda makes the following remark in his eulogy contained in the cremation volume of Khasem's father. Khasem was his classmate at Amnuaisin Junior High School. Khasem's home was near Sommanat Temple in central Bangkok. In those days when Suchinda and other classmates came home from school late, they stayed overnight at Khasem's home and got to know Khasem's family very well. Even after he enrolled in the Royal Military Academy, he often stopped

by the house near the Academy and changed between his uniform and civilian clothes (Suchinda 1992). Besides Suchinda, some of the Class 5 graduates including Itsaraphong frequented Khasem's home. It clearly suggests that Khasem had a close relationship with Suchinda, even though he was not a graduate of the Royal Military Academy.

9 However, Khasem was forced to resign as secretary-general on 9 April 1992 due to disagreement with the party leadership.

10 The visa issue surfaced only after the general election. However, Suchinda later commented that such information was received at the time of the Chatchai administration. He claimed that the CIA had replied to the enquiry from Thailand that there had been such a report but that Narong was not the key figure. Further, Suchinda stated that Thailand's Narcotics Suppression Bureau had confirmed that the allegation was completely groundless, and considering Narong's personality and financial situation, he thought that it could not be true. Suchinda added that, in hindsight, it should have been possible to appoint Narong as Prime Minister without making too much fuss about the allegation (Watsana 2002b: 254, 278). Among major party politicians, Narong was relatively lacking in leadership qualities and he would have been no more than a puppet of the military had he become prime minister. Sombun of the Chat Thai Party shared a common trait of poor leadership abilities.

11 There is a view that the appointment of Suchinda as Prime Minister was planned from the time of the 1991 coup (Kawamori 1997: 148). This theory is slightly strained, because if this was the case, it would mean that Air Force Commander-in-Chief Kaset had spent a large sum of money on maneuvering political parties for Suchinda.

12 According to Watsana's master's thesis, submitted to Thammasat University in 2002, Wirot Saengsanit, then at the top rank of the Army, later remarked that Suchinda needed a reason to go back on his words; he would have to accept if there was a royal will; and His Majesty thought favorably of Suchinda. When Watsana asked Suchinda about this point, 'Suchinda became upset and denied, "It's a lie. You should not believe it. His Majesty would never get involved (in real politics). Do not mention His Majesty"' (Watsana 2002a: 269). The appendix of her thesis which contained this account was excluded from the book (Watsana 2002b) published later. The formation of the Suchinda administration in April 1992, when virtually everyone was eligible to become prime minister in the absence of a law requiring that the prime minister be a MP, in itself can be interpreted as evidence of the King's approval of the appointment.

13 The same thing happened when Sangat, the Navy admiral who led the coup d'état on 20 October 1977, was denied the premiership because he

was from the Navy not the Army. In addition to a power struggle between the Army and the Air Force within the military, there was some subtle discord within the National Peace-Keeping Council. It was the job of the chairman to recommend a prime ministerial candidate to the King. Chairman Sunthon was one of the Class 1 graduates and a close friend of Chawalit. Sunthon was reportedly scheming for the appointment of Chawalit as prime minister from time to time. However, Sunthon was not powerful enough to be able to force his opinion within the council. Such differences of opinion suggest that the appointment of Suchinda as prime minister was not regarded as a foregone conclusion by the military leadership at the time of the coup.

14 The comment that 'the timing of mobilization against a military regime coincided with surfacing internal divisions within Army ranks (e.g., 1973–1976 and 1992)' (Hedman 2001: 929) is totally incorrect.

15 In the process of the prime ministerial selection of the cabinet formation, there were some attempts to split the ruling coalition which accounted for 195 of the 360 seats in the lower house. For example, Chawalit, the leader of the New Aspiration Party, approached the Social Action Party to change sides in exchange for the post of interior minister. This helped the Social Action Party increase its bargaining power within the ruling coalition (*Matichon Sutsapda*, 10 April 1992)

16 Chalat is a politician elected to the House of Representatives in 1979 and 1986. He went on a hunger strike in 1980 to protest against the petroleum policy and in 1983 against the military-led constitutional amendment. His hunger strike in 1994 served as an embryonic movement toward political reform.

17 Among dailies, *Sayam Rat* reported the crowd number at 6:00 p.m. as 200,000 (*Sayam Rat*, 7 May 1992) while *Matichon* reported it at 80,000 at 4:30 p.m., 100,000 at 7:00 p.m. and 150,000 at 9:00 p.m (*Matichon*, 7 May 1992). English-language paper *The Nation* reported a conservative estimate of 70,000–100,000 at the peak time (*The Nation*, 7 May 1992).

18 See Suehiro (1993) for a comparison with the October 1973 uprising.

19 Various figures were reported as to the scale of the rally on the night of 8 May. *The Nation* reported that there were 150,000 people at 7:30 p.m (*The Nation*, 9 May 1992). Other estimates ranged from 500,000 shortly before 8:00 p.m. to 800,000 at 8:15 p.m (*Phuchatkan*, 9–10 May 1992), one million at 8:00 p.m (*Ban Mueang*, 9 May 1992), 200,000 at 4:00 p.m (*Matichon*, 9 May 1992), 100,000 at 5:20 p.m (*Daily News*, 10 May 1992), and 50,000 at 6:30 p.m (*Thai Rat*, 9 May 1992).

20 It should be noted that, in Thailand, the term 'NGO' is used in a much broader sense and includes (non-government and non-party) political organizations such as the Campaign for Popular Democracy, student organizations such as the Student Federation of Thailand, associations of professionals such as teachers and lawyers, and labor unions, as well as organizations working for human rights, the environment, development, education and so on.

21 The Capital Security Command was set up within the headquarters of the first Army region in August 1981, consisting of personnel from the Army, Navy, Air Force and police. The Commander-in-Chief of the Army served as its commander and the commander of the first Army region served as the commander of its Army units.

22 Since the rally organizers were concerned about a drop in the number of participants every morning, they dispatched a vehicle carrying Chalat to tour around the city for a few hours on the morning of 9 May to ask the people to participate in the rally (*Matichon*, 10 May 1992; *Daily News*, 11 May 1992).

23 It was 100,000 according to the Crime Suppression Division and 60,000–70,000 according to the security police (*Matichon*, 10 May 1992). Some newspapers reported that the number was over 200,000 at 11:00 p.m (*Matichon*, 10 May 1992) and 500,000 at its peak (*Naeona*, 10 May 1992).

24 In order to inform the crowd of the decision to dissolve the rally, 'Chamlong and Khothom got up on the stage. However, they realized that the participants were full of determination to continue their fight until they won. Chamlong consulted Khothom. Khothom advised that it would be impossible for them to clearly inform the crowd of the decision; that the participants appeared to be full of enthusiasm and they would not be satisfied unless they achieved a satisfactory outcome; dissatisfaction could lead to violence. To this Chamlong replied that they should give it another thought' (*Naeona*, 10 May 1992).

25 The military hired the mobile toilets ostensibly for a concert to be held at the military stadium on 17 May. However, there was no need for the military to hire them at all since the stadium was fully equipped with toilets.

26 On 15 May, thirty-five representatives of workers' groups led by a labor leader close to a government minister visited the Prime Minister to express their support.

27 The rotary plaza with the statue of King Taksin on the Thon Buri side.

28 A newspaper owned by a government minister reported an exaggerated figure of 50,000 (*Daily Mirror*, 18 May 1992).
29 *Matichon* reported the crowd number at 8:00 p.m. as 150,000 as well as 200,000 (*Matichon*, 18 May 1992) and *Thai Rat* reported it as over 250,000 (*Thai Rat*, 18 May 1992). Some reported that it exceeded 300,000 at 7:00 p.m. and 7:30 p.m. (*Phuchatkan*, 18 May 1992; *Daily News*, 18 May 1992). *Phuchatkan* reported that it reached 500,000 by 8:10 p.m. (*Phuchatkan*, 18 May 1992).
30 A newspaper reported that the sound of about 100 gun shots was heard in the vicinity of Phan Fa Bridge at 1:15 a.m. and that three people were killed and several dozen were injured (*Naeona*, 18 May 1992).
31 Upon receiving this order, English-language paper *Bangkok Post* published its morning edition on 18 May with the top half of page 2 (the bottom half had advertisements), almost one half of page 3 (one quarter had advertisements), and one third of page 4 left blank.
32 The commander of the first division came to negotiate with the rally organizers at 6:00 a.m. and asked them to go back to Sanam Luang. The organizers were unable to reach a decision and continued to hold the rally at Ratchadamnoen Avenue (*Naeona*, 19 May 1992; *Thai Rat*, 19 May 1992).
33 Five-hundred-and-ninety-four men and 119 women were arrested and brought to the police school at 5:15 p.m. (*Matichon*, 19 May 1992).
34 There were 800–1000 motorcycles according to the Interior Ministry (Mahatthai n. d.: 7).
35 Another was the gun. On 20 May, rumors were flying around that anti-mainstream factions of the military were fighting against the government forces in order to save the people.
36 Khothom was teaching at Chulalongkorn University.
37 Some argue that it was the NGOs, not Chamlong, that took the leadership role (Callahan 1998: 97; Callahan 2000: 96–98; Suthy 1995; Gawin 1995; Amara 1995; Prudhisan and Maneerat 1997; Kawamori 1997: 157–170; Kawamori 1998: 148–154). Although it is true that NGOs were members of the rally organizing group, their own mobilization capability was only enough to organize a rally of the size of their April 1992 protest which did not pose a threat to the Prime Minister at all.
38 There were five key terrestrial transmission television stations in Bangkok. Two were owned by the Army (Channel 5 and Channel 7), two were owned by the Mass Communication Organization of Thailand (MCOT) (Channel 3 and Channel 9) and one was owned by the Public Relations Department (Channel 11). The Army and the MCOT respectively leased

one of their stations (Channel 3 and Channel 7) to private companies. The Army-controlled Channel 5 most closely represented the position of the government and the military.

39 There were no government-controlled general newspapers even though some dailies were owned by political party executives.
40 At 5:00 p.m. on 18 May, Suchinda and the commanders of the three forces had an audience with the King to explain the situation (*Thai Rat*, 20 May 1992). At 11:30 p.m. on the same day, a newspaper received a telephone call inquiring whether the BBC report claiming that Prem had an audience with the King was true (*Krungthep Thurakit*, 19 May 1992). There was a report of Prem's audience with the King at 4:45 a.m. on 19 May (*Krungthep Thurakit*, 20 May 1992).
41 It was necessary to persuade the Army.
42 See note (12) of this chapter.
43 For this reason, many people remained in a gloomy mood for some time after this intervention. It was not until Anan was appointed as the new Prime Minister by discreet royal will on 10 June that everyone shouted with delight (Murray 1996: 187).
44 A newspaper claimed that Chamlong intended to reach the Chitlada Palace and ask the King to dismiss Suchinda (*Phuchatkan*, 9–10 May 1992). Another newspaper reported it in more detail (*Matichon*, 10 May 1992). Chamlong expected that the number of participants would increase by 8 May. He thought that they should take this opportunity to apply more pressure to Suchinda and began to move the crowd. His plan was, upon reaching the Chitlada Palace, to distribute the 100,000 candles to the participants, to sing the royal anthem with the candles lit, and to appeal to the King to dismiss Suchinda. In anticipation that Chamlong would go on the offensive on 8 May, the government had set up three layers of barricades.
45 The husband of Prathip stated, 'I asked Prathip on the night of 16 May about their plan for the rally on the next day; She told me, on the condition that I would not tell anyone, that they were going to march after the rally' (Hata 1993: 185). This statement clearly suggests that the demonstration march out of Sanam Luang on 17 May was preplanned.
46 Various criteria, including occupation, income level, education level and lifestyle, are used to determine who belongs to the middle class. The bounds of the middle class change depending on which criteria are used. In reality, it is a matter of the self-perception of the individual. Simply put, middle-class people are those who do not think that they are part of the masses or the upper class. In Thailand, they represent no more than, say,

20% of the total population even though their number has been increasing. They are a well-to-do minority residing in urban areas centering on the capital. Their political attitudes are by no means uniform. See Asami (1998), Ockey (1999), and Funatsu and Kagoya (2002) for discussions on the Thai middle class.

47 Cellular phones were not so ubiquitous because they cost more than 20,000 baht at that time. Only a small percentage of people could afford to own them.

48 It is common practice to import Thailand-originated news from foreign media agencies because the foreign versions of news have a greater impact (McCargo 1999: 554). Chamlong gave priority to foreign media over the local media when giving interviews during the rally.

49 To the author's knowledge, this paper was the only daily newspaper which reported the results of the survey. According to *Phuchatkan*, an MC announced from the stage in Sanam Luang at around 5:50 p.m. on 17 May that the Social Science Association of Thailand would be conducting a survey using about 100 assistants, and asked for rally participants' cooperation (*Phuchatkan*, 18 May 1992).

50 The starting monthly salary for a university graduate civil servant exceeded 5000 baht for the first time in April 1992.

51 It includes professional and technical workers, administrative and managerial workers, and clerical workers (in the narrow classification) and sales workers (in the broad classification). According to Funatsu, the middle class represented 13.0% of the national population based on the narrow classification and 25.3% based on the broad classification (Hattori et al. 2002: 289). In the capital, it was 33.4% based on the narrow classification and 52.8% based on the broad classification (Funatsu and Kagoya 2002: 204).

52 The Center for Southeast Asian Studies, Kyoto University, held a seminar on the subject of the May incident on 22 March 1993. Professor Shizuo Suzuki (deceased) of the University of Shizuoka, who had worked in Bangkok as a journalist in the 1970s, remarked as soon as he watched video footage of the incident that 'These are not middle class people.'

53 They include English-language papers and *Matichon* as well as business papers. People can read them openly in any location. Conversely, the middle class might hesitate to read 'tabloid newspapers' such as *Thai Rat* and *Daily News* in public.

54 English-language daily *The Nation* had a sister Thai-language business daily *Krungthep Thurakit* and its weekly magazine version. The name of this weekly magazine was changed to the same name as the English paper.

55 Anek argues that the middle class was not sleeping, but because an ideal form of democracy was not realized, the middle class criticized democracy during democratic periods to pave the way for a coup d'état and criticized military juntas during military government periods (Anek 1993: 63). One thing is certain: the middle class are not always pro-democracy.
56 In his speech on the night of 10 September at the final stage of the election campaign, Chamlong fiercely criticized the tactics used by the Democrat Party. 'Rival politicians are putting up posters to vilify me everywhere. They tell you to elect Chuan if you do not want to regret or cry. It is a malicious slander against me that I have led people to death' (*Matichon Sutsapda*, 4 December 1992).
57 The national total for the Phalang Tham Party increased from forty-one seats in March 1992 to forty-seven seats in September 1992. The party secured sixteen seats in Bangkok (twenty-three nationally) in the 1995 general election, thanks to a great deal of effort by party leader Thaksin Chinnawat. However, in the 1996 general election after Thaksin left the party, it suffered a devastating loss in that it only managed to win one seat for Sudarat Keyuraphan. The party was left with no seats in 2001 after Sudarat resigned from the party.
58 After the election, a New Aspiration Party executive commented that the Phalang Tham Party was actually defeated and 'although Thais dislike dictatorship, they also dislike the political parties which fight against dictatorship; I am not sure why but perhaps they like someone who does nothing' (*Matichon Sutsapda*, 25 September 1992).
59 Three members of the CFD committee stood as candidates in the Bangkok electoral district (eighteen seats) in the March 2000 Senate election, as discussed later. Only Prathip was elected in tenth place with 40,228 votes. Weng finished twenty-fourth with 13,448 votes and Chalat came 108th with only 3405 votes. Prathip's votes were less than one tenth of the 421,515 votes won by the top candidate and only 1.8 times larger than the 22,925 votes won by the lowest ranked winner. The dominance of the middle class leadership theory which does not recognize the contributions made by the rally organizers and behind-the-scenes supporters may be partly responsible for the poor results.
60 Pasuk was referring to this point when she pointed out that 'the print media grew stronger and bolder' since 1992 (1999: 13).
61 In the views which emphasize the role of NGOs in the rally as mentioned earlier (in note (37) of this chapter), 'civil society' is considered to be a much broader category which includes the masses (for example, Kawamori 1998). However, it does not change the fact that the masses did not have much say in the subsequent debate on political reform.

Chapter Two

1 Only six of them were elected MPs at the time of their appointment.
2 The total number of years for which elected MPs occupied the prime minister's office was only about five years.
3 There was little research prior to the 1980s when the military played a major role in politics and there was even less after the early 1990s, when its role diminished. Of the work that has been produced, Itō's research (1999) stands out as a useful overview of the military's retreat from center stage.
4 See Tamada (2002: 121–4) for factors that contributed to the military's withdrawal from politics that are not directly associated with the May incident.
5 There seem to be several reasons for the military's continuing popularity. First, there is a long history of military involvement in Thai politics, and memories of these interventions are not necessarily negative. For instance, people think surprisingly highly of Sarit Thanarat—whose name is almost synonymous with military government in Thailand—because the people have great admiration for strong leaders. He is the most respected of the seven prime ministers who held office in the 1960s and '70s (IDE 1995: 72). Second, during its long history of political intervention, the military has gained control over the broadcast media and used it to great effect in self-promotion. Third, many people believe that the military is more clean and honest than other political forces. This is evident in Funatsu et al.'s survey (IDE 1995). In response to the question, 'How trustworthy do you think information is that emanates from the following institutions?,' the proportion of respondents who answered 'moderately trustworthy' was 21% for politicians, 47% for the government, 31% for the police, 48% for the media and 59% for the military—even among the metropolitan residents who have a generally unfavorable view of the military (IDE 1995: 68). Fourth, the military is in many respects a merit-based, rather than pedigree-based, competitive and equitable organization. While there are certainly many officers whose fathers were also military officers, there are nevertheless more students from provinces and ordinary families at military academies than at universities. Needless to say, most of the rank and file comes from rural families; and a good pedigree does not help one's promotion as much as it does in administrative agencies. For example, the sons of former Prime Minister Phot Sarasin, except the eldest son who became a businessman (then entered politics and became a minister), successfully attained very high positions. The second son became the

police chief, the third son became a permanent secretary of Finance and the fourth son became a permanent secretary of Foreign Affairs. In contrast, the fifth son joined the Army and, although he reached the rank of general, was never appointed to any prominent post. A similar contrast between promotion in the military and in the administrative agencies can be witnessed among the members of the royal family. Fifth, a sense of balance may be at work when people support the military as a counterforce against the increasing power of party politicians in politics.
6 The Ministry of Defense is not an attractive agency for party politicians in the sense that it does not contribute to the day-to-day administration of the government as do the Interior Ministry and the Ministry of Finance, nor does it provide the sort of lurks and perks that can be had from the Ministry of Transport and Communications or the Ministry of Agriculture and Cooperatives.
7 Likhit argues that the key to success or failure of a coup is the strength of unity within the military (1992: 234).
8 Takeda's explanation that 'factional dynamics' holds military interference in check is right on the mark (2001: 91-3).
9 See also Tamada (1998).
10 The fiscal year for Thai government agencies begins on 1 October, which is therefore also the date of the annual personnel reshuffles in administrative agencies.
11 The Thai military has a large number of generals. It was reported that there were 1450 active generals and eighty full generals (including field marshals) as of January 1997 (*Matichon Sutsapda*, 10 February 1997). Since the 1990's the Thai Armed Forces has been in the process of downsizing, slowing the rate of promoting commissioned officers to generals.
12 Any transfer from the Army to the Supreme Command or the Office of the Defense Permanent Secretary must be agreed to by the receiving agency. Although occasionally people are transferred from these agencies to the Army, the overwhelming majority of transfers are in the opposite direction, to such an extent that it is virtually one-way traffic.
13 Of course some officers plead special cases in their attempts to stay on beyond the retirement age, and there have been some precedents of such postponement. However, each case has drawn harsh criticism from within the military itself. The most recent case of a Commander-in-Chief postponing his retirement was Athit in 1985.
14 This is related to the attitude of Thai people toward power (Tamada 1991). Former commanders-in-chief are unable to continue to exert any influence

on the military if they rely only upon their legacy from the past. Hence if they want to continue to exercise power they must find a new source of authority through posts such as prime minister, defense minister or privy councilor. Under these circumstances, ambitious subordinate officers look forward to the mandatory age retirement of their superiors.

15 School grades are also important for career advancement. For example, Commanders-in-Chief Chawalit (Class 42 of the College), Suchinda (Class 44), Itsaraphong (Class 45) and Surayut (Class 52) and Chief of Staff Chan (Class 51) were each the top graduates in their respective classes at the Command and General Staff College for Cadet Officers (CPR 1987).

16 Officers who did not graduate from a military academy were sometimes handicapped in their quests for promotion. Those who were commissioned as officers after graduating from normal universities are a typical example. Those who commenced their studies at the academy, and received good enough grades to travel abroad to complete their studies were also disadvantaged, because they did not finish the academy. Examples of this latter group include Phichit and Wichit of Class 2, who went to the US Military Academy at West Point and Thawan of Class 7, who went to the Philippines.

17 Former Prime Ministers Prem and Chatchai were both former cavalry (tank) officers. After Manun (who later changed his name to Manunkrit), the leader of Class 7 which supported Prem, participated in the coups of 1981 and 1985 with his tank unit, and Chatchai later reinstated Manun to check moves from the Class 5 cadre, the mainstream of the military came to regard cavalry officers as dangerous. Subsequently, in the 1990s, very few of them were promoted to the Army leadership. Its change of status is clearly indicated by the fact that the cavalry unit, the star of past coups, was not involved in the 1991 coup.

18 Suchinda was the first Prime Minister since Plaek Phibunsongkhram and the first Army Commander-in-Chief since Soem Na Nakhon to have an artillery background. However, Suchinda was only in the Artillery Division for a few years after his graduation from the Academy, before moving to the General Staff Division. Hence, the Artillery Division did not provide his primary support base.

19 There are many instances of fathers and sons or brothers graduating from the same military academy. In addition, there are many cases in which officers marry a classmate's sister. This is not only for the political reason of strengthening the unity of a class, but also because close friendships with a classmate's family provide valuable opportunities to meet members of

the opposite sex. Of course, some military leaders also arrange marriages for their children in order to consolidate their own power.

20 The post of brigade commander (*mae thap noi*) was created in the First to Third Army Regions during the 1980s. It was explained that the post was set up so that fighting units could be organized into brigades in times of emergency and the brigade commander could take charge on behalf of a busy regional commander. However, no emergency was genuinely anticipated; the post was merely created as a convenient stepping stone to provide a large number of major-generals the chance to advance to the rank of lieutenant-general.

21 The First Division is essentially an infantry division, although its name does not have 'infantry' (*thahan rap*) in it.

22 The Second Special Warfare Division was abolished at the end of September 2001.

23 When one leading faction is forced to give way to another, the promising officer in this post is, more often than not, seen as a threat and sidelined through demotion to a nominal post. In contrast, general staff officers (such as the Director of Operations) are often perceived as 'harmless,' and thus advance their careers without obstacle.

24 Assuming, that is, that power is not excessively concentrated in the post of commander-in-chief, but is somewhat distributed among the different officer groups. When the commander-in-chief is more dictatorial, he will typically try to preserve his power by dividing and ruling his subordinates.

25 Real power does not directly correspond to the administrative ordering explained earlier. The Commanders-in-Chief of the three forces have the greatest levels of real power, followed by the Supreme Commander, the Minister of Defense, and then the Permanent Secretary of Defense.

26 Preparatory Class 7 was the last group to graduate from the old academy, and was followed by Class 1 of the new academy the next year.

27 Suchinda had always had postings as an immediate subordinate of Chawalit. Suchinda was appointed Deputy when Chawalit was made Director of Operations in October 1981. He became Director of Operations when Chawalit was promoted to Assistant Chief of Staff in Charge of Operations in October 1982. He became the Assistant Chief of Staff in Charge of Operations when Chawalit was promoted to Chief of Staff in October 1985. Of course, none of the classes was ever monolithically united, and naturally some of the Class 5 officers were aligned with the Athit faction. The key question in this regard is which member of the class

forms the dominant or mainstream faction. In the case of Class 5, Suchinda became the most successful member and formed the dominant faction.

28 We have to go as far back as Praphat Charusathian in 1963 to find an Army Commander-in-Chief who was younger than Chawalit at the time of appointment. Most of the Army Chiefs since then had only three years or less before they reached the retirement age. Quite a few of them had only one year in office. Chawalit's tenure of six years was extremely unusual. This was part of the reason why he voluntarily retired before he reached the mandatory age, which was also extremely unusual for a top military officer or government official.

29 Itsaraphong's father was the metropolitan police commander Lieutenant-General Chat. Itsaraphong's younger sister Waruni married Suchinda. The Nunphakdi clan has produced many military officers, including Lieutenant-General Prayun, who held the post of First Divisional Commander, as did Itsaraphong.

30 '01' refers to the Buddhist calendar year 2501 (1958 CE) in which they graduated from their academies, '3' refers to the three military forces and '4' refers to the three military forces plus the police force. The club reportedly began in 1981 as a get-together to celebrate the promotion of classmates (*Khao Thai*, 21 December 1992). As far as I have been able to confirm, a list of officers who graduated from the military academies of the three forces and were commissioned on 11 February 1958 had already been published in 1988 at the initiative of Air Force officers (*Thamniap 1988*).

31 There are many analysts who think that the military carried out the 1991 coup to restore its political power, which had declined during the 1980s, and planned from the beginning to put a military man in the Prime Minister's Office. This view implies that the military had been eagerly awaiting a chance to regain its political power. I do not subscribe to this view. The military's clumsy manner of execution on the day of the coup suggests that it was a spur-of-the-moment action with little preparation. The coup leaders did not even have an agreed plan for a post-coup government. Hence, it seems that more than anything else, the coup was a defensive action to prevent the Prime Minister from dismissing military leaders (Tamada 1992a). As Interior Minister Praman Adireksan, a brother-in-law of then Prime Minister Chatchai, explained: 'When the dismissal of the Army Commander-in-Chief and the Supreme Commander of the Armed Forces was rumored, the officers were displeased at the appointment of (former Army Commander-in-Chief) General Athit Kamlangek as the Deputy

Minister of Defense and mounted a coup d'état. They made up the five-point statement to justify their action afterwards' (Praman 1999: 48).
32 'At first, many were pleased to see the end of a corrupt civilian government' (Hewison 1997: 1).
33 Another strong candidate to succeed Itsaraphong was Wimon of Class 5. Wimon became a divisional commander in October 1982 at the same time as Itsaraphong and one year before Wirot, then became a regional commander in October 1986 at the same time as Itsaraphong. Wimon joined the Five Tigers in April 1990 at the same time as Wirot and six months after Itsaraphong. In other words, Wimon had slightly less seniority than Itsaraphong and slightly more than Wirot. In the contest for the post of commander-in-chief, Wimon was a formidable rival for Itsaraphong and even more so for Wirot. Hence, Wimon was transferred to the Supreme Command as the Deputy Supreme Commander in the October 1991 reshuffle. This significantly cleared the way for Itsaraphong to assume the top job after Suchinda's retirement and enabled Wirot to feel relatively secure while awaiting Itsaraphong's retirement.
34 He was promoted to major-general shortly before his retirement.
35 Some have attributed the 1985 coup, the 1991 coup and the May 1992 incident all to rivalry between Class 5 and Class 7. Certainly, rivalry between these two groups is said to have begun when they were still in the academy and became publicly apparent after the 1970s, when Class 7 emerged as a major force. However, following the failed coup of 1981, Class 7 officers were regarded as dangerous and were thoroughly purged from all important posts in the Army. Subsequently, the disparity in power between the fallen Class 7 and the prospering Class 5 was far too great for them to be real rivals. This contest between Chamlong, Chawalit and Suchinda arose because both Chamlong and Chawalit were more daring than the run-of-the-mill party politicians—probably in no small part due to their military background—rather than because of any rivalry between these two classes.
36 Many officers in the Second Region were loyal to Privy Councilor and former Prime Minister Prem, and the Phran Soldier Unit (a unit of volunteer soldiers organized in preparation for deployment on the frontline in the fight against communism), which was loyal to Chawalit, was also stationed in the Second Region. The Special Warfare Unit was under the command of Surayut, who was close to Prem. These formed the basis for such speculations, as they were the first units that came to mind when one looked for the possible appearance of anti-Suchinda units.

37 In this tense situation, some Class 4 officers paid a visit to Prem. Deputy Commander of the First Army Region Prayun Midet (Class 8), who was openly opposed to the violent suppression operation, also visited Prem to offer encouragement (*Khao Thai*, 10 August 1992). Among the fifteen privy councilors, Prem had the most extensive connections to the military and politicians. Mention of the name of Prem made everyone think of a privy councilor close to the King, and encouragement offered to Prem was considered to be equivalent to encouragement offered to the King who was behind or above him.

38 The decree provided immunity to both the government and the protesters from liability for all of the acts committed in relation to the rally from 17 to 21 May. A court action was filed some time later to challenge the constitutionality of this decree, but it was almost impossible that the decree issued for the political purpose of appeasing the military would be ruled unconstitutional by the court.

39 The televised announcement of his resignation was reportedly recorded on 22 May (*Khao Thai*, 1 June 1992).

40 The military also mobilized a hard-line group (which called itself the 'defenders of the royal house of Chakri (*aphirak chakri*)') to criticize Chawalit and Chamlong who belonged to minority parties. This group had clashed with Chawalit and other soft-liners at the Internal Security Operations Command (ISOC) in the 1980s over anti-Communist measures, insisting on all-out armed suppression rather than the softer conciliatory approach of their opponents. Some of the rancor involved in this contest arose from the fact that some of the officers involved continued to be disgruntled about a severe downsizing of the organization orchestrated by Chawalit, following the destruction of the Communist Party in the late 1980s (*Lak Thai*, 1 September 1988).

41 The parliament passed four constitutional amendment bills simultaneously on 10 June 1992. Three concerned reducing the authority of the Senate, etc. and the fourth bill stipulated that the prime minister should be an elected MP. The former were promulgated on 29 June and put into force on the following day. The latter was scheduled for promulgation on 10 September and enforcement on 13 September—a grace period of three months. The interim prime minister was appointed on 10 June, immediately after the constitutional amendment bills were passed. Anan, who was not an elected MP, was appointed to serve for this grace period. This was a highly political decision which was clearly contrary to the spirit of the constitutional amendment. Nevertheless, the public's favorable reaction

to the appointment of the unelected prime minister seems to have been indicative of a growing desire for political reform.
42 San Siphen, who was promoted from Assistant Commander-in-Chief to Deputy Commander-in-Chief at this time, was also a member of Class 5; but he had reportedly walked out of the countermeasures meeting on the night of 17 May in protest against the deployment of troops (*Khao Thai*, 6 July 1992).
43 See Aphiwat's (1998) commemorative book marking Chettha's sixtieth birthday for his personal history.
44 Of the fifteen or so privy councilors, he was only the second, following Prem, to have held a high military position. This was presumably because the Privy Council learned from the experience of the May crisis that the military could not be adequately controlled by Prem alone.
45 Phaibun was the Assistant Director of the Army Weapons Production Control Center (major-general, 1983), the Deputy Director (1985) and the Director (lieutenant-general, 1989) before becoming a general assigned the post of Head of the General Staff Corps attached to Commander-in-Chief Wimon in October 1992. In comparison, although Pramon became a major-general in 1985, he held the post of Director of Operations on the elite track within the Army, and then became a lieutenant-general as the Assistant Chief of Staff in 1988, the Deputy Chief of Staff in April 1990 and a general as the Chief of Staff in April 1992. The difference between their respective career paths was evident. It is worth recalling that Chawalit, Suchinda and Pramon had each followed almost identical career paths in succession.
46 Samphao's classmates from Class 12 were appointed to the post of Anti-Aircraft Division Commander from October 1991 to September 1995 and to the post of Artillery Division Commander from October 1993 to September 1996, quite possibly with the aim of reinforcing his power base. It can be assured that Samphao was a member of the Suchinda faction, since he continued to attend Suchinda's birthday party every August, even after the May 1992 incident.
47 When Surayut was a lieutenant-colonel, he became a member of the House of Representatives Development Budget Committee, created on 11 April 1980 immediately following the formation of the Prem administration (Somkhit et al. 1998: 58), because he was trusted by Prem as an intellectual. It seems likely that Prem's nomination of Surayut as Commander-in-Chief was not unrelated to Prem's own political situation over and above his friendship with Surayut and high regard for his ability and character. Prem,

who joined the Privy Council after he stepped down as Prime Minister, had been appointed President of the Privy Council on 4 September 1998, only days before Surayat was appointed Commander-in-Chief (the military personnel reshuffle of 1 October 1998 was announced on 18 September). While many privy councilors were jurists or members of the royal family, Prem had no high lineage, wealth nor legal knowledge to speak of. His most valuable resource would seem to have been his influence over the military and politicians. By getting Surayut appointed as Commander-in-Chief with a long term in office, Prem could prolong his influence over the Army.

48 This reshuffle has set a new precedent and may potentially disrupt future selections of the commander-in-chief by opening the field of candidates to officers who do not hold any of the Five Tiger posts. In the process, it has created more opportunities for party politicians to interfere in military personnel matters, as will be described later.

49 Chawalit stayed in office for less than four years, appointed in May 1986 and retiring in March 1990. Surayut was due to exceed this span in August 2002.

50 It may suffice to point to the appointment of such an officer to the post of commander-in-chief to establish the hypothesis of the declining political power of the military.

51 None of the Class 11 officers who held divisional command posts in the First Army Region during the May 1992 incident were subsequently appointed to important posts. However, Nopphadon Inthanya of Class 17, who was directly implicated in the suppression operation as the Chief of Staff of the First Division at the time, was given the First Divisional Command in October 1998.

52 Bandit was the commander of the First Infantry Regiment at the time of the September 1985 coup and remained with Phichit at the First Regional Command while pro-government (anti-coup) military leaders gathered at the Eleventh Infantry Regimental Command. Phichit was believed to be one of the masterminds of this coup, and hence many of the field officers in his faction were subsequently sidelined to nominal posts.

53 Mongkhon was promoted to Supreme Commander of the Armed Forces, Oraphan Watthanawibun was appointed Chief of Staff of the Armed Forces, Watthana Sanphanit became Superintendent-General of the Armed Forces and Yutthasak Sasiprapha became Defense Permanent Secretary.

54 The results of this analysis are the same whether one officer remained in a particular post for three years or three officers each held the post for one year, as the purpose of the analysis is to determine the distribution of power among different classes.

55 The list included former Defense Permanent Secretary Yutthasak, former Army Commander-in-Chief Chettha and former Army Deputy Commander-in-Chief Thawan in the Thai Rak Thai Party; former Supreme Commander of the Armed Forces Wirot, former Special Warfare Unit Commander Hom and former Air Force Commander-in-Chief Amon in the Chat Thai Party; and former Third Army Regional Commander Surachet and Commander of Engineering Corps Naruenat in the Democrat Party. The person who attracted the most attention in this election campaign was Supreme Commander Mongkhon, who was due to retire in September 2000. Although he was invited by many parties, he declined to enter politics, instead accepting a position as Chairman of the Board of the New Bangkok International Airport Corporation (NBIA) that was to prepare and manage the new Suwannaphum Airport.

56 Chaiyasit had an engineering background, and had risen to the rank of major-general in October 1996 before being promoted to lieutenant-general as a Special Advisor to the Army in April 2001. He then moved to the Supreme Command of the Armed Forces in October 2001 to become Deputy Commander of the Development Headquarters, and was then promoted to the rank of general as a Special Advisor to the Supreme Command in April 2002. In short, he joined the Five Tigers through the back door.

57 Likewise, in the Navy, the next commander-in-chief was appointed against the wishes of the retiring incumbent. Since the Army had clashed with the Prime Minister over its policy concerning relations with Myanmar (Burma) many times, Surayut had been prepared to be sidelined from the Army to the post of Supreme Commander of the Armed Forces in October 2002 (*Nation Sutsapda*, 29 July 2002). However, he believed that according to custom, he would still have the leading role in selecting officers for the October 2002 reshuffle (*Thai Rat*, 9 August 2002). The Five Tigers envisaged by Surayut were Commander-in-Chief Watthanachai (Assistant Commander-in-Chief, Class 12), Deputy Commander-in-Chief Somthat (Chief of Staff, Class 14), Chief of Staff Phongthep (Deputy Chief of Staff, Class 15), and Assistant Commanders-in-Chief Sirichai (Deputy Chief of Staff, Class 15) and Chirasak (Second Regional Commander, Class 14) (*Nation Sutsapda*, 5 August 2002).

58 Thammarak (Class 10), because he had a debt of gratitude to Chawalit, was actually chosen by Chawalit as his own replacement from several MPs of the Thai Rak Thai Party. As suggested in an analysis by the weekly *Matichon*, however, Thammarak would side with Prime Minister Thaksin if there was any disagreement between Thaksin and Chawalit (*Matichon Sutsapda*, 14 October 2002).

59 In the October 1975 reshuffle, Defense Minister Praman of the Chat Thai Party promoted Chalat to Deputy Commander-in-Chief of the Army even though he had been promoted to the Deputy Chief of Staff only a year earlier. This appointment generated strong resentment within the Army, and Chalat was effectively demoted to the Supreme Command on 1 May 1976. He was later executed for his failed coup attempt of March 1977.

60 Commander-in-Chief Chettha commented at the time: 'Please do not ask me to mount a coup d'état... [E]ven if we seized power, we would not be able to solve economic problems' (*Athit*, 15 August 1997). Moreover, since the most powerful man in the military, Mongkhon, was close to Prime Minister Chawalit, it was far more likely that Chawalit would have resigned voluntarily before the coup was launched, just as Prime Minister Kriangsak had done in 1980. In other words, the Prime Minister and the military leadership of the time were on good terms.

Chapter Three

1 In the early 1990s, both the budget and the number of local government employees accounted for less than 10% of those of the national government. Interior Ministry officials, including the provincial governors, played the key roles in this centralized system of local administration. One of the main aims of the decentralization campaign was to replace provincial governors appointed by the Interior Ministry with popularly elected local government heads. However, the provincial governors' offices were very important within the Interior Ministry bureaucracy, being equal in rank and prestige to the ministry director's post. Thus for many Interior Ministry officials, such an appointment is the highlight of their career. It was only natural, therefore, that the ministry should stubbornly resist. Furthermore, decentralization was not only a problem for the Interior Ministry, but would affect almost all of the ministries and departments of the central government. Although some ministries actually welcomed the prospect of less supervision by the Interior Ministry officials, they attempted to protect themselves from the waves of decentralization by delegating authority to local agencies (deconcentration). Many party politicians were not very enthusiastic about decentralization, either. One reason was that they had long relied upon the cooperation of bureaucrats in elections. More importantly, though, decentralization would reduce the powers of ministers, and thus the vested interests of party politicians. As a result, a compromised form of decentralization was agreed upon in 1994 that was

to upgrade about 7000 small administrative wards (*tambon*) throughout the country to municipal government status. The Tambon Council and Tambon Administrative Authority Law came into force on 1 March 1995. Further decentralization occurred thereafter. Prior to these changes, rural areas other than cities and sanitary districts had been governed by the province as local administrative units. Since rural areas came under the governance of *tambon* administrative authorities, the provincial governments were reorganized (on 1 November 1997) to preserve themselves. Also, based on provisions concerning decentralization in the 1997 Constitution, there was a wholesale revision of related laws and regulations on local government. For the decentralization of the local government system, see Hashimoto (1999a: 1999b). On the decentralization implementation process, Nagai (2001) is useful.

2 This is the same Chalat who went on hunger strike in April 1992.

3 Prawet was the vice president of Mahidon University at the time. He was a prominent intellectual who had received the Magsaysay Award in 1981 and an active commentator on political and social issues. According to Bowonsak, a jurist who was the leading figure in constitutional drafting work, Prawet could be called 'the first person who mentioned political reform' (1999: 88).

4 Prawet reports that he happened to be sitting with the Prime Minister at Sinlapakorn University on the afternoon of 7 June when the PM told him that the government was planning to set up a special committee on political reform. Although the ruling Democrat Party rejected such a move at a meeting that same evening, the Speaker of the House announced the establishment of the Committee on Developing Democracy on 9 June (Prawet 1997b: 57–8).

5 The title and author of each volume are as follows: (1) 'Constitutional rights and freedom' (Woraphot Witsarutphit); (2) 'The constitution court and constitutional case review procedures' (Kamonchai Rattanasakawawong); (3) 'The system for the investigation of corruption by people in high offices' (Bowonsak Uwanno); (4) 'Neutral state institutions' (Witsanu Waranyu); (5) 'Appropriate political means to supervise the government' (Suraphon Nitikraiphot); (6) 'An alternative election system to reduce vote buying and give good people more opportunities to run for election' (Phaithun Bunyawat); (7) 'The establishment of support organizations for the implementation of honest and fair elections' (Phaithun Bunyawat); (8) 'The improvement of the political party system' (Bunsi Miwongukhot); (9) 'An administrative system to neutralize the secretariat of the parliament' (Montri Rupsuwan); (10) 'The form of economic

and social advisory and consultation bodies to be included in the draft constitution' (Thiwa Ngoenyuang); (11) 'Form and method of constitutional revision' (Phunsak Waisamruat); (12) 'The national referendum model' (Nanthawat Boromanan); (13) 'The constitution enforcement law' (Somkhit Loetphaithun); (14) 'Procedures to introduce and consider finance-related laws' (Oraphin Phonsuwan Sabairup); and (15) 'The improvement of work efficiency of parliamentary committees' (Thongthong Chanthrangsu). Of the fourteen authors (one author wrote two volumes), thirteen are legal scholars from Chulalongkorn, Thammasat and Ramkhamhaeng Universities. Nine of them received law doctorates in France, two in Germany and one in the US. The only non-scholar was a senior Interior Ministry official (provincial governor) with a Ph.D. in political science from the US. Although these are relatively short booklets of fifty to 100 pages, all of them contain specific suggestions on how to proceed with political reform. They are therefore useful references for those who are interested in political reform. Their contents later lead directly to the enactment of the new constitution. Significantly, five of the eight law scholars who were later elected to the CDA were among these thirteen researchers. The researchers were mainly invited by Bowonsak and in this sense were his associates.

6 According to Prawet, issues such as poverty, traffic congestion, air pollution, environmental and resource conservation and morals cannot be resolved unless political reform is achieved 'because bad politics is like a virus that destroys the immunity of all social systems' (Prawet 1997a: 81–2).

7 These are administrative officials at or above the C8 level. Administrative officials are classed from C1 to C11. Permanent secretaries are classified as C11, directors-general and deputy permanent secretaries as C10 and university fresh graduates as C3. C8 corresponds to division heads within the ministries.

8 It should be noted that the narrower term 'urban middle class' was used instead of 'urban residents.' It was the urban middle class, rather than urban residents *per se*, that was contrasted with rural residents.

9 This rule was included in the 1978 Constitution to stop the proliferation of small parties. It effectively eliminated many left-wing parties.

10 The Provincial Development Budget (also called *ngop. so. so.*, the MP's budget) had been distributed evenly among all lower house MPs, including those who were elected from urban electoral districts. Additionally, the capital city had the Bangkok Metropolitan Council with far greater powers and a larger budget than any other local council, and members of the Bangkok Metropolitan Council received a development budget similar to

the one distributed to elected MPs. The metropolitan residents enjoyed more benefits than rural residents in terms of development funds received via MPs and therefore had no right to criticize rural residents or rural-constituency MPs. In short, the claim that only rural areas received benefits was completely incorrect; city residents demonstrated their ignorance and arrogance by accepting the claim without question.

11 Nevertheless, the proposal included measures to facilitate introducing expenditure-related bills to the lower house, and the lower house MPs' participation in preparing the budget (CDD 1995: 71–3).

12 For example, sweeping reorganization of central government ministries and agencies has typically only been conducted in the absence of a popularly elected parliament (Tamada 1996: 73–5).

13 As per Article 81 of the Basic Law for the Federal Republic of Germany (Abe and Hata (eds) 1998: 268).

14 As per Article 67 of the Basic Law for the Federal Republic of Germany (Abe and Hata (eds) 1998: 265).

15 The other two recommendations were as follows. Fourth, restrictions should be put on the number of questions MPs can ask the government. The number of useless questions is to be reduced and ministers are expected to be able to reply (CDD 1995: 79). Fifth, rules should be changed to allow the government to reorganize its administrative agencies without introducing new legislation, provided it is lower than bureau level and it does not involve establishing new agencies (CDD 1995: 79).

16 An additional 3000 copies were printed in December 1997.

17 This expression became widely known when the military cited it as one of the justifications for the February 1991 coup.

18 Prawet stated elsewhere that political reform was to make politics honest and efficient (Prawet 1997a: 25, 38–9).

19 Banhan stated on 12 June 1995, 'the Chat Thai Party supports the CDD's proposal that the people should participate in the constitutional revision and therefore a committee should be set up for the purpose of amending Article 211 of the Constitution.' He insisted on 26 June, 'I think it is absolutely vital to carry out political reform based on Dr Prawet's guidelines and I will amend Article 211 of the Constitution' (*Matichon Sutsapda*, 8 August 1995). He also stated on 2 July, 'If I am elected to office, I will amend Article 211 of the Constitution to realize political reform' (Nikon 2000: 23). Banhan used to say that political reform was necessary because 'so much money is spent on politics these days that we will not be able to survive without political reform' (Nikon 2000: 22).

20 This campaign promise did not necessarily contribute to their victory.

21 The amendment of Article 211 was needed because only a partial revision was allowed for by the 1991 Constitution. Hence, new procedures had to be set in order to constitutionally conduct a full revision.
22 There are two particularly interesting points to be made about this remark. First, Banhan stresses that people in cities and rural areas view politics very differently. Second, former Prime Minister Anan was very popular among both the media and the people in Bangkok. In this regard, Banhan and Anan were considered to be completely opposite types.
23 Prior to this bill, draft proposals were submitted by the government and the committee respectively and met with various criticisms (*Nation Sutsapda*, 23–29 August 1996).
24 On this point, among seventy-six provincial representatives and twenty-three experts, the latter would not be elected from any particular areas, but it is reasonable to regard all of them as representatives of Bangkok.
25 The *tambon* councils were gradually upgraded to administrative organization status, but some remained *tambon* councils headed by *kamnan*.
26 The abstainers were Sit Chirarot and Michai Ruchuphan. As mentioned earlier, Sit was the chairman of the committee investigating unusually rich politicians in 1991. Michai had been the 'head legal advisor' for the Prem and Chatchai administrations for the long ten years as the minister attached to the Prime Minister's Office in charge of legal affairs. Members of the Seritham Party were absent as they were skeptical about the feasibility of political reform.
27 Breakdown of 760 provincial representatives by occupation:

Occupation	Number	%
Lawyer	270	35.5
Businessperson	174	22.9
Bureaucrat	138	19.5
Employed	88	11.6
Farmer	35	4.6
Politician	9	1.2
Other	36	4.7

Source: *Nation Sutsapda*, 20 December 1996.

28 Then Senate Speaker Michai observes that 90% of CDA members were elected according to the government's wishes (Michai 2001: 21). As others

have observed, however, they did not necessarily act as the government wanted them to (Connors 1999: 214).

At around this time, Prawet whipped up the public into support for the political reform by claiming that political reform through the enactment of a new constitution was a matter of life and death.

> [If the politics is] left as it is, it will eventually result in bloodshed. [Even if political reform begins,] if it does not work out due to conflicts, it will again result in bloodshed. Thailand is a Buddhist country and more than 90% of its population is Buddhist. However, it is faced with the problem of moral hazard... Politicians engage in corruption, merchants engage in exploitation. We cannot trust anyone. We cannot trust politicians, bureaucrats, and even doctors. We have become a nation in which no one can be trusted. Once political reform is successfully completed, other systems must be reformed. However, [once the constitutional revision is finalized,] other reforms will become easy... The survival of this nation depends on this political reform. If successful, our homeland will make tremendous progress. If unsuccessful, our homeland will plunge into a state of violence. (*Nation Sutsapda*, 27 December 1996)

He often repeated the argument that sharp divisions would lead to bloodshed—evoking the May 1992 incident—in order to put pressure on the opposition to compromise.

29 Many members of the Constitution Drafting Committee also served on the Draft Constitution Amendment Committee. Since the CDA had only ninety-nine members, it was inevitable that some members had to participate in more than one committee. However, twelve of twenty-nine Drafting Committee members were included in the Amendment Committee, which means that twelve of thirty-three Amendment Committee members were members of the Drafting Committee, and both committees were chaired by Anan. Since those who had prepared the draft were unlikely to raise objections in the Amendment Committee, they could be counted as supporters of the draft. That is, more than one-third of members of the Amendment Committee supported the draft from the beginning. Besides, two persons who had been part of the research group organized by the CDD were also included in the Amendment Committee, and could also be considered to be supporters too. Thus, over 42% of members were supporters of the draft before the committee even began to consider it. Once the draft was prepared, any discussion in the Amendment Committee was merely a

formality and the likelihood of any radical amendments to the draft was considered to be small.

30 It was reported that 200,497 people expressed their views by mail and 600,873 people did so verbally or by other means (Montri et al. 1999: 35). Public comments were collected at seminars, forums, briefings and by questionnaires in various parts of the country.

31 Reportedly 629,232 people participated in the public comment process in the provinces, 122,584 people attended provincial public hearings, 3,828 people attended regional public hearings and 87,912 people responded to questionnaires—a grand total of 843,556 people (SR 1997: 100).

32 Some researchers point out that, although public hearings and meetings were held in the drafting process, they were 'an excellent means of public relations' and the draft generally followed a blueprint that had been drawn up beforehand (Connors 1999: 217).

33 Article 65 provided for the right for peaceful resistance against unconstitutional seizures of power (meaning military coups).

34 All constitutions since 1949 have had a section called 'Directive Principles of State Policies.' The section initially had nineteen articles but ended up with thirty-five in the 1991 version after a series of additions. The state policies provided in the constitution became very similar to the policies of each administration. Since it was considered inappropriate to include detailed stipulations in the constitution, it was decided that the section in the 1997 version should be called the directive principles of 'fundamental' state policies and only include carefully selected provisions (Kramon 1998: 217–18).

35 The most undesirable of all would be a law which was harmful to the monarchy. There were vociferous calls for direct popular election of the prime minister in the course of the drafting. Constitution drafters tried frantically to deny it. If a referendum result was given binding authority, there was a possibility that such a system might be adopted. With the fear of the possibility that the constitutional monarchy might be replaced by a republican system, constitution drafters were absolutely against giving a referendum binding authority.

36 One of the pretexts for the traditional government appointment of senators was a vocational representation system. Assemblyman Khanin argues that the vocational representation system has lost its meaning in this global information age. He observes that it paid no more than lip service in the first place, as the representatives of particular vocations actually accounted for one-third of the senators, and only two to three representatives of farmers and laborers were selected even though they accounted for a large

majority of the population (Khanin 1998: 237–8). It is true that the majority of senators were military or administrative officials under the government appointment system. However, it is also true that some representatives of farmers and laborers were included. The globalized information age does not seem to have anything to do with the argument that a vocational representation system is no longer necessary. Due to the newly added university qualification rule of the 1997 Constitution, it has become almost impossible for farmers and laborers to run for election. In comparison with the CDD recommendation, which attempted to retain the vocational representation system (perhaps largely out of consideration for the existing government-appointed senators), this proposal was a significant backward step.

37 Decho also called it the 'parliament solely for inspection' (1998: 117).
38 Parliamentary seats were distributed to each province in proportion to its population. The maximum number of seats per electoral district was three. If four or more seats were allocated to a province, the province had two or more electoral districts. Single-seat districts were avoided as much as possible. A province would have one three-seat district if it had three seats, two two-seat districts if it had four, one three-seat district and one two-seat district if it had five, two three-seat districts if it had six, one three-seat district and two two-seat districts if it had seven, and so on. If the population of a province was less than the total population divided by the number of parliamentary seats, that province was allocated one seat.
39 Voters used to be provided as many votes as seats allocated to their district. Hence, there was inequality as those who lived in a three-seat district could vote for three candidates whereas those who lived in a single-seat district could only vote for one candidate.
40 This story about influential figures who decide who will win the election is a real story based on Uthai's own electoral district, Chon Buri Province, not Songkhla Province. Uthai had fought against these influential figures and won several times but his last victory was the September 1992 general election.

The illegal lottery game method has been used frequently. The lottery operator does not always hold a superior position to the candidate. The following is a model case in respect of the January 2001 general election reported by *Matichon*. At the time of twice-monthly sale of official lottery tickets by the government, illegal private lottery tickets are also sold in various places throughout the country. Election candidates use the operators of these illegal lottery games. Following the change to the single-seat electoral district system, a candidate now only needs 20,000 to 25,000 votes to win. Even if he spends 1000 baht per voter to buy his or her vote, the total outlay of 20 million to 25 million baht is not too large a sum for a candidate who desperately wants to win. All the candidate has to do is to give this amount to the lottery operator. Just like the usual illegal lottery tickets, tickets are sold through sellers for 10 baht each. Bets are made on candidate numbers. If candidate No. 5 wins, voters who purchased the tickets will receive a payout of 1000 baht per ticket. Voters who purchased the tickets will enthusiastically cast their votes for candidate No. 5 in the hope that they can receive prize money one hundred times more than their bet. Moreover, they will encourage their family and friends to vote for candidate No. 5. The number of tickets one voter can purchase is limited to two because the more voters purchase the tickets, the higher the chance of this candidate winning the election. The proceeds of the sale of ten-baht tickets become the income of the operator and his sellers. The sellers try hard to sell many tickets for sales commission. In short, the more illegal election lottery tickets on a particular candidate are sold, the greater the chance of this candidate winning the election. The candidate can estimate the number of votes he or she is likely to get based on the number of tickets sold before a vote count. The candidate can claim that the betting was organized by the lottery operator without his knowledge and he had nothing to do with it, and therefore he will not be charged with a violation of the election law. At the same time, the lottery operator is always 'protected' and thus never charged with illegal acts (*Matichon*, 14 November 2000). This lottery method does not work if a candidate is considered to have no hope of winning and no one purchases his or her tickets.

41 Under the constitution, only the prime minister must be a lower house MP before his appointment. Other cabinet members do not have to be lower house MPs. In an extreme case, all cabinet members, except the prime minister, might be appointed from outside of the House of Representatives. This is very different from, say, the Japanese constitution which provides that a majority of state ministers (cabinet members other than the prime minister) must be members of the Parliament.

42 Cabinet members do not have the right to vote in parliament (Khanin 1998: 264–5).

43 Article 184 has a similar aim, concerning an interpellation to ministers. When questions are submitted to the parliamentary speaker in writing, ministers must reply orally on the floor on the same day. Due to this rule, ministers must do their homework and gain full knowledge of the areas

under their responsibility in order to prepare their replies. A minister cannot ask another minister to stand in for him (Khanin 1998: 255). This rule is intended to promote the appointment of suitable people to ministerial posts.

44 However, a large-scale kingpin who deals in votes for the whole of a district should still be able to deliver the number of votes he promises, even if he cannot monitor the vote counting at each polling station.

45 Murray quoted these points from a newspaper: 'Powerful groups buy political parties; parties buy politicians and *chao pho*; the MPs and *chao pho* buy canvassers—particularly *kamnan* (*tambon* leaders) and *phuyaiban* (village headmen) and canvassers in turn buy/coerce/arrange votes' (1996: 89). The 'powerful groups' that provide funds are almost invariably businesspeople, with the National Peace-Keeping Council in the March 1992 general election being the only exception.

46 This provision was not applicable for the first general election after the enforcement of the 1997 Constitution due to transitional provisions in the constitution, as discussed in this chapter.

47 According to data compiled by the Department of Community Development, Interior Ministry (Mahatthai 1995: 497), of 23.79 million people living in rural communities in 1994, 20.56 million people have only completed compulsory primary education. Only 430,000 people (1.8%) have completed higher education (i.e., beyond secondary education, including vocational schools and junior colleges). The number of bachelor's degree holders is only a small proportion of this.

48 Because the drafting process became a major event and some of the provisions were innovative, the 1997 Constitution received considerable publicity and many more books have been written about it in comparison with previous constitutions.

49 The then Education Minister Chingchai Mongkhontham commented in September 1997: '90% of the comments heard at public hearings conducted by the CDA wanted direct popular election for the prime minister. Why doesn't the CDA do it? Why doesn't it include the provision in the constitution?' He then sarcastically remarked that if the CDA should insist that many people wanted lower house MPs 'to have a bachelor's or higher degree...we might as well go with a doctorate' (*Athit*, 19 September 1997).

50 Election supervisors in the original sentence has been omitted here. He has included 'bureaucrats' elsewhere (Prawet 1997a: 96).

51 This is in stark contrast to the 1978 Constitution, which was harshly criticized for its education qualification rule concerning the political rights

of those who had non-Thai fathers. Under the 1978 Constitution (Articles 92 and 94) and the 1979 Election Code (Articles 18 and 19), such persons had to have completed lower secondary education (junior high school graduates) in order to vote and upper secondary education (high school graduates) in order to be eligible for election. The 1980 revision lowered the requirement for them to vote down to the completed compulsory primary education. The 1991 Constitution removed the education requirement for them to vote but kept the upper secondary education requirement for their eligibility to be elected (Articles 109 and 110). The 1997 Constitution removed these provisions for those who had non-Thai fathers all together but instead added the university graduate requirement for all candidates. The requirement became far stricter under the 1997 Constitution than before. The difference in the responses is perhaps due as much to qualitative and quantitative changes among intellectuals who perceive the eligibility restriction as their own pain. Although twenty years ago they felt the restriction was a frontal attack on themselves (since many intellectuals in Thailand are Chinese-Thais), they probably do not in the 1990s because it does not directly affect them.

52 It appears that many of these independent bodies had other political functions in addition to inspection. Until 1992, the King could influence the appointment of prime minister to some extent because the prime minister did not have to be an elected MP or the leader of the parliamentary majority. However, the King no longer had a say in the matter after Anan's appointment in 1992. His distance from the prime minister's appointment would be made concrete under the 1997 Constitution, which provided that the prime minister should be elected by a majority vote in Parliament. It seems that the creation of these independent inspection bodies would bridge this gap to some extent, as the selection of commissioners and judges continues, in a way, to be conducted behind closed doors. There is thus some room for intervention. In the process, the decisions of the Constitution Court and the National Counter Corruption Commission may also be influenced. In this sense, at least, the creation of inspection bodies to oversee politicians was advantageous to the King. Of course, whether the King actually exercises his influence in such a way or not is a different question.

53 Besides politicians, those who may be investigated by the NCCC include the President of the Supreme Court of Justice, the President of the Constitution Court, the President of the Supreme Administrative Court, the Prosecutor General, Election Commissioners, Ombudsman, members of the State

Audit Commission, judges of the Constitution Court, judges of the Court of Justice, public prosecutors and high ranking government officials.

54 The three-instance court system is a judicial system that allows litigants to have three trials at different levels of courts; for example, Provincial Court, Court of Appeal and Supreme Court.

55 There are other independent inspection bodies as well, including Ombudsman, the national Human Rights Commission and the Accounting Audit Commission, but the inspection of improper conduct by politicians is not the direct aim of these bodies.

56 This reasoning is not very convincing. The real aim of the separation is to stop single-seat electorate MPs from joining the cabinet.

57 Two of the five laws were promulgated and enforced in November 1999, which was after the two year deadline; therefore the Democrat Party government at the time was in breach of the constitution. It should be noted that the Democrat Party government was also very late in holding the first general election under the new constitution; it took four years rather than the initially expected one year.

58 Because inspecting politicians was not the primary purpose of either the Ombudsman or the State Audit Commission, no detailed provisions were included in the constitution. See Imaizumi's study (2002) for judicial system reforms required by the 1997 Constitution.

59 Somchai (1997) points out that the constitution drafting process excluding MPs was modeled on France's 1958 Constitution. The 1958 draft constitution received overwhelming support in a referendum, with a high voter turnout of 85% and 79% of votes in favor. On this point, a researcher specializing in French political history states:

> Even if the reality was that most voters were not interested in the contents of the draft constitution but they simply voted in favor to express their support for the anti-left-wing campaign, or for the government policy on Algeria, or for Charles de Gaulle himself, the fact that it was approved by an overwhelming majority enabled the government to assert a high degree of legitimacy of the new constitution. (Morimoto 1997b: 185)

In France at the time, there was report of a looming coup d'état by troops stationed in Algeria and General de Gaulle was touted as the person who was capable of resolving the situation peacefully. The parliament and political parties realized their lack of problem-solving ability and began to accept de Gaulle (Morimoto 1997a: 181). In Thailand in 1997, the currency crisis and the draft constitution played similar roles as did the Algerian problem and de Gaulle in France, respectively.

60 For the currency crisis, see a series of studies by Suehiro (1998b; 1998c; 1999; 2000: chapter 3).

61 According to Surachat, middle-class discontent was as strong as the entrepreneurs' because it was the first time since the 1930s that so many middle-class workers were laid off at once in Thailand. Middle-class people in the 1930s were government bureaucrats. The government laid off many bureaucrats due to the Depression and a fiscal deficit. This was one of the principal reasons for the coup on 24 June 1932. The subsequent increase in the number of white-collar workers was gradual, both in the public and private spheres, and large-scale dismissals did not occur (Surachat 1998a: 157).

62 As political scientist Somchai (1997: 18) observed:

> Whether or not the draft constitution of the CDA will be approved is important not only because it will determine the direction of future Thai politics but also because it will impact on the survival of the Thai economy today and in future... Rejection of the draft constitution, or even a mere delay in decision-making, will certainly destabilize politics and have an adverse impact on the economic crisis. Therefore the draft constitution is also important for the resolution of the economic crisis.

63 Anan was awarded the Magsaysay Award on 10 July 1997, the sixteenth Thai to win the Award. Undoubtedly, this award raised his reputation further and supplied a nice tailwind for the draft constitution.

64 For example, 'The economic predicament provided a stimulus needed for the passage of the draft constitution. Under normal circumstances, there would have been little possibility for the draft to be approved by both the Senate and the House of Representatives, because some of the drastic changes contained in the draft would be damaging for the existing members of the Parliament' (Chaianan and Parichart 1998: 166–7). Further, 'This controversial Constitution, which was opposed by most politicians since it restricted their powers, was finally pushed through due as a reaction to the financial and economic crisis' (Callahan 2000: 165).

65 Chawalit carried out a cabinet reshuffle on 24 October 1997. He drew up a blueprint to enact the organic laws immediately, dissolve the parliament at the end of the year and hold a general election in January 1998. However, former Prime Minister Chatchai of the ruling coalition Chat Phatthana Party felt aggrieved at the reshuffle and began to plot his return to the

premiership. Amid mounting criticisms against these moves, Chawalit finally decided to resign (*Matichon Sutsapda*, 11 November 1997).

66 The Democrat Party managed to split the Prachakon Thai Party, one of the ruling coalition parties in the Chawalit government, into five pro-coalition members and thirteen pro-Democrat Party members.

67 Partial revision of the constitution was undertaken six times for the 1991 Constitution, three times each for the 1932 and 1947 Constitutions, twice for the 1978 Constitution and once for the 1974 Constitution (Decho 1998: 86–7). Although the 1991 Constitution was revised rather frequently, a higher frequency of full revision than partial revision is characteristic of Thailand.

68 To borrow Kawamori's expression, this was the group interested in resolving the 'economic issue of income disparities' (1997: 180).

69 Although both the urban middle class and farmers have received few benefits from party politics, the middle class compensates for this by dominating political debates while farmers must resort to less effective measures such as demonstrations and rallies (Pasuk and Baker 1997: 35, 37). National politics seldom reflects the voice of farmers, who are rarely organized, with a few exceptions such as sugar cane growers, despite their large numbers (Yamamoto 1998: 218–22; 2000: 186–205). Many lower house MPs are elected from rural electoral districts but almost all of them live in regional cities. The only benefits of electoral politics for rural residents were the money they were paid for their votes and the thinly and broadly distributed public works projects. Accordingly, Bowonsak's view that includes farmers alongside the urban middle class as beneficiaries of party politics is one-sided.

70 Because only a small number of intellectuals such as scholars were eligible to be members of these inspection bodies the principal beneficiary would be a group of urban intellectuals, which was even more limited than the urban middle class. Needless to say, Bowonsak was a leading figure of this group.

71 Asami (2002) concisely summarizes contemporary Thai politics since the 1960s from the perspective of this axis of conflict between the urban middle class and farmers.

72 At a regional rally of the Chat Thai Party in the lead up to the September 1992 general election, a speaker's cry, 'We are second-class citizens,' was met with cheers from the audience, indicating that rural residents are well aware that their status is lower than that of metropolitan residents.

73 The major reason for the increase in the proportion of rural-constituency MPs in the cabinet was the growing proportion of lower house MPs in

the cabinet throughout the 1980s. At the same time, as mentioned, the executive offices of the major parties were occupied by rural-constituency MPs. In the Social Action Party, Khuekrit and Sit (party leaders elected from Bangkok), and Bunchu and Phong (party secretaries elected from rural constituencies but who had managed large corporations in Bangkok) were replaced by Montri, who was promoted from party secretary to party leader. In the Chat Thai Party, the Ratchakhru clan (party leaders Praman and Chatchai) was replaced by party secretaries Banhan and Sano who began to wield more power. In the Democrat Party, party secretary Sanan began to exert more influence.

74 Wiengrat Netipho (1997) criticizes the impressionist view of *chao pho* in her empirical study, which is very informative.

75 Pasuk and others report that twenty to thirty MPs operate highly illegal businesses (Pasuk, Sungsidh and Nualnoi 1998: 262).

76 However, many of the prominent local families of lower house MPs dispatch their children to leading universities at home and abroad and send many of them to the civil service. Their social and economic circumstances are better than the middle class in Bangkok and they deserve to be called local notables.

77 Although the advocates of political reform tended to suggest that politicians had a monopoly on corruption, this was patently not true. The CDA chairman Uthai likens national budget to an ice cream given by the government to the people: Ministries and departments lick it, provinces lick it, districts lick it and *tambon* leaders (*kamnan*) lick it, so when the ice cream reaches the residents, only a small amount of melted cream is left on the stick which is of no use for anyone other than ants. He further points out that whether it is true or not, the government budget is allegedly reduced by 15% at the provincial level, 10% at the district level, 5% at the *tambon* level and contractors take 20% for profit, making it only 30 to 40% in the worst case when it reaches the residents (Uthai 1998: 30–1).

As mentioned earlier, because of the extremely centralized administrative structure, the central ministries and departments execute much larger budgets than do local governments. The people who execute the budget are national civil service officials, and they are the one who lick the budget like an ice cream in the capital, provinces and districts.

78 Some saw these arguments for political reform as merely an internal squabble among capitalists. If capitalists are divided into provincial and metropolitan capitalists, those who came to control the parliament at this time were representatives of the provincial capitalists. The large-scale capitalists in Bangkok who acted in partnership with foreign capital were

dissatisfied with this situation, calling the party politicians 'electoralists' (*nak lueaktang*), and arguing that the prime minister and other cabinet members should be expert business managers to run the national government. For example, Anan remarked in August 1997 that 'we need the proportional representation system because we need people who are not electoralists' (*Matichon Sutsapda*, 18 August 1997).

Sane Chamarik, a political scientist, harshly criticizes this dichotomy, arguing that it was none other than expert business managers who overemphasized industry, aggravated economic disparities between city areas and rural areas and eventually brought about the economic crisis. Whether provincial or metropolitan, these 'experts' are all capitalists who neglect the populace. Local areas, he continues, form the very foundations of democratic political regimes around the world and it is wrong to belittle them (Sane 1997: 398–410; Sane 1998: 1–32). Although Sane is undoubtedly correct, it is nevertheless true that many people became increasingly critical of the economic management skills of the party politicians during the Banhan administration and there was growing expectation among urban residents for a dream team who could 'save' them. In this context, the conflict was between urban residents and rural-constituency MPs rather than between competing groups of capitalists.

79 Specifically, the English-language *Bangkok Post* and *The Nation*, economic papers *Phuchatkan* and *Krungthep Thurakit*, general quality paper *Matichon*, and weeklies *Matichon Sutsapda*, *Nation Sutsapda* and *Sayam Rat Sapdawichan*.

80 Asami points out that the media began to represent the views of the urban middle class strongly in the late 1980s when the economy began its period of rapid growth:

> Since the late 1980s, many corporations began to focus on selling products that targeted the middle class as their main purchasers. The main readership of newspapers and magazines was also the middle class, which became an important market for many of the corporations that advertised in newspapers, magazines and on television. In the late 1980s, new newspapers and magazines were launched one after another and competed to publish articles and columns more appealing to the middle class. (2002: 50)

81 The economic newspaper *Phuchatkan* was a notable exception.
82 The first time government agencies, educational institutions and the media competed to forecast election results based on opinion polls was the general election of September 1992.

83 One weekly magazine, based on analyses of company shareholders and managers, points out that the media abandoned its free and unbiased stance toward the government in 1992. Since then, it has begun an attempt to achieve political changes, such as change of government, by supporting certain interest groups (*Athit*, 24 September 1997).
84 The Thai word '*man*' is a third person pronoun (derogatory when used for people) but also means a potato and fat. Although Chawalit actually used the word to mean 'them' or 'that lot,' he played the innocent by replying 'potato' in English when asked by reporters.
85 Anan's ideal was 'good governance (*thammarat*)' in the sense of 'a government or a ruler that is honest, sincere, moral, acts with the interests of the majority in mind, constructs a highly transparent system and is accountable' (Anan 1998: 45).
86 Pasuk and Baker sarcastically observe that the 'interests of the nation' are the 'interests of the capital city' (2000: 118).
87 Under Thailand's Criminal Code, the penalty for bribe-givers is imprisonment of up to five years or a fine of up to 10,000 baht or both (Article 144 of the Criminal Code) while the penalty for bribe-takers ranges from a fine of 2000 to 40,000 baht and imprisonment for five years to life, or death (Article 149 of the Criminal Code). In comparison with penalties under the Japanese Criminal Code which are imprisonment for five to seven years for bribe-takers and imprisonment of up to three years or a fine of up to ¥2.5 million for bribe-givers (Articles 196, 198 of the Criminal Code), the penalties in Thailand are clearly more severe. However, prosecution of bribe-takers is rare and prosecution of bribe-givers is even rarer in Thailand.

Chapter Four

1 See Kato (2000) for details of Senate reform.
2 The breakdown of appointed senators by occupation from 1933 to 1988 is based on a table compiled by Rangsan (1989: 174–8). Incidentally, the appointment of senators in 1975 was not made by the party cabinet.
3 There were eighty-five serving public officials and fifty-three retired public officials. As of June 1995 prior to the election, there were 110 serving and eighty-four retired public officials: 72.7% of the total 267 senators (SLW 1995: 166).
4 Businesspeople accounted for only 14.2% as of June 1995 (appointed by the National Peace-Keeping Council in March 1992 and subsequently to fill occasional vacancies created due to death or resignation) but more than

doubled to 30.4% in the Senate appointed by a party cabinet in March 1996 (SLW 1995: 166; SLW 1996: 154).

5 Another curious phenomenon is a marked decline in the proportion of military officials to below 20% after 1973 and 1996. Except for these periods, the number of military officers almost always exceeded the number of administrative officials. For example, there were 147 generals out of 270 senators (54.4%) in March 1992 and 141 of 267 (52.8%) in June 1995 but only fifty-one of 260 (19.6%) in November 1996 (calculated on the basis of lists in Kromkanpokkhrong 1992; SLW 1995; SLW 1996). This reflects the decreasing importance of the military to the administration, or in other words, the diminution of the military's political power.

6 The bureaucratic polity was, in reality, a regime ruled by the military with the cooperation of the administrative bureaucracy (Girling 1996: 25). Although the proportion of military officials in the Senate declined dramatically as mentioned above, administrative officials filled the gap and the aggregate proportion of military and administrative officials did not decrease markedly, indicating that the administrative bureaucracy is an indispensable collaborator with political party governments as well as with military governments.

7 Although the proportion of senators to lower house seats has varied widely, sometimes equal, other times three-quarters or two-thirds of the lower house, the proportion of two-fifths of the lower house MPs provided by the 1997 Constitution was relatively small.

8 This provision does not mean that there was no association between senators and lower house MPs. There were about 100 former lower house MPs among the candidates and twenty-nine among the winners. There were also many relatives of lower house MPs. For example, the first Senate president appointed after the election was the older brother of a serving lower house MP, and most winners leaned towards or had an affiliation with a political party.

9 According to data published on the website of the Election Commission at the time of the 2000 Senate election (http://www.ect.go.th/newthai/senate/).

10 The question of how to enforce compulsory voting received a great deal of attention. Deciding what sanctions to apply to voters who failed to vote was not a task that anyone welcomed, hence, the Election Commission and Parliament each tried to pass this responsibility to the other (Sombat 2002: 206). In the end, it was decided that Section 23 of the 1998 Election Act should be amended (promulgated on 17 November 1999) to deny the following eight rights to those who fail to vote without prior notice:

1. the right to file a complaint about parliamentary or local government elections;
2. the right to file a complaint about *kamnan* or village chief elections;
3. the right to run for parliamentary or local government elections;
4. the right to run for *kamnan* or village chief elections;
5. the right to sign a petition for the enactment of a law;
6. the right to sign a petition for the enactment of an ordinance;
7. the right to sign a petition to the Senate for dismissal of a corrupt politician;
8. the right to sign a petition for dismissal of a member of local council.

These sanctions were effective until the voter cast a vote in the next election. In the 2001 general election, some applicants were denied candidacy under this rule, so it was not meaningless or 'toothless.' However, for the majority of voters who became ineligible for national office, these sanctions were negligible because they did not include loss of voting rights. The loss of voting rights, however, was not one of the sanctions because that would contradict the purpose of the compulsory voting provision.

11. Voter turnout was on a slow upward trend at 62.0% in the 1995 general election and 62.4% in the 1996 general election.
12. Even if a candidate lost miserably in the first round of voting and did not expect to gather more votes regardless of how many more ballot rounds he or she might attempt, the candidate was not allowed to withdraw his or her nomination. For highly recognizable public officials, including former generals and provincial governors, this could be quite humiliating, not to mention a waste of money.
13. Constitution Court decision No. 24 of 2000 (http://www/concourt.or.h/decis/y2000d/d002443.html).
14. Nitisak Ratchanit, who came ninth in the first round, died during the election period and was disqualified from the third round onwards.
15. *Bangkok Post* reported that in the Senate election, as a nation-wide trend, money made a difference in the first round but power, influence and patron-client relations were more important in the second round of voting on 29 April (*Bangkok Post*, 17 May 2000).
16. At the time of the 2000 Senate election, the Election Commission released personal data of all candidates (http://202.183.254.190/report/) and more detailed personal data of successful candidates (http://202.183.254.190/information/show_senate.asp). For example, even the nationalities of successful candidates' parents were released. Unfortunately, the Commission later took such data off the website and released far less

personal information about candidates and winners in the subsequent 2001 lower house election.

17 The police tend to come under the Defense Ministry in countries with a politically powerful military. Although the military had been a powerful political force in Thailand for a long time, the police had been under the Interior Ministry ever since the modern bureaucracy was organized at the end of the 19th century. Police officers are administrative officials. However, the police separated from the Interior Ministry to form an independent agency called the National Police Office under an ordinance enforced in October 1998. Thus many of the former police officers who ran for the Senate had served their entire career as part of the Interior Ministry. Nevertheless, they are counted separately from the Interior Ministry officials here because the police force was independent from the Interior Ministry at the time of the 2000 election.

18 There were some peculiarities with the way the Commission classified occupations. One was the seemingly high number of unemployed and farmers (ten of each). Which of the winners fell under these categories remains a mystery. There was a separate category for doctors but the five winners were all former state-run hospital directors and officials of the Ministry of Public Health. One of them was sixty-two years old, but the other four were all under the mandatory retirement age of sixty, and therefore had probably held their posts until immediately before the election. Among those classified as legal professionals, there were former public officials such as judges, prosecutors and national university lecturers.

19 There were thirty-eight people whose personal data did not clearly state whether they had worked in the public sector or not. Looking at the remaining 162 election winners, former public officials accounted for over two-thirds of them. It should be noted that 55.5% is a conservative estimate.

20 For example, a more detailed examination of the personal history of the senators appointed in March 1996 reveals that about ten people who had been in key posts such as bureau director did not state their occupation as serving or former public officials (SLW 1996: 1–133).

21 There are rumors that systematic election campaigns were conducted by the police organization. That is, police officers reportedly engaged in vote-gathering for their former bosses.

22 Data published on the National Statistical Office website (www.nso.go.th/pop2000/table/tadv_tab5.xls).

23 Only 5.1% of the total population of 60,606,000 in 2000.

24 Data published on the National Statistical Office website (www.nso. go.th/pop2000/table/tadv_tab6.xls).
25 Data published on the National Statistical Office website (www.nso. go.th/thai/stst/migrat/tmigra.htm).
26 Since Bangkok had always recorded low voter turnouts in past national elections, it was hard to say that the high turnout of the 2000 Senate election candidates was a reflection of a strong political awareness.
27 Based on data published by the Civil Service Commission (http://www. ocsc.go.th/PersPoli/manpower/manth/slide7.htm).
28 According to the Civil Service Commission, the national government had 1,245,000 regular staff, while local governments had 93,000 (http://www. ocsc.go.th/PersPoli/manpower/manth/slide2.htm and http://www.ocsc. go.th/PersPoli/manpower/manth/slide3.htm).
29 According to the Civil Service Commission, there were 299,000 non-regular full-time employees in the central government and 45,000 in local governments, a total of 343,000 in 1997 (http://www.infonews. co.th/CSC/stat/gvszp_t/htm).
30 According to the Civil Service Commission (http://www.ocsc.go.th/ PersPoli/manpower/manth/slide7.htm).
31 Some people have obtained a qualification from universities with no entrance examination or open universities in their adulthood, sometime after completing secondary education. However, the number of these people is small.
32 Data published by the National Statistical Office (http://www.nso.go.th/ thai/stat/pop-hou/tab6.htm).
33 They were followed by private-sector company employees and lawyers.
34 Pasuk and Baker argue that many of the election winners were retired public officials, politicians or members of a political clan because of these restrictions on electioneering (Pasuk and Baker 2000: 235).
35 The candidate who attracted the highest number of votes (422,000 votes) in the country was former Irrigation Department chief Pramot Maiklat, who frequently appeared in the media as a close aide to the King, and had an interest in water utilization. Damrong Phuttan, who came second with 388,000 votes, and Choemsak Pingthong, who came third with 197,000 votes, were both hosts of popular television programs. Sophon Suphaphong, who came fourth with 163,000 votes, was well-known via the media as a state-run corporation manager with a keen interest in environmental issues. The fifth-ranked winner only attracted 71,000 votes, which was less than one-half of the fourth-ranked winner's votes, perhaps because the top four candidates were celebrities who made headlines in the media.

36 Comparison between the list of the CDA members and that of Senate election candidates reveals that nearly one half of the CDA members, forty-seven out of ninety-nine, ran for the Senate. A majority of them were provincial representatives but there were five expert members as well. This means that many of the CDA members made a bid for election under the rules made by them to suit themselves. Only eleven out of forty-seven were successful, though, and one received a red card.

37 As discussed in Note 51, Chapter Three, an education qualification rule in the 1978 Constitution provided that a candidate whose father was a foreign national should at least have an upper secondary education. This aroused strong opposition at the time. It was interpreted that the rule was intended to impose a certain limit on the increasing number of Chinese-Thai businesspeople going into politics. In the 2000 Senate election, data from the Election Commission website (http://202.183.254.190/information/show_senate.asp) indicated that sixteen of 188 successful candidates after the second round of voting had a father with Chinese nationality (eleven had a mother with Chinese nationality as well). No information was available on the nationality of the parents of the 2001 lower house MPs but it was highly likely that there were more Chinese-Thai people among the lower house MPs as it was almost certain that more businesspeople nominated their candidacy in the lower house election than in the Senate election. The reason why an education qualification requirement was condemned in 1978 but barely mentioned in 1997 was perhaps that the circumstances of the target or victims of the provision were different. There were many Chinese-Thai residents not only among businesspeople but also among intellectuals, who responded angrily to restrictions that directly impinged on their lives. Farmers did not have such advocates who would speak up on their behalf.

38 Ignominiously, he was sentenced to imprisonment for sixteen years in the first trial in September 2002.

39 The number of candidates in each province was nine in Khon Kaen, eight in Phayao, nine in Ayutthaya, eight in Ranong, twelve in Lop Buri, thirteen in Si Sa Ket, nine in Ubon Ratchathani and ten in Surat Thani. The election on 21 April failed to produce a winner in Si Sa Ket province and another election was held on 26 May.

40 There were only two previous senators among the winners, indicating that eight previous senators failed.

41 There was a House of Representatives election between the original Senate election and this Senate by-election. This highlighted both the unsubstantial nature of the ban on political party affiliation and the

fragility of political parties. There are two examples worth discussing here. The candidate who won this by-election with 159,170 votes in Khon Kaen province was the same candidate who ran as a Chat Phatthana Party candidate for Khon Kaen's Constituency 2 in the January 2001 general election. Although he gathered 23,576 votes, he came second to a leader who gathered 29,721 and failed. In another case, the winner in Lop Buri by-election was a loser in the 2000 Senate election. He came third with 30,290 votes in the two-seat province. The second-ranked winner obtained 69,463 votes, more than twice his count. He also ran for the January 2001 general election as a Democrat Party candidate in Constituency 4 of the province but only managed to gather 10,611 votes, well short of the 49,692 votes of the district winner. In view of the eligibility rule that requires Senate candidates to sever ties with political parties at least twelve months prior to election, these two candidates were supposed to have given up their party connections immediately after the general election.

42 However, if disqualification and by-election are repeated at irregular intervals, it will be difficult to stay well prepared for by-elections. Also, former lower house MPs (who failed in the previous election) who switch to the Senate will be powerful competitors for the public officials. For example, the winner in Si Sa Ket province in the May 2001 Senate by-election was a businesswoman (who openly boasted that she had donated over 200 million baht to Buddhist rites in Si Sa Ket province since 1995) (*Krungthep Thurakit*, 2 November 2002). The winner in the February 2002 by-election in Samut Prakan province was a businessperson who had held a seat in the House of Representatives for the province for nine terms. The by-election winner in the Nakhon Si Thammarat province in August 2002 was a former public official who had entered politics and won six lower house elections.

43 The same applies to the winners of the 2001 lower house elections. Lower house MPs may attempt to amend the law in order to reduce the uncertainty of disqualification.

Chapter Five

1 The Election Commission explains the party-list proportional representation election as follows. Each party submits a list of up to 100 ranked candidates. The listed candidates must not be candidates in single-seat constituencies or candidates of other parties. The candidates must be sourced evenly from all regions. They should not come only from Bangkok or any particular region. A number is allocated to the list of each party (http://202.183.203.226/neo/new/mp/newect12.html). This is the same number used by each party in the

single-seat constituencies. For example, the Democrat Party was No. 16 in both systems in the 2001 general election.

2 When Germany adopted this 5% rule, it was to prevent the emergence of ultra-right political parties. Thailand's 5% rule is intended to exclude left-wing parties.

Of the major parties, four candidates were disqualified from the Democrats, one from New Aspiration, two from Chat Thai, two from Chat Phatthana and one from the Ratsadon Party.

3 *Bangkok Post* also reported about some disqualified party-list candidates. For example, Chalat who was a central figure in a series of rallies that demanded the resignation of Prime Minister Suchinda in April 1992, and sparked the political reform movement in May 1994, was the first-ranked proportional representation candidate of the Phalang Tham Party. However, he was disqualified because he had not voted in the Senate revote in the previous year in his constituency of Bangkok (*Bangkok Post*, 3 December 2000).

4 Polling was conducted at 112 locations in sixty-five countries. There were 42,445 people or 6% of about 700,000 overseas nationals registered to vote, a 65% increase on the 26,058 registered voters for the Senate election. However, only 14,989 of them voted between 3 and 30 December, only 45% more than the 10,302 who voted in the Senate election. The cost of conducting the overseas polls was 27 million baht for the Senate election and 22 million baht for the House of Representatives election (*Bangkok Post*, 28 December 2000 and 4 January 2001). Michai writes approvingly of the concept behind this system, but criticizes it for being too great a burden on tight national finances (2001: 40–1).

5 Voter turnout in general elections, 1933–2001

Voter turnout, 1933–2001

	Election date	Voter turnout (%)		Election date	Voter turnout (%)
1	Nov 1933	41.45	11	Apr 1976	43.99
2	Nov 1937	40.22	12	Apr 1979	43.90
3	Nov 1938	35.03	13	Apr 1983	50.76
4	Jan 1946	32.52	14	Jul 1986	61.43
5	Jan 1948	26.54	15	Jul 1988	63.56
6	Feb 1952	38.76	16	Mar 1992	59.35
7	Feb 1957	57.50	17	Sep 1992	62.02
8	Dec 1957	40.10	18	Jul 1995	62.04
9	Feb 1969	49.16	19	Nov 1996	62.42
10	Jan 1975	47.17	*	Mar 2000	72.08
			20	Jan 2001	69.95

Source: Chaowana (1998: 121)
Note: The March 2000 election was the Senate election.

6 The invalid vote rate exceeded 20% in six electoral constituencies, with the eighth constituency of Chiang Mai recording the highest at 28.41%. In addition to invalid votes, the blank vote rate was 1.77% in the proportional representation and 3.55% in the single-seat constituencies. It was over 10% in four electoral constituencies, with the highest being 11.37% in the first constituency of Chiang Mai (Kho. Ko. Tho. 2001b: 22, 113, 117). One reason for the high rates of blank votes was a campaign by some intellectuals to cast blank votes as a protest about the absence of suitable candidates.

7 Some problems were encountered during the counting of votes for the 6 January election at polling stations in two provinces, including discrepancies between the numbers of voters and the numbers of votes. Re-voting was conducted on 13 January at two polling stations in the fourth constituency and four polling stations in the fifth constituency of Maha Sarakham province, and seven polling stations in the first constituency and one polling station in the fourth constituency of Kanchana Buri province.

8 The 1997 Constitution requires candidates to have a university or higher education qualification. However, former members of the House of Representatives or the Senate are exempted from this rule, which is why there are a few candidates with no university qualification. Nevertheless, more than 40% of successful candidates in the single-seat constituencies and 60% in the proportional representation system have a master's or higher degree.

Educational qualifications of the 2001 election candidates and winners

	Single-seat district		Party-list	
	Candidates	Winners	Candidates	Winners
Total number	2,782	400	940	100
Below bachelor's degree	4.7%	16.0%	3.8%	6.0%
Bachelor's degree	67.6%	41.0%	59.4%	34.0%
Master's degree	24.8%	40.8%	26.7%	43.0%
Doctorate	2.9%	2.3%	10.1%	17.0%
	100.0%	100.0%	100.0%	100.0%

Source: Compiled from Election Commission data (Kho. Ko. Tho. 2001b: 29, 40, 150, 159).

9 The proportional representation system is a nationwide constituency and does not represent particular provinces or regions. Each party was required to source their candidates evenly from all regions (See Note 1 above). The table below shows the ratio of proportional representation candidates by place of residence. In comparison with the single-seat constituencies

where the ratio is proportional to the population distribution, the ratio of successful proportional representation candidates based in the central region is disproportionately high. It is not difficult to imagine that most of them reside in the metropolitan area.

Regional breakdown of the 2001 election winners

Region	Party-list Candidates	Winners	Single-seat district Winners
Central	51.8%	64.0%	33.0%
South	10.2%	10.0%	13.5%
North	14.8%	6.0%	19.0%
Northeast	23.2%	20.0%	34.5%
	100%	100%	100%

Source: Compiled from Election Commission data (Kho. Ko. Tho. 2001b: 30–1, 151, 161).

10 There was strong rivalry within the Phalang Tham Party between the temple faction (*sai wat*) led by an unorthodox Buddhist sect, Santi Asok, and the laity faction (*sai ban*). Following the retirement of party leader and conciliator Chamlong, leading figures in the laity faction (Winai Somphong, Bunchu Rotchanasathian, Thaksin Chinnawat, etc.) left the party and Sudarat Keyuraphan of the laity faction was the only winner in the 1996 general election. The party was left with no seat when Sudarat moved to the Thai Rak Thai Party. Many of the candidates who ran for this election from the Thai Rak Thai Party in the Bangkok constituency were former members of the Phalang Tham Party.

11 The allocation of seats in a party-list proportional representation system is calculated as follows. Call the total number of valid votes in the proportional representation system 'A'. Any party that fails to poll at least 5% of 'A' does not get any seat. 'B' is the total number of votes gathered by all the parties that poll at least 5% of 'A'. Then 1/100 of 'B' is the number of votes required to secure one seat. Election winners are chosen from the list of each party in descending order to the number of seats secured by each party. If the number of winners is below 100 after this allocation, the remaining seats are allocated to the parties in descending order of fractions until all 100 winners are chosen.

12 The occupations of successful candidates were similar to those in the previous general elections. In the new proportional representation, 43% of successful candidates were politicians, 22% businesspeople, 18% bureaucrats, 6% legal professionals, 2% other salaried workers and 9% others (based on Kho. Ko. Tho. 2001b: 148, 157). Of the Election Commission's classification, state-run corporation employees and local

government employees were counted as bureaucrats, self-employed and traders were counted as businesspeople, and political public servants were included in politicians.
13 The Seritham Party ranked sixth with 807,902 votes, or only 2.82%.
14 It has often been pointed out that Thailand's administrative structure is extremely centralized and having control of its core organization, the Interior Ministry, is highly advantageous in an election. However, the 1969 election proved that the vote-gathering power of the Interior Ministry was limited. The parties holding the Interior Minister's post have not always won subsequent elections.
15 MPs' private offices had traditionally been used as their party branch offices, therefore when these MPs switched parties, their offices also changed into new branch offices of the new parties. Although, whether this was still the case at the time of the 2001 general election is unclear.
16 For example, the Thin Thai Party, an urban party that emphasized environmental issues and fielded candidates in many electoral constituencies, had seven branches and only sixteen registered party members as of 20 December 2000. These numbers remained unchanged as of 1 February 2001. This suggests that membership size would remain relatively small if parties did not shamelessly engage in membership drives to recruit nominal members.
17 Based on Election Commission data (http://202.183.203.226/neo/new/party/p2-1.html and http://202.183.203.226/neo/new/party/p2-2.html).
18 The Thin Thai Party was judged to be ineligible for the subsidy as it failed to submit the report to the Election Commission and thus did not satisfy the requirements of the Political Parties Act.
19 Election Commission data (http://222.ect.go.th/newthai/election/party/dunda1.html). The budget allocated to the Fund for Development of Political Parties increased from 300 million baht in 2000 to 350 million baht in 2001. Accordingly, the amount distributed to political parties increased from 216 million baht to 252 million baht (http://www.ect.go.th/newthai/party/fund.html).
20 The total donation to the Thai Rak Thai Party in 2001 was 71.93 million baht according to the Election Commission data on donations to all parties for the four years from 1998 (http://www.ect.go.th/newthai/party/give/41-44.htm). However, when the figures in a more detailed list of donations and donors to the Thai Rak Thai Party on another web-page (http://www.ect.go.th/newthai/party/amout/44/trtp44.html & /trtp2.html) are totaled, the figure almost doubles to 140.07 million baht. This list shows that

Photchaman contributed 60 million baht each on 3 and 29 January 2001, a total of 120 million baht.
21 Chotchoi ran for the Senate in 2000 in Bangkok and won a seat in the second round of voting. Since electioneering was prohibited in a Senate election, she did not have to sweat under the sun. In a general election held in September 1992, Akon Huntrakun, the owner of Thailand's leading hotel chain Imperial Group at the time, surprised everyone by conducting a street preaching-style election campaign. When he sold his hotel chain, except three small properties, in 1994, it was a large scale sale of over 3000 rooms in ten properties. People thought such an election campaign was beneath a wealthy person like Akon.
22 Phothiphong is not a member of the main branch of the Lamsam family under Chot, but is the son of Chulin, Chot's younger brother.
23 The late Phot Sarasin served as prime minister in 1957. His first son Phong was a businessperson who had been a Member of the House of Representatives and the cabinet. See Note five of Chapter Two for the Sarasin family.
24 Chatri Sophonphanit, the second son of Chin Sophonphanit, who had succeeded his father as the head of the clan after his death, contributed 600,000 baht, Chin's first daughter and newly elected senator Chotchoi contributed 150,000 baht, and Kanlaya, the wife of Chin's fourth son Chot, contributed 2 million baht.
25 This became a political problem when suspicions were raised that Kao Pinyo was a foreign company. The Political Parties Act banned political donations from corporation with more than 25% foreign ownership. A more serious issue, however, was the fact that Sawat used the company as a conduit for political donations despite his enormous debts.
26 See *Prachachat Thurakit* (13–15 November 2000) and *Matichon Sutsapda* (20 November 2000) for the businesspeople on the proportional representation list of each party. According to these reports, the Thai Rak Thai Party's list included Wirachai Wiramethikun of M Group, school operator Phongsak Raktaphongphaisan and BMW importer Sirikon Manilin. The New Aspiration Party's list included Phiphat Phanianwet, the president of the Thai President Company, famous for 'Mama' instant noodle products. The Chat Thai Party's list included Sony Thailand executive Thamma Pinsukanchana.
27 Some dubious cases were found among the disclosed donations. For example, a donation of 600,000 baht from timber merchant Sunthon Ratsamiloekset of Kanchana Buri province, reported by the Democrat

Party on 25 October 2000, later raised suspicions that the money was gained through illegal business activity (*Bangkok Post*, 17 December 2000).

28 The legal limit each candidate could spend on the election campaign cost was one million baht.
29 This case became public because Pancha did not distribute these funds, thus angering the other candidates. Even though the Chat Phatthana Party spent this much money, none of its candidates, including Pancha, were elected in the province.
30 Chuchip Hansawat, the unsuccessful candidate in the party-list system discussed here, was nevertheless appointed Minister of Agriculture, as one of the central figures of the Sano faction in the Thai Rak Thai Party. Hence the clan was still represented in cabinet.
31 However, one of the reasons that Tun polled fewer votes than Chatri was the difference in the vote-gathering power of their respective parties. Tun polled over 10,000 votes more than his party attracted on the party-list basis in the new eleventh constituency while Chatri polled over 10,000 votes fewer than his party did on the party-list basis. Since the number of seats in the constituency was reduced from three to one, the number of votes received by a winner was also reduced to approximately one-third.
32 Vote brokers were sometimes attacked by the supporters of opposing candidates. One newspaper reported that twenty brokers were killed in the lead up to the March 1992 general election, eighteen brokers prior to the September 1992 general election and dozens of local politicians such as village chiefs and provincial councilors were murdered in relation to general elections (*Prachachat Thurakit Kanmueang*, 13–16 September 1992). However, it is not appropriate to link all of these murders to elections as not a few of these brokers were the type of people who might be targeted for a variety of reasons unrelated to their election activities.
33 Needless to say, the provision of such benefits amounts to an election fraud only during the election period.
34 The narrower northern region is the upper northern region of seven provinces, including Chiang Mai, Chiang Rai, Lamphun, Lampang, Mae Hon Song, Phrae and Nan. This region came under Bangkok's control through the centralization processes which began at the end of the nineteenth century. In contrast, the residents of the lower northern region to the north of Nakhon Sawan province considered themselves to be part of the upper central region and did not respond as strongly to the prospect of a northerner for prime minister.

35 Thaksin was accused of unreported assets of a total of 4.54 billion baht in his declaration in November and December 1997 and December 1998.
36 There may be a counterargument that even a ruling party executive had been punished. Sanan Khachonprasat, the Interior Minister and secretary-general of the Democrat Party was disenfranchised for five years following a similar allegation of asset concealment in 2000. However, this was said to be the outcome desired by the main faction executives of the Democrat Party. The party had built a stable support base in the southern region since the 1980s, followed by the less stable metropolitan region with many swinging voters. The party leadership was dominated by the southern faction, which had an upper hand in factional struggles against the metropolitan faction. This southern bias was hindering the party's national expansion. Sanan from Phichit province was appointed secretary-general in an attempt to overcome this problem and extend the party's influence beyond the southern and metropolitan regions. Thanks to Sanan, the Democrat Party had steadily expanded during the 1990s. However, it seemed that the southern faction came to regard Sanan's increasing influence as a threat and moved to oust him.
37 There were an additional seven former MPs from the 1990s in the lower half of the list.
38 Both Thanin and Bunyat expressed their support for Thaksin before the general election and became advisors to the Finance Minister in Thaksin's administration. Finance Minister Somkhit had been an advisor to the Saha Phatthana Group for many years and his brother Som worked as an advisor for CP.
39 The Sano faction became a major faction in Thai Rak Thai, second only to the party leader's main faction. In this sense, Sano could be called a power broker or a king maker. Perhaps partly because Sano switched allegiance to Thai Rak Thai, he sold his golf course to Thaksin for 500 million baht. Sano had bought the land for 130 million baht and developed a golf course but was losing money on it. It would not be entirely wrong to interpret this high value disposal as the cost Thaksin paid to buy off Sano. This transaction became an issue after the Thaksin administration was formed, as the land was allegedly owned by a temple and should not have been bought or sold.
40 It is hard to overlook the fact that the introduction of the single-seat constituency system favored the two parties with the most incumbent MPs, namely Thai Rak Thai and the Democrats.
41 Sia Leng commented that he would not get involved in his son's election campaign because he might be prosecuted for election law violations if

he helped his son (*Bangkok Post*, 3 January 2001). But since he should not be prosecuted if he conducted a legitimate election campaign, his claim can be interpreted to mean that he would employ all available measures to help his son's and his party's election prospects. See Tamada (1988: 297) for Sia Leng's ability to gather votes.

42 Pakon's younger brother Praphan came third but failed in a by-election round. He ran for this general election as the ninth-ranked party-list candidate of the Ratsadon Party.

43 Somphong had been elected for consecutive terms since 1986. His elder brother, former Police Chief Sawat Amonwiwat, won a Senate seat in Chiang Mai province in 2000 with the help of Somphong's support base. Chat Thai was planning to back Somphong in a single-seat constituency of Chiang Mai in the 2001 general election. When Thai Rak Thai tried to poach him as its party-list candidate, it drew strong protests from Chat Thai. Somphong was still undecided about which party to run for at the deadline for candidacy applications and ended up not running at all. Thus the Thai Rak Thai Party had managed to eliminate its most powerful rival in Chiang Mai province.

44 However, he defeated a candidate from the Hansawat family and won a seat.

45 This mass resignation was intended to urge the ruling party to dissolve the parliament early.

46 In the general election of March 1992, two new parties won many seats. One of them, the New Aspiration Party, had reportedly spent a total of 55 million baht up to January 1992 recruiting incumbent MPs and the other, the Sammakkhitham Party, paid 3.5 million baht per person (Murray 1996: 38, 41). It appears that the price of an incumbent MP jumped more than tenfold over the next ten years.

47 The Chinnawat family (Thaksin, Photchaman and three children) owned 21.9 billion baht in assets according to a declaration made in 1997 (*Nation Sutsapda*, 17 July 2000) and was capable of injecting a lot of money into the party. The family's declared assets at the time of his appointment as Prime Minister in March 2001 were worth 15.1 billion baht (for the couple and two children, as the eldest son was an adult by then) (Computed from data in Chumphon 2002: 21–38).

48 According to information obtained from a reliable source in March 2001, the Thai Rak Thai Party paid 30 to 40 million baht to an incumbent MP candidate in a certain province in the central region as well as 18 million baht to a new candidate who was this MP's relative.

49 Many MPs dream about belonging to a government party and joining the cabinet. Hence parties that are likely to remain in opposition are not attractive to these MPs. There are two types of parties that can become a government party. One is the leading party, the one with the most seats in the house. The other is medium-sized to small parties that may be invited to be a coalition partner. As mentioned in the text, no single party has ever won a majority of seats in any general election in Thailand since the 1970s, and therefore coalition governments have been the norm. Hence, for example, the Social Action Party, a small party with only twenty or so seats, was consistently a member of the ruling coalitions throughout the 1990s. For those MPs who might not stand out enough in a large party to secure a cabinet post, becoming the leader or executive of a minor party is a way to join the cabinet. It is better to be a big fish in a small pond than a small fish in a big pond.

50 The three people mentioned from this family joined Thai Rak Thai and won (two on the constituency basis and one on the party-list basis).

51 More than a few MPs are of the opinion that Section 107(4) of the constitution should be amended. However, the Thai Rak Thai executives are extremely unlikely to support the idea, since such a move could be the death knell for the party. Amon, one of the people who triggered the political reform movement, commented at a symposium in November 2002 that independent MPs should be allowed (*Bangkok Post*, 25 November 2002; *Prachachat Thurakit*, 28 November 2002).

52 *Dokbia* (February 2001: 29–30) estimates the amount of funds required for each election promise at 210 to 230 billion baht for the moratorium on farmers' debt repayments, 70 billion baht for the Village Development Fund, 30 billion baht for the reduction of medical fees and 600 to 700 billion baht for the Thai Asset Management Corporation (TAMC) to dispose of bad loans.

53 The Election Commission had trouble with election fraud in the 2000 Senate election and took several months to confirm the election of all 200 senators. Based on this experience, the 1998 Election Act was revised and promulgated in November 2000. The Senate hid this compensation provision in 'Section 4—Penalties' in the amendment bill and approved it on 6 October 2000. Forty-three MPs complained that Section 113/1 of the revised Election Act might be unconstitutional and asked the Constitution Court for a ruling. They claimed that the compensation provision was unfair in that it only applied to constituency MPs and that it gave wealthy MPs and parties an advantage. They also claimed that

it was unjust to penalize constituency MPs for accepting cabinet posts, which was not an offence. The Constitution Court ruled on 31 October 2000 that the compensation provision was constitutional on the grounds that the Constitution did not guarantee constituency MPs the right to enter the cabinet, that parties had the freedom to choose which constituency to field candidates in, and that the obligation to pay the cost of by-elections was not a penalty (www.concourt.or.th/decis/y2000d/d05643.html). Normally, an MP who has committed an election offence and triggered a by-election is forced to pay for the cost. The Election Commission had demanded compensation from three candidates who were red-carded in the Senate election in October 2000, thus giving rise to revotes. The total amount demanded was 48.68 million baht including 18.31 million baht for two revotes in Chon Buri province, 8.63 million baht for two revotes in Angthong province and 21.74 million baht for five revotes in Ubon Ratchathani province (*Matichon Sutsapda*, 30 October 2000). It is probably not appropriate to compare the Senate election directly with the constituency election because the former is a province-wide constituency and had several revote rounds. However, based on the figure for Angthong province, which has only one seat in the Senate and one constituency for the House of Representatives, the cost would not exceed 10 million baht each. Considering that MPs in the ruling coalition's Chat Thai Party accused each other of selling and buying cabinet posts for 50 or 100 million baht, 10 million baht is not a prohibitive cost for constituency MPs who want to join the cabinet (*The Nation*, 7 July 2000; *Bangkok Post*, 7 July 2000; Sombat 2002: 215).

54 There was a comprehensive cabinet reshuffle in October 2002. The new cabinet had thirty-six members, including the prime minister, comprised of thirty-two party-list candidates (twenty-five successful and seven unsuccessful), one single-seat candidate (unsuccessful) and three non-candidates. In other words, twenty-five elected MPs, eleven non-MPs and no single-seat MP.

55 Revote was held in sixty-two single-seat constituencies. The number of votes polled by each candidate in the revote differed from the original polls. However, the votes in the original election are used here for both the party-list and the constituencies for the purpose of comparison.

56 The share of votes of the Thin Thai Party was twice as high in the party-list election as in the single-seat election, in no small part because the party aimed to win in the party-list and did not field any strong candidates in the constituencies. The party's highest number of votes polled by a candidate was 8803, far below the winning range. It finally won one constituency

in a revote on 29 January, the second constituency of Roi Et province, but this win was not due to any effort or ability on the part of the candidate or the party. The Thai Rak Thai candidate, who had far out-polled his competitors in the election on 6 January with 35,085 votes, was red-carded and disqualified. Usually, the second or third candidate would come first in the revote. This time, however, the Thin Thai candidate, who had polled a mere 240 votes in the original election, received the highest number of votes, at 19,271. Voter turnout in this constituency had decreased from 64% to 49% and the number of valid votes decreased from 62,200 to 47,800 but the candidate managed to poll nearly 20,000 more votes than in the first round. Since Thin Thai gathered only 399 votes for the party-list in this constituency, these additional votes were obviously not attracted by the party itself. This strange election result came about because the red-carded Thai Rak Thai candidate directed his votes to the Thin Thai candidate who was least likely to be a strong rival in the next general election. This suggests that the votes belonged to individuals rather than parties.

Election results in the 2nd district of Roi Et province, 2001

Candidate's party affiliation	Original votes	By-election votes
Thai Rak Thai	35,085	0
New Aspiration	9,367	15,437
Democrat	9,046	6,747
Seritham	6,311	5,160
Chat Phatthana	1,305	768
Chat Thai	323	125
Prachakon Thai	298	151
Ratsadon	279	139
Thin Thai	240	19,271

Source: Compiled from Election Commission data
(http://202.183.203.226/sorsor/sh_kate_city2_47_2%20.htm).

57 Similarly in the eastern province of Chon Buri, the Thai Rak Thai Party polled the highest number in party-list ballot in four electoral constituencies, the Democrat Party in two constituencies and the Chat Thai Party in one constituency while the Chat Thai Party won in six single-seat constituencies and the Thai Rak Thai Party in one. This clearly demonstrated that many of the voters cast their votes differently for the single-seat constituency and the party-list.

58 McCargo notes that of the winners in single-seat constituencies, many of the newcomers were relatives of Senators and former MPs (McCargo 2002: 248–9). This suggests that electoral success was highly dependent on the candidates' own ability to gather votes. Almost half of the winners

in Bangkok were incumbent MPs and almost half of the Thai Rak Thai winners were either incumbent MPs, former MPs or their relatives.

59 One reason for the increase in the success rate of incumbent MPs during the 1980s was that the development funds were distributed evenly to all sitting MPs, thus strengthening their vote-gathering ability, as discussed shortly.

60 As demonstrated by the error committed by the Seritham and Ratsadon parties, perhaps because it was the first party-list election in Thai history, a party could not win a seat if it did not poll at least 5% of the total votes no matter how many attractive potential cabinet ministers it had on its party candidate list. The Ratsadon Party nominated six incumbent MPs, including its four executives, for the party-list. Consequently, it only managed to win one single-seat constituency (i.e., none of the incumbents were re-elected).

61 If the administration remains stable enough to complete its four-year term, single-seat MPs will press even harder for cabinet posts toward the end of the term. As the next general election approaches, the risk of losing a parliamentary seat in exchange for a cabinet post and becoming unemployed if dismissed from the cabinet will decrease. The same applies when MPs can guess when the parliament is likely to be dissolved.

62 The balance of power between parties and factions had been traditionally measured by the number of MPs and cabinet posts. However, now that single-seat constituency MPs were not included in the cabinet, the balance of power between factions within the Thai Rak Thai Party was measured by the number of posts such as private secretary and assistant secretary to a minister, advisor to a minister and committee chairperson (*Nation Sutsapda*, 9 July 2001).

63 A Chat Thai MP commented in July 2000 that the party used to pay a monthly allowance of 50,000 baht to its MPs but had increased it to 100,000 baht when Thai Rak Thai increased its recruitment activity (*Matichon Sutsapda*, 10 July 2000).

64 Thaksin worked hard to contain the powerful Sano faction from the very beginning of his administration. He, for example, absorbed the New Aspiration Party, which had been at odds with the Sano faction. In March 2002, a conflict of interests between the Sano faction and the Somsak faction sparked a round of mutual accusations of impropriety. A constituency MP of the Sano faction first alleged that Somsak, the Minister for the Office of Prime Minister in charge of the Tourism Authority of Thailand, was involved in impropriety in relation to the expenditure of

6 billion baht budgeted for tourism promotion. Further, Sano expressed opposition to a budget of 1.2 billion baht to upgrade the Public Relations Department's TV station under the jurisdiction of Somsak. Somsak countered that there was no impropriety. His wife, a constituency MP, said, 'MPs of the Sano faction might not have had a hand in the allocation of a tourism budget but might have taken part in the allocation of other budgets, an Agriculture Ministry budget for instance. MPs are not doing their job if they do not get involved in any budget.' A constituency MP of the Somsak faction who was criticized for licentious spending of a tourism promotion budget hit back, saying that if an audit was to be carried out on tourism budget administration, the budgets of all ministries and agencies should also be audited, particularly the Agriculture and Cooperative Ministry under the Sano faction minister (*Krungthep Thurakit*, 12 March 2002).

65 A 20% rise in MPs' salary proposed in August 2002 appears to have been at least partly intended to keep them quiet.

66 In addition to the development budget, the power to allocate public works is an important reward for MPs. For example, when an MP for Lampang province was about to leave the Chat Thai Party for the Thai Rak Thai Party in June 2000, party leader and former Prime Minister Banhan threatened to cancel a public works budget earmarked for Lampang province, and he actually did (*Matichon Sutsapda*, 10 July 2000).

67 The Communist Party has always been an illegal political organization except for a short period after the Second World War.

68 The party's founding manifesto placed so much emphasis on equality and fairness that it had to explicitly declare that it was 'not socialist' (SAP 1974).

69 This is supported by the fact that, after twenty years of implementation of general elections at almost regular intervals, political parties have made few inroads into local government sectors such as provincial and city councilors, with Bangkok being almost the only exception. The parties did not feel the need to reach out to local politicians and did not develop any ability to involve themselves in local political communities. Some local politicians may join the local faction of an MP but that is typically as far as it goes. Since MPs are always switching parties, local politicians do not belong to particular parties either. This is in part because local governments are small and do not provide many privileges. Also, the parties can extend their influence into local communities via the centralized administrative structure if they secure ministerial posts. Bangkok is an exception for two reasons. First, it has a much larger local government which has broad

powers. Second, candidates cannot rely on vote-gathering brokers in the metropolitan region, so the parties must take the initiative in winning votes there.

70 The New Aspiration Party became the leading party in the November 1996 election and secured the prime minister's post. It went into opposition after its leader Chawalit resigned from premiership in 1997 and yet lost dismally in the 2001 general election.

71 This provision was adopted because no confidence motions had been routinely submitted against cabinet members, often aimed simply at triggering a cabinet reshuffle which might make room for the motion's instigator to join the cabinet. The repeated deployment of this tactic contributed to continuing government instability.

72 Specifically, the daily newspaper *Naeona* and the English-language paper *The Nation* came under attack. Foreign magazines that criticized the Thaksin administration (*Far Eastern Economic Review* and *Economist*) were occasionally prohibited from selling or importing specific issues on the grounds of *lese majesty*. Some NGO leaders were also investigated on alleged suspicions of money laundering.

73 Photchaman does not hold public office but carries a lot of weight within the Thai Rak Thai Party and the cabinet, and can therefore be regarded as Thaksin's co-proprietor.

Chapter Six

1 During the course of these political changes, the word 'businesspeople (*nakthurakit*)' came into common usage, largely replacing 'merchant (*phokha*)' and 'capitalist (*naithun*).' The new name not only sounded better, but perhaps more accurately reflected the fact that those who entered politics from the business world were not only business owners but also salaried executives. A typical example is Bunchu Rotchanasathian, president of the Bangkok Bank, who was elected to the House of Representatives and then appointed Treasurer. The number of professional business managers like Bunchu who entered politics continued to increase in the 1990s. Terms such as 'political business (*thurakit kanmueang*)' and 'political merchant (*nakthurakit kanmueang*)' also came into general use in the 1980s. Many political merchants, so-called because they profited from special relationships with the government and politicians, had been around long before the 1980s. In this sense, they were actually 'bureaucratic merchants' who took advantage of relationships with the military and government

bureaucrats. One of the characteristics of the political merchants of the 1970s is that they used political parties as profit-making enterprises.
2 According to Surin, 'The citizenry tacitly but clearly supported the military coup' (1999: 362).
3 Former diplomat Anan was an eloquent and effective self-promoter who gave eloquent speeches and interviews. These personal factors no doubt contributed to his high regard.
4 There was one more thing that was rejected: actions that would drag the King into mundane political matters.
5 The expansion of print media companies into broadcasting media during the booming economy until the mid-1990s also increased their transmission capability and influence.
6 Sakagami's discussion of the birth of public opinion in France and the distinction between the 'opinion of the populace' and 'public opinion' is very useful (Sakagami 1999: chapter 3).
7 As mentioned above, each multiple-seat electoral district under the previous system always contained both city and rural areas and therefore the city area tended to be a minority constituency. Under the new single-seat system, provincial capitals and other cities form individual electoral districts. This has increased the possibility of urban representatives being elected.
8 A coup staged by Army officers of Class 7 on April 1, 1981 was a good example. Although they succeeded in seizing the capital city, they were forced to give in to the government just because the monarchy did not approve their attempt. The royal disapproval encouraged military forces that did not agree with or were neutral to the coup to support the government. In contrast, the NPKC staged a successful coup on February 23, 1991. As the NPKC had a thorough grip on the military, no military forces could defeat them and there was little possibility of royal disapproval (see Chapter Two).

Bibliography

Abe, Teruya and Hiroyuki Hata (eds). 1998. *Sekai no kenpō shū (dainihan)* (Constitutions of the world, second edition): Yushindō.

Akon Huntrakun. 2000. 'Prachaphichan' in *Akon ramluek: thiraluek nai wara khlai wankoet khun akon huntrakun*, Bangkok: Phikkhanet Printing Center: 139–140. (Originally published in *Matichon*, 10 June 1997)

Amara Pongsapich. 1995. 'Strengthening the role of NGOs in popular participation' in Jaturong Boonyarattanasoontorn and Gawin Chutima (eds), *Thai NGOs: The Continuing Struggle for Democracy*, Bangkok: Thai NGO Support Project: 9–50.

Anan Panyarachun. 1998. 'Rabop prachathipatai kap sangkhom lok lae prathet thai,' in Khana So. So. Ro., *Ruam sara ratthathammanun chabap prachachon*, Bangkok: Matichon: 37–49.

Anderson, Benedict R. 1977. 'Withdrawal symptoms: social and cultural aspects of the October 6 coup,' *Bulletin of Concerned Asian Scholars*, 9: 13–30.

—— 1990. 'Murder and progress in modern Siam,' *New Left Review*, 181: 33–48.

Anek Laothammathat (Anek Laothamatas). 1992. *Business Associations and the New Political Economy of Thailand: From Bureaucratic Polity to Liberal Corporatism*, Boulder: Westview Press.

—— 1993. *Mop muethue: chonchan klang lae nakthurakit kap phatthanakan prachathipatai*, Bangkok: Matichon.

—— 1995a. *Song nakkhara prachathipatai: naeothang kanpatirup kanmueang setthakit phuea prachathipatai*, Bangkok: Matichon.

—— 1995b. 'Patirup kanmueang setthakit: sang phanthamit prachathipatai' in Chalong Suntharawanit (ed.), *Wiphak sangkhom thai*, Bangkok: Amarin Book Center.

—— 1996. 'A tale of two democracies: conflicting perceptions of elections and democracy in Thailand' in R. H. Taylor (ed.), *The Politics of Elections in Southeast Asia*, New York: Woodrow Wilson Center Press.

—— 1997. 'Development and democratization: a theoretical introduction with reference to the Southeast Asian and East Asian cases' in Anek Laothamatas (ed.), *Democratization in Southeast and East Asia*, Singapore: ISEAS: 1–20.

—— 1999. 'Suan ruam thi mi chai rat: khwammai khong prachasangkhom' in Anuchat Phueangsamli and Krittaya Achawanitkun (eds), *Khabuankan prachasangkhom thai: khwamkhlueanwai phak phonlamueang*, Bangkok: Amarin Printing and Publishing: 36–61.

—— 2006. *Thaksina-prachaniyom* (Bangkok: Matichon)
Aphiwat Phothisit. 1998. *Charuek wai nai khwamsongcham phonek chettha thanacharo 23 singhakhom 2541*, Bangkok: Sinsayambanchuphan lae kanphim.
Arghiros, Daniel. 2001. *Democracy, Development and Decentralization in Provincial Thailand*, Richmond, Surrey: Curzon.
Asami, Yasuhito. 1998. 'Chūkansō no zōdai to seiji ishiki no henka (Expansion of the middle class and changes in political awareness)' in Toshio Tasaka (ed.), *Ajia no daitoshi (1) Bangkok* (Major cities of Asia (1) Bangkok): Nihon Hyōronsha: 305–328.
—— 2002. 'Tai: kaihatsu to minshuka no paradokusu (Thailand: the paradox of development and democratization)' in *Iwanami kōza tōnanajia shi 9 'kaihatsu' no jidai to 'mosaku' no jidai* (Iwanami course on Southeast Asian history (9): the age of 'development' and the age of 'search'): Iwanami Shoten: 33–63.
At Sasiprapha. 1972. *Anuson nai kanphraratchathan phloengsop phontho at sasiprapha*, Bangkok: Krungthepkanphim.
Bowonsak Uwanno (Bavornsak Uvanno). 1997. 'Political culture vs. CDA charter,' *Bangkok Post*, 26 September 1997.
—— 1998. 'Phap ruam khong ratthathammanun chabap mai' in Khana So. So. Ro. (ed.), *Ruam sara ratthathammanun chabap prachachon*, Bangkok: Matichon: 50–79.
—— 1999. *Ratthathammanun naru: ruam sara-kham athibai lak kotmai ratthathammanun chak sathani witthayu krachai siang haeng prathet thai*, Bangkok: Samnakphim Winyuchon.
Bowie, Katherine A. 1997. *Rituals of National Loyalty: An Anthropology of the State and the Village Scout Movement in Thailand*, New York: Columbia University Press.
Bunce, Valerie. 2000. 'Comparative democratization: big and bounded generalizations,' *Comparative Political Studies*, 33 (6/7): 703–734.
Bunloet Khachayutthadet. 1998. 'Nathi khong chao thai' in Khana So. So. Ro. (ed.), *Ruam sara ratthathammanun chabap prachachon*, Bangkok: Matichon: 210–216.
Callahan, William A. 1998. *Imaging Democracy: Reading 'The Events of May' in Thailand*, Singpore: ISEAS.
—— 2000. *Pollwatching, Elections and Civil Society in Southeast Asia*, Aldershot: Ashgate.
CDD (Committee on Developing Democracy, Khanakammakan phatthana prachathipatai). 1995. *Khosanoe krop khwamkhit nai kanpatirup kanmueang thai*, Bangkok: Samnakngan kongthun sanapsanun kanwichai.

Chai Uengphakon et al. 2000. *Kanmueang thai nai thatsana latthi mak*, Bangkok: Chulalongkorn University Press.

—— (Ji Giles Ungpakorn). 2002. 'From tragedy to comedy: political reform in Thailand,' *Journal of Contemporary Asia*, 32(2): 191–205.

Chaianan Samutthawanit (Chai-anan Samudavanija). 1987. 'The bureaucracy' in Somakdi Xuto (ed.), *Government and Politics of Thailand*, Singapore: Oxford University Press: 75–109.

—— 1989. 'Thailand: a stable semi-democracy' in Larry Diamond, Juan J. Linz, and Seymour Martin Lipset (eds), *Democracy in Developing Countries, Volume 2: Asia*, Boulder: Lynne Rienner: 305–346.

—— 2000. *Wisaithat thai nai sangkhom lok*, Bangkok: Amarin.

Chaianan Samutthawanit (Chai-anan Samudavanija) and Parichat Chotiya. 1998. 'Beyond transition in Thailand' in Larry Diamond and Marc F. Plattner (eds), *Democracy in East Asia, Baltimore*: The Johns Hopkins University Press: 147–167.

Chamlong Simueang. 1993. *Tai ni minshushugi wo* (Democracy for Thailand). Translated by Hajime Kitamura and Eiko Sasaki. Saimaru Shuppankai.

Chaowana Traimat. 1998. *Khomun phuenthan 66 pi prachathipatai thai*, Bangkok: Sathaban Nayobaisueksa.

Chatcharin Chaiwat. 1998. *Chutfai nai nakhon: phachoen na lokaphiwat*, Bangkok: Samnakphim Samaphan.

Chattawa Klinsunthong (ed.). 1995. *Ratthahburut chue prem*, Bangkok: J. Plus Image and Publishing.

Chaturong Chaisaeng, Konlayut Chaisaeng, Wutthiphong Chaisaeng lae Thitima Chaisaeng. 1996. *Dae pho mae duai duang chai*, Bangkok: Statenews.

Chumphon Phatthraphon. 2002. *Thaksin ruai thaorai nae: Ching rue chaek ngoen wan la lan pa ik ko mai mi wan mot*, Bangkok: Thanaban.

Compton, Robert W., Jr. 2000. *East Asian Democratization: Impact of Globalization, Culture, and Economy*, Westport: Praeger.

Connors, Michael Kelly. 1999. 'Political reform and the sate in Thailand,' *Journal of Contemporary Asia*, 29(2): 202–226.

—— 2003. *Democracy and National Identity in Thailand*, London: Routledge Curzon.

CPR. 1987. *100 pi rongrian nairoi phrachunlachomklao, phak 2–3*, Bangkok: JNT.

—— 1998. *Thamniap nakrian nairoi khroprop 111 pi rongrian nairoi phrachunlachomklao*, Bangkok: Mangkon Kanphim.

Decho Sawananon. 1998. 'Chotmaihet chabap yo ratthathammanun haeng

ratchaanachak thai phutthasakkarat 2540' in Khana So. So. Ro., *Ruam sara ratthathammanun chabap prachachon*, Bangkok: Matichon: 80–120.
Diamond, Larry. 1999. *Developing Democracy: Toward Consolidation*, Baltimore: The Johns Hopkins University Press.
Doner, Richard F. and Ansil Ramsay. 2000. 'Rent-seeking and economic development in Thailand' in Mushtaq H. Khan and Jomo K. S. (eds), *Rents, Rent-seeking and Economic Development: Theory and Evidence in Asia*, Cambridge: Cambridge University Press: 145–181.
Endō, Mitsugu. 2000. 'Afurika "shimin shakai" ron no tenkai (Development of African "civil society" theory)' in Nihon Kokusai Seiji Gakkai (ed.), *Tenkanki no afurika (kokusai seiji 123)* (Africa at a turning point (international politics 123)): 13–29.
Fujiwara, Kiichi. 1987. 'Firipin ni okeru "minshushugi" no seido to undō (The "democratic" system and movement in the Philippines),' *Shakai Kagaku Kenkyū* (Social science research) 41(1): 1–94.
―― 1994. 'Seifutō to zaiyatō: tōnanajia ni okeru seifutō taisei (Government party and opposition party: government party rule in Southeast Asia)' in Yoshiyuki Hagiwara (ed.), *Kōza gendai ajia 3-kan – Minshuka to keizaihatten* (Course on contemporary Asia vol. 3 – democratization and economic growth): Tokyo Daigaku Shuppankai.
Funatsu, Tsuruyo and Kazuhiro Kagoya. 2002. 'Tai no chūkansō: toshi gakureki erīto no seisei to shakai ishiki (Thai middle class: formation of the urban educated elite and social awareness)' in Tamio Hattori, Tsuruyo Funatsu and Takashi Torii (eds), *Ajia chūkansō no seisei to tokushitsu* (The formation of the middle classes in Asia and their characteristics): Ajia Keizai Kenkyūjo: 201–234.
Gawin Chutima. 1995. 'Thai NGOs and civil society' in Jaturong Boonyarattanasoontorn and Gawin Chutima (eds), *Thai NGOs: The Continuing Struggle for Democracy*, Bangkok: Thai NGO Support Project: 135–144.
Girling, John. 1996. *Interpreting Development: Capitalism, Democracy, and the Middle Class in Thailand*, Ithaca: Cornell University Southeast Asia Program.
Hashimoto, Takashi. 1999a. 'Tai ni okeru chihō seido kaikaku no dōkō to kadai (1) (Trends and issues of local government reform in Thailand (1)),' *Doshisha Hōgaku* (Doshisha Law Review), 50(4): 1–38.
―― 1999b. 'Tai ni okeru chihō seido kaikaku no dōkō to kadai (2, kan) (Trends and issues of local government reform in Thailand (2, conclusion)),' *Doshisha Hōgaku* (Doshisha Law Review), 50(5): 74–143.

Hata, Tatsuya. 1993. *Bankoku no atsui kisetsu* (Season of passion in Bangkok), Iwanami Shoten.
Hattori, Tamio, Tsuruyo Funatsu and Takashi Torii (eds). 2002. *Ajia chūkansō no seisei to tokushitsu* (The formation of the middle classes in Asia and their characteristics): Ajia Keizai Kenkyūjo.
Hedman, Eva-Lotta E. 2001. 'Contesting state and civil society: Southeast Asian trajectories,' *Modern Asian Studies*, 35(4): 921–951.
Hewison, Kevin. 1993. 'Of regimes, state and pluralities: Thai politics enters the 1990s' in Kevin Hewison, Richard Robison and Garry Rodan (eds), *Southeast Asia in the 1990s: Authoritarianism, Democracy & Capitalism*, NSW: Allen & Unwin: 161–189.
—— 1997. 'Introduction: power, oppositions and democratization' in Do (ed.), *Political Change in Thailand: Democracy and Participation*, London: Routledge: 1–20.
Heywood, Paul. 1997. 'Political corruption: problems and perspective,' *Political Studies*, 45(3): 417–435.
Higashi, Shigeki. 1998. 'Sangyō seisaku to kokusai kyōsōryoku no kaizen (Industrial policy and improvement in international competitiveness)' in Akira Suehiro (ed.), *Taikoku jōhō (bessatsu) Tai – keizai būmu, keizai kiki, kōzō chōsei* (Thailand country information (supplementary volume) Thailand – economic boom, economic crisis and structural adjustment): Zaidanhōjin Nihon Tai Kyōkai.
Horikoshi, Hisao. 1997. 'Tai ni okeru puremu shushō jidai no seitō no hattatsu (Development of political parties in prime minister Prem's era in Thailand),' *Gaimushō chōsa geppō* (Ministry of Foreign Affairs monthly report), 2: 21–70.
Huntington, Samuel Paul. 1991. *The Third Wave: The Democratization in the Late Twentieth Century*, Norman: University of Oklahoma Press.
—— 1993. 'American democracy in relation to Asia' in Robert Bartley, Chan Heng Chee, Samuel P. Huntington and Shijuro Ogata, *Democracy & Capitalism: Asian and American Perspectives*, Singapore: ISEAS: 27–43.
—— 1995. *Daisan no nami* (The third wave), translated by Minoru Tsubogō, Hisakazu Nakamichi and Yūzō Yabuno: Sanrei Shobō.
IDE (Institute of Developing Economies). 1995. *Hattentojōkoku kankyō mondai sōgō kenkyū hōkokusho: chūgoku & tai kankyō ishikichōsa no shūkeihyō* (Comprehensive research report on environmental issues in developing countries: tabulated results of environmental awareness studies in China and Thailand): Ajia Keizai Kenkyūjo.
Imaizumi, Shinya. 2002. 'Tai no saiban seido kaikaku no genjō to kadai

(Current state of Thai court system reform and its problems)' in Masayuki Kobayashi and Shinya Imaizumi (eds), *Ajia shokoku no shihō kaikaku* (Judicial reform in Asian nations): Ajia Keizai Kenkyūjo: 91–128.

Itō, Nobufumi. 1999. *Minshuka to gunbu: tai to firipin* (Democratization and the military: Thailand and the Philippines): Keio Gijutu Daigaku Shuppankai.

—— 2002. *Tōnanajia no minshuka* (Democratization of Southeast Asia): Kindai Bungeisha.

Iwasaki, Ikuo. 1998a. 'Ajia shiminshakairon: gainen, jittai, tenbō (Asian civil society theory: concept, reality, outlook)' in Ikuo Iwasaki (ed.), *Ajia to shiminshakai: kokka to shakai no seiji rikigaku* (Asia and civil society: political dynamics of the state and society): Ajia Keizai Kenkyūjo: 3–28.

—— 1998b. 'Shingapōru: Ittō shihai taiseika no kibishii seiyaku (Singapore: strong constraints under the one-party regime)' in Ikuo Iwasaki (ed.), *Ajia to shiminshakai: kokka to shakai no seiji rikigaku* (Asia and civil society: political dynamics of the state and society): Ajia Keizai Kenkyūjo: 77–108.

—— 2001. *Ajia seiji wo miru me* (Observing Asian politics): Chūkō Shinsho.

Jackson, Peter A. 1989. *Buddhism, Legitimation, and Conflict: The Political Functions of Urban Thai Buddhism*, Singapore: ISEAS.

Jain, R. K. 1984. *China and Thailand 1949–1983*, New Delhi: Radiant.

Jones, David Martin. 1997. *Political Development in Pacific Asia*, Oxford: Polity.

Kasem Sirisamphan. 2002. 'Khwamlomsalai khong khwamwangmai,' *Nation Sutsapda*, 4 February 2002, p. 28.

Kasian Tejapira. 2002. 'Post-crisis economic impasse and political recovery in Thailand: the resurgence of economic nationalism,' *Critical Asian Studies*, 34(3): 323–356.

Katō, Kazuhide. 1995. *Tai gendai seijishi* (History of contemporary Thai politics): Kōbundō.

—— 2000. 'Tai ōkoku no jōin kaikaku to gikaiseiji no hensen (Senate reform and changes in parliamentary politics in the Kingdom of Thailand), *Gikaiseiji kenkyū* (Parliamentary politics research), 54: 27–43.

Katsuda, Kichitarō. 1970. *Minshushugi no gensō* (Illusions of democracy): Nihon Keizai Shimbunsha.

—— 1979. *Jiyūshakai no byōri: gensō no naka no jiyū to byōdō* (Pathology of free society: illusory freedom and equality): Tamagawa Daigaku Shuppanbu.

—— 1994 (1969). 'Gendai minshushugi no kadai' in *Katsuda Kichitarō chosakushū dairokkan* (Kichitarō Katsuda collection vol. 6): Minerva Shobō: 41–76.

Kawamori, Masato. 1997. *Tai: henyōsuru minshushugi no katachi* (Thailand: changing form of democracracy): Ajia Keizai Kenkyūjo.

—— 1998. 'Tai: kōdo keizaiseichō to shiminshakai no keisei katei (Thailand: rapid economic growth and the process of civil society formation)' in Ikuo Iwasaki (ed.), *Ajia to shiminshakai* (Asia and civil society): Ajia Keizai Kenkyūjo: 139–164.

Khan, Mushtaq H. 2000. 'Rents, efficiency and growth' in Mushtaq H. Khan and K. S. Jomo (eds), *Rents, Rent-seeking and Economic Development: Theory and Evidence in Asia*, Cambridge: Cambridge University Press: 21–144.

Kho. Ko. Tho. (Samnakngan khanakammakan lueaktang). 1999. *Raingan kandamnoen kitchakan khong phakkanmueang nai rop pi B. E. 2541*, Bangkok: Phimdi 39.

—— 2000a. 'Raingan phon nap khanaen so. wo. 37,' *http://202.183.254.190/report/*.

—— 2000b. 'Raingan phon kanruam khanaen lueaktang samachik wutthisapha khet lueaktang changwat [number],' *http://202.183.254.190/report/Show001.ASP?ID=[number]*.

—— 2000c. 'Ekkasan naenam tua phusamak changwat,' *http://202.183.254.190/information/showappeal.asp?SSN=[number]&Ename=[province]*.

—— 2000d. *Khomun sathiti lae phonkanlueaktang samachik wutthisapha B. E. 2543*, Bangkok: Khanakammakanlueaktang.

—— 2000e. *Raingan kandamnoen kitchakan khong phakkanmueang nai rop pi B. E. 2542*, Bangkok: Teens Team.

—— 2001a. *Raingan wichai kanlueaktang samachik wutthisapha B. E. 2543*, Bangkok: Khanakammakanlueaktang.

—— 2001b. *Khomun sathiti lae phon kanlueaktang samachiksaphaphuthaen ratsadon B. E. 2544*, Bangkok: S2R Group.

Khanakammakan Yat Wirachon Phruetsapha 35. n. d. *Ramluek 5 pi phruetsapha pracha tham: Kanchamla prawatisat khong prachachon*, Bangkok: Khletthai.

Khana So. So. Ro. 1998. *Ruam sara ratthathammanun chabap prachachon*, Bangkok: Matichon.

Khanin Bunsuwan. 1998. 'Krabuankan tham ngan khong rabop ratthasapha nai ratthathammanun chabap mai' in Khana So. So. Ro., *Ruam sara ratthathammanun chabap prachachon*, Bangkok: Matichon: 225–282.

Khian Thirawit. 1993. *Wikritkan kanmueang thai: karani phruetsapha mahawippayok B. E. 2535*, Bangkok: Matichon.

—— (Khien Theeravit). 1997. *Thailand in Crisis: A Study of the Political*

Turmoil of May 1992, Bangkok: The Thailand Research Fund & The Institute of Asian Studies, Chulalongkorn University.

Kimura, Masaaki. 1993. *Yūtopia igo no seiji* (Politics after a utopia): Yūhikaku.

—— 1996. *Indo gendai seiji: sono hikari to kage* (Contemporary politics in India: light and shadow): Sekai Shisōsha.

Kitahara, Atsushi. 2002a. 'Gendai higashiajia no shakaihendō to sono tenbō (Social changes and outlook in modern East Asia)' in Atsushi Kitahara (ed.), *Kōza higashiajia kingendaishi 6 hendō no higashiajia shakai* (Modern and contemporary history of East Asia course 6 changing East Asian societies): Aoki Shoten: 13–41.

—— 2002b. 'Tai kindai ni okeru shōnō sōshutsuteki tochi seisaku heno michi (jō) (A road to small farm creation policy in modern Thailand vol. 1),' *Keizai kagaku* (Economic science), 50(2): 21–40.

—— 2002c. 'Tai kindai ni okeru shōnō sōshutsuteki tochi seisaku heno michi (ge) (A road to small farm creation policy in modern Thailand vol. 2),' *Keizai kagaku* (Economic science), 50(3): 21–40.

Kramon Thongthammachat. 1998. 'Neaonayobai phuenthan haeng rat' in Khana So. So. Ro., *Ruam sara ratthathammanun chabap prachachon*, Bangkok: Matichon: 217–224.

Kriangkrai Attanan. 1973. *Anuson nai ngan phraratchathan phloengsop chomphon kriangkrai attanan*, Bangkok: 21 Century Watthanatham Kankha.

Kromkanpokkhrong. 1992. *Thesaphiban chabap phiset lueaktang 22 minakhom 2535*, Bangkok: Rongphim suanthongthin kromkanpokkhrong.

—— 1995. *Thesaphiban chabap phiset lueaktang 2 karakkadakhom 2538*, Bangkok: Rongphim suanthongthin kromkanpokkhrong.

—— 1996. *Thesaphiban chabap phiset lueaktang 17 phruetsachikayon 2539*, Bangkok: Rongphim suanthongthin kromkanpokkhrong.

Likhit, Thirawekhin (Likhit Dhiravegin). 1992. *Demi-Democracy: The Evolution of the Thai Political System*, Singapore: Times Academic Press.

—— 1998. 'Khanaratthamontri tam ratthathammanun 2540' in Khana So. So. Ro., *Ruam sara ratthathammanun chabap prachachon*, Bangkok: Matichon: 286–307.

Mahatthai, Krasuang. 1992. *12 duean nai mo. tho.*, Bangkok: Rongphim suanthongthin kromkanpokkhrong.

—— n. d. *Krasuang mahatthai kap hetkan phruetsapha 35*, Bangkok: Rongphim ongkan songkhro thahan phan suk.

—— 1996. *Tarang khomun sathiti prakop ekkasan khomun mahatthai chut 'khomun choeng nayobai samrap phu borihan radap sung' (lem thi 2)*,

Bangkok: Sunsansonthet, samnakngan palatkrasuang mahatthai, krasuang mahatthai.

Mann, Michael. 1993. *The Sources of Social Power*, Volume II, Cambridge: Cambridge University Press.

Manut Watthanakomen. 1986. *Khomun phuenthan phakkanmueang patchuban lae phakkanmueang kap kanlueaktang pi 2522–2529*, Bangkok: Samakhomsangkhommasat haeng prathet thai.

Matichon. 1989. *Tamnan ratthaban thai*, Bangkok: Matichon.

McCargo, Duncan. 1997. *Chamlong Srimuang and the New Thai Politics*, London: Hurst.

—— 1999. 'The international media and the domestic political coverage of the Thai politics,' *Modern Asian Studies*, 33 (3): 551–579.

—— 2002. 'Thailand's January 2001 general elections: vindicating reform?' in Do (ed.), *Reforming Thai Politics*, Copenhagen: Nordic Institute of Asian Studies: 247–259.

Michai Ruchuphan. 2001. *Khwamkhit seri khong michai*, Bangkok: A. R. Business Press.

Montesano, Michael J. 2000. 'Market society and the origins of the new Thai politics' in Ruth McVey (ed.), *Money and Power in Provincial Thailand*, Singapore: ISEAS and Chiengmai: Silkworm: 97–122.

Montri Rupsuwan, Kanchanarat Liwirot, Ruthai Hongsiri, Manit Chumpa lae Khomsan Phokhong. 1999. *Chetanarom khong ratthathammanun*, Bangkok: Winyuchon.

Morell, David and Chai-anan Samudavanija. 1981. *Political Conflict in Thailand*, Cambridge: Oelgeschalager, Gunn & Hain.

Morimoto, Tetsurō. 1997a. 'Daiyon kyōwasei (The fourth republic)' in Kazuyuki Watanabe, Mitsuhiko Minami and Tetsurō Morimoto, *Gendai furansu seijishi* (The history of contemporary French politics): Nakanishiya Shuppan: 148–184.

—— 1997b. 'Daigo kyōwasei (The fifth republic)' in Kazuyuki Watanabe, Mitsuhiko Minami and Tetsurō Morimoto, *Gendai furansu seijishi* (The history of contemporary French politics): Nakanishiya Shuppan: 185–226.

Moriyama, Shigenori. 1998. *Kankoku gendai seiji* (Contemporary Korean politics): Tokyo Daigaku Shuppankai.

Murashima, Eiji. 1980. '70-nendai ni okeru tai nōmin undō no tenkai (Development of the Thai farmers' movement during the 1970s),' *Ajia keizai* (Asian economy), 21(2): 2–30.

—— 1982. '1970-nendai no taikoku ni okeru gakusei undō to kyōsanshugi

(Students' movement and communism in the 1970s Thailand),' *Ajia keizai* (Asian economy), 23(12): 24-49.

---- 1987. 'Tai ni okeru seiji taisei no shūkiteki tenkan (Cyclical transition of the Thai political regime)' in Nobuyuki Hagiwara and Eiji Murashima (eds), *ASEAN shokoku no seiji taisei* (Political regimes in the ASEAN countries): Ajia Keizai Kenkyūjo.

Murashima, Eiji, Nakharain Mektrairat and Somkiat Wanthana. 1991. *The Making of Modern Thai Political Parties*, Tokyo: IDE.

Murray, David. 1996. *Angels and Devils: Thai Politics from February 1991 to September 1992 – A Struggle for Democracy?* Bangkok: White Orchid Press.

Nagai, Fumio. 2001. 'Tojōkoku no chihōbunkenka no genjōhōkoku: tai ni kansuru kēsusutadī (Report on the current state of decentralization in developing countries: case studies in relation to Thailand)' in Kokusai Kyōryoku Jigyōdan, *'Chihōgyōsei to chihōbunken' hōkokusho* (Report on 'local government and decentralization'): Kokusai Kyōryoku Jigyōdan Kokusai Kyōryoku Sōgō Kenshūjo: 47–108.

Narong Phetprasoet. 1997. 'Naksetthasat sithao fangthong ngoen kap sue 2 yang ni yuet amnat dai leo,' *Nation Sutsapda*, 12 September 1997: 10–11.

Nikon Chamnong. 2000. *Borihan ngan satai banhan*, Bangkok: Matichon.

NSO (National Statistical Office). *Statistical Yearbook Thailand*.

Ockey, Jim. 1999. 'Creating the Thai middle class' in Michael Pinches (ed.), *Culture and Privilege in Capitalist Asia*, London: Routledge: 230–250.

Okazaki, Hisahiko, Akihiko Fujii and Junko Yokota. 1993. *Kūdetā no seijigaku: seiji no tensai no kuni tai* (Political science of coup d'état: Thailand, the country of political genius): Chūkō Shinsho.

O'Loughlin, John, Michael D. Ward, Corey L. Lofdahl, Jordin S. Cohen, David S. Brown, David Reilly, Kristian S. Gleditsch, and Michael Shin. 1998. 'The diffusion of democracy, 1946–1994,' *Annals of the Association of American Geographers*, 88(4): 545–574.

Parichart Chotiya. 1997. 'The changing role of provincial business in the Thai political economy' in Kevin Hewison (ed.), *Political Change in Thailand: Democracy and Participation*, London: Routledge: 251–264.

Pasuk Phongpaichit. 1999. *Civilising the State: State, Civil Society and Politics in Thailand* (The Wertheim Lecture 1999), Amsterdam: Centre for Asian Studies Amsterdam.

Pasuk Phongpaichit and Chris Baker. 1995. *Thailand: Economy and Politics*, Kuala Lumpur: Oxford University Press.

—— 1997. 'Power in transition: Thailand in the 1990s' in Hewison (ed.),

Political Change in Thailand: Democracy and Participation, London: Routledge: 21–41.

—— 2000. *Thailand's Crisis*, Chiang Mai: Silkworm.

Pasuk Phongpaichit, Sungsidh Piriyarangsan and Nualnoi Treerat. 1998. *Guns, Girls, Gambling, Ganja: Thailand's Illegal Economy and Public Policy*, Chiang Mai: Silkworm.

Pathan Suwannamongkhon (ed.), n. d. *Prawat samachik ratthasapha thai B. E. 2529*, Bangkok: Social Science Association of Thailand.

Pei, Minsin. 1998. 'The fall and rise of democracy in East Asia' in Larry Diamond and Marc F. Plattner (eds), *Democracy in East Asia*, Baltimore: Johns Hopkins University Press, chapter 5.

Phongthep Thepkanchana. 1998. 'San tam ratthathammanun chabap patchuban' in Khana So. So. Ro., *Ruam sara ratthathammanun chabap prachachon*, Bangkok: Matichon: 308–319.

Phuchatkan. 1992. *Phruetsapha Thamin*, Bangkok: Phuchatkan.

Phumiphonadunyadet. 1991. *Phraratchadamrat phraratchathan kae khanabukkhon tangtang thi khaofao thawai mongkhon nai okat wan chaloemphraratchaphansa wan thi 4 thanwakhom 2534* (Royal Speech Given to the Audience of Well-Wishers on the Occasion of the Royal Birthday Anniversary Wednesday December 1991), Bangkok: Amarin Printing Group.

Poguntke, Thomas and Webb, Thomas. 2005. 'The Presidentialization of Politics in Democratic Societies: A Framework for Analysys,' in Poguntke, Thomas and Webb, Thomas (eds) *The Presidentialization of Politics: A Comparative Study of Modern Democracies*, Oxford: Oxford University Press: 1–25.

Potter, David. 1993. 'Democratization in Asia' in David Held (ed.), *Prospects for Democracy: North, South, East, West*, Stanford: Stanford University Press: 355–379.

—— 1997. 'Explaining democratization' in David Potter, David Goldblatt, Margaret Kiloh, Paul Lewis (eds), *Democratization*, Cambridge: Polity: 1–40.

Praman Adireksan. 1999. *Chiwit thi phop phan lae phan phon khong phonek/ phontamruatek praman adireksan* (phim phuea pen thiraluk nai wara ayu khrop 84 pi), n. p.: Munlanithi phuea sangkhom thai.

Pramuan Rutchanaseri. 2005. *Phraratchaamnat*, Bangkok: Sumet Rutchanaseri.

Praphat Charusathian. 1998. *Amuson ngan phraratchathan phloengsop chomphon praphat charusathian*, Bangkok: Arunkanphim.

Praphat Pintoptaeng. 1988. *Kanmueang bon thanon 99 wan samatcha khon chon lae prawatisat kandoenkabuan chumnum prathuang nai sanghom thai*, Bangkok: Mahawitthayalai Kroek.

Prasong Sunsiri. 1989. *726 wan tai banlang prem*, Bangkok: Matichon.

Prasoet Patthamasukhon. 1974. *Ratthasapha thai nai rop si-sip-song pi 2475–2517*, Bangkok: Cho. Chumnumchang.

Prawet Wasi. 1995. *Kanpatirup thang kanmueang: thang ok khong prathet thai*, Bangkok: Mochaoban.

——— 1997a. *Kandoen thang haeng khwamkhit: patirup kanmueang*, Bangkok: Mochaoban.

——— 1997b. *Bonsenthang chiwit*, 7, Bangkok: Mochaoban, bot thi 90: 51–62.

Prudhisan Jumbala. 1992. *Nation-Building and Democratization in Thailand: A political History*, Bangkok: Chulalongkorn University Social Research Institute.

Prudhisan Jumbala and Maneerat Mitprasat. 1997. 'Non-governmental development organizations: empowerment and environment' in Kevin Hewison (ed.), *Political Change in Thailand: Democracy and Participation*, London: Routledge: 195–216.

Randolph, R. Sean. 1986. *The United States and Thailand: Alliance Dynamics, 1950–1985*, Berkeley: Institute of East Asian Studies, University of California.

Rangsan Thanaphonphan. 1989. *Krabuankan kamnot nayobai setthakit nai prathet thai: botwikhro choeng prawatisat setthakit kanmueang B. E. 2475–2530*, Bangkok: Samakhomsangkhommasat haeng prathet thai.

——— 1993. *Anitchalaksana khong kanmueang thai: setthasat wikhro waduai kanmueang*, Bangkok: Phuchatkan.

Ratchakitchaanubeksa, 91. pt. 159, p. special 12, 92, pt. 203, p. special 7, 93, pt. 78, p. 1221.

Riggs, Fred W. 1966. *Thailand: The Modernization of a Bureaucratic Polity*, Honolulu: East-West Center Press.

RPKP (Raingankanprachum khanakammakan phitcharana rang ratthathammanun), 21 mithunayon 2540.

RPRS (Raingan kanprachum ruamkan khong ratthasapha), khrang thi 3, 4 and 7, duan kanyayon, B. E. 2540.

RPSR (Raingan prachum sapha rangratthathammanun), khrang thi 29 and 24.

RT (Ratthaban Thai, Khanakammakan truat sop kho thetching). 1992. *Raingan phon truat sop kho thetching kiaokap kankratham khwamphit lae samruat khasiahai nueangnai kanchumnumkan rawang wan thi 17–20 phruetsaphakhom 2535*.

Rueschemeyer, Dietrich, Evelyne Huber Stephens, and John D. Stephens. 1992. *Capitalist Development & Democracy*, Cambridge: Polity.

Sakagami, Takashi. 1999. *Kindaiteki tōchi no tanjō: jinkō, yoron, kazoku* (The birth of modern government: population, public opinion, family): Iwanami Shoten.

SAP (Phak Kitchasangkhom = Social Action Party). 1974. *Pratya lae chutprasong khong phak kitchasangkhom*, Bangkok: Rongphim Yanhi.

Sane Chamarik. 1997. *Kanmueang thai kap phatthanakan ratthathammanun*, Bangkok: Munlanithi khrongkan tamra sangkhommasat lae manutsayasat.

—— 1998. *Than khit su thang lueak mai khong sangkhom thai (Withithat chut phumipanya 3)*, Bangkok: Amarin.

Sangsit Phiriyarangsan and Phasuk Phongphaichit (eds). 1993. *Chonchan klang bon krasae prachathipatai*, Bangkok: Sunsuksa Setthasat Kanmueang.

Sapharangratthathammanun. 1998. 'Prachachon cha dai arai chak (rang) ratthathammanun' in *Anuson nai ngan phraratchathan phloengsop nai phan bunyachit*: Mai prakot thi phim: 117–149.

SC (Siam Chotmaihet). 1999. *Siam Chotmaihet CD-ROM: Banthuek khaosan lae hetkan rawang 1 mokkarakhom 2519 thung 31 thanwakhom 2541*, Bangkok: Progress Information.

Shiraishi, Takashi. 2000. *Umi no teikoku* (Empires of the sea): Chukō Shinsho.

SKT (Samakhom nak khao haeng prathet thai). 1992. *Banthuek yiao khao na samonraphum thanon ratchadamnoen phruetsaphakhom 2535*, Bangkok: Dokbia.

SLN (Samnak lekhathikan nayokratthamotri). 1992a. *Ngan khong ratthaban anan panyarachun lem 1*, Bangkok: J. Film Process.

—— 1992b. *Ngan khong ratthaban anan panyarachun lem 2*, Bangkok: Amarin Printing Group.

SLR (Samnak lekhathikan ratthasapha). 1989. *Thamniap samachik saphaphuthaenratsadon 2532*, Bangkok: Kongkanphim Samnaklekhathikanratthasapha.

SLW (Samnakngan lekhathikan wutthisapha). 1995. *Thamniap samachik wutthisapha 2538*, Bangkok: Kongkanphim, Samnakngan Lekhathikan Ratthasapha.

—— 1996. *Thamniap samachik wutthisapha 2539*, Bangkok: Kongkanphim, Samnakngan Lekhathikan Ratthasapha.

SNNT (Sunklang nisit naksueksa haeng prathet thai). 1974. *Khabuankan prachachon tulakhom 2516*, Bangkok: Krungsayam Kanphim.

Sombat Chanthonwong. (Sombat Chantornvong) 2002. 'The 1997 Constitution and the politics of electoral reform' in Duncan McCargo (ed.), *Reforming Thai Politics*, Copenhagen: Nordic Institute of Asian Studies: 203–222.

—— 2006. 'Reforming Thailand: Kho sanoe kiaokap kanlueaktang 2550' (*http://www.onopen.com/2006/01/1352*, posted on 28 Dec 2006).
Sombat Chantornvong and Montri Chenvidyakarn. 1991. 'Constitutional rule and the institutionalization of leadership and security in Thailand' in Stephen Chee (ed.), *Leadership and Security in Southeast Asia*, Singapore: ISEAS: 141–178.
Somchai Phakhaphatwiwat, 'Kanpatirup kanmueang thai kap ngueankhai thang setthakit,' *Nation Sutsapda*, 29 August 1997, p. 18.
Somkhit Loetphaithun, Bunsi Miwongukhot lae Sakon Waranyuwatthana. 1998. *Raingan kanwichai rueang ngop phatthana changwat khong samachik sapha phuthaen ratsadon*, Bangkok: Kongkanphim Samnaknganlekhathikan Saphaphuthaenratsadon.
Sonoda, Shigeto. 1998. 'Shakai kaisō no kōzō henyō: taitōsuru ajia no chūkansō (Structural changes in social classes: the emerging middle classes in Asia)' in Satoshi Amako (ed.), *Ajia no 21-seiki: rekishiteki tenkan no isō* (Asia in the 21st century: the historical transition phase): Kinokuniya Shoten: 97–128.
—— 2002. 'Yutakasa no nakano kakusa (Disparities in wealth)' in Atsushi Kitahara (ed.), *Kōza higashiajia kingendaishi 6 hendō no higashiajia shakai (Modern and contemporary history of East Asia course 6 changing East Asian societies)*: Aoki Shoten: 77–101.
SPR (Khanakammakan sueksa lae sanoenae mattrakan phoem prasitthiphap kanborihan chatkan rabop kanngoen khong prathet). 1998. *Raingan phon kanwikhro lae winitchai kho thetching kiaokap sathanakan wikkrit thang setthakit*, Bangkok: Munlanithi sathaban wichai phuea phatthana prathet thai.
SR (Sapha rang ratthathammanun). 1997. *(Rang) ratthathammanun haeng ratchaanachak thai chabap prachachon*, Bangkok: Khanakammathikan prachasamphan, Sapha rang ratthathammanun.
Suchinda Khraprayun. 1992. 'Kham wai alai' in *Anuson ngan phraratchathan phloengsop khunpho kamon kraisan*, Bangkok: Arunkanphim.
Suchit Bunbongkarn. 1996. *Thailand: State of the Nation*, Singapore: ISEAS.
Suehiro, Akira. 1993. 'Tai no gunbu to minshuka undō: 73-nen "10-gatsu seihen" kara 92-nen "5-gatsu ryūketsu jiken" he (The Thai military and democratization movement: from the 1973 "October uprising" to the 1992 "May bloody incident"),' *Shakai Kagaku Kenkyū* (Social science research), 44 (5): 48–95.
—— 1998a. 'Rōdōryoku chōsa (Workforce survey)' in do (ed.), *Tai no tōkei seido to shuyō keizai seiji dēta* (Thailand's statistical system and main economic and political data): Ajia Keizai Kenkyūjo: 73–100.

—— 1998b. 'Keizai no kakudai to baburukeizaika (Economic expansion and economic bubbles)' in Do (ed.), *Taikoku jōhō (bessatsu) Tai – keizai būmu, keizai kiki, kōzō chōsei* (Thailand country information (supplementary volume) Thailand – economic boom, economic crisis and structural adjustment): Zaidanhōjin Nihon Tai Kyōkai: 13–46.

—— 1998c. 'Toripuru kiki no hassei to keizai saiken no mosaku (The outbreak of a triple crisis and a search for economic rebuilding)' in Do (ed.), *Taikoku jōhō (bessatsu) Tai – keizai būmu, keizai kiki, kōzō chōsei* (Thailand country information (supplementary volume) Thailand – economic boom, economic crisis and structural adjustment): Zaidanhōjin Nihon Tai Kyōkai: 47–77.

—— 1999. 'Tai no keizai kiki to kinyū sangyō no jiyūka (Thai economic crisis and financial and industrial deregulation),' *Keizai kenkyū* (Economic research), 50 (2): 120–132.

—— 2000. *Kyacchiappugata kōgyōkaron* (Catch-up-style industrialization theory): Nagoya Daigaku Shuppankai.

Surachat Bamrungsuk (Surachart Bamrungsuk). 1998a. *Thahan kap prachathipatai thai: chak 14 tula su patchuban lae anakhot*, Bangkok: Sun wichai lae phalit tamra, Kroek University.

—— 1998b. 'Changing patterns of civil-military relations and Thailand's regional outlook' in David R. Mares (ed.), *Civil-Military Relations: Building Democracy and Regional Security in Latin America, Southern Asia, and Central Europe*, Boulder: Westview: 187–205.

—— 2000. *Thahan kap kanmueang thai nai satttawat na: phatthanakan lae khwamplianplaeng*, Bangkok: Chulangkorn University.

—— 2001. 'Thailand: military professionalism at the crossroad' in Muthiah Alagappa (ed.), *Military Professionalism in Asia: Conceptual and Empirical Perspectives*, Honolulu: East-West Center: 77–91.

Surin Maisrikrod. 1992. *Thailand's Two General Elections in 1992: Democracy Sustained*, Singapore: ISEAS.

—— 1997. 'The making of Thai democracy: a study of political alliances among the state, the capitalists, and the middle class' in Anek Laothamatas (ed.), *Democratization in Southeast and East Asia*, Singapore: ISEAS.

—— 1999. 'Changing forms of democracy in Asia?: some observations on the Thai and Philippine constitutions,' *Asian Studies Review*, 23(3): 355–373.

Surin Maisrikrod and Duncan McCargo. 1997. 'Electoral politics: commercialization and exclusion' in Kevin Hewison (ed.), *Political Change in Thailand: Democracy and Participation*, London: Routledge: 132–148.

Suthachai Yimprasoet. 2001. 'Prawatisat khong phak naeo thang sangkhomniyom' in Somphon Chanthonchai (ed.), *Prachachon tong pen yai nai phaendin: ramluek 25 pi dr. bunsanong bunyothaya*, Bangkok: Dueantula: 96–110.

Suthy Prasatset. 1995. 'The rise of NGOs as critical social movement in Thailand' in Jaturong Boonyarattanasoontorn and Gawin Chutima (eds), *Thai NGOs: The Continuing Struggle for Democracy*, Bangkok: Thai NGO Support Project: 97–134.

Takahashi, Masaki. 1997. 'Kanbojia funsō to taikoku kyōsantō no hōkai: chiiki shisutemu to tai kokka shisutemu (Cambodian conflict and the collapse of the Communist Party of Thailand: the regional system and the state system of Thailand),' *Chuo Daigaku Shakai Kagaku Kenkyūjo Hōkoku dai-18-go* (Chuo University Institute of Social Sciences Report 18).

Takahashi, Takuma, Chi Hung, Kwan and Tetsuji Sano. 1998. *Ajia kinyū kiki* (Asian financial crisis): Tōyō Keizai Shimpōsha.

Takeda, Yasuhiro. 2001. *Minshuka no hikaku seiji: higashiajia shokoku no taisei hendō katei* (Comparative politics of democratization: the process of regime change in the East Asian countries): Minerva Shobō.

Tamada, Yoshifumi. 1988. 'Tai no jitsugyōka seitō to gun (Thailand's business-political parties and the military),' *Tōnanajia kenkyū* (Southeast Asian studies), 26(3): 293–307.

——— 1991. 'Itthiphon and Amnat: an informal aspect of Thai politics,' *Tōnanajia kenkyū* (Southeast Asian studies), 28(4): 455–466.

——— 1992a. 'Tai no kūdeta, 1980–1991: gun no dōkisei, naibu kōsō, tai seifu kankei (Military coups in Thailand, 1980–1991: military classmates, internal conflicts, government relations),' *Tōnanajia kenkyū* (Southeast Asian studies), 29(4): 389–421.

——— 1992b. '"Bōgyaku no 5-gatsu" jiken to chamurōn sīmuan no hansuto sengen (The "barbarian May" incident and Chamlong Simueang's hunger strike action),' *Tōnanajia kenkyū* (Southeast Asian studies), 30(3): 376–377.

——— 1996. *Tai gyōsei soshikishi 1892–1993: kyoku ijō no soshiki no hensen* (Thailand's administrative organizations 1892–1993: organizational changes to agencies on and above the bureau level) (1995 Ministry of Education scientific research grant general research (C) research paper): Kyoto Daigaku Tōnanajia Kenkyū Sentā.

——— 1998. 'Guntai no seijiryoku to jinji idō (Political power of the military and personnel changes)' in Akira Suehiro (ed.), *Tai no tōkei seido to shuyō keizai seiji dēta* (Thailand's statistical system and main economic and political data): Ajia Keizai Kenkyūjo: 287–313.

——— 2001. 'Tai no kaihatsu jigyō ni okeru chūōshūken to chihōbunken (Centralization and decentralization of power in development projects in

Thailand),' *Tojōkoku no chihōbunken to kaihatsu* (Decentralization and development in developing countries), (scientific research grant foundation research (B)(2) research paper, research leader Michio Muramatsu): 1–19.

——— 2002. 'Taigun no jinji idō to seijiryoku teika (Personnel changes in the Thai military and a decrease in political power),' *Ajia afurika chiiki kenkyū* (Asia and African area studies), 2: 120–172.

Thahan Kao. 1978. *Phanathan hoi*, Bangkok: P. G. Press.

Thak Chaloemtiarana. 1989. *Tai – dokusaiteki onjōshugi no seiji* (Thailand – the politics of despotic paternalism), Translated by Yoshifumi Tamada: Imura Bunka Jigyōsha.

Thamniap. 1988. *Thamniap naithahan thi samret kansueksa B. E. 2501*, Bangkok: Rongphim Kromsarabanthahanakat.

Thirayut Bunmi. 1994. *Suan nueng khong khwamsongcham 20 pi 14 tula lae pai khang na*, Bangkok: Winyuchon.

Tilly, Charles. 1992. *Coercion, Capital and European States, AD 990–1992*, Oxford: Blackwell.

——— 2000. 'Process and mechanism of democratization,' *Sociological Theory*, 18(1): 1–16.

Tsunekawa, Keiichi. 2000. 'Joron "minshuka" to kokusai seiji keizai (Introduction "democratization" and international politics and economy) in Nihon Kokusai Seiji Gakkai (ed.), *'Minshuka' to kokusai seiji keizai (kokusai seiji 125)* ('Democratization' and international politics and economy (international politics 125)): 1–13.

Uthai Phimchaichon. 1998. 'Ratthathammanun chabap prachachon miti mai nai sangkhom thai' in Khana So. So. Ro., *Ruam sara ratthathammanun chabap prachachon*, Bangkok: Matichon: 1–36.

Vishnu Cholitkul. 1992. 'A professional association,' *Manager* (42) (June 1992).

Wanmuhamatno Matha. 1998. 'Khamnam chak prathan ratthasapha' in Khana So. So. Ro., *Ruam sara ratthathammanun chabap prachachon*, Bangkok: Matichon: 15–21.

Watsana Nanuam. 2002a. *Khwamkhit thang kanmueang khong phonek suchinda khraprayun*, M. A. thesis: Faculty of Political Science, Thammasat University.

——— 2002b. *Banthuk khamhaikan suchinda khraprayun: Kamnoet lae awasan ro. so. cho.*, Bangkok: Matichon.

Wiangrat Netipho. 1997. *Chaopō: chihō kara mita tai seiji no renzokusei* (Cao pho: the continuity of Thai politics viewed from the provinces), M.A. thesis: Kyoto University Graduate School of Law.

Wiraphong Ramangkun. 2001. *Khon doen trok*, Bangkok: Matichon.
Withaya Sucharitthanarugse. 1983. 'The Thai concept of power' in Ernest E. Boesch (ed.), *Thai Culture: Reports on the Second Thai-European Research Seminar 1982*, Saarbrucken: University of the Saar: 493–537.
Yamakage, Susumu. 2001. 'Anteisei shinwa no kokufuku ni mukete (To overcome the stability myth),' *Ajiken wārudo torendo* (Ajiken world trends), July 2001: 2–5.
Yamamoto, Hiroshi. 1998. *Tai tōgyōshi: yushutsu taikoku heno kiseki* (History of the Thai sugar industry: the path to a major exporting country): Ochanomizu Shobō.
—— 2000. 'Tōgyō seisaku: buntōhō to seifu, nōmin, kōjō (Sugar industry policy: profit distribution policy and the government, growers and mills)' in Akira Suehiro and Shigeki Higashi (eds), *Tai no keizai seisaku: seido, soshiki, akutā* (Economic policy of Thailand: systems, organizations and actors): Ajia Keizai Kenkyūjo: 179–213.
Yuenyat Chaisamut. 1997. 'Khit yang ratthaburut,' *Nation Sutsapda*, 8 August 1997, p. 20.

Newspapers and magazines

Dailies: (Thai language) *Ban Mueang, Daily Mirror, Daily News, Dao Sayam, Khao Sot, Matichon, Naeona, Phuchatkan, Sayam Rat, Thai Rat, KT (Krungthep Thurakit), Thai Post, Prachachat Thurakit*, (English language) *The Nation, Bangkok Post*.
Weeklies: (Thai language) *Athit, Khao Thai, Krungthep Thuraki Sutsapda, Lak Thai, Matichon Sutsapda, Nation Sutsapda, Sayam Rat Sapdawichan, Su Anakhot*, (English language) *BPWR (Bangkok Post Weekly Review)*.

Name Index

Individuals

Adisai Photharamik 214, 224
Akon Huntrakun 218, 319
Amon Chantharasombun 117, 126, 129, 165, 323
Amon Raksasat 146
Anan Kalintha 36, 274
Anan Panyarachun 15, 24–25, 89–92, 128, 131, 152, 160–162, 172, 195, 251, 279, 288, 296, 297, 302, 304, 307, 308, 329
Anek Laothammathat 4, 13, 167, 172, 262, 269, 281
Athit Kamlangek 81, 286

Banhan Sinlapaacha 25, 35–36, 100, 126–131, 169, 172, 212, 218–219, 225, 274, 295, 296, 306, 307, 327
Banyat Banthatthan 222
Bowonsak Uwanno 119, 126, 132, 134, 135–136, 140, 142, 144, 166–167, 197, 293–294, 305
Bunchai Bencharongkhakun 224
Bunchu Rotchanasathian 317
Bunyasit Chokphatthana 224

Chaianan Samutthawanit 3, 108, 129, 163, 164–165, 177, 262, 271
Chainarong Nunphakd 84–86, 88, 90, 92, 93, 96, 98–99
Chaiyasit Chinnawat 107, 248, 191
Chalat Hiransiri 19, 271, 292
Chalat Worachat 39, 44, 46, 110, 116–117, 165, 276, 277, 281, 293, 315

Chaloem Yubamrung 129
Chamlong Simueang 26, 31, 39–46, 48–49, 51–60, 63–67, 86–87, 89, 252–253, 277, 278, 279, 280, 281, 287, 288, 317
Chan Bunprasoet 93–96, 101, 284
Chatchai Chunhawan 21, 24, 35, 83–84, 197, 284, 286, 304, 306
Chatri Sophonphanit 224, 319
Chawalit Yongchaiyut (Chavalit Yongchaiyudh) 5, 25, 35, 41, 44–45, 50, 65, 66, 68, 72, 75, 82–84, 87–93, 95–96, 99–101, 103, 106, 108, 131, 160, 162–163, 172, 273, 276, 284, 285, 286, 287, 288, 289, 290, 291, 292, 304–305, 308, 328
Chettha Thanacharo 90, 93–94, 96, 98, 101, 103, 291, 292
Chotchoi Sophonphanit 182
Chuan Likphai 25, 65–66, 90, 96, 101, 163, 221–222, 230, 281,

Itsaraphong Nunphakdi 37–38, 84–86, 88, 90, 93, 98, 101, 273, 275, 284, 286, 287

Kasem Sirisamphan 149, 249
Kaset Rotchananin 36–38, 273, 274, 275
Kasian Techaphira 258
Khasem Kraisan 36
Khothom Ariya 43–44, 52–53, 277, 278
Khuekrit Pramot (Kukrit Pramoj) 18, 41, 46, 270, 306
King, the 14, 18, 20–21, 25, 34, 39, 42,

Name Index

45, 47, 51, 55–57, 58, 75, 88–89, 99, 108, 119, 129, 136, 138, 156, 262–264, 271, 272, 276, 277, 279, 288, 302, 312, 321, 328
Kriangsak Chamanan 18–20, 23, 240, 292,
Krit Siwara 17, 270

Michai Ruchuphan 162, 296
Montri Phongphanit 36, 42, 306

Narong Wongwan 35–37, 275

Parinya Thewanaruemitkun 43
Phaibun Emphan 92
Phichit Kunlawanit 91–92, 99, 284, 290
Phongthep Thepkanchana 147, 150
Photchaman Chinnawat (Pojaman Shinawatra) 212
Phothiphong Lamsam 213
Phriophan Damaphong 248
Plaek Phibunsongkhram 205, 284
Pracha Malinon 214, 224
Praman Adireksan 36, 218, 271, 286, 292, 306
Pramon Phalasin 85, 92–93, 98, 101, 103, 289
Praphat Charusathian 17, 18, 78, 286
Prawet Wasi 117, 126, 155, 268, 293, 294, 295, 297,
Prem Tinsulanon 5, 16, 19–21, 38, 51, 56, 75, 82, 89–90, 96, 99, 107, 241, 263, 271, 272, 273, 274, 279, 284, 287, 288, 289, 290, 296
Princess Sirinthon 53, 56

Samak Sunthorawet 36, 270
Samphao Chusi 86, 93
Sane Chamarik 172, 307

Sangat Chaloyu 18
Sano Thiangthong (Snoh Thienthong) 131, 171, 218, 225, 306, 321, 326–327
Sanya Thammasak 18, 272
Sarit Thanarat 84, 245, 262, 272, 282
Seni Pramot 18, 270
Sit Chirarot (Sitthi Chirarochana) 34
Soeharto 11, 245
Sombun Rahong 36, 89
Somchai Wongsawat 248
Somkhit Chatusiphithak 214
Somphong Amonwiwat 228
Somsak Thepsuthin 214
Somthat Attanan 97, 107
Suchinda Khraprayun 24–25, 31, 33–42, 45–46, 49, 55–59, 64, 66–67, 69, 82, 83–94, 98–99, 101, 252–253, 273, 274, 275, 276, 279, 284, 285, 286, 287, 289, 315,
Suchit Bunbongkan 137
Surayut Chulanon 86, 94, 96–98, 101, 103, 106, 107, 284, 287, 289, 290, 291
Suwat Lippataphanlop 212

Thaksin Chinnawat ix, 26, 106–109, 212, 221, 222–225, 228, 231, 240, 247–249, 260–266, 281, 291, 317, 321, 322, 326
Thanin Chiarawanon (Dhanin Chearavanont) 5, 224
Thanin Kraiwichian 19, 271, 272
Thanom Kittikhachon 17, 18, 71, 78, 205, 242

Uthai Phimchaichon 131, 140, 142, 212, 299, 306

Weng Tochirakan 128

Wimon Wongwanit 90, 92–93, 98, 101, 104, 287, 289
Wirot Saengsanit 85, 275

Yaowapha Wongsawat 228
Yutthasak Sasiprapha 97, 290

Organizations

Administrative Court 120, 139, 156–157, 199, 302
Air Defense Unit 79, 85–86
Air Force 36–37, 74, 84, 274, 286, 291
Aphirak Chakri 117
Army 17, 19, 24, 33–35, 37–38, 41, 51, 72–74, 77, 79, 81–101, 104, 106–108, 186, 191, 248, 261, 263–264, 270–271, 276, 283–292
Army Academy (Chunlachomklao Royal Military Academy) 51

Bangkok Metropolitan Authority (BMA) 46
Bureau of Budget 199

Campaign for Popular Democracy (CPD) 34, 39, 41, 43–45, 52–53
Capital Security Command 44–45, 48, 50, 87–88, 277
Chamber of Commerce 121, 140
Charoen Phokkhaphan (CP) 5, 224
Chulalongkorn University 63, 119, 161, 274, 278
Chunlachomklao Royal Military Academy 51, 77
Civil Service Commission 151, 192, 199, 312
Committee on Developing Democracy (CDD) 116, 117, 119–120, 125–127, 132, 135–136, 297, 299
Confederation for Democracy (samaphan prachathipatai: CFD) 46–48, 52–53, 58–59, 65, 68, 281
Constitution Court 120, 156–157, 160, 180, 197, 222, 248, 302–303, 310, 323–324
Constitution Drafting Assembly (CDA) 112, 116, 131–136, 144, 146, 148–150, 152, 154, 162–164, 171, 196–197, 212, 217, 294, 296, 297, 301, 304, 306, 313
Council of State 132, 165, 199

Election Commission 108, 139, 142–143, 145, 155, 159–160, 163, 179, 183–184, 186, 199, 202–203, 206, 212, 215, 218–219, 221, 232, 302, 309–310, 313–314, 317–318, 323–324

Federation of Industry 121
First Division 79, 84, 92, 99, 107, 263, 285–286, 290
Fourth Cavalry Battalion 264

Government House 48, 58, 88, 172, 264

IMF 161

Mass Communication Organization of Thailand 56, 96, 278
Ministry of Finance 160, 283
Ministry of the Interior (Interior Ministry) 4–5, 42, 46, 48, 65, 66, 115, 117, 130, 142, 186, 188, 190, 199, 218, 225, 273, 278, 283, 292, 294, 301, 311, 318

National Administrative Reform Council 18–19
National Counter Corruption Commission 139, 156–157, 160, 302
National Peace–Keeping Council 24, 33, 84, 276, 301, 308
National Statistical Office 170, 191, 312
Navy 18–19, 74, 84

Phuchatkan 57, 61–62, 68, 117, 165, 278–280, 307
Political Reform Committee 116, 126–128
Public Health Ministry 186, 188, 190
Public Relations Department 47, 50, 56, 278, 327
Ramkhamhaeng University 51
Revenue Department 50

Santi Asok 51, 55, 60, 67, 317
Second Cavalry Division 79, 263–264
Second Infantry Division 79, 92, 107, 191
Social Science Association of Thailand 61–62, 280
Special Warfare Unit 79, 85–86, 88, 96, 287, 291
Student Federation of Thailand (SFT) 39
Supreme Commander of the Armed Forces 18, 37–38, 74, 90–91, 95–97, 99, 101, 107, 274, 286, 290–291
Supreme Court 19, 120, 156–157, 197, 199, 263, 302–303

Thammasat University 18, 117, 256, 275

The Council for Democratic Reform under a Constitutional Monarchy 261

Political Parties

Chat Phatthana Party 109, 204–206, 212, 214, 218–219, 227–228, 235, 238, 249, 304, 314, 320
Chat Thai Party 21, 25, 35–37, 47, 89, 116, 126, 131, 203–207, 212–214, 217–220, 227, 231, 235, 244–245, 249, 271, 274–275, 291–292, 295, 305–306, 319, 324–325, 327

Democrat Party 18, 25, 34, 37, 64–66, 96, 98, 101, 115, 127, 160, 163, 201, 204–206, 213, 218–219, 221–223, 227, 270–271, 281, 291, 293, 303, 305–306, 314–315, 321, 325
Democratic Socialist Party 22–23

Ekkaphap Party 35

New Aspiration Party 25, 34–35, 37, 41, 50, 64, 131, 203–207, 209, 211–212, 221–222, 227–228, 231, 238, 249, 273–274, 276, 281, 319, 322, 326, 328
New Force Party 22–23, 272

Phalang Tham Party 34, 37, 40, 43, 51, 64–66, 86–87, 117, 129, 205, 281, 315, 317
Prachakon Thai Party 36–37, 225, 305

Ratsadon Party 215, 234, 315, 322, 326

Sahapracha Thai Party 205
Sammakkhitham Party 36–37, 238, 273, 322
Seri Manangkasila Party 205
Seritham Party 204, 207, 211–212, 231, 296, 318
Social Action Party 18, 36–37, 42, 65, 115, 205, 211, 235, 243, 249, 276, 306, 323
Socialist Front Party 22, 272
Socialist Party 22–23, 272

Thai Rak Thai Party 26, 202–207, 209, 212, 214, 216–218, 220–225, 227–228, 239–240, 246, 249, 260–261, 291, 317–320, 322, 325–328
Thin Thai Party 318, 324

Locations

Buri Ram 145, 219–220, 238

Chachoengsao 217
Chanthaburi 66, 235
Chiang Mai 51, 79, 192, 216, 222, 228, 316, 320, 322
Chitlada Palace 45, 58, 279
Chon Buri 217, 299, 324–325

Democracy Monument 43–44, 49

East Asia 13

Indonesia 11, 245

Khon Kaen 51, 220–221, 227, 235, 313–314

Laos 11

Malaysia 11, 13
Myanmar (Burma) 245, 291

Nakhon Ratchasima 146, 182, 192, 219
Nakhon Sawan 151, 235, 320
Nakhon Si Thammarat 148, 192, 314

Phan Fa Bridge 39, 43–44, 48–50, 66, 278
Phetchabun 214, 217, 238
Philippines, the 10
Ratchadamnoen Avenue 39, 43, 45, 50–51, 53, 58–59, 278
Ratchadamnoen Nok Avenue 48–49
Roi Et 23, 238, 325
Royal Hotel 50, 54
Royal Plaza 39, 41

Sakon Nakhon 238
Samut Prakan 215, 314
Sanam Luang 34, 39, 41–48, 50, 57–59, 65, 278–280
Singapore 11, 13
Songkhla 51, 140, 150, 217, 299
South Korea 10–13, 56
Southeast Asia 10, 13, 259, 280
Sukhothai 191, 217
Suphan Buri 169, 219

Taiwan 10–12

Ubon Ratchathani 180, 192, 216, 313, 324
Udon Thani 192
US 10–11, 18, 37, 59, 269, 284, 294

Vietnam 11, 18, 20

Subject Index

14 October 1973 uprising 17, 41, 60–61, 65, 87, 250, 270, 276
1978 Constitution 19, 22, 33
1991 Constitution 33, 125–128, 130–131, 134–136, 141, 175, 178, 296, 302, 305
1991 coup 16, 25, 39, 70, 81, 94, 99, 251, 273, 275, 284, 286–287, 295
1997 Constitution i, 1–2, 26, 112–113, 115–116, 122, 132–134, 136, 138–139, 141, 144, 157, 164–165, 173–175, 177, 184, 188, 191, 194, 196–197, 201–202, 206, 214, 218, 221, 229–231, 242, 247, 249, 255–260, 264–265, 293, 299, 301–303, 309, 316
6 October 1976 incicident 18–19

artillery 77, 86, 284

bachelor clause 121–122, 138, 144–145, 147–148, 151–152, 154–155, 162, 196
Bangkok Governor 51
bloodshed 6, 30, 49, 51, 55–59, 63–64, 72, 94, 99, 297
broadcast media 53–54, 56, 170, 282
Buddhism 41–42, 119
bureaucracy 2–4, 100, 115, 121, 165, 177, 254, 260, 292, 309, 311
bureaucratic polity 2–4, 115, 176, 250, 309
business associations 4
business community 3, 5, 12, 20–21, 155, 168, 223–224, 242, 250, 254, 257, 259, 268

cabinet minister 4, 117, 138, 151–152, 172, 239–240, 326
cavalry 77, 284
censorship 53–54
CEO 5, 247–249
Channel 11 47, 278
Channel 5 41, 45, 50, 53, 278–279
chao pho 169, 173, 217, 301, 306
checks and balances 75, 121, 245, 260
China 11, 18, 20, 181, 191
civil society 6, 9–11, 13–14, 68, 254, 269, 281
Class
  Class 1 77, 82–84, 101–102, 107, 274, 276, 285, 290–291
  Class 5 34, 81–86, 88, 90–93, 98–102, 273, 275, 284–287, 289
  Class 7 19, 51, 81, 93, 98–99, 102, 284–285, 287, 329
  Class 8 83–85, 93, 99, 102–103, 288
  Class 11 84–86, 88, 92–93, 96, 98, 102–103, 191, 290
  Class 12 85, 93–94, 96–97, 101–103, 289, 291
  Class 14 92, 97, 291
  Class 21 107
class structure 8, 256
Cold War 11, 84, 97
Commander–in–Chief of the Army 17, 19, 73, 90–91, 97, 100–101, 248, 261, 263, 270–271, 292

communist 19, 21–22, 41–42, 50, 53, 87, 168, 256
conservative pact 2, 19
consolidation phase 2, 8, 14, 16, 24–26
constitutional amendment 45, 47, 55, 58, 89, 127, 276, 288
constitutional monarchy 14, 69, 298
corruption 35, 41, 70, 112, 119, 126, 138–139, 142, 154, 156–157, 159, 167, 174, 240–241, 244–245, 293, 306
coup 18, 19, 27, 43, 64, 69, 77, 82, 84, 96, 98, 100, 106, 107–109, 113, 123, 127, 165, 174, 281, 283, 292, 303
  1932 coup 69, 144, 304
  1947 coup 175, 270
  1957 coup 205
  1971 coup 71, 242
  1976 coup 14, 18, 74, 243, 256, 270
  1977 coup 19, 275
  1981 coup 81, 98, 99, 287, 329
  1985 coup 82, 287, 290
  1991 coup 16, 25, 33, 35, 38, 39, 70, 81, 84, 94, 99, 251, 273, 275, 276, 284, 286–287, 295, 329
  2006 coup ix, 250, 260–261, 263–266
Crown Prince 56

Defense Minister 17, 36, 38, 74–75, 89–90, 92–93, 95–97, 99–101, 106, 108, 232, 270–271, 292
democracy i, 1–2, 4, 7–13, 15–17, 19, 22, 26–27, 30, 44, 55, 59, 62–64, 66–67, 70, 100, 108, 112, 125, 144, 166–169, 172, 196–197, 231, 244, 250, 252–253, 255–256, 258–260, 265–266, 269, 271, 273, 281

discursive power 2, 26, 253, 257, 266

economic crisis i, 26, 96, 160–164, 174, 213, 222, 231, 241, 304, 307
economic growth 6, 8, 10–13, 30, 60
education 8, 12, 61–62, 117, 120–121, 129, 132, 134–135, 139, 143–147, 150–152, 154, 156, 159, 162–163, 170, 178–179, 191–192, 194, 196–197, 202, 277, 279, 301–302, 307, 312–313, 316
electoral politics i, 5, 24, 257, 259, 305
extra–bureaucratic forces 3

farmers 13, 64, 67, 121, 144, 150, 155, 162–165, 167, 188, 196, 223, 256, 268, 298–299, 305, 311, 323
Five Tigers (*ha suea*) 38, 77–85, 92–98, 101–103, 176, 287, 290, 291

huakhanaen (see vote broker)
hunger strike 39–40, 42, 44–46, 51–55, 57–58, 116, 165, 252, 276, 293

infantry 77, 84, 86, 92, 285
Interior Minister 34, 36, 38, 171, 222, 251, 286, 318, 321

kamnan 137, 296, 301, 306, 310

liberal democracy 258
lower class 2, 13, 27, 66–67, 165, 213, 257, 265, 269
Magsaysay Award 10, 54–55, 108, 155, 169–170, 253, 268, 293, 304
managed transition 10, 16
mass democracy 258
May 1992 incident 1–2, 7, 16, 27, 36, 63–64, 81, 87, 96, 108, 112, 117,

Subject Index

125, 170–171, 191, 251–253, 257, 272, 287, 289–290, 297
middle class 1–2, 4, 6–8, 10–13, 16, 25–27, 30, 55, 59–64, 66–68, 115–116, 121, 171–172, 252–254, 257–258, 265–269, 272, 279–281, 305–306
military i, 2–4, 7, 10–11, 13–21, 24–25, 27, 30–31, 33–35, 37–39, 41, 45–46, 48–50, 54–59, 62, 65–66, 69–77, 81–82, 84–90, 92, 96–101, 106–109, 112, 115, 121, 127, 138, 166, 168, 170, 175–177, 184, 186, 188, 190–192, 197, 199, 223, 241, 245, 248, 250–254, 256, 259–260, 263–264, 270–271, 274–279, 281–290, 292, 295, 298–299, 309, 311, 328–329
military government 11, 17–18, 22, 74, 87, 141, 256, 260, 281–282, 309
Minister of the Interior 34, 42, 46, 66, 274
modernization approach 6, 8, 11, 30
monarchy 16, 20–22, 64, 144, 245, 248, 256, 261–265, 298, 329

newspaper 42, 48, 53–54, 57, 60–63, 67, 117, 127, 170, 195, 277–280, 301, 307, 320, 328
NGO 6, 43, 46, 52–53, 60, 68, 125, 155, 165, 167, 197, 254–255, 258, 265, 268, 277–278, 281, 328

October 14th generation 17, 63
Ombudsman 120, 139, 302–303
organic law 159, 163, 304

Parliament 2, 14, 26, 33–34, 38–42, 47, 64–66, 86, 89, 99, 108, 112, 116–117, 119–121, 123–124, 126–131, 134–135, 137–138, 140, 142–146, 155–163, 165, 174–176, 178, 195, 201, 229–230, 241–243, 245–247, 250, 256, 261, 263, 299–300, 302, 304, 309
parliamentary politics i, 4, 17, 19, 22, 64–65, 68, 165, 253
party politician 4–5, 24, 100, 106, 108, 115, 126, 161, 165, 168–169, 173, 197, 199, 245, 251, 254–255, 257, 265, 271, 274–275, 283, 287, 290, 292, 307
political participation 4
political reform i, 1, 15, 25–27, 30, 64, 66, 68, 70, 112, 115–117, 119–120, 125–129, 143, 145, 155, 159–161, 163, 165–170, 172–173, 175, 177, 196–197, 201, 231, 242, 254–259, 268, 276, 281, 289, 293–297, 306, 315, 323
popular uprising 9
population 2, 7, 61–62, 67, 71, 139, 143–144, 163, 165, 168, 171, 178, 191, 194, 202, 217, 223, 254–255, 280, 299, 311, 317
populist 231
presidentialization of politics 261
print media 53–54, 60, 62, 71, 170, 252–253, 265, 281, 329
Privy Council 18, 56, 263–264, 270, 272, 289–290
Privy Councilor 18, 21, 56, 91, 99, 264, 270–272, 287
protest rally 26, 30, 33, 39, 41–42, 47, 50, 53–57, 62–63, 86–87, 252
provincial administrative organization 130
public opinion 68, 71, 170–172, 253–255, 329

ratthaburut 21
red card 179–180, 221, 313
referendum 125, 129, 134, 136–138, 154–155, 159, 161, 163, 294, 298, 303
riot 41–42, 45, 48–50, 53, 59
royalist 19, 256, 261–263, 265–266, 270, 272

sanitary district 130, 293
Senate 33, 47, 117, 121, 132, 139, 144, 156–157, 162, 175–178, 182, 184, 188–189, 192, 194–197, 199–200, 218, 230, 264, 288, 296, 304, 308–311, 313–316, 319, 322–324
Senate election 27, 112–113, 139, 175, 177, 179–180, 183–184, 188, 192, 194–197, 199, 202–203, 218, 227–228, 281, 309–310, 312–315, 319, 323–324
Senior Statesman 21, 272
socialism 22
structural approach 8–9, 268
student 3, 10, 17–18, 22, 42, 44, 46, 60–61, 63–64, 66, 87, 100, 144, 167, 250, 256, 267, 270, 277, 282

tambon administrative organizations 130
teacher 12, 60, 142, 167, 186, 188–189, 192, 197, 199, 273, 277
transition approach 8, 14, 269
transition phase 2, 8, 17, 26
urban middle class 1, 6, 12, 26, 98, 121, 166–167, 170, 172, 251, 254–255, 259, 268, 294, 305, 307

vote broker 22–24, 143, 227, 243–244, 320

vote–buying 23, 142, 155, 199–200, 214–215, 218, 221, 273

workers 12, 18, 22, 60, 150, 164–166, 188, 219–220, 250, 256, 268, 273, 277, 280, 304, 317

yellow card 179–182